"Baseball endures not only because of the heroics of a Babe Ruth or a Shohei Ohtani but also because of its lesser-known heroes and heroines—those in the game who fought against its unjust status quo, be it unfair labor practices or the exclusion of people of color, women, and LGBTQs. *Baseball Rebels* digs deep into history to honor the stories of the men and women who, often at great sacrifice, fought to forge a better path for the national pastime."

—Jean Hastings Ardell, author of *Breaking Into Baseball* and coauthor (with Ila Jane Borders) of *Making My Pitch: A Woman's Baseball Odyssey*

"A rich, informative account of individuals associated with professional baseball—players, managers, umpires, executives, union organizers—who voiced dissenting, nonconformist views. As a game hidebound by tradition, proud of its conservatism, and draped in the American flag, these rebels brought various perspectives of social justice to a game that was often recalcitrant to reform and resistant to revolution. A necessary read for anyone interested in baseball for something more than stats and nostalgia."

—Gerald Early, author of *A Level Playing Field: African American Athletes and the Republic of Sports*

"You do not have to be a baseball fan to appreciate *Baseball Rebels*. Providing yet more evidence of the ways baseball mirrors the evolution of American society, Dreier and Elias have crafted a well-researched and enlightening analysis of efforts to challenge the status quo in the generally conservative world of professional baseball. Their lineup includes prominent innovators such as Jackie Robinson and Branch Rickey as well as lesser-known figures, men and women, who have dared to confront issues of inequity within the national pastime and society."

—Lawrence Baldassaro, author of *Tony Lazzeri: Yankees Legend and Baseball Pioneer*

"Baseball players are not particularly known for their political activism, but that may be about to change. In *Baseball Rebels,* seasoned baseball historians Peter Dreier and Robert Elias have compiled the little-known and untold stories of the reformers, radicals, and nonconformists in baseball and their ties to the broader progressive movements of their times. The authors reveal the personal stories of players who chose to push back against injustice and discrimination. There is something here for every fan and student of the game: compelling baseball stories, new material about fascinating little-known players, and thoughtful consideration of the role baseball continues to play in American life."

—Marty Lurie, creator of AmericanInnings.org and host of the San Francisco Giants' KNBR 680 radio program *Talking Baseball*

"You need to read *Baseball Rebels* because it tells a story about baseball you probably don't know but should. Baseball is better because of the people in this book—Octavius Catto, Sam Nahem, 'Doc' Sykes, 'Mudcat' Grant, George Gmelch, Toni Stone, Ila Borders, Sean Doolittle, and Terry Cannon—and so is America."
—Chris Lamb, author of *Conspiracy of Silence* and *Stolen Dreams*

"Dreier and Elias have given us the most comprehensive history to date of social activism in professional baseball. But *Baseball Rebels* is not just a landmark study backed by impressive research. It's also a riveting read full of stories, some hopeful, others dismal, that explode the standard narrative that baseball is a conservative sport. Essential reading for baseball and history enthusiasts."
—Michael G. Long, editor of *42 Today: Jackie Robinson and His Legacy*

"In *Baseball Rebels* Dreier and Elias tell the tales of the men and women who in ways both blunt and subtle pushed back against baseball dogma by demonstrating time and again that the perceived wisdom isn't the only wisdom. And often it isn't even wisdom at all. Through their portrayals of rebels both well-known and little known, they shed valuable light on how baseball is America after all, although not quite the way those who run things would have you believe."
—Mitchell Nathanson, author of *A People's History of Baseball* and *God Almighty Hisself: The Life and Legacy of Dick Allen*

"Though Jackie Robinson's leap across the color line in 1947 was the catalyst to change on and off the field, Major League Baseball has invariably resisted those objecting to its entrenched conservative and hierarchical ways. Yet, as Peter Dreier and Robert Elias explain, the game has long had its rebels—women and men willing to challenge the status quo. Like E. P. Thompson in *The Making of the English Working Class*, *Baseball Rebels* seeks to rescue its subjects 'from the enormous condescension of posterity.' At a moment when athletes and those who care about sport are raising their voices, this history is a compelling reminder to look to the past and draw strength from those who came before us."
—Rob Ruck, author of *Raceball: How the Major Leagues Colonized the Black and Latin Game*

BASEBALL REBELS

BASEBALL REBELS

The Players, People, and Social
Movements That Shook Up the
Game and Changed America

PETER DREIER AND ROBERT ELIAS
FOREWORD BY DAVE ZIRIN

UNIVERSITY OF NEBRASKA PRESS | LINCOLN

The University of Nebraska Press is part of a land-grant institution
with campuses and programs on the past, present, and future
homelands of the Pawnee, Ponca, Otoe-Missouria, Omaha,
Dakota, Lakota, Kaw, Cheyenne, and Arapaho Peoples, as well as
those of the relocated Ho-Chunk, Sac and Fox, and Iowa Peoples.

Library of Congress Cataloging-in-Publication Data

Names: Dreier, Peter, 1948–, author. | Elias, Robert, 1950–,
    author. | Zirin, Dave, author of foreword.
Title: Baseball rebels: the players, people, and social movements
    that shook up the game and changed America / Peter
    Dreier and Robert Elias; foreword by Dave Zirin. Includes
    bibliographical references and index.
Identifiers: LCCN 2021038179
ISBN 9781496217776 (Hardback: acid-free paper)
ISBN 9781496231765 (ePub)
ISBN 9781496231772 (pdf)
Subjects: LCSH: Baseball—Political aspects—United States. |
    Baseball—Social aspects—United States. | Discrimination in
    sports—United States. | Racism in sports—United States. |
    Social change—United States—History—20th century. |
    Social justice—United States—History—20th century. |
    BISAC: Sports & Recreation / Baseball / History | Social
    Science / Discrimination
Classification: LCC gv863.a1 d75 2022 | DDC 796.3570973—dc23
LC record available at https://lccn.loc.gov/2021038179

This book is set in Arno by TIPS Technical Publishing, Inc.

To the memory of Terry Cannon,
Jackie Robinson, Bill Veeck, Curt Flood,
and Helen Callaghan Candaele St. Aubin.
May their lives be an inspiration.

CONTENTS

A paradox beats in the heart of baseball. This is a sport that is culturally about as conservative as the day is long. It is a sport constantly looking backward at old heroes, musty records, and a code of conduct at odds with our "look at me" world of "likes" and "clout." If you dare flip a bat or stroll around the bases after a home run, vengeance will be acted upon you or your teammates in the form of a one-hundred-mile-per-hour fastball. The code of baseball is practically biblical. You are to speak in clichés, run the bases with your head down, and occasionally spit something.

Yet therein lies the paradox in our national pastime. This conservative sport has also produced some of the most important rebels in sports and US history. Maybe it's the resistance to that pressure to conform that forces these erstwhile rabble-rousers into public view. However it happened and whatever the calculus, baseball is the sport that has produced people like Jackie Robinson, Roberto Clemente, and Curt Flood. It has given us ground-breaking tell-all books like *Ball Four* by Jim Bouton and *The Bronx Zoo* by Sparky Lyle. Dr. Martin Luther King Jr said of Robinson, who of course smashed Major League Baseball's color line in 1947, that he was "a sit-inner before sit-ins and a freedom rider before freedom rides."[1]

Now Major League Baseball, once a year, bathes in the memory of Robinson, as well as Clemente, and speaks about itself as if it is a force for progressive good. Former commissioner Bud Selig even called baseball "a leader in the Civil Rights Movement," pointedly ignoring that Robinson integrated in spite of Major League Baseball and its racist owners, fans, and players. It is revisionist history writ large. Major League Baseball co-opts the history of Robinson precisely because he is too big to hide, too grand a figure to toss down the memory hole.

But if we can all agree that Robinson is too big to be buried, doesn't that imply that there were others who weren't? This is how our grossly unequal system treats rebels off the field: either you are thrown down the memory hole or your political teeth are extracted—a veritable political root canal—that turns you into a harmless icon. This is why *Baseball Rebels* is as radical and important a baseball book as I've read in such a long time. It restores a history that the minders of baseball would soon have us forget. This history is not at all just one of resisting baseball's racist practices, although sometimes it feels that just those are the only battles baseball permits us to remember.

As *Baseball Rebels* reminds us, there were also fights over labor, gender equity, LGBTQ rights, and the uses of baseball as a tool for US empire. As the introduction to *Baseball Rebels* puts so aptly, "America's battles over race, labor, immigration, and gender have all been reflected on the baseball field, in the executive suites, in the press box, and in the community. While most sports fans are aware of baseball's better-known rebels, like Jackie Robinson, Marvin Miller, and Curt Flood, many others are either forgotten or known primarily for their sports achievements. All Americans—whether or not they are baseball fans—can learn from this history."[2]

That is absolutely right. If you don't know names like Octavius Catto, Moses Fleetwood Walker, Frank "Doc" Sykes, Wendell Smith, Lester Rodney, Bill Veeck, Sam Nahem, Alta Weiss, Mildred "Millie" Deegan, Glenn Burke, Dave Pallone, and Ila Borders, then you don't know baseball history.

Maybe we don't know this history precisely because it is such a radical reimagining of what we know baseball—and all of sports—to be. These athletes are among the host of characters, many of them new to me, who took fusty old baseball and turned it on its head. Learning about them is part of the joy of this volume, but I will say that as a student of the game, I was struck by how much of this history I did not know.

It is vital to know this history because we are living in a time when there is a renaissance of rebels across the world of sports, driven primarily by street movements for racial justice and the struggle for Black lives in the face of remorseless police brutality. I had once thought that this struggle had affected baseball the least of all the major sports. Only one player had kneeled during the anthem over the four years since Colin Kaepernick had taken that fateful step, and that player, Oakland A's catcher Bruce Maxwell, found himself quickly shuttled out of the league, getting little to no solidarity from his fellow players. It seemed grim. But then, after the police shooting of Jacob Blake in Kenosha, Wisconsin, in August of 2020, the Milwaukee Brewers were the first team outside of basketball to actually go out on strike in solidarity with protesters. Other teams followed suit. It showed that the rebel heart still beats inside the chests of many Major League players.

I hope each and every one of them gets to read *Baseball Rebels*. With this book in their hands, they will see that they are not building this platform from scratch but that they stand on the shoulders of forgotten giants (and Giants) and are part of a story more than a century old of athletes who took this priggish world of baseball and turned it on its head.

—Dave Zirin, author of *The Kaepernick Effect*

ACKNOWLEDGMENTS

This book combines my two passions: baseball and politics. But it wouldn't have been written without the support and friendship of many people. I hope this book—and its companion, *Major League Rebels*—reflects the spirit of Terry Cannon, the founder of the Baseball Reliquary, to whom the book is dedicated. The Reliquary is an organization of baseball fans (or fanatics) who love the game but not the business of baseball and who admire the sport's mavericks and iconoclasts. I'm particularly grateful to Kelly Candaele, with whom I have shared many baseball adventures and written many articles on various aspects of the sport. Over the course of many years, I have appreciated the encouragement and help of Jean Ardell, Alan Barra, Peter Bjarkman, Clifford Blau, Jim Bouton, Jim Buzinski, Mary Cannon, Bill Carle, Merritt Clifton, Warren Corbett, Rory Costello, Dave Davis, Neil deMause, Dan Gordon, Steve Greenhouse, Bill Hickman, Neil Lanctot, Jon Leonoudakis, Bob Locker, Lee Lowenfish, John McReynolds, Marvin Miller, Ivan Nahem, Bill Nowlin, Jennifer Piscopo, Jacob Pomrenke, Steve Rosenthal, Rob Ruck, William Simons, Willie Steele, Christian Trudeau, Bob Tufts, and Dave Zirin. I met some of these folks through my membership in the Society for American Baseball Research, a serious group of baseball fanatics with a wealth of knowledge and a willingness to share it through their research, writing, and correspondence. Jim Gates and Cassidy Lent at the Baseball Hall of Fame's Giamatti Research Center have been very helpful. For research assistance, I want to thank Occidental College students Andrea Mateo and Chiaki Ma. For instilling in me the love of baseball, grateful thanks to the late Ted Dreier (my father), Bernie and Augie Dreier (my uncles), and Joe Black (my former baseball coach). For their patience and tolerance, as well as their love of baseball, I thank my wife, Terry Meng, and our daughters, Amelia and Sarah.

—Peter Dreier

After long years devoted to other academic pursuits, I've returned in more recent times to my childhood obsession: baseball. It's been a pleasure exploring it not merely as a player and fan but also as a serious scholarly endeavor via my recent baseball books. For this one, I thank Michael Bloch, George Gmelch, Howard Nemerovski, Brian Weiner, Bill Hoynes, and Miles Theeman for their supportive friendship. My thanks to my research assistants, Clowie Ang and Kirsten Saldana at the University of San Francisco and June Gleed at McGill University. I appreciate the inspiration and insights provided by fellow baseball writers George Gmelch, Ron Briley, Dave Zirin, Jon Leonoudakis, Bill Lee, Mitchell Nathanson, Rob Fitts, the late Peter Bjarkman, Jean Ardell, Lawrence Baldassaro, and my fellow members of the Society for American Baseball Research. I'm indebted to the helpful staff at the Giamatti Research Center of the Baseball Hall of Fame, the Negro Leagues Baseball Museum, the Gleeson Library of the University of San Francisco, the San Francisco Public Library, the Norfolk Public Library, and the Mill Valley Public Library. Grants from the University of San Francisco Faculty Development Fund provided valuable financial assistance. Many thanks to Dan Gordon for his valuable editorial work. I'm also thankful for University of Nebraska Press editor Rob Taylor, for his patience, flexibility, and guidance, and for associate editor Courtney Ochsner for her assistance. Most of all, I'm grateful for the support and love of my immediate family: "Baseball" Jack, Madeleine, Andre, Smalley, and my wife, Jennifer.

—Robert Elias

A week after his inauguration in 2016, Donald Trump signed the first version of his travel ban, sparking nationwide protests. "These refugees are fleeing civil wars, terrorism, religious persecution, and are thoroughly vetted for two years," tweeted Sean Doolittle, at the time an Oakland Athletics pitcher, in response. "A refugee ban is a bad idea. . . . It feels un-American. . . . And also immoral."[1] St. Louis Cardinals outfielder Dexter Fowler, whose wife emigrated from Iran, told ESPN that he opposed the executive order. In response to angry comments from fans, Fowler tweeted, "For the record. I know this is going to sound absolutely crazy, but athletes are humans, and not properties of the team they work for."[2]

Doolittle and Fowler's comments reflect a long but little-known tradition of dissent and rebellion among professional ballplayers. Compared with their counterparts in football and basketball, baseball players have tended to be cautious about speaking out on controversial social and political issues, but throughout the sport's history, some players—alongside executives, sportswriters, and managers—have challenged the status quo.

Baseball's rebels, reformers, and radicals took inspiration from the country's dissenters and progressive movements, speaking and acting against abuses both within their profession and in the broader society: racism, sexism, homophobia, poverty, war, repression of civil liberties, undue corporate power, worker exploitation, militarism, and imperialism.

Dissent has played a central role in American history. Every reformist crusade since the Boston Tea Party has drawn on this legacy: the abolitionists who helped end slavery; the Populist farmers who sought to tame the banks, railroads, and other big corporations; the progressives who fought slums, sweatshops, and epidemic diseases; the suffragists who won the vote for women; the labor unionists who demanded an eight-hour workday, safe working conditions, and a living wage; the civil rights pioneers who helped dismantle Jim Crow; and other activists who have won hard-fought battles for environmental protection, women's equality, gay rights, and decent conditions for farmworkers.

Ballplayers and owners have often voiced skepticism and even opposition to progressive or radical movements. Hall of Famer (and Ku Klux Klan member) Rogers Hornsby claimed that "any ballplayer that don't sign autographs for little kids ain't American. He's a Communist."[3] Ty Cobb, another hardcore racist Hall of Famer, chastised a shirking pitcher, "Don't you turn Bolshevik on me."[4]

In the late 1940s, Brooklyn Dodgers president Branch Rickey condemned ballplayers' decision to join the Mexican League and reject Major League Baseball's stingy salaries as a "communist plot."[5] In the 1950s, the Cincinnati "Reds" changed their name to the "Redlegs" to escape the nation's anticommunist hysteria.

In 1976, during a game at Dodger Stadium, two protesters ran into center field and tried to set fire to an American flag. Cubs center fielder Rick Monday grabbed the flag to thunderous cheers from the fans. When he came to bat the next inning, he got a standing ovation from the crowd while the scoreboard behind the left-field bleachers flashed the message, "Rick Monday . . . You Made A Great Play." In 1998, Dodgers manager Tommy Lasorda testified before Congress in support of an amendment to the Constitution to ban desecration of the American flag.[6] Broadcaster and former major league pitcher Curt Schilling compared Muslims to Nazis and called for Hillary Clinton to be "buried under a jail somewhere."[7]

America's battles over race, labor, immigration, and gender have all been reflected on the baseball field, in the executive suites, in the press box, and in the community. While most sports fans are aware of baseball's better-known rebels, like Jackie Robinson, Marvin Miller, and Curt Flood, many others are either forgotten or known primarily for their sports achievements. All Americans—whether or not they are baseball fans—can learn from this history.

In *Baseball Rebels: The Players, People, and Social Movements That Shook Up the Game and Changed America*, we develop several broad themes. Baseball rebels have resisted American racism: battling Jim Crow, building Black institutions, laying the foundation for breaking the color line, fighting against the lingering discrimination after integration, and defending civil rights. The Civil War ended slavery, but by the 1870s, segregation replaced Reconstruction's promises. For almost a century, Black Americans and their white allies fought against Jim Crow laws in all walks of life: politics, education, transportation, public facilities, and sports. Baseball had its own anti–Jim Crow rebels long before Jackie Robinson, and also for decades after he broke the color line.

Baseball rebels have also resisted sexism and homophobia, promoting women's role in the sport and taking courageous stands for sexual identity and equality. We describe the battles that women fought, beginning in the mid-1800s, to play organized baseball, including the pioneering women who played in the All American Girls Professional Baseball League during and after World War II. In the 1970s, as the feminist movement was gaining momentum, women asserted themselves in baseball positions both on and off the field. They were soon joined by gay and lesbian movement activists who pressured Major League Baseball for inclusion, one's sexuality notwithstanding. Baseball rebels include mavericks whose impact has spanned the sport's history and others who increasingly stand up to confront America's current, most pressing problems. A few have helped blow the lid off of a stodgy, conservative sport and introduced it to the realities of the twenty-first century.

In *Major League Rebels: Baseball Battles Over Workers Rights and American Empire* (Rowman & Littlefield, Inc., 2022), a companion volume to this book, we profile baseball rebels who have resisted labor exploitation, both inside and outside the sport: challenging worker repression in the Gilded Age, fighting baseball's corporate monopoly, and inspiring player resistance to the indentured servitude of the reserve clause.

Baseball paralleled the economic struggles happening in the wider society. By the 1880s, a few industrialists—Rockefeller, Carnegie, and Vanderbilt, to name just three—controlled most of the nation's wealth. Developing ruthless monopolies, these so-called robber barons deployed every tactic, no matter how vicious, to enhance their power and profits. They cut wages, repressed unions, and bribed politicians. This ushered in the Gilded Age: riches for the few, misery and exploitation for the rest. A group of unscrupulous baseball club owners mimicked the industrial magnates' strategies. At the same time that a growing labor movement was pushing back against oligarchy, baseball players began demanding more rights and better pay. During the post–World War II economic boom, the labor movement gained members and strength, helping lift millions of workers into the middle class. But baseball players remained poorly paid, with little control over their working conditions, until a courageous few fought back, suing Major League Baseball, organizing a serious baseball union, and, in some cases, risking their careers to finally produce their enviable position as workers, which big leaguers have now enjoyed for the last several decades.

That companion book, *Major League Rebels*, also examines baseball radicals who have resisted US empire: challenging America's past wars, contesting America's current wars, and protesting US imperialism in Latin America and elsewhere. While organized baseball has always waved the flag and supported all of America's wars, some players have resisted that version of patriotism. Even as early as World War I, protests emerged and continued through World War II. The baseball establishment embraced America's military adventure in Vietnam, even as the antiwar movement grew and sheltered its players from combat via stateside National Guard assignments. But the sport couldn't isolate itself from the growing dissent over the war. While players risked being labeled troublemakers and being dropped from their teams, a few spoke out against the war. Others followed with later protests against the Gulf War, the Iraq War, and the War on Terror.

Sports both reflect and shape US society. Athletes in other sports have stood up to protest injustices: track stars such as Tommie Smith and John Carlos, boxers like Muhammad Ali, tennis players such as Billie Jean King and Arthur Ashe, basketball players like LeBron James and Steve Nash, and football players such as Dave Meggyesy and Colin Kaepernick. Since the Civil War, baseball activists have also challenged the status quo in baseball and in the country, contributing to the kind of dissent that creates a more humane society. These are their stories.

PART ONE

Resisting Racism

CHAPTER ONE

Battling Jim Crow

The election of President Abraham Lincoln in 1860 provoked the Southern states to secede. The North states resisted, seeking to preserve the Union. The Civil War began at the Battle of Fort Sumter (near Charleston, South Carolina) in April 1861. While historians still debate the different causes of the war, the struggle over slavery was not the only, or the immediate, objective. In the war's early years, even free Blacks were banned from Northern armies. Despite being barred, some Blacks formed militias and began training and drilling for combat. Other Blacks claimed they would fight (if allowed) only if the Union's primary objective changed from maintaining the Union to eliminating slavery. It wasn't until Lincoln's 1863 Emancipation Proclamation that abolishing slavery was formally added as a motivation for the war. Thousands of Blacks rallied to join the North's war effort, but their reception was not what they were expecting.

The Civil War Game

As with everything else, the Civil War disrupted America's pastimes and recreations. While references to "base ball" (as it was written in the early years) date back to the 1790s, organized teams emerged by the 1830s, led by the Olympic Ball Club of Philadelphia in 1831. The first baseball game using modern rules is attributed to the New York Knickerbockers and the New York Nine in 1846. Although hundreds of baseball clubs soon emerged, they competed with even greater numbers of clubs that played cricket, a sport imported from England. Yet even as early as the mid-1850s, baseball had prevailed and was already being described by reporters and sports enthusiasts as the "national pastime."[1] In addition to the informal teams in every American town and city (at least in the Northeast), the top amateur clubs were organized into the National Association of Base Ball Players (NABBP) in 1857.

Baseball was dominated by white men, who were dedicated to the sport for fitness and entertainment. Yet free Blacks also played the game, segregated from white teams and leagues. For African Americans, baseball was more than recreation. It became a vehicle for Black civil and political rights. On July 4, 1859, a white antislavery Republican congressman from Ohio played in a game with African Americans to show his support for desegregation and equality. The first known game between Black teams occurred later that year, when the Henson Club of Queens defeated the Unknowns of Brooklyn, 54–43. Thereafter, Black teams began a long quest for integration.

The Civil War disrupted the nation's baseball mania, but the game survived and even thrived during the war years. Northern soldiers played baseball as their primary recreation, and games were arranged in the prisoner-of-war camps on both sides of the conflict. In 1862, two New York regiment teams played a game in Hilton Head, South Carolina, and drew as many as forty thousand spectators. Many Confederate soldiers got their first initiation to baseball during the war, and after it ended they helped spread the game in the Southern states. Black teams persisted during the war as well, gaining some respect from whites despite ongoing segregation and racist stereotypes.

Martyr: Octavius Catto

The battle over baseball segregation was a fight Blacks would continue after the war. Baseball would be integral to the post–Civil War movements for Black liberation after the official elimination of slavery with the Thirteenth Amendment in December 1865. During the war, a new generation of Black leaders emerged to continue the struggle for freedom that abolitionists such as Frederick Douglass and Harriet Tubman had begun. Among them was Octavius Catto, a Renaissance man who pioneered Black education, integrated Philadelphia's streetcars and the US military, was a leader of the city's civic and intellectual life, and promoted Black voting rights—for which he died as a martyr. He was also the founder, captain, and star shortstop of the Black Pythian Base Ball Club, which became a major vehicle for his work as a civil rights activist.

Catto was born in 1839 in Charleston, South Carolina to a free Black mother, Sarah Cain, and William Catto, who was born a slave but won his freedom and became a Presbyterian minister. William moved his family to Baltimore, intending to move to Liberia as a missionary in 1848. But when church officials discovered a letter he wrote that they believed threatened to "excite discontent and insurrection among the slaves,"[2] the Catto family fled to Philadelphia to escape an arrest warrant. There, William became an active abolitionist and civil rights advocate through the 1850s, profoundly influencing his son, Octavius.

Philadelphia had become a primary destination for freed slaves, but it was not the paradise they envisioned. Frederick Douglass claimed that no Northern city was more prejudiced against Blacks than Philadelphia, the "City of Brotherly Love," and yet it "held the destiny of our people."[3] Philadelphia had the largest Black population of any Northern city. It was also a hotbed of the nation's amateur baseball.

In 1854, Octavius Catto attended the Institute for Colored Youth (ICY), Philadelphia's only Black high school, which later became the nation's first historically Black college, Cheyney University. The Institute was a focal point for Black civil rights. Catto was a star student and valedictorian at the ICY, where he also played cricket, town ball, and base ball. After pursuing further studies of languages and the classics in Washington, DC, Catto returned to Philadelphia in 1859, when he was hired by the ICY to teach English, mathematics, Greek, and Latin.

In 1864, Catto delivered the school's commencement address. He challenged the insensitivity of white teachers toward Black students and argued that education had to be combined with political activism to advance the cause of Black freedom. He rallied support for a Northern victory in the Civil War, claiming it would not only liberate Blacks but also ensure America's promising future: "It is for the good of the Nation that every element of its population be wisely instructed in the advantages of a Republican Government."[4] Catto had hoped to be appointed head of the ICY, but the school's Quaker trustees, fearing his militancy, derailed his bid.

With a growing reputation for scholarship and teaching, Catto was offered the post of principal at Black schools in both New York and Washington, DC, but he chose to remain at the Institute. With Philadelphia as his base, Catto expanded his ties with the city's intellectuals. He was soon interacting with leading thinkers and writers from around the nation and the world, speaking repeatedly at events and gatherings to expose the harsh reality of racism.

Besides education, Catto's next target was the US military. Lincoln's 1863 Emancipation Proclamation invited Blacks to enlist in the war effort. As the ICY alumni association president, Catto rallied graduates and other Philadelphia Blacks to join up: "Men of color to arms! Now or never!"[5]

Like Douglass, Catto believed that Blacks' service in the war would help ensure their rights once the war ended. Catto tirelessly rallied Black recruitment, leading the effort to raise eleven regiments of US Colored Troops for the Union Army. He helped establish a Free Military School, joined the Pennsylvania National Guard, supported Black troops at Camp William Penn, and quickly became a major and inspector for the Fifth Brigade.

Toward the end of the war, Catto broadened his activism. In 1864, he met in Syracuse, New York, with hundreds of Blacks from the North and South to form the National Equal Rights League, the first US group devoted to promoting Black equality. Catto helped form and was then elected secretary of the Pennsylvania Equal Rights League. In 1865, he served as the vice president of the State Convention of Colored People in Harrisburg. He worked zealously alongside Douglass and other abolitionists to pass the Thirteenth Amendment, which ended slavery. He traveled to Washington, DC, to help develop Black school curricula there, and to advocate for the Fourteenth Amendment, which would require due process and equal protection from the states.

After the war ended, Catto addressed a large crowd at Philadelphia's Independence Hall to send off the Twenty-Fourth US Colored Troop, which had been assigned to help occupy postwar Richmond, Virginia. Speaking to many of his former students and recruits, Catto praised the two hundred thousand Black Americans who, despite prejudices, had nobly fought for the Union, "trusting to a redeemed country for the full recognition of their manhood." Unfurling a flag with the words "Let Soldiers in War be Citizens in Peace," he hoped that during Reconstruction, "the votes of the blacks could not be lightly dispensed with."[6]

While maintaining his ICY teaching position, Catto crusaded for Black rights by participating, and sometimes integrating, Philadelphia's civic, literary, patriotic, and political groups, such as the Philadelphia Library Company, the Fourth Ward Black Political Club, and the Union League Association, which he addressed in a January 1865 speech. An eloquent, powerful and charismatic speaker, Catto claimed, "It is the duty of every man, to the extent of his interest and means to provide for the immediate improvement of the four or five millions of ignorant and previously dependent laborers, who will be thrown upon society by the reorganization of the Union."[7]

Catto became a member and officer of the Banneker Institute, a Black literary society for Philadelphia's intellectual elite. Besides discussing scholarly subjects such as philosophy and mathematics, Banneker members debated social justice issues such as emancipation, equal wages, voting rights, and

Republican Party politics. He successfully pushed to get the Banneker members admitted to the previously all-white City-Wide Congress of Literary Societies. Catto also integrated the Franklin Institute, a major center for science and education. Despite Blacks' military service and the postwar Amendments, Black Philadelphians continued to face blatant discrimination. For example, they were banned from the city's streetcars. After the city's powerbrokers ignored his public appeals, Catto resorted to civil disobedience. On May 18, 1865, he was ordered to leave a streetcar, but he refused and explained his reasoning. The conductor unhitched the car and left Catto sitting there alone all night. In the morning, a crowd and the press gathered, giving the injustice great visibility.

Unable to budge streetcar operators, Catto took his cause to the Pennsylvania legislature. Enlisting the help of Republican Congressmen Thaddeus Stevens and William D. Kelley, Catto devised a "Bill of Rights" for public transportation, which became state law in 1867. When Catto's fiancée, the renowned educator Carrie Le Count, was subsequently barred from a streetcar, she sued and won, and the operators finally gave in. Catto and Le Count achieved desegregation for Philadelphia streetcars ninety years before Rosa Parks and other Black citizens of Montgomery, Alabama dismantled bus segregation after a year-long boycott.

Through baseball Octavius Catto pursued yet another avenue for Black civil rights. A star player on his ICY baseball team, Catto loved playing the game, but he wanted something more. In 1866, he cofounded and became the captain and star infielder for the Pythian Base Ball Club, tapping players from his ICY, Banneker Institute, and the Equal Rights League. Many of the players belonged to the Knights of Pythias Lodge, and thus the team became the Pythians (derived from a mythical priestess at the Greek Temple of Apollo). Besides Catto, the Pythian leadership included other prominent Blacks who emerged from Underground Railroad families. Club president James W. Purnell worked with abolitionists John Brown and Martin Delany, and vice president Raymond W. Burr descended from the American revolutionary Aaron Burr and was the son of a prominent Black activist.

While only the second Black team in Philadelphia, after the Excelsiors, the Pythians quickly dominated. They ended with a 9–1 record and were considered the best Black team in Philadelphia and perhaps the nation. Black teams began to proliferate, such as the Monitors of Long Island, the Blue Skies of Camden, the Monrovia of Harrisburg, and the Uniques of Chicago.

The Pythian games against Washington's Black teams were particularly spectacular and a boon to Black pride. White reporters covered the contests sympathetically, and white ballplayers watched the games. They drew big crowds and Black leaders from both cities, including Frederick Douglass, whose sons were active players. Frederick Douglass Jr. was a founder of Washington's Alerts Base Ball Club. Another son, Charles, became a clerk with the Freedman's Bureau in Washington and played third base for the Alerts. He then joined—as a player and eventual president—the city's other Black team, the Mutuals. His father was made an honorary team member.

In 1867, the "Pyths" became even stronger by recruiting players from other Black teams. Led by Catto, they won ten of thirteen games that year and went undefeated in 1868. The club report claimed the team "performed their labors with zeal and with an ardent desire to do all in their power to sustain our character and reputation as a base ball club and as an association of gentlemen."[8]

While winning games was rewarding, Catto pursued baseball for loftier goals. He sought equal participation and recognition for Blacks and believed that baseball "built community ties, pushed racial boundaries, and established local and national networks of support."[9] Catto sought to lure and organize young Black men into his activist circles, and baseball was the best vehicle for doing so. For the Pythians, he drew from middle class Blacks involved with cultural and civic institutions who, if not already activists for Black equality, could be enlisted in the cause of Black self-improvement, allowing African Americans to demonstrate their skills, independence, and right to full citizenship.

When Catto and his team traveled the Black baseball circuit in the Northeast and mid-Atlantic (often to towns that had provided safe houses on the Underground Railroad), Catto spoke to players and fans of the opposing teams about current political issues and recruited them as allies in the struggle for Black rights. The games were played with a spirit of friendship, followed by meals and parties uniting both visiting and home teams. Shut out from other institutions, sports and politics were closely linked for Black athletes.

Pythian baseball helped make Philadelphia a major hub for the emergence of Negro League baseball. It also helped inspire a role for Black women in baseball. Observing the success of Black teams, John Lang—an enterprising white barber—established three teams of Black women, two of which survived as the Dolly Vardens. Their first game in 1883 drew a large, enthusiastic crowd, and while ultimately viewed as a novelty, the women were applauded for their toughness and surprising skills. With most Black women relegated to domestic labor, these ballplayers broke the mold and bravely took some first steps on the road to equality.

Promoting Black teams, including Black women teams, was a boon for African American institutions and civil rights organizing, but Catto had more ambitious plans. Despite the Civil War Amendments to the Constitution, Black teams were often blocked from equal access to baseball resources and fields. Catto viewed integration on the baseball diamond as a vehicle to help Blacks assimilate into white society.

In Philadelphia, Catto secured accounts with the white A.J. Reach Sporting Goods Company and scheduled Pythian games at white fields, such as the field maintained by the city's white Athletics club. After the Pythians' great 1867 season, Catto petitioned the Pennsylvania chapter of the NABBP for membership. He wanted his Black team accepted as an equal member in the otherwise all-white league. Despite support from the Athletics at the Harrisburg convention, the Pythians were denied membership (and even a vote), while 265 new white teams were all admitted.

Leading up to the NABBP's national convention in Philadelphia later that year, Catto mounted another campaign, dubbed "Catto's Proposal." Although the white Athletics delegates continued their support, the Pythians were again denied. The official explanation indicated that "if colored clubs were admitted there would be, in all probability, some division of feeling, whereas by excluding them no injury would result to anyone." Colored clubs were defined as any team with "one or more colored players."[10]

In 1869, the NABBP formally voted to deny membership to the Pythians. The official color line would not be lifted for another eighty years. It was a terrible lost opportunity for baseball to serve as a pathbreaker. For many white European immigrants, playing America's game was often a route to assimilation in mainstream culture, but this was denied to African Americans.

The failure to integrate white baseball leagues was obviously motivated by racism and perhaps anger against Catto, the militant equal rights agitator. But the Pythians' exclusion from the NABBP was also the best way "to keep out of the Convention the discussion of any subject having a political bearing."[11]

Many Northerners and Southerners alike viewed baseball as a common denominator between the two regions, one that could be used to heal the nation after the Civil War. Contests on the ballfield would replace conflicts on the battlefield. But this required amateur, and then professional, baseball leagues to set terms acceptable to Southern teams. Allowing Black teams to play white teams would be unacceptable to Southern ballplayers. Ironically, Black athletes were excluded from key baseball leagues in order to promote national unity among whites.

Some Black leaders couldn't see the significance of baseball in the struggle for racial equality. William Still, the great abolitionist and Underground Railroad leader, wrote to the Pythians, "Our kin in the South . . . have claims too great and pressing for frivolous amusements."[12] But Catto persisted, sensing the game's eventual value as a wedge against racial discrimination. After the NABBP rejection, he shifted his strategy. The white leagues might exclude the Pythians, but they could at least break another barrier: playing a white team. Competing against "our white brethren" on a "field of green"[13] would force whites to take Black athletes seriously—and perhaps even acknowledge that, at least on the ballfield, Blacks and white were equal.

White ballplayers had mixed feelings about playing with African Americans. Aside from prejudice, white players felt that if they won, it would be expected, but if they lost, their superiority would be questioned. One white reporter thought Blacks might be better ballplayers than whites and "in hot weather . . . play a stronger game."[14] Would a white club take the risk?

The Pythians had an advocate in Thomas Fitzgerald, a white publisher who was also a founder of Philadelphia's Athletics Ball Club and had some clout in baseball and city politics. Progressive on race relations, Fitzgerald used his newspaper, City Item, to argue relentlessly for universal voting rights. Soon the Athletics ousted him for his outspoken views. It was one thing to promote racial progress in the South, but Black voting rights in Philadelphia went too far. Even so, Fitzgerald used his newspaper to lobby for a Black-white baseball contest. In 1869, he wrote ardently about the Black teams, and was particularly fond of Catto and the Pythians. He asked, "Who will put the ball in motion?"[15] A forerunner of Branch Rickey, Fitzgerald challenged the Athletics, in particular.

In August 1869, the white Masonics team agreed to play the Pythians, claiming, "There is a desire on the part of a great majority of the admirers of the game of base ball to have some club, composed of players of the Caucasian race, play a game with the famous Pythian club, composed of colored gentlemen."[16] Suddenly other white clubs expressed interest: the Keystones, the Experts, the Franklins, even the Athletics. Yet it was all talk, as fears rose about being the first white squad to lose to a Black team.

Fitzgerald and Catto persisted, and finally the Olympic club accepted the challenge. Aside from Fitzgerald's influence, Catto had nurtured relationships with white businessmen and white ballplayers, despite their political differences.

On September 3, 1869, the Pythians met the Olympics on the latter's home field, and Fitzgerald served as the game's umpire. Ready to watch the unthinkable, a large and enthusiastic crowd of Black and white fans looked on, comprising the Olympics' biggest crowd since playing the nation's first professional team, the Cincinnati Red Stockings, earlier that year. The Pythians took an early lead, but their star pitcher, John Cannon, was injured and didn't play well. Back then, with only one umpire on the field, it was left to the players themselves to call safes and outs. The umpire was limited to hearing appeals when a team thought a bad call had been made. The Pythians decided beforehand not to argue any plays. Any appeals would amount to a Black man challenging a white man's word in front of five thousand people. The Pythians "acquitted themselves in a very creditable manner,"[17] but lost the game 44–23. The next day's newspapers applauded the Pythians' gentlemanly play, noting that had the Pythians challenged a series of bad calls, they might have won.

The *New York Times* described the contest as "A Novel Game in Philadelphia," but it was much more than that.[18] It was the first recorded game between formal Black and white teams. To complete the picture, however, the Pythians wanted a victory to show that Black ballplayers were as good as white ballplayers. On October 16, 1869, the Pythians defeated the white City Item Club, 27–17, and a form of equality was achieved on the diamond.

The Pythian games bridged racial divides, and interracial contests sprung up throughout the Northeast. On September 20, 1869, for example, the Black Alerts met the white Olympics of Washington, DC, on a field overlooking the White House. In subsequent decades, when Blacks and whites lived, worked, socialized, studied, and worshiped separately, the ball field was sometimes among the few places where the races mixed. It was a site for Blacks to dispel stereotypes, achieve fair treatment, and prove themselves.

Catto wasn't done crusading. In his baseball travels and equal rights campaigns throughout the Northeast, he valued one right above all others: the right to vote. In 1838, Pennsylvania's constitution denied the vote to free Blacks. Catto became a ceaseless advocate for the Fifteenth Amendment and helped push Pennsylvania to adopt it. Catto encouraged Blacks to register as Republicans because the party had supported the Amendment. In 1870, Philadelphia's Black citizens voted for the first time and elected Republican candidates.

In Philadelphia, Blacks were concentrated in a neighborhood adjoining an Irish community. The Irish district was strongly Democratic and controlled by a political machine that was key to Democratic Party victories citywide. Black voting was viewed as a threat to its power and economic well-being since African Americans supported the Republicans, known as the party of Lincoln. The Democratic machine responded with voter intimidation against Black voters, abetted by Philadelphia police officers, who were predominantly Irish themselves and allied to the Democratic mayor.

Violence against Blacks during the 1871 mayoral election was particularly rampant. The night before election day, on October 9, two Black citizens were beaten and shot, one fatally. Despite the intimidation, Catto rallied Black voters to show up at the polls. Seeking to vote himself, Catto neared his home when he passed two men, one of whom whirled and shot him, then ran away, in front of a passing streetcar filled with Blacks and whites. Catto, only thirty-two years old, died immediately. He was one of ten Black men shot that day, yet news of Catto's death spread quickly and the Republican candidate easily won the mayoral election. Years later the Black radical, W. E. B. DuBois observed, "And so closed the career of a man of splendid equipment, rare force of character, whose life was so interwoven with all that was good about us, as to make it stand out in bold relief, as a pattern for those who have followed after."[19]

Many whites were outraged at Catto's murder in his quest for civil rights. His funeral procession was the largest since Lincoln's assassination and unprecedented for a Black man. Over the three-mile route, tens of thousands of Black and white Philadelphians watched in reverence for a fallen hero. More than 125 carriages paraded by, containing Congressmen, military leaders, local politicians, students, colleagues, soldiers, ballplayers, and fellow civil rights activists. Frank Kelly, an Irish thug, was the known assassin, but the police helped him escape, and he wasn't arrested for another seven years, when he was extradited from Chicago. In 1877, despite many eyewitnesses, Kelly was acquitted by an all-white jury.

Catto's assassination left a mixed legacy. In the short run, it broke the Democratic Party machine, elevated the Black vote, and redirected resources to the African American community. Republican political clubs flourished, and Black candidates were elected to some offices. But Catto's murder robbed the freedom movement of a charismatic and strategic leader. Without his leadership, the Equal Rights League stalled and militant Black activism declined by the late 1870s and the end of Reconstruction. With the emergence of Jim Crow laws and the rise of the Ku Klux Klan and other white supremacist organizations, most Blacks adopted a more defensive posture, as reflected in the rise of the accommodating self-help strategy advocated by Booker T. Washington starting in the 1880s.

A similar self-help development arose in baseball. In Philadelphia, the Pythians continued playing after Catto's death through the 1870s and 1880s. Rather than resume the battle to enter white Organized Baseball leagues, it joined other Black clubs to begin building separate amateur, and then professional, baseball institutions of their own. In 1887, the Pythians became charter members of the National Colored Base Ball League (NCBBL). While the association folded within weeks, it demonstrated the Black community's determination to mirror white leagues of their own, and it anticipated the Negro Leagues of the next century. In the meantime, Black clubs operated independently and grew in number. Philadelphia had become a hotbed for the expansion of Black baseball, and the Pythians inspired future Black players and teams.

In the early years after Catto's death, his name was memorialized at schools, university dorms, Masonic lodges, and other civic organizations. Thereafter, he was largely forgotten until around 2010, when annual remembrances, new headstones, and an Octavius Catto Medal (awarded by the Pennsylvania National Guard) were inaugurated. The Negro Leagues Baseball Museum also recognized Catto's importance in the history of Black baseball, and the City of Philadelphia finally celebrated Catto's contributions. On September 26, 2017, a twelve-foot bronze statue of Catto, entitled "Quest for Parity," was erected and dedicated at Philadelphia's City Hall, 140 years after his death. Lamenting our historical amnesia, Philadelphia's white mayor, Jim Kenney, led the drive for the Catto statue, asking, "How in God's name did I not know this man? He was the Dr. King and Jackie Robinson of his day."[20]

Fleet: Moses Fleetwood Walker

In 1879, William Edward White, an African American, played one major league game for the Providence Grays in 1879. But the light-skinned White lived his life as a white man, and nobody knew he was Black. The distinction of being the first openly Black player in the major leagues remains with Moses Fleetwood Walker, who broke the color line in 1884. Another Black athlete wouldn't play on a big league roster until 1947, when Jackie Robinson broke in with the Brooklyn Dodgers.

Walker made his mark in baseball but also transcended the sport. After the Civil War, American Blacks were free but considered distinctly inferior. Walker, who was born at the Underground Railroad stop of Mount Pleasant, Ohio, in 1856, was among the few Blacks to attend college. He entered Oberlin College in 1880, where he excelled as a student and catcher on the baseball team. In the summer of 1881, he joined a Cleveland semipro team, but when it traveled to Kentucky, the St. Cloud Hotel—where his white teammates were staying—refused Walker service. Moreover, the Louisville club refused to play against Cleveland if Walker was on the field. This prejudice, and racist taunts from fans and players, became common. Walker transferred to the University of Michigan, where he studied law and led the baseball team to a winning season with his strong hitting (batting .308) and spectacular defense.

In 1882, Walker joined the New Castle Neshannocks, located outside of Pittsburgh, for his first extended professional experience. The local press welcomed him with glowing reviews, calling him "one of the best catchers in the country" and "a gentleman in every sense of the word both on the ball field and off." Unlike other newspapers, the New Castle press never mentioned Walker's color, and when he left the team to resume his studies at Michigan, they described him as having been "brilliant behind the plate."[21]

In the spring of 1883, Walker became a full-time professional ballplayer with the minor league Toledo Blue Stockings after the Northwestern League narrowly rejected a proposal to ban Blacks. Walker was the particular target, and it was reported that "the motion that would have expelled him was fought bitterly but finally laid on the table."[22] During the season, Walker rarely missed games, even though he caught barehanded and only a mask protected him behind the plate. He quickly became known for his speed on the bases and his shotgun arm, helping his team win the pennant. According to the *Toledo Daily Blade*, "Walker has played more games and has been of greater value behind the bat than any catcher in the league."[23] *Sporting Life* agreed, claiming that "Toledo's colored catcher is looming up as a great man behind the bat."[24] Walker's backup was Deacon McGuire, who caught for another twenty-six years in Major League Baseball.

But as Walker traveled the minor league circuit, his color was always an issue. At an August 1883 exhibition game, the ardent racist and future Hall of Famer Cap Anson refused to let his Chicago White Stockings play against Walker. Relenting only to avoid losing gate receipts, the influential Anson vowed never to play with a "n––" again,[25] which began the unwritten but widely agreed-upon Black exclusion from white major league baseball.

The Toledo club joined the major league American Association in 1884. Back in Louisville, amidst abuse from fans, the press, and players, Walker nevertheless broke the color barrier on May 1. While his teammate Tony Mullane claimed Walker "was the best catcher I ever worked with," he hated Blacks and repeatedly threw Walker pitches he wasn't expecting. One time, after throwing a fastball when Walker had called for a curve, Walker confronted Mullane on the mound, saying, "I'll catch you without signals, but I won't catch you if you are going to cross me when I give you signals."[26] Walker caught Mullane for the rest of the season without knowing what was coming.

Even so, Walker quickly became an outstanding catcher. Some thought he was "greater even than his contemporary, [Hall of Famer] Buck Ewing."[27] But racial pressures and death threats persisted. Before traveling to play a team in Virginia in 1884, Walker's Toledo manager received a letter, saying, "We the undersigned, do hereby warn you not to put up Walker, the Negro catcher, the evenings that you play in Richmond, as we could mention the names of 75 determined men who have sworn to mob Walker if he comes to the ground in a suit. We hope you will listen to our words of warning, so that there will be no trouble: but if you do not, there certainly will be. We only write this to prevent much blood shed, as you alone can prevent."[28] Injuries prematurely ended Walker's season, so the threat was avoided, but the Jim Crow mentality was obviously influencing professional baseball.

In 1885, Walker took ownership of the LeGrande House, a hotel-theater-opera house in Cleveland. Then, after two years back in the minors with teams in Cleveland in the Western League and Waterbury in the Eastern League, Walker joined the Newark club in 1887 in the top minor league, the International Association (IA), forming the first African American battery in organized baseball with the pitching star George Stovey. After playing against the duo in an exhibition game, the New York Giants captain John Montgomery Ward lobbied management to sign Walker, but Walker's skin color ultimately dissuaded management from doing so.

Then, before a July exhibition game that same year, Walker again encountered Cap Anson, who insisted that he and Stovey not play. That same day, International Association owners voted to exclude any new Blacks from future contracts. Already under contract, Walker moved in 1888 to the Syracuse Stars, helping them to a pennant. Anson again drove him from the field late that season. The American Association and National League banned Blacks in 1889, institutionalizing Jim Crow in baseball and driving Walker from the game. He became the last Black athlete to play in the International League until Jackie Robinson joined the Montreal Royals in 1946.

In 1891, Walker was violently attacked in Syracuse by white men hurling racist insults. Walker stabbed one of his assailants to death. Walker was tried for murder, but he claimed he acted in self-defense. An all-white jury acquitted him, but Walker emerged bitter. Returning to Ohio, he bought the Union Hotel in Steubenville and joined the Knights of Pythias. Then Walker not only purchased an opera house and theater in nearby Cadiz but also patented three of his inventions to improve motion picture equipment. He also patented his exploding artillery shell, which the US military soon began to use in its arsenal.

Alienated by Jim Crow, social Darwinism, and escalating violence, Walker was also disillusioned with both the moderate Black self-help leader Booker T. Washington and the more radical Black integrationist W. E. B. DuBois. Instead, Walker became a Black nationalist and began editing *The Equator*, a newspaper that covered Black issues. In 1908, Walker published a book, *Our Home Colony*, which his biographer, David Zang, described as "certainly the most learned book a professional athlete ever wrote."[29] In the book, Walker concluded that "the only practical solution of the race troubles in the U.S. is entire separation by emigration of the Negro from America."[30] Anticipating by a decade the Back to Africa Movement led by Black nationalist Marcus Garvey, Walker became an agent for the relocation of American Blacks to Liberia. He returned to Cleveland in 1920 to manage the Temple Theater, and he died there in 1924 of pneumonia at age sixty-eight.

As David Zang has observed, "As with his baseball career, Walker's radicalism anticipated a future moment that couldn't be willed into an earlier arrival."[31] Like the dashed hopes for an integrated America, the prospect of integrated baseball arose and died with Fleet Walker, both dreams postponed for several more generations.

CHAPTER TWO

Building Black Institutions

I n the hotly contested presidential election of 1876, Democratic candidate Samuel Tilden, governor of New York, won 260,000 more votes than his Republican rival, Ohio Governor Rutherford B. Hayes. But the nineteen electoral college votes in three states—Louisiana, Florida, and South Carolina—were in dispute, and both sides claimed victory. The outcome was decided by the US Congress, which reached a compromise between the Democratic-controlled House and the Republican-run Senate. The Democrats agreed to hand the White House to Hayes on the condition that the Republicans end Reconstruction—ceding control of the Southern states to the segregationist Democrats. This opened the door for the Democrats to reimpose white supremacy on former Black slaves. White segregationists overturned the promise of racial equality embodied in the Thirteenth, Fourteenth, and Fifteenth Amendments to the Constitution. Without federal government supervision, the Democrats stripped Blacks of their voting rights and adopted strict Jim Crow laws that mandated racial separation in every facet of Southern life. In 1887, for example, Florida became the first state to mandate segregated railroad cars; other Southern states soon followed Florida's example.

Coping with Segregation

Baseball was not immune from the racial intolerance growing across the country after the Civil War. By 1884, Blacks were banned from the major leagues. Moses Fleetwood Walker was the last African American to play in the big leagues until Jackie Robinson joined the Brooklyn Dodgers in 1947.

Even so, at least fifty-five Blacks played in the mostly white minor leagues between 1883 and 1898. While the International League banned African American ballplayers after 1887, other leagues were less rigid. Most Black athletes played for only one season, but some lasted longer. Frank Grant starred at second base for three years with the Buffalo Bisons and hit .366 in 1887.

That same year, George Stovey won thirty-four games for the Newark Giants, and Bud Fowler (who had switched to second base) hit .350 for Birmingham. Fowler, who was born—ironically—in Cooperstown, New York, excelled for twelve teams in seven different leagues. George Wilson won twenty-nine games for the Adrian Demons (also known as the Reformers) in the Michigan State League in 1895, but none of the team's Black players were rehired the following year.

Some minor leagues had all-Black teams that played against all-white clubs. The most successful was the all-Black Cuban Giants, who played in the Middle States League and other circuits. Other prominent African American teams included the Philadelphia Giants, the New York Gorhams, and the Chicago Unions. The Page Fence Giants (based in Adrian, Michigan) won 118 of their 154 games against mostly white competition in 1895. The last gasp for a Black team playing in white organized baseball was the Acme Colored Giants of Celeron, New York, who played in the Iron and Oil League in 1898. That same year, the Black southpaw, Bud Jones, pitched in the Kansas State League and became the last African American to play in the minor leagues until Jackie Robinson joined the Dodgers' Triple-A squad in Montreal in 1946. Bill Galloway was the last Black player in the Canadian League when he played for the Woodstock, Ontario, club in 1899.

In 1896, the US Supreme Court, in its infamous *Plessy v. Ferguson* decision, ruled that segregation, including separate facilities and institutions for Blacks and whites, didn't violate the US Constitution's equal protection clause. The ruling enshrined the doctrine of "separate but equal" as a constitutional justification for segregation, guaranteeing the persistence of the Jim Crow South for the next half-century. Southern whites launched a terrible period of racial violence to maintain the racial caste system. Lynchings of Blacks became a frequent occurrence. More than 4,000 Black people were lynched between 1877 and 1950, mostly in the South.[1] Ku Klux Klan (KKK) membership rose to record numbers. The Jim Crow laws and white terrorism ended progress toward Black civil rights until the mid-1900s.

Rube: Andrew Foster

By the end of the nineteenth century, African Americans had been banned as individual players on white teams, and Black teams couldn't sustain themselves in white leagues, even when they were allowed. If Black baseball was going to survive, it needed another approach: a sustained effort at organizing and maintaining Black leagues. Despite his nickname, Andrew Foster was no "rube." In the early twentieth century, Rube Foster made an unlikely aspect of American culture—baseball—central to the Black activism and intellectual ferment of that era.

Foster was born in Calvert, Texas, in 1879. Foreshadowing his future role, it was said that Foster was running a baseball team while he was still in grade school. His mother died when he was young, and when his father—a minister—remarried, Foster ran away from home. At age fourteen, Foster was pitching for a Fort Worth team against major leaguers during spring training. He began his professional career in 1897 with the Waco Yellow Jackets, which toured the South playing other Black teams. Seeking to escape from Southern racism, Foster moved north and joined the Chicago Union Giants in 1902, winning fifty-one games. He got his nickname from out-pitching the future Hall of Famer Rube Waddell in an exhibition game against the Philadelphia Athletics. His screwball mesmerized batters, and he became a pitching sensation in segregated baseball.

In 1903, Foster joined the Cuban X Giants, based in Philadelphia. The legendary Philadelphia Athletics manager Connie Mack sought Foster's advice. New York Giants manager John McGraw noted his talent, claiming he would gladly hire Foster but for the color barrier. As Robert Peterson observed in *Only the Ball Was White*, "If the talents of Christy Mathewson, John McGraw, Ban Johnson and Judge Kenesaw Mountain Landis were combined in a single body, and that body was enveloped in a black skin, the result would have to be named Andrew 'Rube' Foster."[2] McGraw allegedly sought out Foster to teach future Hall of Famer Christy Mathewson how to throw the screwball, then known as the "fadeaway" pitch. These relationships fueled Foster's desire to achieve an equal footing with the white magnates and players.

The Cuban X Giants beat the Philadelphia Giants five games to two for the 1903 Black baseball championship, with Foster winning four of those contests. He then jumped to the Philadelphia Giants, leading them to the 1904 championship, winning two of the team's three victories. In 1905, Foster went 51–4 for the Giants, with wins over both Black teams and white major league teams, including the New York Giants, Philadelphia Athletics, and Brooklyn Superbas.

In 1906, Foster moved back west, joining the Chicago Leland Giants. He was soon not only booking and managing the team's games but also turning it into a powerhouse, winning 110 of their 120 games in 1907. Foster dominated as a player, posting a lifetime 2.44 earned run average, and even earned praise from white Hall of Famers. Rogers Hornsby called Rube "the smoothest pitcher I've ever seen," which was remarkable coming from someone who openly boasted about his KKK membership. Honus Wagner called him "one of the greatest pitchers of all time." Frank Chance claimed Foster was "the most finished product I have ever seen in the pitcher's box."[3] The *Albany Times Union* called Foster the "Black Mathewson of the national game."[4] Baseball's color barrier, however, forced Foster to give up his major league aspirations early on, even though he continued pitching until 1917. Foster had other plans.

As a player-promoter, Foster arranged exhibitions against white teams and insisted on a 50–50 split of the proceeds to increase Black salaries. He took over ownership of the Leland Giants in 1910, turning it into the Chicago American Giants, which sometimes outdrew Chicago's major league clubs, the Cubs and White Sox.

Foster succeeded through a series of astute moves. He relocated the team to the old White Sox ballfield, South Side Park. Committed to putting the best possible players on the field, he inaugurated the first spring training trips for a Black team. Foster's ballplayers traveled tens of thousands of miles each year on barnstorming tours, including West Coast swings where they won California Winter League and East-West Colored titles. Foster's American Giants steamrolled the competition for the next decade, winning championships nearly every season. Their phenomenal success turned them into "Black America's Team,"[5] generating enormous racial pride while creating the first national Black baseball heroes worshipped by Black America.

Foster bought a Pullman railroad car to allow the team to travel in luxury and insisted that his players present themselves as dignified to both whites and Blacks. In *Invisible Men*, Donn Rogosin describes Foster's barnstorming tours: "Nothing was as imposing as the sight of the Pullman, fully loaded with the nattily attired young men, pulling into a Deep South city." Pullman cars had symbolic importance to Blacks. The Pullman Company was the largest employer of African Americans. In 1925, its employees organized the first significant African American labor union, the Brotherhood of Sleeping Car Porters, under the leadership of socialist A. Philip Randolph. According to Rogosin, "Pullman meant wages; but it also meant being a servant. Blacks thrilled to see other blacks as passengers on a Pullman car."[6]

By the 1910s, Black participation in baseball had significantly increased. Previously, Black ballplayers relied on clowning to promote their teams, turning the game into a circus or comic farce. Instead, Foster insisted on selling Black baseball as equal to white baseball: based on athletic skills.

Foster revolutionized the sport with "inside baseball," emphasizing smarts and speed over power and conventional strategies. His trademark plays were the drag bunt, and the bunt and run, where the runner had the potential to go from first to third on the play. Foster studied his pitchers meticulously, detecting the slightest flaws in their mechanics. He schooled them in rules of geometry, physics, and psychology. "If you haven't got the intelligence to fit into this kind of play," his third baseman Dave Malarcher quoted him as saying, "then you can't play here."[7]

Foster refused to regard himself and his fellow Black ballplayers as inferior athletes of color. While prejudiced white America sought to keep Black athletes subordinated, Foster pushed back, seeking to elevate Black baseball permanently into the American sports fabric. He not only innovated but also propagandized for the game, endlessly speaking and writing to promote the sport. The force of his personality and his conviction about his God-ordained prominence in the game often shocked even Black baseball, generating fear but also respect for his wisdom. While the door to the major leagues remained firmly closed, Foster's efforts undermined racist stereotypes and contributed to the eventual integration of baseball.

Foster was building Black baseball at the same time that Black boxer Jack Johnson was generating headlines and controversy. In 1910, Johnson knocked out white heavyweight champion Jim Jeffries, called the "Great White Hope," a major blow against white assumptions about Black inferiority. While the knockout provoked white-initiated race riots, it inspired Foster, who sought the same kind of symbolic statement for Blacks through baseball.

In 1912, Johnson was falsely convicted by an all-white jury of violating the federal Mann Act, which forbade transporting a woman across state lines for "immoral purposes." In the eyes of white America, his relationship with his white girlfriend fit that description. While his team was on a road trip to Canada in 1913, Foster suited Johnson up as a Chicago American Giant player and smuggled him out of the United States. Foster's initiatives coincided with the rise of the "New Negro" movement and the Harlem Renaissance, a flowering of Black culture, including poetry, theater, music, painting, and journalism.

On the heels of the Great Migration of Blacks from the South to northern cities, voices of resistance emerged from the Black community against the passive acceptance of American racism throughout the country, not just the South. Laws and customs forced the growing Black population to live in segregated neighborhoods, often called ghettoes, in America's cities. To address these inequities, Booker T. Washington, the best-known Black leader in the early 1900s, advocated Black enterprise, arguing that rather than integration and social equality, African Americans should develop their own businesses and skills. Marcus Garvey promoted a similar emphasis on Black self-reliance through his Universal Negro Improvement Association, the African Communities League, and the Negro Factories Corporation.

W. E. B. DuBois—a prolific sociologist, historian, and activist who in 1895 was the first Black person to earn a PhD from Harvard University— also supported the development of Black institutions. He helped found the Negro Businessmen Leagues and the Niagara Movement, which emphasized the need for Black business cooperation. But he split with Washington and Garvey on segregation. A founder of the National Association for the Advancement of Colored People (NAACP) in 1909, DuBois argued that economic progress for Blacks would be impossible without political rights. He condemned Washington's "accommodationist" stance, which implicitly accepted the Negro race as an inferior caste. DuBois wanted nothing less than full enfranchisement and integration for Blacks in American society. As Blacks faced white resistance to integration, DuBois became more radicalized, arguing that capitalism was at the root of racism and that African Americans should ally with white workers and labor unions to challenge the business class that sought to divide workers by race and weaken their collective power.

Other Black intellectuals agreed that Black Americans had to become more assertive to gain their freedom. John Hope—a cofounder of the Niagara Movement and the first Black president of Morehouse College—argued that "the white man has converted the Negro's labor and money into capital . . . [and an] immense section of the developed country [is] owned by whites and worked by coloreds . . . We must take in some, if not all, of the wages, turn it into capital, hold it, increase it."[8] Alain Locke, one of the leaders of the Harlem

Renaissance, insisted that the standing of African American culture relied on identifying the beauty, genius, and uniqueness of the Black experience.

Foster wanted to elevate Black baseball as part of this growing movement. But which of these approaches would guide his aspirations for the sport? Certainly he supported the development of Black institutions and would be instrumental in creating some of the most vibrant and enduring enterprises in Black America. But Washington's philosophy carried a danger: he seemingly accepted segregation, which whites used to continue denying basic rights for Blacks and which white baseball officials used to end Black petitions to enter the major leagues. Instead, for baseball, Foster wanted Blacks to operate in more than a parallel universe. He wanted baseball institutions that would prove the equal, if not the superior, skill of Black ballplayers as a wedge for opening the major leagues to African Americans.

Foster had become an owner, had a great team, and had his own ballpark, which was unique for a Black baseball entrepreneur. White interests controlled almost all the venues where Black teams might play, charging extortionate percentages at the gate in exchange for permission to play. Then white booking agents began pushing out Black owners altogether. Foster was increasingly isolated, but he refused to accept the usurpation of his sport. Instead, he would form his own league.

Foster's effort came amidst a time of terror and opportunity. White vigilantes lynched nearly one hundred Blacks in 1917 and 1918 alone. A race riot broke out in St. Louis when whites objected to Black employment in a defense plant. KKK membership skyrocketed. Many businesses purged their Black employees. In 1919, there were at least twenty-five white-initiated race riots in America. Many African Americans, including Moses Fleetwood Walker, the last Black major leaguer, were so disillusioned they believed a return to Africa was the only solution.

Rube Foster was not among them. In 1917, the *Freeman*, a Black newspaper in Indianapolis, printed an appeal for a "Moses to lead the baseball children out of the wilderness."[9] Three years later, Foster answered the call. Black baseball needed organization. Two earlier attempts to form a Black league had failed. But in 1919, appealing through a series of newspaper articles entitled "Pitfalls of Baseball," Foster proposed the Negro National League (NNL), noting the high caliber of Black play and spectator interest; the league needed only wise management, business support, and press coverage to flourish. In February 1920, after a year of lobbying financial backers and the Midwest's best Black ball clubs, Foster and other baseball leaders signed a constitution in Kansas City, creating the governing board of the National Association of Colored Professional Base Ball Clubs. Foster wanted a league that would feature tough competition and organized championships. He sought to establish an occupation for Black players equal to any other profession. He wanted Black championship teams that would eventually play white teams in the World Series and a future where his league would accept white teams and vice versa.

Foster borrowed the NNL's motto, "We Are the Ship, All Else is Sea," from Frederick Douglass's description of the Republican Party after the Civil War. The original teams included the Chicago American Giants, Chicago Giants, St. Louis Stars, Dayton Marcos, Detroit Stars, Indianapolis ABCs, Cincinnati Cuban Stars, and Kansas City Monarchs.

Foster proposed and organized the NNL not only for baseball but also for "racial uplift and progress."[10] Influenced by Marcus Garvey, Foster saw profitable Black enterprise and property ownership as the solution for "the mire of prejudice and scorn"[11] and thus declared his intention to operate without white financial participation. In practice he couldn't be so absolute. To ensure Black baseball as a profitable business, he'd have to negotiate with the white business and political power structure. The real issue for Foster wasn't Black versus white but rather "good white" versus "bad white" and, later, "good Black" versus "bad Black" (when a new Black league began raiding his team).

The timing of Foster's new league corresponded to a rise in Black business enterprise. The Black newspapers encouraged African Americans to patronize Black businesses, thus creating an expanding Black consumer market. The NNL teams competed on the field, but they joined forces to keep the league alive, to thwart outside competition from other leagues, and to keep players from jumping from team to team for higher pay. The NNL was immediately successful, drawing big crowds, reaping profits for the owners, and providing star players wages that were almost incomprehensible compared with other Black workers.

Foster was the brains behind the league's success, and the club owners elected him as the first NNL commissioner. He enhanced competition, recognizing the promotional possibilities of pennant races and urban rivalries. Rather than promoting only his own team, he sent one of his players, Pete Hill, to manage the Detroit team and one of his stars, Oscar Charleston, to Indianapolis to strengthen another club to ensure that the teams were competitive. He ordered equalizing trades among other teams. To guarantee timely payrolls, Foster took out loans or paid salaries from his own pocket. He made sure the NNL looked professional, both on and off the field, bolstering a sense of Black pride as well as demanding respect for Black athletes among white Americans.

White sportswriters reluctantly began acknowledging the physical skills of Black ballplayers. But they argued that baseball also required quick thinking and acting, qualities they claimed that African Americans lacked. On the playing field the Black players challenged these stereotypes. The Black press highlighted the evidence that "Negroes play the game with much more thought and snap than the average white player."[12] As for managerial strategy, Foster was favorably compared to the New York Giants' highly regarded John McGraw.

The New Negro movement emphasized Black manliness and gentlemanliness but also included physical prowess. Rather than being passive, the New Negro challenged the color line whenever possible, assuming what scholar Marlon Ross called the "cool pose of racial trespassing."[13] Foster took on this role as an outspoken "race man" while acting as the gentleman race ambassador. Foster was the public face of a rising Black institution. Black periodicals described him as embodying manliness and race success, praising his moral character within a segregated sport.

The New Negro institutional world included the NAACP, the National Urban League, blues and jazz music, Black literature, and Black newspapers, some of which reached readers across the entire country. The movement's leaders included editors such as Robert Vann at the *Pittsburgh Courier* and Robert Abbot at the *Chicago Defender*; literary figures such as Langston Hughes, Claude McKay, Zora Neale Hurston, and Countee Cullen; and political agitators such as DuBois, A. Philip Randolph, and Chandler Owens. But beyond its poets, intellectuals, journalists, and jazz musicians, no list of New Negro trailblazers should exclude Foster. Under his leadership, organized Black baseball powerfully symbolized Black accomplishment in business and society.

In the NNL's first years, Foster's Chicago American Giants continued their success, winning pennants in 1920, 1921, and 1922. Inspired by the NNL, the Southern Negro League emerged in 1920, with teams in Atlanta, Memphis, Nashville, Birmingham, and New Orleans. Less successful than the NNL, it nevertheless supplied the northern teams with some of its greatest stars, including George "Mule" Suttles, Norman "Turkey" Stearns, and Leroy "Satchel" Paige.

In 1923, six teams—the Baltimore Black Sox, Philadelphia Hilldale Athletics, New York Lincoln Giants, New York Cuban Stars, Brooklyn Royal Giants, and the (Atlantic City) Bachrach Giants—organized the Eastern Colored League (ECL), and soon began raiding NNL teams for top players. Eventually the two leagues agreed to respect each other's contracts and even to play a World Series to determine the championship of Black baseball. Black teams also played against white major league teams in barnstorming games in cities and towns across the country, frequently defeating the white clubs. This made Major League Baseball Commissioner Kenesaw Mountain Landis nervous. He banned white major league teams from playing exhibition games against Black teams, telling Foster, "Mr. Foster, when you beat our teams, it gives us a black eye."[14] But Landis's order was frequently ignored as Black teams continued to play white major league clubs during the off-season, which helped to elevate the visibility of Black stars like Satchel Paige and Josh Gibson among white fans and sportswriters.

In May 1925, Foster was in Indianapolis for a series between his Giants and the local Black team, the ABCs. In his hotel room, a gas pipe ruptured. Foster became asphyxiated and lay on the floor, near death, when a player dropped by and saved him. After a brief hospital stay, he returned home to Chicago to recuperate, but the effects of this incident and his baseball obligations began to take a toll.

In 1926, at age forty-seven, Foster had a mental breakdown. His wife told doctors that he was imagining things, often acting oddly. He began hallucinating, claiming he was seeing baseballs flying outside his window along Madison Avenue or insisting he was needed to pitch in the World Series. He was committed to a psychiatric hospital in Kankakee, Illinois, and died there in 1930 at age fifty-one. More than three thousand grieving mourners—Black and white, rich and poor—attended his funeral in rain and snow, and his body lay in state in Chicago for three days. During the services, his casket was closed at the usual hour a ballgame ends, and then a long solemn procession followed him to the graveyard. The American Giants Booster Association presented a huge wreath featuring a green baseball diamond with white carnations for the base paths. The *Chicago Defender*, a leading Black newspaper, observed that Foster "had died a martyr to the game, the most commanding figure baseball had ever known."[15]

To some, Foster was a heavy-handed commissioner who sometimes abused his power, yet even his critics acknowledged that without his domineering leadership, a Negro league wouldn't have existed, much less succeeded. He took precarious, independent Black teams and disciplined them into a thriving league, vastly improved playing facilities, created a Negro World Series, and increased attendance, player wages, and owner profits. In Foster's absence thereafter, the NNL encountered increasing problems, as well as the challenges of the Great Depression, and it finally folded in 1931.

Long recognized as the father of Black baseball, Foster was belatedly inducted into the Cooperstown Hall of Fame in 1981. He transformed baseball for Black Americans, taking African American ball playing from obscurity to respectability, giving professional opportunities to Black ballplayers, and ultimately becoming integral to American baseball. While not completely free of white influence, Foster showed that the sport could be run as a successful business without white interference in management. He inspired a generation of African American baseball entrepreneurs, who would soon create a new Negro National League in 1933 and a Negro American League in 1937—both of which would briefly last beyond baseball's integration. Those leagues pioneered innovations such as portable lighting systems for night games. And they included a female owner, Effa Manley, who became the first woman inducted into the Cooperstown Hall of Fame in 2006.

El Diablo: Willie Wells

Another sign of Foster's greatness was his relentless effort to pass on his hard-earned baseball knowledge. Even though Foster lost him as a player in a dispute with another team, Willie Wells was one of Foster's star pupils. Wells visited Foster often in Chicago and would sit for hours absorbing his baseball insights and stories. Foster called Willie the "Little Ranger," but Wells was more often known as "El Diablo" ("the Devil") for his intensity on the field.

Wells was born in 1906 and grew up in a shack in South Austin, Texas. He played ball and hung around Dobbs Field, where Black teams frequently played. One of Wells's most thrilling childhood memories was meeting the rising Black star, Biz Mackey, who allowed Wells to carry the team equipment to the ballpark and sit on the team bench. In the 1920s, Negro League teams trained in Central Texas. Playing on local sandlots, Wells led an all-star team that challenged Black teams during spring training in 1924, and he attracted the attention of both the Chicago American Giants and the St. Louis Stars.

Wells had graduated from high school and was attending college when several teams bid for his services. With his mother struggling financially, Wells dropped out of college and began a twenty-five-year career as a player and manager. Wells played with the St. Louis Stars from 1924 to 1931, setting a Negro League single-season record of twenty-seven home runs in 1926 along the way. He moved around a lot thereafter, playing for the Detroit Wolves, Homestead Grays, and Kansas City Monarchs in 1932 alone. He joined the Chicago American Giants from 1933 to 1935, and in his second year, he was selected as the West shortstop in the 1934 East-West All-Star Game.

Wells was the premier Negro League shortstop into the mid-1940s. According to Hall of Famer Monte Irvin, Wells was the "Shakespeare of Shortstops"[16] since he knew where balls would go before each pitch was hit. He knew all the fine points of the game and how to teach them. Playing with the Newark Eagles from 1936 to 1939, Wells and third baseman Ray Dandridge formed what was dubbed the "million-dollar infield,"[17] so called because if they were white they'd be worth a million dollars to any major league team.

Wells made two important contributions to how baseball is played. In one game against the Baltimore Elite Giants, Wells was beaned by pitcher Bill Byrd, knocking him unconscious. He survived, and in his next at bat against Byrd, in a time before players used helmets, Wells came up to the plate with a hard hat borrowed from a nearby construction site. Eventually, other ballplayers followed suit. Wells also watched Negro League catcher Pepper Bassett redesign his glove. With its pillow-like shape, the conventional glove made it difficult for Bassett to get a quick release for throwing out runners trying to steal. Wells took Bassett's new squeezer-style catcher's mitt one step further, cutting a hole in the center of his glove, opening the palm, and enhancing both his fielding and release at shortstop. It was the prototype for today's infielders' gloves.

While Negro League stars had played in Cuba and elsewhere in the Caribbean in the off-season, Mexico became an even more significant haven beginning in 1938. Besides allowing them to make additional pay, playing in Mexico provided Black players with an immense relief from America's Jim Crow discrimination. The Mexican League began to lure Negro League, as well as white major league, stars to play during the regular season, offering bigger salaries. Major League Baseball teams collaborated to limit white players from jumping to the Mexican League, imposing lifetime bans, and strong-arming winter leagues in Cuba and Puerto Rico to prohibit white major league players who jumped to Mexican League teams. But the Negro League teams couldn't stop the exodus. In 1940, Wells joined other Black stars, including Martin Dihigo, Cool Papa Bell, Josh Gibson, Buck Leonard, Quincy Troupe, Sam Bankhead, Hilton Smith, and Ray Dandridge, signing on with the Veracruz Blues. Wells played for the Blues for two years, posting a career high .347 batting average in 1941.

In 1942, Newark Eagles owner Effa Manley persuaded Wells to return to the United States to join her team. He became player-manager, guiding the first of several teams he would lead.

Despite his success in Newark, the attractions of Mexico were too strong, and Wells headed back there in 1943 to play for the Tampico Lightermen. Then, in 1944, the Veracruz Blues recruited native Texan and KKK member Rogers Hornsby to manage the team. When he demanded that the team's four Black players be released, he was instead fired and Wells replaced him as player-manager. As a Black man, playing in the integrated Mexican League was a major milestone. But being the manager of both Black and white ball-players, and being successful doing so, was groundbreaking—more evidence against racist assumptions of Black inferiority.

In Mexico, Negro Leaguers were sometimes homesick, and they found the food strange and the language difficult. But it was an opportunity to earn money and escape second-class status in the United States. In 1944, when *Pittsburgh Courier* journalist Wendell Smith asked Wells why he returned to Mexico, Willie spoke for all the Blacks who had left. In Mexico, Wells observed, Black players stayed in the best hotels, ate in the best restaurants, and could go wherever they wanted. He added,

> I didn't quit Newark and join some other team in the States. I quit and left the country. I've found freedom and democracy here, some-thing I never found in the U.S. I was branded a Negro in the States and had to act accordingly. Everything I did, including playing ball, was regulated by my color. They wouldn't even give me a chance in the big leagues because I was a Negro, yet they accepted every other nationality under the sun. Well, here in Mexico, I am a man. I can go as far in baseball as I am capable of going.[18]

Despite the lure of Mexico, many Black players, including Wells, still held out hope for a more tolerant, post–World War II America, including baseball. In 1945, Wells returned to his native country to play and manage the Newark

Eagles. In 1946, he played for the Baltimore Elite Giants. The next year he played shortstop and managed the Indianapolis Clowns and the following year he played for the Memphis Red Sox along with his son, Willie Wells Junior—the second father-son duo to play on the same Negro League team.

After the Brooklyn Dodgers brought Jackie Robinson to the majors in 1947, the Negro Leagues fell on hard times. Major league teams were slow to hire Black players, but Black fans gradually abandoned the Negro League teams to attend major league and minor league games that featured the first wave of Black ballplayers. As the Negro League teams collapsed, many Black ballplayers were abandoned, too. The Manitoba-North Dakota League (called ManDak), with teams in North Dakota, Minnesota, and Canada, which lasted from 1950 through 1957, served as a refuge for many unemployed Black ballplayers, including Leon Day, Ray Dandridge, Satchel Paige, and Wells. The teams were racially integrated and played at a high level of competition. In 1950–1951, Wells was hired as the player-manager of Canada's Winnipeg Buffaloes. With the help of future Hall of Famer Leon Day, Wells led the Buffaloes to the league championship. Wells managed Winnipeg again in 1951 and then managed another ManDak League team, the Brandon (Ontario) Greys, in 1952 and 1953.

Wells liked to teach the game as well as play and manage it. He took ballplayers such as Ernie Banks and Don Newcombe under his wing. In 1947, he was approached by Jackie Robinson at the Brooklyn Dodgers spring training camp. While he was actually a shortstop, Robinson played first base in his sensational first season with the Dodgers' minor league Montreal Royals. "Now," Robinson complained to Wells, "they got me playing second base, and I don't even know how to pivot."[19] Wells taught him how.

Willie was inducted into the Mexican Baseball Hall of Fame and the Cuban Baseball Hall of Fame before he died in 1989. Wells hit over .320 in the Negro, Mexican, and Cuban leagues. He was finally elected posthumously to the Cooperstown Hall of Fame in 1997. Wells proved his skills worthy of accolades, but his contributions to baseball's racial integration deserve just as much attention.

Doc: Frank Sykes

Baseball rebels often make a mark on their sport, speaking out against injustice when others remain silent, ignoring the wrath of their managers, owners, and fans. Some ballplayers take even greater risks beyond the game. Such was the case for Frank Sykes, who embroiled himself in one of America's most controversial criminal trials.

Sykes was born in Decatur, Alabama, in 1892, the son of former slaves. He grew up playing baseball with his five brothers. Sykes graduated from Morehouse College, the historically Black school in Atlanta, and then attended medical school at Howard University in Washington, DC. Although he also played at Morehouse, Sykes was a standout baseball and basketball player at Howard, and as a pitcher he never lost a game. In 1914, while continuing his studies to become a dentist, Sykes was signed by the New York Lincoln Giants. He pitched in the 1917 Negro League's World Series, and played for the Lincoln Giants through 1919, a year after his medical school graduation.

Sykes went on to pitch for several other Negro League teams, including the Philadelphia Giants, the Brooklyn Royal Giants, the Hilldale Daisies, and the Baltimore Black Sox. For the latter team, for which he played between 1920 and 1926, he had a 13–3 season in 1921 and a 30–6 season in 1922, during which he pitched a no-hitter against the Atlantic City Bachrach Giants. It was said that Sykes was "a pitcher hitters did not want to face." Tutored by Rube Foster, Sykes learned to stop trying to blow pitches by batters and rather to vary speeds and location, about which Foster observed, "Well, college, I see you're learning some sense."[20]

Besides winning games, Sykes also helped improve economic conditions for his fellow ballplayers. During the 1930s, in the midst of the Great Depression, Black teams took their players off fixed wages and adopted the "co-plan," in which the owners received 25 to 30 percent of each game's net profits and the players had to share the rest. Sykes organized other players to demand that team owners pay all players fixed salaries. When his Baltimore Black Sox played a Major League All-Star team, he protested that Blacks were receiving lower pay than the whites. While playing ball, Sykes also maintained his dental practice in Baltimore until 1927, when he ended his thirteen-year Negro League career and moved his office and family back to his hometown of Decatur, Alabama.

In March 1931, after a fight broke out on a Southern Railroad freight train in Jackson County, Alabama headed for Chattanooga, Tennessee, police arrested nine Black teenagers, ranging in age from thirteen to nineteen, on a minor charge. When deputies questioned two white women, Ruby Bates and Victoria Price, they accused the young men of raping them while onboard the train. The nine teenagers—Charlie Weems, Ozie Powell, Clarence Norris,

Andrew and Leroy Wright, Olen Montgomery, Willie Roberson, Haywood Patterson, and Eugene Williams—were transferred to the local county seat, Scottsboro, to await trial. They quickly became known as the "Scottsboro Boys." After a week-long trial, eight of the teenagers were convicted and sentenced to death, triggering a nationwide protest movement.

The trial was an outrageous miscarriage of justice. The local newspapers proclaimed the teenagers' guilt even before the trial began. The defense attorney at the trial had no criminal law experience and was inebriated. The convictions and sentences were reached by an all-white jury. Teenagers were tried as adults. They had been falsely accused, but even if they had committed the crime, they would have been victims of a racist criminal justice system. In the South, capital punishment for rape was reserved exclusively for Black men.

As it turned out, the alleged victims had been drinking and had been involved sexually with some white boys on the train. Concerned about being arrested for prostitution and coerced by the white sheriff's deputies to lie, they accused the Black teenagers in order to deflect attention from themselves. In a letter later written by Ruby Bates, she admitted that the Black young men had not raped her or her friend.

The International Labor Defense (ILD), the legal wing of the American Communist Party, took on the case, hoping it would galvanize public opinion against racism. The Communist Party and other leftists also mobilized a movement to "free the Scottsboro Boys," organizing rallies, speeches, parades, and a letter-writing campaign to protest the verdict. Despite this effort, the Alabama Supreme Court upheld the convictions of seven of the defendants, granting Williams a new trial because he was a minor at the time of his conviction.

In November 1932, the US Supreme Court ruled in *Powell v. Alabama* that the Scottsboro defendants had been denied the right to counsel, which violated their right to due process under the Fourteenth Amendment. It ordered a new trial. That trial took place in the circuit court in Decatur, fifty miles west of Scottsboro and Frank Sykes's hometown.

Decatur was not alone among Southern towns in excluding Blacks from the jury rolls. In response, Sykes led a movement to protest this injustice, even though such initiatives could threaten his livelihood and even his life. "Action, not words, counted most with him and he wasted neither,"[21] said journalist Bill Gibson about Sykes. Preparing for the new trial, Samuel Leibowitz, a prominent New York attorney who had taken on the case, claimed that Blacks were systematically excluded from juries. He called Sykes to testify, and Sykes revealed a list of two hundred Black citizens in Decatur who were qualified to serve on a jury but hadn't been called.

The challenge of providing the Scottsboro Boys a strong defense increased when the indictments were split and separate retrials were pursued for the different defendants. Patterson and Norris were again convicted and sentenced to death in 1933; the Alabama Supreme Court affirmed those verdicts in 1934. Thinking back, Sykes couldn't understand how the whites on the jury—some of whom he knew—could convict obviously innocent Black young men and still "call themselves Christians. I supposed they didn't think any more of a Negro than they did a dog."[22] In 1935, however, the US Supreme Court again overturned the convictions in the landmark case of *Norris v. Alabama*. Influenced by Sykes's testimony, the Supreme Court agreed that excluding Black citizens from the jury (which the lower court had done again) was discrimination and a violation of Constitution.

Unfortunately, the Alabama courts wouldn't relent, and they pursued several more trials against the young men. During one of them, Sykes housed Black journalists for Northern newspapers who were reporting on the case and shifted them from home to home when they were threatened with violence. Sykes himself was targeted by white racists and was involved in a high-speed chase to avoid a car full of KKK members. When the KKK burned a cross on his front lawn, Sykes felt he had to protect his family, and they returned to Baltimore in 1937. He resumed his dental practice there and died in 1986 at the age of ninety-four.

While charges were dropped against several of the Scottsboro Boys after six years of wrongful imprisonment, Norris was again sent to death row, Andrew Wright was sentenced to ninety-nine years, and Patterson and Weems received seventy-five years each. The US Supreme Court declined to review those convictions despite persistent evidence of racism. Those sentences were eventually reduced, but the trials persisted into the early 1950s. Despite the continuing injustice in these cases, the resistance by Sykes to all-white juries contributed significantly to the emerging "due process revolution" of the Supreme Court led by Chief Justice Earl Warren in the 1950s and 1960s.

Sykes knew what was at stake in the Scottsboro trials for himself and all African Americans, and with a growing national and international audience watching, he stepped up to help reform American criminal justice amidst a seriously hostile environment. His son, Larry Sykes, later observed, "Even though his money [livelihood] was generated in the Southern cotton economy as a dentist, my father knew he had a responsibility to testify."[23] "You can bet," observer Bill Gibson recounted, that Sykes's actions "took more nerve than it required for him to set down the Bachrach Giants [in his no-hitter] in 1922."[24]

CHAPTER THREE

Before Jackie Robinson

I n February 1933—when Jackie Robinson was fourteen years old and living in Pasadena, California—Heywood Broun, a syndicated columnist at the *New York World-Telegram*, addressed the annual dinner of the all-white New York Baseball Writers Association. If Black athletes were good enough to represent the United States at the 1932 Olympic Games, Broun said, "It seems a little silly that they cannot participate in a game between the Chicago White Sox and St. Louis Browns." There was no formal rule prohibiting Black players from the major leagues, he continued, but instead a "tacit agreement" among owners. He questioned, "Why, in the name of fair play and gate receipts should professional baseball be so exclusive?"[1]

That same month, Jimmy Powers, a popular columnist for the *New York Daily News*, the nation's most circulated newspaper, interviewed baseball executives and players, asking if they would object to having Black players on their teams. National League (NL) President John Heydler, Yankees owner Jacob Ruppert, and star players Herb Pennock, Lou Gehrig, and Frankie Frisch, told Powers they didn't object. Only New York Giants manager John McGraw—who, ironically, had tried to hire a Black player (posing as a Cherokee Indian) when he managed the Baltimore Orioles in 1901—told Powers he opposed the idea. In his February 8, 1933, column, Powers predicted that Blacks would eventually play major league baseball. Powers wrote, "I base this upon the fact that the ball player of today is more liberal than yesterday's leather-necked, tobacco-chewing sharpshooter from the cross roads."[2]

Later that month, Chester Washington, sports editor of the influential Black newspaper the *Pittsburgh Courier*, coordinated a four-month series reporting the views of major league owners, managers, and players about baseball segregation. It began with an interview with Heydler, who said, "I do not recall one instance where baseball has allowed either race, creed, or color to enter into the question of the selection of its players." The paper quoted Philadelphia Phillies President Gerry Nugent: "Baseball caters to all races and creeds. . . . It is the national game and is played by all groups. Therefore, I see no objections to negro players in the big leagues."[3] Commissioner Kenesaw Mountain Landis refused to respond to the *Courier*, but his assistant Leslie O'Connor said there was no rule against Black players. Hiring decisions were made by owners, not the commissioner, he said.

The saga of how Robinson broke baseball's color line in 1947 has been told many times in books, newspaper and magazine articles, and Hollywood films. It is typically told as the tale of two trailblazers—Robinson, the combative athlete, and Dodgers president and general manager Branch Rickey, the shrewd strategist—battling baseball's, and society's, bigotry.

The Jackie Robinson Story, released in 1950 at the height of the Cold War, five years before the Montgomery bus boycott, celebrated Robinson's feat as evidence that America was a land of opportunity where anyone could succeed if he had the talent and will. The movie opens with the narrator saying, "This is a story of a boy and his dream. But more than that, it's a story of an American boy and a dream that is truly American."[4] Rickey is portrayed as a benevolent do-gooder who, for moral and religious reasons, believes he has a responsibility to break baseball's color barrier.

Most books and articles about this saga ignore or downplay the true story of how baseball's apartheid system was dismantled. Rickey's plan came to fruition only after more than a decade of protest to desegregate the national pastime. It was a political victory brought about by a progressive movement.

During America's two biggest crises of the twentieth century—the Great Depression and World War II—Americans of conscience joined forces to battle against the nation's economic class and racial caste system. Baseball played an important role in these overlapping struggles for social justice. Given its endorsement of Jim Crow and the owners' longstanding "gentlemen's agreement" to bar African Americans, baseball seemed like an unlikely site of antiracist resistance.

The Great Depression and the Color Line

The Depression began in October 1929 when the stock market crashed and lasted until the United States entered World War II in 1941. The Depression was hard on almost every American, but it imposed even greater hardships on Blacks than whites. At least one out of five Americans was out of work, but the unemployment rate of African Americans was double or even triple that of white Americans.

Between 1910 and 1940, 1.5 million African Americans left the South, primarily for destinations in northern and Midwestern cities. The exodus accelerated during World War I, when northern companies recruited Blacks to work in factories making clothes, weapons, and food for the war effort. Even so, 77 percent of all African Americans still lived in the former Confederate states in 1940. Most worked as menial labor on plantations or as household domestic workers. Jim Crow laws governed their day-to-day lives. The few Black children who went to school attended segregated, underfunded, and overcrowded schools. Restaurants, parks and playgrounds, and other institutions were strictly segregated. Blacks couldn't vote or serve on juries. The subjugation of Negroes, wrote sociologist Gunnar Myrdal in a 1944 report, *An American Dilemma,* was "the most glaring conflict in the American conscience and greatest unsolved task for American democracy."[5]

The Blacks who fled the South were not only looking for better jobs, but also for better education and escape from the daily indignities and violence of Jim Crow. Once they arrived in the northern and Midwestern cities, or in California, Black Americans discovered that they hadn't fully escaped segregation. They were limited to finding homes in mostly-Black inner cities, sending their children to mostly-Black schools, and working in the lowest-paying and dirtiest jobs.

Cities outside the South had their own version of Jim Crow. Houses in mostly white neighborhoods were off-limits to Blacks. Whites often resorted to organized mob violence to resist having Black families move into white areas, even as late as the 1960s.

Every African American living in the United States, even those who had escaped the South, knew about the terror of lynching. Between 1882 and 1930, lynch mobs killed at least 1,844 African Americans in the Southern states. During the 1930s alone, 113 African Americans were victims of lynching. This brutal practice continued into the next decade. In 1940, for example, a Black man named Jesse Thornton was lynched in Luverne, Alabama, simply for referring to a white police officer by his name without the title of "mister." By 1937, Gallup polls showed overwhelming white support for antilynching legislation, but Congress consistently refused to pass numerous proposed antilynching bills.

Lynching was only one aspect of the violence that whites employed to maintain the racial caste system. In 1940, word spread in Brownsville, Texas that Elbert Williams, a thirty-one-year-old laundromat attendant, was going to host a meeting of the local NAACP in his home to discuss mobilizing Black citizens to register to vote. Before the meeting took place, the local police took Williams from his home, but not to the local jail. Two days later, he was found in a nearby river, tied down to a log and with two bullet holes in his chest. On his death certificate the coroner wrote, "cause of death unknown," but the cause was clear: it was a warning to Brownsville's Black residents who might want to mobilize and vote.

The Protest Movement for Economic and Racial Justice

Throughout the 1930s, millions of workers, consumers, and farmers engaged in protest about the economic hardships they experienced during the Great Depression. The protest movement reflected the nation's mood: a combination of anger, fear, and hope.

The labor movement grew dramatically, particularly among workers in mass-production industries like automobiles, rubber, electrical equipment, steel, and textiles. The movement was led by a new umbrella organization, the Congress of Industrial Organizations (CIO). The slogan "black and white, unite and fight" captures the attitude of most CIO unions.[6]

Franklin Roosevelt's election as president in 1932, with 57 percent of the vote, added an element of hope to the national mood and helped catalyze the union upsurge. His New Deal program not only gave workers the right to unionize (via the National Labor Relations Act) but also included the minimum wage, a massive government-funded jobs program that put people back to work, and provided Social Security, subsidies to troubled farmers, and stronger regulation of banks and other businesses. FDR lifted the nation's spirit. For most Americans, New Deal reforms were a welcome relief to the suffering all around them. In 1936, they reelected FDR in an even bigger landslide, with 61 percent of the vote.

Black Americans generally supported FDR, even though few New Deal programs directly challenged racial segregation. Roosevelt depended on support from segregationist Southern Democrats in Congress to pass his New Deal programs. In 1934, FDR told Walter White of the NAACP, "If I come out for the anti-lynching bill, the Southern Democrats will block every bill I ask Congress to pass to keep America from collapsing. I just can't take that risk."[7]

Most Southern politicians didn't mind adopting some progressive policies so long as they didn't disrupt the South's Jim Crow system of segregation.

As a result, poor Black Southerners were excluded from Social Security and minimum wage laws (which originally didn't cover agricultural workers and domestic workers like maids and nannies, the principal occupations of Southern Blacks). The New Deal allowed cities to segregate public housing and to discriminate against Blacks through the Tennessee Valley Authority, which brought electricity to many rural areas.

A second wave of Black migration occurred during World War II. Blacks again fled the South to escape Jim Crow and were lured to northern, Midwestern, and western cities to work in the war effort. There, they faced constant hostility from whites at work, in neighborhoods, and at the beaches and playgrounds. But the war mobilization also dramatically expanded union membership, from 8.7 million in 1940 to over 14.3 million in 1945—about 36 percent of the work force. For the first time, large numbers of Black factory workers, male and female, joined unions.

Racial tensions erupted in a series of riots in 1943 in Detroit, Los Angeles, New York, Mobile (Alabama), Beaumont (Texas), and other cities, sparked by white resistance. The Detroit riot began on June 20 and lasted three days. It was initiated by white youths, most of them unskilled and poorly educated, who resented the competition for jobs and apartments from newly arrived African Americans. More than six thousand federal troops were ordered into the city to restore peace. A total of thirty-four people (twenty-five of them Black) were killed, most at the hands of white police or National Guardsmen. The riots left 433 people wounded, 75 percent of them Black. Property valued at about $2 million ($31 million in 2021 dollars) was destroyed, most of it in Black neighborhoods that had been invaded by white rioters.

Growing Radicalism

The collapse of America's economy had radicalized millions of Americans, or at least opened their minds to the possibility that something was seriously wrong with the capitalist system. Many African Americans, as well as many white Americans, began to question an economic system that pitted whites and Blacks against each other for scarce jobs and housing.

A growing number of Americans viewed FDR's New Deal as a half measure. To them, the New Deal programs helped relieve much suffering, but they didn't challenge the root cause of the problem. Although in 1932, 1936, and 1940 the presidential candidates of both the Socialist Party and the

Communist Party (CP) received few votes, their radical ideas sparked the curiosity of a growing number of Americans.

During the 1930s and 1940s, the CP —although never even approaching one hundred thousand members—had had a disproportionate influence in progressive and liberal circles. It attracted many idealistic Americans— including many Jews and African Americans—who were concerned about economic and racial injustice. In the United States, the CP took strong stands for unions and women's equality and against racism, anti-Semitism, and emerging fascism in Europe. It sent activists to the Jim Crow South to organize sharecroppers and tenant farmers. The CP was part of the broader civil rights movement that involved campaigns against lynching, police brutality, and Jim Crow laws. The CP and civil rights groups led campaigns to stop landlords from evicting tenants and push for unemployment benefits. In Harlem, they launched the "Don't Buy Where You Can't Work" campaign, urging consumers to boycott stores that refused to hire Black employees. Few Black Americans were CP members, but many rank-and-file Black citizens participated in protests and campaigns that were led or influenced by communists. Some prominent Black artists, intellectuals, and activists, including Paul Robeson, Richard Wright, Alice Childress, Claude McKay, Loraine Hansberry, and Langston Hughes, were either CP members or participated in political and artistic circles influenced by the CP.[8]

The campaign to integrate baseball, which began in the 1930s, was part of that broader effort. It was led by the Negro press, civil rights groups, the CP, progressive white activists, labor unions, and radical politicians. The coalition of forces was a broad umbrella that included some unlikely allies who disagreed about political ideology, but they found common ground in challenging baseball's Jim Crow. They recognized that baseball was, by far, the most popular sport in the country. They believed that if they could push baseball to dismantle its color line, they could make inroads in other facets of American society.

With a few exceptions, sportswriters for white-owned newspapers ignored the Negro Leagues during the 1930s and 1940s. Readers who relied on these papers for sports news learned almost nothing about the Negro Leagues' outstanding players, nor did they learn about the burgeoning protest movement against baseball's color bar.

In contrast, readers of the nation's many African American papers were well-informed about the players and the protest. These papers did not simply report about these people and events. They were actively engaged as advocates for civil rights, including the integration of the national pastime. Between 1933 and 1945—when the Dodgers signed Robinson to a contract—the Negro papers published hundreds of articles and editorials calling for an end to baseball's color line.

Reporters for African American papers, especially Wendell Smith and Chester Washington of the *Pittsburgh Courier*, Fay Young of the *Chicago Defender*, Joe Bostic of the *People's Voice* in New York, Sam Lacy and Art Carter of the *Baltimore Afro-American*, Mabray "Doc" Kountze of Cleveland's *Call and Post*, Dan Burley of New York's *Amsterdam News*, and Lester Rodney, sports editor of the communist *Daily Worker*, took the lead in pushing baseball's establishment to hire Black players. They published open letters to owners, polled white managers and players, brought Black players to unscheduled tryouts at spring training centers, and kept the issue before the public.

A few white journalists for mainstream papers joined the chorus for baseball integration. They reminded readers that two Black athletes— Jessie Owens and Mack Robinson (Jackie's older brother)—had embarrassed Hitler in the 1936 Berlin Olympics by defeating Germany's white track stars. The next year, boxer Joe Louis—called the "Brown Bomber" by sportswriters—knocked out James Braddock in the eighth round to win the heavyweight championship. On the night of June 22, 1938, Louis fought the German Max Schmeling—whom Hitler touted as evidence of white Aryan superiority—at Yankee Stadium before a crowd of 70,043. Louis knocked Schmeling out in two minutes and four seconds of the first round. About 70 million people in the US, and over 100 million people around the world, listened to the fight on radio. Many Americans, white as well as Black, cheered Louis' victory. Although he continued to confront discrimination in his daily life, his defeat over Schmeling made him a national hero.

The issue of baseball's bigotry was an obvious cause for the left, including the CP. In 1938, the American Youth Congress, a group led by CP activists, passed a resolution censuring the major leagues for its exclusion of Black players. In 1939, New York State Senator Charles Perry, who represented Harlem, introduced a resolution that condemned baseball for discriminating against Black ballplayers. In 1940, sports editors from college newspapers in New York adopted a similar resolution.

America Enters World War II

As the nation geared up to enter World War II, African Americans were consistently excluded from well-paying jobs with private defense contractors. A. Philip Randolph, the founder of the Brotherhood of Sleeping Car Porters (the largest all-Black labor union) and a leading civil rights figure, had an idea to challenge segregation in the war industries. He and Walter White (the head of the NAACP) met with FDR in June 1941 to ask him to open up defense employment to Blacks. They came armed with a threat—a march on Washington, DC with over one hundred thousand protesters. FDR relented. A week later, on June 25, he signed Executive Order 8802, which Randolph helped draft. It stated, "There shall be no discrimination in the employment of workers in defense industries or government because of race, creed, color, or national origin."[9] The order also created a Fair Employment Practices Committee (FEPC) to investigate reports of discrimination. Randolph called off the march. This successful campaign to break the color line in private industry was part of the larger civil rights movement, which included the effort to integrate baseball.

The United States officially entered World War II after the Japanese bombed Pearl Harbor on December 7, 1941. Not surprisingly, many African Americans had mixed feelings about supporting the war effort when they faced such blatant discrimination in their own country. When he was drafted, Nate Moreland, a pitcher in the Negro Leagues, complained, "I can play in Mexico, but I have to fight for America, where I can't play."[10] An editorial in the *New Negro World* in May 1942 reflected similar frustrations: "If my nation cannot outlaw lynching, if the uniform [of the army] will not bring me the respect of the people that I serve, if the freedom of America will not protect me as a human being when I cry in the wilderness of ingratitude; then I declare before both God and man . . . To Hell With Pearl Harbor."[11] On Opening Day in 1945, activists carried picket signs at Yankee Stadium, asking, "If we are able to stop bullets, why not balls?"[12]

A month after the bombing of Pearl Harbor, James Thompson, a cafeteria worker in Kansas, coined the phrase "Double Victory" in a letter to the African American newspaper, the *Pittsburgh Courier*. "The V for victory sign is being displayed prominently in so-called democratic countries which are fighting for victory over aggression, slavery and tyranny," Thompson wrote. "If this V sign means that to those now engaged in this great conflict, then let we colored Americans adopt the VV for a double victory. The first V for victory over our enemies from without, the second V for victory over our enemies from within. For surely those who perpetrate these ugly prejudices here are seeking to destroy our democratic form of government just as surely as the Axis forces."[13]

Blacks enlisted in the war effort in great numbers, but faced the reality that America's armed forces were as segregated as the rest of the country. Most Black men who served in the Army were relegated to segregated combat support groups. Even the nation's blood program was segregated. The Red Cross collected blood from millions of Americans that the military shipped to soldiers fighting overseas. But blood donated by Black Americans could not be used to save the lives of white soldiers, nor could blood from white donors be used to help Black soldiers—never mind that the director of the Red Cross's blood program was an African American scientist named Dr. Charles Drew.

After the United States entered the war, Black papers escalated their campaign to integrate baseball. They enthusiastically supported the "Double V" campaign and made baseball part of a larger crusade to confront Jim Crow laws. Cumberland "Cum" Posey, owner of the Negro League's Homestead Grays, went so far as to suggest in his weekly *Courier* column, "Posey's Points," that every Negro League player wear a Double V symbol on his uniform.

Unions played an important part in this crusade. The New York Trade Union Athletic Association, a coalition of progressive unions, organized an "end Jim Crow in baseball" day of protest at the 1940 World's Fair.[14] Unions and civil rights groups picketed outside Yankee Stadium, the Polo Grounds, and Ebbets Field in New York, and Comiskey Park and Wrigley Field in Chicago. The speakers included Congressman Vito Marcantonio of New York and Richard Moore of the left-wing National Negro Congress. Over several years, these activists gathered more than a million signatures on petitions, demanding that baseball tear down the color barrier. In 1943, similar pickets occurred outside Wrigley Field in Los Angeles, where the minor league Angels played.[15] Angels President Pants Rowland wanted to give tryouts to several Black players. He and Philip Wrigley, owner of the Chicago Cubs, the parent team, met with William Patterson, a civil rights lawyer and Communist Party member. But Wrigley nixed the tryout idea, saying he favored integration but "I don't think the time is now."[16]

In June 1942, large locals of several major unions—including the United Auto Workers and the National Maritime Union, as well as the New York

Industrial Union Council of the CIO—sent resolutions to Landis demanding an end to baseball segregation. The union leaders told Landis's secretary, Leslie O'Connor, that unless he let them address the owners' meeting, they would take the issue to the FEPC, the federal agency created by FDR in 1941 to investigate discrimination in the defense industry and other sectors.[17] Landis and the owners refused to meet with them.

The unions' protest made headlines in both Black and white newspapers across the country. The stories mostly focused on Landis's refusal to meet with them, but just getting the issue in the news helped them build public support for their cause.[18] The movement gained an important ally when Chicago's Catholic bishop, Bernard Shiel, announced he would urge Landis to support integration.[19] In July 1942, Landis summoned Leo Durocher to a meeting in Chicago, and rebuked him for his comments claiming that baseball banned Black players. Landis issued a statement claiming that "there is no baseball rule—formal, informal, or otherwise—that says a ball player must be white."[20] Most newspapers took Landis at his word, but the Black papers and the *Daily Worker* called him a hypocrite.

That December, ten CIO leaders went to the baseball executives' winter meetings in Chicago to demand that major league teams recruit Black players, but Landis again refused to meet with them.[21] Only Chicago Cubs owner Phil Wrigley broke ranks. After the official meeting ended, Wrigley invited union leaders to his office and told them he favored integration and revealed that, contrary to his fellow owners' claims, there was, in fact, a "gentlemen's agreement" among them to keep Blacks out of major league baseball. "There are men in high places," he told them, "who don't want to see it."[22] Frustrated by the lack of progress, in February 1943, a broad coalition of unions, left-wing groups, and religious and civil rights organizations—including the Urban League and the NAACP—met in Chicago and adopted a resolution demanding the integration of baseball to send to Landis, team owners, and President Roosevelt.[23]

Crusader: Wendell Smith

Wendell Smith, one of the leading crusaders within the Black press, was born and raised in Detroit. His father moved from Canada to Detroit, where he worked as a dishwasher and then a cook, eventually becoming auto magnate Henry Ford's personal chef. His father took Smith to Ford's mansion, where he played baseball with the tycoon's sons. The Smiths lived in an integrated neighborhood, but Wendell was the only African American student at Detroit's Southeastern High School, where he played on the school's baseball team and on an American Legion team. During the summer of 1933, Smith pitched his American Legion club to a 1–0 victory in the playoffs. After the game, a scout for the Detroit Tigers, Wish Egan, signed Smith's catcher Mike Tresh (who went on to play in the majors for twelve years) and the losing pitcher on the opposing team. "I wish I could sign you, too, but I can't," Egan told Smith.

Egan's words "broke me up," Smith later recalled. "It was then I made a vow that I would dedicate myself to do something on behalf of the Negro ballplayers. That was one of the reasons I became a sportswriter."[24]

At West Virginia State College, Smith not only played on the baseball team but also served as the school paper's sports editor during his junior year. Smith began working at the *Pittsburgh Courier* immediately after graduating in 1937, first as a sportswriter and then as the sports editor the following year.

During the 1930s and 1940s, the *Courier* had the largest circulation of any Negro newspaper, growing from 46,000 readers in 1933 to over 250,000 in 1945. Reaching readers across the country, it established itself as a leading voice against baseball's racial divide.

Like other Negro papers, the *Courier* extolled the talents of Black players as equal to their white counterparts. As evidence, they pointed to the outcomes of exhibition games between Negro teams and white players. On October 20, 1934, for example, the Negro Leagues' Kansas City Monarchs beat a team of major leaguers, which included the St. Louis Cardinals' ace pitcher Dizzy Dean. A week later, Satchel Paige and the Pittsburgh Crawfords defeated the same contingent of major leaguers. The headline in the *Pittsburgh Courier* read "Satchell Outhurls Dizzy!"[25] In 1938, Dean told the *Courier* that Paige was "the pitcher with the greatest stuff I ever see."[26] In 1939, Dean—who grew up in rural Arkansas—told Smith that Paige, Josh Gibson, and Oscar Charleston were among the best players he'd ever seen. "I have played against a Negro all-star team that was so good we didn't think we had a chance," he said.[27]

In 1937, Paige proposed that the winner of the major league World Series play against a team of Negro League all-stars, including Josh Gibson, Cool Papa Bell, and Paige on the mound. He suggested that the profits from the game go directly to the winning players. The mighty Yankees of Lou Gehrig,

Joe DiMaggio, Bill Dickey, Red Ruffing, and Lefty Gomez won the American League (AL) pennant with a 102–52 win-loss record and then vanquished the New York Giants four games to one in the World Series. A contest between the Yankees and Negro Leaguers would have sold out any big-league stadium and generated much excitement. But the Yankees never took Paige up on his offer, perhaps worried that they might lose and undermine a key justification for baseball segregation—the alleged inferiority of Black ballplayers.

After Smith joined the paper, he expanded its efforts to protest segregation in baseball and other professional sports. In his first column on the issue, published on May 14, 1938, Smith criticized Black Americans for their economic support of major league baseball, spending their hard-earned money on teams that prohibited Black players. Smith wrote, "We know they don't want us, but we keep giving them our money. Keep on going to their ball games and shouting til we are blue in the face—we pitiful black folk. Yes, sir—we Black folk are a strange tribe."[28] He also criticized Black Americans for not patronizing the Negro League teams, putting them in constant financial jeopardy. In this way, Smith was echoing the demand among civil rights leaders at the time to boycott businesses that refuse to hire or show respect for Black Americans.

In 1939, Smith conducted an interview with National League president Ford Frick, who claimed that the only reason major league teams didn't employ Black athletes is because white fans would not accept them. It would take an education campaign to change white public opinion, he told Smith. He also noted that Black players wouldn't be allowed to travel with their teams during spring training or in certain major league cities because Southern hotels, restaurants and trains would not accept them—a reality that, Frick said, would undermine team spirit.[29]

Frick's comments inspired Smith to interview eight managers and forty National League players, which he published in a series entitled "What Big Leaguers Think of Negro League Baseball Players" between July and September. Among the managers, only the Giants' Bill Terry said he believed that Blacks should be barred from major league teams. Dodgers manager Leo Durocher said he'd put Black players on his team but noted that "the decision as to whether or not they shall play is not up to the managers but ball club owners."[30] Other managers agreed with Durocher's view, while some players expressed the hope that Black players would one day play alongside them.

Smith was writing primarily for a Black audience, since the *Courier* had few white readers. But as part of a broader movement, Smith recognized that his goals were shared by progressive whites. In fact, Smith's 1939 interviews with major league managers and players inspired the New York Trade Union Athletic Association to plan its "end Jim Crow in baseball" day of protest at the World's Fair the following summer.

Once the United States entered World War II, Smith escalated his campaign, drawing on the obvious hypocrisy of a country that asked Black Americans to fight in a war for democracy while practicing racism at home. Throughout the war years, Smith continued to use the *Courier* as an instrument to voice outrage against the baseball establishment.

In a July 1942 column Smith wrote that "big league baseball is perpetuating the very things thousands of Americans are overseas fighting to end, namely, racial discrimination and segregation."[31] The next year, he called on Roosevelt to adopt a "Fair Employment Practice Policy" for major league baseball, similar to the one he'd adopted in war industries and governmental agencies.

Smith spent much of 1943 quarreling with Washington Senators owner, Clark Griffith for his blatantly racist view of Black ballplayers. While other owners refused to publicly voice their segregationist views, Griffith was outspoken in his opposition to allowing Blacks in organized baseball. Griffith insisted that Blacks should focus on improving their own leagues. Smith recognized that Griffith was profiting handsomely by renting his ballpark to Negro League teams.

Later in 1943, Smith took the initiative to ask Landis to meet with the publishers of some of the nation's leading Black newspapers at the December meeting of major league owners at the Roosevelt Hotel in New York City. Landis agreed, pressured in part by a resolution sponsored by a New York City council member demanding that major league baseball recruit Black players. This was the first time that representatives of the Black community had the chance to meet directly with baseball's establishment and demand an end to its racial segregation.

Smith brought seven newspapermen along with Paul Robeson, a prominent Black actor, singer, activist, and former All-American athlete at Rutgers. Landis began the meeting by insisting that he wanted it "clearly understood that there is no rule, nor to my knowledge, has there ever been, formal or informal, or any understanding, written or unwritten, subterranean or sub-anything, against the hiring of Negroes in the major leagues."[32]

Then Landis introduced Robeson, who was perhaps the most famous American in the world at the time. Robeson gave an impassioned twenty-minute appeal, referencing his experience in college and professional football and his current work as an actor, dispelling the idea that desegregation creates chaos. "They said that America never would stand for my playing Othello with a white cast, but it is the triumph of my life," he declared. "The time has come when you must change your attitude toward Negroes. . . . Because baseball is a national game, it is up to baseball to see that discrimination does not become an American pattern. And it should do this this year."[33] The owners gave him a rousing applause, but Landis had instructed them to ask him no questions.

Landis next introduced John Sengstacke, president of the Negro Newspaper Publishers Association and the publisher of the *Chicago Defender*. Sengstacke called the ban against Black players "un-American" and "undemocratic." Then Ira Lewis, president of the *Courier*, told the owners it was simply untrue that major league players would refuse to play against Black athletes, based on Smith's many interviews. He also noted that Black players could compete with white players at the same level, reminding the owners that Black teams had defeated teams of major leaguers in various exhibition games.[34]

Not one of the baseball owners and executives asked the Black publishers any questions. After the meetings were over, however, they issued an official statement repeating Landis' claim that each team is free to employ Black players if they want to do so. In his columns, Smith continued to taunt Landis for his hypocrisy and disingenuousness. After Landis died in November 1944, Smith wrote a column criticizing him for refusing to use his office to challenge discrimination against Black players, pointing out that it was the one issue that Landis in his almost twenty-five years as baseball's powerful commissioner "never faced with the courage and exactness that he faced others."[35]

In 1944, Smith wrote several sympathetic stories to help publicize the court-martial of a Black soldier at Fort Hood, Texas—a former UCLA four-sport athlete—for refusing to go to the back of a military bus. The soldier was Jackie Robinson, who befriended Smith and was grateful for his support.

Press Box Red: Lester Rodney

No white journalist played a more central role in baseball's civil rights crusade than the *Daily Worker*'s Lester Rodney. He grew up in Brooklyn, where he became a Dodgers fan, covered sports for his high school newspaper, and played basketball and ran track. His father, a staunch Republican, owned a silk factory but was ruined financially by the 1929 stock market crash, losing both his business and his home. Rodney earned a partial track scholarship to Syracuse University, but he had to turn it down because his family could not afford the other half of his tuition. To supplement the family income, he took odd jobs and attended night school at New York University (NYU) in the mid-1930s.

Rodney was radicalized by his family's experience and by the enormous suffering he witnessed during the Great Depression. A pivotal moment, which Rodney referred to as his "political epiphany," came one day when he was walking near Grand Central Station and encountered a man making a speech. "He was a Communist. But he wasn't at all like the popular image I had of Communists . . . he wasn't shouting," Rodney remembered. "The way he talked was more like chatting with a circle of maybe thirty or forty people." Rodney recalled him saying, "Don't you think it's ridiculous for a country as rich as ours to have to many people out of work? We Communists believe there are reasonable alternatives to the callous capitalism that benefits the few and keeps creating wars and economic crises." When the speaker stopped, Rodney approached him. They had a long talk, "and from then on I began seriously examining the political ideas I was encountering."[36]

While at NYU, a young CP recruiter handed Rodney a copy of the *Daily Worker*, "which stirred up some latent anti-capitalist feelings in me."[37] He agreed with its political perspective but was appalled by its failure to take sports seriously. The paper had occasionally written about union-sponsored and industrial baseball leagues, but not professional sports.

Rodney wrote a letter to the paper's editor, criticizing its sports coverage. "I've begun to read your paper," he explained, "and I've become interested in what it has to say. But I cringe a little when I read the sports pages because I'm a sports fan." He made some suggestions, but mainly argued that they needed a change in attitude. Rodney continued,

> You guys are focusing on the things that are wrong in sports. And there's plenty that's wrong. But you wind up painting a picture of professional athletes being wage slaves with no joy, no élan—and that's just wrong. Of course there's exploitation, but . . . the professional baseball player still swells with joy when his team wins. . . . that's not fake. That's beyond the social analysis of the game. The idea of people coming together, blending their skills into a team,

getting the best out of each other—and winning. That's a remarkable thing. . . . The way I would write about sports . . . that would never be absent. Along with social criticism. They're not contradictory.[38]

In response, the higher-ups at the *Daily Worker* asked him to write a column, and soon they made him the paper's first sports editor. He served in the capacity from 1936 to 1958, when he quit the Communist Party. To the leaders of the Communist Party, sports, like religion, was seen as an opiate for the masses—a distraction from dealing with their oppression. But like most Americans, rank-and-file Communists loved baseball. Rodney argued that if you wanted to appeal to bedrock Americans, then you had to take sports, especially baseball, seriously.

It is not surprising that the CP—which regarded itself as the "Party of Negro and White"—took up the cause of opposing baseball's color ban. The Communists had been a leading force against racism since the 1920s, and thus many prominent Blacks were attracted to the Party. Communist Party leaders believed they could win the hearts and minds of Black Americans if they were seen as leading the fight to desegregate professional baseball.

Rodney was an enthusiastic and well-informed baseball fan. Hardnosed baseball manager Leo Durocher once told him, "For a fucking Communist, you sure know your baseball."[39] For a dozen years, Rodney was one of the few white sportswriters to cover the Negro Leagues and to protest baseball segregation. One of his editorials attacked "every rotten Jim Crow excuse offered by the magnates for this flagrant discrimination."[40]

In an open letter to Landis published in the *Daily Worker* in May 1942, Rodney wrote, "Negro soldiers and sailors are among those beloved heroes of the American people who have already died for the preservation of this country and everything this country stands for—yes, including the great game of baseball. . . . You, the self-proclaimed 'Czar' of baseball, are the man responsible for keeping Jim Crow in our National Pastime. You are the one refusing to say the word which would do more to justify baseball's existence in this year of war than any other single thing."[41]

According to Rodney, "Every story we did had a purpose and the *Daily Worker* was on the desk of every other newspaper." The paper "had an influence far in excess of its circulation, partly because a lot of our readership was trade union people."[42]

Like Smith and other sympathetic reporters, Rodney interviewed players and managers to shoot down the argument that they all opposed the integration of major league baseball. A typical *Daily Worker* story ran on July 19, 1939, with the headline: "Big Leaguers Rip Jim Crow." It quoted members of the Cincinnati Reds, whose manager Bill McKechnie said that "I'd use Negroes if I were given permission." Reds' star pitcher Bucky Walters declared them "some of the best players I've ever seen."[43] Johnny Van der Meer, another pitching ace, said: "I don't see why they're banned."[44] In an interview with Yankee slugger Joe DiMaggio, the All-Star outfielder told Rodney that Satchel Paige was the best pitcher he ever faced. Getting these views out in the open was instrumental in breaking down the color barrier, over a period of years.

Rodney had great rapport with the players and even recruited two of them to write for the *Daily Worker*. In 1937, members of the Newspaper Guild, including reporters and other staffers, launched a strike against the publishers of the *Brooklyn Eagle* to protest pay and working conditions. The *Daily Worker* helped organize a citizens' committee in support of the fifteen-week strike, and to protest the beating of the *Eagle* sports reporter and labor leader, Ed Hughes, by antiunion thugs. Several big-league ballplayers joined the picket line against the publisher, including Yankees stars Joe DiMaggio, Lou Gehrig, Lefty Gomez, Bill Dickey, Red Ruffing, and Red Rolfe. None of those players was a radical, but they were friendly with Hughes and they sympathized with "working stiffs," according to Rodney.[45] Perhaps the most progressive Yankee of all was Rolfe, the star third baseman, a Dartmouth College graduate, and ardent New Dealer at a time when President Roosevelt's opponents called him a Socialist and a Communist.

Rodney developed a close relationship with Rolfe, and later that year, Rodney convinced him to write stories for the *Daily Worker*. Rolfe, who got his nickname from his hair color, not his politics, knew the *Daily Worker* was a communist paper but kept politics out of his writing. He insisted on writing all his own material. On October 7, 1937, Rolfe's account of the first game of the World Series between his Yankees and the New York Giants appeared on the front page. As Rodney's biographer, Irwin Silber, claimed, "The fact that a major-league ballplayer would be willing to write for the *Daily Worker* signified a degree of legitimacy for the Communist Party—or at least its newspaper—that could hardly have been imagined a few years earlier."[46] Thereafter, Rolfe wrote a regular column for the newspaper. But Rodney didn't press

Rolfe to write about baseball's color barrier. He didn't want to jeopardize the coup of having a baseball star writing for a communist newspaper.

On the days when Rolfe's column appeared, the *Daily Worker* sold thousands more copies at the newsstands. "The way I thought about it at the time," Rodney recalled, "was that the main value of getting Red Rolfe . . . was to show that we were a real sports section on a real newspaper." Rodney claimed that "if I had said to Rolfe, 'what do you think about the Negro players? Shouldn't the Yankees have a Negro player?' Somebody would have said, 'See. They only wanted you to get the n–– question in.'"[47]

In 1938, Rodney commissioned Chicago Cubs first baseman Ripper Collins to write a column for another communist newspaper, the *Midwest Daily Record*, an offshoot of the *Daily Worker*. Collins had been a mine worker before entering professional baseball. A member of the militant United Mine Workers union, he had leftist sympathies. For the newspaper, he covered the 1938 pennant race and the Cubs contests against the Yankees in the World Series. Like Rolfe, Collins avoided writing about politics or controversial issues, especially baseball's color ban.

According to Rodney, "Readers loved it, of course, but the really fascinating thing was the next day after a story would come out. I'd go into the dressing room before the game—and just picture this—there are the Yankees—the New York Yankees—sitting around the dressing room reading the *Daily Worker*. If Colonel Rupert [the Yankees owner] had walked in, he would have had a heart attack." And there was "not a word of red-baiting" of Rolfe or Collins by their teammates.[48]

Despite avoiding any political commentary in his columns, Rolfe received hostile letters and threatening phone calls for writing for a communist paper. That only strengthened his resolve. "Can you imagine those people?" he asked. "I'll write whatever I want for whoever I want."[49] In 1939, however, Yankee manager Joe McCarthy complained that Rolfe was spending too much time on his column and ordered him to quit.

Over the next few years, Rodney interviewed Negro players to challenge the myth that they preferred playing in the Negro Leagues to breaking into Major League Baseball. By doing so, he also exposed the exploits and talents of Black ballplayers to the mostly white readers of the *Daily Worker*. Rodney recalled an interview with Satchel Paige in which the Negro Leagues' premier pitcher was brimming with ideas about how to make baseball integration happen. "Let the winners of the World Series play an all-star Negro team just one game at Yankee Stadium and if we don't beat them before a packed house they don't have to pay us a dime," Paige told Rodney.[50]

Rodney didn't just write about baseball's color ban. He was also active in the "End Jim Crow in Baseball" campaign. In 1941, he and sport writers for Negro newspapers sent telegrams to team owners asking them to give tryouts to Black players. In 1942, the Chicago White Sox reluctantly invited the Negro League pitcher Nate Moreland and UCLA's multi-sport athlete and All-American football star Jackie Robinson to attend a tryout camp in Pasadena, California. Manager Jimmy Dykes raved about Robinson. "He's worth $50,000 of anybody's money. He stole everything but my infielders' gloves."[51] Yet the two ballplayers were dismissed with no follow-up discussions.

Because Pittsburgh was home to two of the best Negro League teams— the Homestead Grays and the Pittsburgh Crawfords—Rodney and Smith pushed Pittsburgh Pirates owner William Benswanger to give tryouts to Black ballplayers. During the summer of 1942, Benswanger scheduled two auditions—one with Roy Campanella, Sammy Hughes, and David Barnhill and another with Josh Gibson, Leon Day, Sam Bankhead, and Willie Wells. But Benswanger broke his promise and cancelled both tryouts.

Despite his strong opposition to communism, Smith acknowledged Rodney's role on behalf of baseball integration. In an August 20, 1939 letter to the *Daily Worker*, Smith wrote that he wanted to "congratulate you and the *Daily Worker* for the way you have joined with us in the current series concerning Negro Players in the major leagues, as well as all your past great efforts in this aspect."[52] He expressed the hope of further collaboration. Over the next eight years, despite their ideological differences, Smith and Rodney joined forces in the battle to integrate baseball.

Maverick: Bill Veeck

Among baseball's owners, Bill Veeck was a maverick. If he had his way, major league baseball would have integrated five years before Robinson signed with the Dodgers.

His father, Bill Sr., was president of the Chicago Cubs. After Bill Sr. died in 1933, the Cubs owner, Philip K. Wrigley, hired the eighteen-year-old Veeck out of a sense of loyalty. He started off as a glorified office boy and jack-of-all-trades, but he gradually began to assume more responsibilities.

Although the major leagues banned Black ballplayers, Veeck was exposed early in life to outstanding African American players. In his early teens, he attended games of the Negro Leagues' Chicago American Giants. In early 1934, while visiting Los Angeles for the Cubs' spring training, he watched Satchel Paige and Dizzy Dean pitch against each other in an exhibition, with Paige's Negro League team squeaking out a 1–0 win. Recalling that experience, Veeck said it was "the greatest pitchers' battle I have ever seen."[53]

Veeck was also aware that in 1934, the Negro League's annual All-Star game, called the East-West Game—held in Chicago's Comiskey Park, home of the White Sox—attracted twenty thousand fans, while only twelve thousand people watched the Cubs play a double-header at Wrigley Field.

Veeck admired Abe Saperstein, the owner of the all-Black basketball team, the Harlem Globetrotters, who played exhibition games in big cities and small towns across the country, drawing big crowds of Black and white fans, who marveled at the players' ball-handling antics. During the 1930s, before the advent of a major professional basketball league, the Globetrotters were the sport's best-known team. Veeck was drawn to Saperstein's promotional genius and the idea that white fans would pay to see outstanding Black athletes.

In 1942, at age twenty-seven, Veeck purchased the Milwaukee Brewers of the American Association, the highest minor league level. During one Brewers' spring training season in Ocala, Florida, Veeck decided to sit in the "colored" section of the stands. The local police showed up, told him he couldn't sit there, and ordered him to move, threatening to arrest him for violating Florida's Jim Crow laws. "I'm not bothering them," Veeck said, according to his 1962 autobiography, *Veeck as in Wreck*. "I'm enjoying our talk and they don't seem to resent me too much. They won't mind if I stay here."[54]

Soon the town's mayor arrived to insist that Veeck leave. "I don't know anything about that," Veeck told him. "What I do know is that if you bother me any more we'll move our club out of Ocala tonight. And we'll tell everybody in the country why," he said, threatening to pull the team's lucrative spring training program. The local officials left him alone after that. "I sat there every day, just to annoy them, without ever being bothered again," Veeck recalled in his autobiography. "Nevertheless, I had already made up my mind to get out of Florida."[55] Most major league teams didn't integrate their spring training facilities in Florida until the 1960s. Veeck's small gesture laid the groundwork for a broader assault on baseball segregation.

In 1942, while he still owned the Brewers, Veeck thought he'd found an opportunity to challenge baseball segregation. He learned that the Philadelphia Phillies were bankrupt and for sale, and he quietly found investors, including the progressive union federation, the CIO, and then made a deal with the Phillies' owner Gerry Nugent to buy the team. He believed that stocking the team with stars from the Negro Leagues could turn the lowly Phillies into a winning club, according to his autobiography.

As he was leaving for Philadelphia to seal the deal, he ran into John Carmichael, a *Chicago Daily News* sports columnist. "Where you going?" Carmichael asked. "I'm going to Philadelphia," Veeck responded. "What're you going to do in Philadelphia?" his friend inquired. "I'm going to buy the Phillies. And do you know what I'm going to do? I'm going to put a whole Black team on the field."[56] But hours before his train departed for Philadelphia, Veeck made the mistake of informing baseball Commissioner Kennesaw Landis, a foe of baseball integration, about his intentions.

Veeck later recounted, "I got on the train feeling I had not only a Major League ball club but I was almost a virtual cinch to win the pennant next year." As Veeck told the story in *Veeck as in Wreck*, Landis and National League president Ford Frick thwarted his plans by orchestrating a quick sale of the Phillies to another buyer. Before he had even reached Nugent's office the next day, Veeck learned that the National League had taken over the Phillies the night before and was seeking a new owner. Veeck was not on their list.[57]

The Movement Escalates

With a large number of progressive unions and civil rights groups, a large African American population, and three major league teams, it was not surprising that throughout the 1930s and 1940s New York City was the center of the movement to end Jim Crow in baseball. On Opening Day of 1944, for example, the Congress of Racial Equality (CORE) organized a demonstration outside Yankee Stadium to enlighten fans and castigate the owners of the game's most powerful franchise for its failure to put a Black player on its roster. Several New York politicians were allies of the campaign to integrate baseball. Running for reelection as a Communist to the New York City Council in 1945, Ben Davis—an African American who starred on the football field for Amherst College before earning a law degree at Harvard—distributed a leaflet with the photos of two Black men, a dead soldier and a baseball player. "Good enough to die for his country," it said, "but not good enough for organized baseball."[58]

In March of 1945, the New York State legislature passed—and Republican Governor Tom Dewey signed—the Quinn-Ives Act, which banned discrimination in hiring, and soon formed a committee to investigate discriminatory hiring practices, including a focus on baseball. In short order, New York City Mayor Fiorello LaGuardia established a Committee on Baseball to push the Yankees, Giants, and Dodgers to sign Black players. Branch Rickey met with LaGuardia but didn't reveal his plan. Left-wing Congressman Vito Marcantonio, who represented Harlem, called for the US Department of Commerce to investigate Major League Baseball's racist practices.

The baseball establishment was feeling the heat. Sam Lacy, a reporter for the *Afro-American*, wrote to all the team owners, suggesting that they set up an integration committee. As power holders often do when they want to deflect a problem causing them bad publicity, the owners reluctantly agreed to study the issue of discrimination in baseball. Rickey (representing the National League) agreed to serve on the committee along with Yankees president Larry MacPhail (representing the American League), Lacy, and Philadelphia judge Joseph H. Rainey, an African American. But, according to Lacy, "MacPhail always found a way to be too busy for us," and the full committee never met. Soon, Rickey told Lacy, somewhat mysteriously, that he was going to work on integrating baseball on his own.[59]

On April 6, 1945, Black sportswriter Joe Bostic of the *People's Voice* appeared unannounced at the Dodgers' Bear Mountain training camp with Negro League stars Terris McDuffie and Dave "Showboat" Thomas and pressured Rickey to hold tryouts for the two players. The next day, Rickey and manager Leo Durocher watched the two athletes perform, but determined that they were not major league caliber. Rickey was furious. He wanted to bring Black players into major league baseball, but he wanted to do it on his terms and his timetable. He didn't want the public to think that he was being pressured into it. "I am more for your cause than anybody else you know," he told Bostic, "but you are making a mistake using force. You are defeating your own aims."[60] But the ploy made the news. The *New York Times* ran a story headlined, "Two Negroes Are Tried Out By Dodgers But They Fail To Impress President Rickey."[61]

Rickey had subscriptions to the major Negro newspapers, which published Negro League box scores, statistics, and schedules and whose sportswriters gave accounts of its best players. In 1945, Rickey gave his scouts a list of play-ers to follow, pretending that he was interested in starting his own all-Black baseball league to compete with the existing Negro Leagues.

Rickey's search for the right player was inadvertently aided by Isadore Muchnick, a progressive Jewish member of the Boston City Council, who was determined to push the Boston Red Sox to hire Black players. Team owner Tom Yawkey was among baseball's strongest opponents of integra-tion. Muchnick knew the Red Sox needed a city permit to be able to play on Sundays, a big turnout day for major league teams. In 1945, he backed Red Sox general manager Eddie Collins into a corner, inquiring why the team had never given a Black player a tryout. He threatened to deny the Red Sox a permit unless the team considered hiring Black players. Working with Wen-dell Smith and white sportswriter Dave Egan of the *Boston Record*, Muchnick persuaded the reluctant Collins to give three Negro League players—Jackie Robinson, Sam Jethroe, and Marvin Williams—a tryout at Fenway Park on April 16.

Robinson had already endured the earlier bogus tryout with the White Sox four years earlier in Pasadena. He was skeptical about the Red Sox's motives now. He and the other two players performed well. Robinson, the most impressive of the three, hit line drives to all fields. "Bang, bang, bang; he rattled it," Muchnick recalled. "Jackie hit balls over the fence and against The Wall," echoed Jethroe. "What a ballplayer," said Hugh Duffy, the Red Sox's chief scout and onetime outstanding hitter. "Too bad he's the wrong color."[62]

After the phony Fenway Park tryout, Smith phoned Rickey to tell him about Robinson's superlative performance. The Dodgers president asked Smith to meet with him at his office. Smith had heard rumors that Rickey wanted to start a new Black league and suspected it might be a camouflage for the bolder idea of integrating baseball. Smith was convinced that among major league owners, Rickey was the desegregation campaign's strongest ally. The meeting cemented the relationship between the two men. Smith kept offering Rickey the names of Black ballplayers, but gave Robinson his stron-gest endorsement.

The pressure on major league teams to give tryouts to Black players gen-erated media publicity and helped raise awareness about baseball segrega-tion. And it helped give Rickey, who did want to hire Black players, a sense of urgency that if he wanted to be baseball's racial pioneer, he would need to act quickly.

In early 1945, a few months after Landis died, baseball's owners selected Albert "Happy" Chandler as the next baseball commissioner. As governor and then senator from Kentucky, Chandler echoed the segregationist views of most white Kentuckians. So when *Pittsburgh Courier* reporter Ric Roberts asked Chandler about allowing Blacks in the big leagues, he was surprised to hear Chandler say that he didn't think it was fair to perpetuate the ban and that teams should hire players to win ball games "whatever their origin or race."[63] Baseball's integration crusaders felt that even if Chandler wasn't an ally, he wouldn't be an implacable obstacle like Landis had been.

Subway Sam: Sam Nahem

During World War II, the American military ran a robust baseball program at home and overseas. President Roosevelt believed it would help soldiers stay in shape and boost the country's morale. The abundance of professional players in the military raised the quality of play. After Germany surrendered in May 1945, the military expanded its baseball program for American troops stationed in Europe. That year, over two hundred thousand American soldiers were playing baseball on military teams in France, Germany, Belgium, Austria, and Britain.

Many of the Negro Leagues' finest ballplayers saw military service during the war, but like other African Americans they faced discrimination and humiliation as soldiers. Most Black soldiers with baseball talent were confined to playing on all-Black teams. Jackie Robinson was stopped from joining the baseball team at Fort Riley, Kansas, and Larry Doby, who would later become the first African American in the American League, was blocked from playing baseball for the all-white Great Lakes Navy team near Chicago. A few African Americans played on racially integrated military teams in the South Pacific but not in other military installations.

One little-known episode in the battle to integrate baseball took place on American military bases in Europe, and it was led by a major league pitcher named Sam Nahem. A right-handed pitcher who embraced left-wing politics, Nahem was a Communist who challenged his sport's racial divide.

Nahem grew up in a family—and in a Brooklyn enclave—of Arabic-speaking Syrian Jews. When he was thirteen, his father, a well-to-do import-exporter, drowned when the British steamship the Vestris, sank off Virginia in November 1928. Nahem pitched for Brooklyn College's baseball team and played fullback on its football team. At the time, Brooklyn College was a center of radical political activism, and Nahem began participating in Communist Party activities there.[64]

In 1935, after his sophomore year, Nahem signed with the Brooklyn Dodgers. He made his Major League debut on the last day of the 1938 season, pitching a complete game to beat the Phillies 7–3 on just six hits. (He also got two hits and drove in one run). Despite his stellar performance, the Dodgers sent Nahem to the minors in 1939 and traded him to the St. Louis Cardinals organization the next year. In 1940, Nahem pitched for the Cardinals' Texas League franchise in Houston where he was 8–6 with a league-leading 1.65 earned run average (ERA). He joined the Cardinals the following season and went 5–2, primarily as a relief pitcher with a 2.98 ERA, the tenth-best in the league. Purchased by the Phillies in 1942, he made thirty-five appearances with a 4.94 ERA.

In his off-seasons, Nahem attended St. John's University, where he earned his law degree before passing the bar exam in 1941. In the minors and majors, he was known to bring books to read into the dugout or bullpen. These weren't pulp fiction novels but serious works of literature, like the writings of Honore de Balzac. He would sometimes quote Shakespeare and Guy de Maupassant in the middle of conversations. Nahem, who was bald and wore glasses, looked more like a professor than a ballplayer. Though better-educated than most other players, he was popular with his teammates.

"That's why he was so political," his daughter, Joanne, explained. "He believed that people deserved more, so he had a great faith in humanity."[65] Few of Nahem's minor league teammates had ever met a Jew or even a New Yorker before. He was known as "Subway Sam" for the rest of his life.

Nahem fervently believed that baseball should be racially integrated. "I was in a strange position," he explained. "The majority of my fellow players were very much against Black ball players. The reason was economic. They knew these guys had the ability to be up there, so they felt their jobs were threatened directly, and they did all sorts of things to discourage black ball players."[66] Nahem talked to some of his teammates to encourage them to be more open-minded. "I did my political work there," he told an interviewer years later. "I would take one guy aside if I thought he was amiable in that respect and talk to him, man to man, about the subject. I felt that was the way I could be most effective."[67]

Nahem entered the military in November 1942. He volunteered for the infantry and hoped to see combat in Europe to help defeat Nazism. But he spent his first two years at Fort Totten in New York. There, he pitched for the Anti-Aircraft Redlegs of the Eastern Defense Command. In 1943, he set a league record with a 0.85 ERA. He also finished second in hitting with a .400 batting average and played every defensive position except catcher. In September 1944, his Fort Totten team beat the Philadelphia Athletics 9–5 in an exhibition game. Nahem pitched six innings, gave up only two runs and five hits, and slugged two homers, accounting for seven of his team's runs.

Sent overseas in late 1944, Nahem served with an antiaircraft artillery division. From his base in Rheims, he was assigned to run two baseball leagues in France, while also managing and playing for his own team, the Overseas Invasion Service Expedition (OISE) All-Stars, which represented the army command in charge of communication and logistics. The team was made up mainly of semipro, college, ex-minor-league players and one other player with major league experience, Russ Bauers, who had compiled a 29–29 win-loss record with the Pirates between 1936 and 1941.

Defying the military establishment and baseball tradition, Nahem insisted on having African Americans on his team. He recruited two Negro League stars—Willard Brown, a slugging outfielder for the Kansas City Monarchs, and Leon Day, a pitcher for the Newark Eagles.

Nahem's OISE team won seventeen games and lost only one, attracting as many as ten thousand fans to its games and reaching the finals against the Seventy-First Infantry Red Circlers, representing General George Patton's Third Army. One of Patton's top officers assigned St. Louis Cardinals All-Star outfielder Harry Walker to assemble a team. Besides Walker, the Red Circlers included seven other major leaguers, including the Cincinnati Reds' six-foot six-inch side-arm pitcher Ewell "The Whip" Blackwell.

Few people gave Nahem's OISE All-Stars much chance to win the European Theater of Operations (ETO) championship, known as the GI World Series. It took place in September, a few months after the defeat of Germany. They played the first two games in Nuremberg, Germany, in the same stadium where Hitler had addressed Nazi Party rallies. Allied bombing had destroyed the city but somehow spared the stadium. The US Army laid out a baseball diamond and renamed the stadium Soldiers Field.

On September 2, 1945, Blackwell pitched the Red Circlers to a 9–2 victory in the first game of the best-of-five series in front of fifty thousand fans, most of them American soldiers. In the second game, Day held the Red Circlers to one run. Brown drove in the OISE's team first run, and then Nahem (who was playing first base) doubled in the seventh inning to knock in the go-ahead run. OISE won the game, 2–1. Day struck out ten batters, allowed four hits, and walked only two hitters.

The teams flew to OISE's home field in Rheims for the next two games. The OISE team won the third game, as the *Times* reported, "behind the brilliant pitching of S/Sgt Sam Nahem," who outdueled Blackwell to win 2–1, scattering four hits and striking out six batters.[68] In the fourth game, the Third Army's Bill Ayers, who had pitched in the minor leagues since 1937, shut out the OISE squad, beating Day, 5–0.

The teams returned to Nuremberg for the deciding game on September 8, 1945. Nahem started for the OISE team in front of over fifty thousand spectators. After the Red Circlers scored a run and then loaded the bases with one out in the fourth inning, Nahem took himself out and brought in Bob Keane, who got out of the inning without allowing any more runs and completed the game. The OISE team won the game, 2–1. The *Sporting News* adorned its report on the final game with a photo of Nahem.[69]

Back in France, Brigadier General Charles Thrasher organized a parade and a banquet dinner with steaks and champagne for the OISE All-Stars. As historian Robert Weintraub has noted, "Day and Brown, who would not be allowed to eat with their teammates in many major-league towns, celebrated alongside their fellow soldiers."[70]

One of the intriguing aspects of this episode is that although both major league baseball and the American military were racially segregated, no major newspaper even mentioned the historic presence of two African Americans on the OISE roster. If there were any protests among the white players, or among the fans—or if any of the Seventy-First Division's officers raised objections to having African American players on the opposing team—they were ignored by reporters. For example, an Associated Press story about the fourth game simply referred to "pitcher Leon Day of Newark."[71]

Having won the ETO World Series, the OISE All-Stars traveled to Italy to play the Mediterranean Theater champions, the Ninety-Second Infantry Division Buffaloes, an all-Black division. Several major league players on the Fifth Army's Red Circlers got themselves added to the OISE All-Stars roster, which meant that some of OISE's semipro, college, and minor league players were left behind. The OISE All-Stars beat the Buffaloes in three straight games, with Day, Keane, and Blackwell gaining the wins. Then Day switched to the all-Black team and beat Blackwell and his former OISE teammates, 8–0, in Nice, France.

Although Rickey knew Nahem when he played for the St. Louis Cardinals, it isn't known if Rickey was aware of Nahem's triumph over baseball segregation in the military. But in October 1945, a month after Nahem pitched his integrated team to victory in the European military championship, Rickey announced that Robinson had signed a contract with the Dodgers.

Aftermath

After the war, Leon Day returned to the Negro Leagues. He also played for racially integrated teams in Mexico and Cuba. In 1951, the Toronto Maple Leafs, a Triple-A minor league team, put the thirty-five-year-old Day on its roster. He pitched in fourteen games, had a 1–1 record and an ERA of 1.58. But his best years were behind him, and he never made the majors. He played two more years in the minors before retiring. The Veteran's Committee elected Day into the Hall of Fame on March 7, 1995. A week later, he died of a heart condition at a hospital in Baltimore. He never got to go to his induction ceremony in Cooperstown.

Willard Brown also returned to the Negro Leagues after the war until he was hired by the St. Louis Browns in July 1947, a few months after Jackie Robinson joined the Dodgers. He appeared in twenty-one games. On August 13, batting against the Detroit Tigers ace Hal Newhouser, he hit an inside-the-park home run—the first homer by an African American batter in the American League. Brown had used a bat belonging to outfielder Jeff Heath. When Brown returned to the dugout, Heath smashed the bat against the wall rather than allow Brown to use it again. That was emblematic of the treatment Brown received, exacerbated by playing in St. Louis, a southern city that didn't welcome Brown or his other Black teammate, Henry Thompson. Both were quickly let go and they returned to the Negro Leagues. Brown played pro ball—in the Negro Leagues, Puerto Rico, Mexico and Venezuela—until 1958. In 2006, Brown was voted into the Hall of Fame by a committee of historians specializing in Negro League players.

In 1947, after Rickey promoted Robinson to the Dodgers, he recruited Wendell Smith to travel and room with the young player to provide comfort and advice during what would surely be a rough experience. The 2013 smash hit film 42 depicts Smith as Robinson's traveling companion and the ghostwriter for Robinson's newspaper column during his rookie season but ignores Smith's key role as an agitator and leader of the long crusade to integrate baseball before Robinson became a household name.

In 1948 Smith left the *Courier* to take a job with the *Chicago Herald-American* (which would later change its name to the *American*), becoming the first Black sportswriter at a major white newspaper. That year he (along with Sam Lacy) became the first Black member of the Baseball Writers' Association of America. In 1961 Smith wrote a series of articles about the continued segregation of Black baseball players in Florida during spring training. Soon, Black players were allowed to share the same hotels and restaurants as their white teammates. In 1964, Smith accepted a job at WGN, one of Chicago's major television stations, working primarily as a sportscaster. He died of cancer in 1972, at the age of fifty-eight. He was posthumously inducted into the writer's wing of the Baseball Hall of Fame in 1994. (Lacy would join him in 1998.)

Under Lester Rodney's leadership, the *Daily Worker* also helped integrate professional basketball, pressuring the Boston Celtics to sign the first Black National Basketball Association (NBA) players in 1950. Rodney's reward for his work was often the typical red-baiting that greeted all radicals of the time. He was singled out for special condemnation by FBI director J. Edgar Hoover in his 1958 book *Masters of Deceit*. He wrote two baseball books for children, but to get them published he had to use pseudonyms.

In 1956, two events—Soviet premier Nikita Khrushchev's speech denouncing the corruption and terrorism of his predecessor Joseph Stalin and the Soviet invasion of Hungary to thwart a democratic protest movement—led many American Communists to leave the party over the next few years. Rodney was one of them. In 1958, he left the *Daily Worker* and the Communist Party and moved to southern California, where he worked first in journalism and advertising and then as a features and religion editor for eleven years with the *Long Beach Press-Telegram*.

Moving to northern California in 1990, Rodney kept active athletically, and in his sixties he was ranked the number one amateur tennis player in California for his age group. Long considered only a footnote, Rodney began receiving attention for his historic role in the early 2000s, taking part in baseball conferences and HBO documentaries on the Brooklyn Dodgers and Joe Louis. In 2005, the Baseball Reliquary—an organization of baseball fans who celebrate the sport's mavericks—inducted Rodney into its Shrine of the Eternals. But many other sportswriters didn't appreciate Rodney's pioneering efforts. In 2009, a month after his death, the Baseball Writers Association of America honored writers who had died that year at their annual dinner. They didn't mention Rodney. He has still not been inducted into the writer's wing of the Baseball Hall of Fame.

After the war, and another brief fling with the Phillies, Sam Nahem practiced law and worked as a longshoreman unloading banana boats on the New York docks while pitching part time for a top-flight semipro team, the Brooklyn Bushwicks. In the fall of 1946, the Bushwicks represented the United States in the Inter-American Tournament held in Venezuela. Against teams representing Mexico, Venezuela, and Cuba, Nahem won three and lost one. He clinched the tournament title for the Bushwicks with a 7–6 win over Cuba. In June 1947, Nahem pitched the Bushwicks to a 4–1 victory over the Homestead Grays of the Negro Leagues. On October 12, 1947, he spun a one-hitter against the World Series All-Stars that included major leaguers Eddie Stanky, Ralph Branca, and Phil Rizzuto. It was his seventeenth win of the season. Nahem played winter ball with the Navegantes del Magallanes club of the Venezuelan Professional Baseball League, where he pitched fourteen consecutive complete games in the 1946–47 season to set a league record that still stands today.

Because of McCarthy-era red-baiting, Nahem had a hard time keeping a job due to his left-wing affiliations. In 1955, he moved with his wife and three children to the Bay Area. He got a job at the Chevron plant in Richmond, California, where he became a head operator, retiring twenty-five years later in 1980. He was an active leader of the Oil, Chemical, and Atomic Workers union and led a successful strike against the corporate giant. After he retired, he volunteered at the University Art Museum in Berkeley. He died in 2004.

CHAPTER FOUR

Crossing the Color Line

With the help of baseball rebels such as Wendell Smith, Sam Lacy, Lester Rodney, Sam Nahem, and Bill Veeck, the protest movement for baseball integration set the stage for Jackie Robinson's entrance into the major leagues. The times were ripe for change, but there was no guarantee that America, or baseball, would confront its racial hypocrisy.

More than 1.2 million African Americans had served in the military during World War II. They initially worked as support troops—doing the hardest, dirtiest jobs—under segregated circumstances. But as white casualties increased, more African Americans became infantrymen, airmen, medics, and even officers. In 1945, Benjamin O. Davis was named commander of Goodman Field in Kentucky, becoming the first African American to command a military base. All-Black or mostly-Black units, such as the Tuskegee Airmen, earned reputations for their courage in combat, even while facing discrimination and segregation on military bases, in military towns, and among white soldiers and officers, as Lieutenant Jackie Robinson discovered when he refused to move to the back of a bus while stationed at Fort Hood in Texas and was court-martialed. Blacks who moved to northern cities to work in defense plants also confronted everyday bigotry and racism.

On both the home front and overseas, African Americans played important roles in winning the war. They hoped, even expected, that when the war was over, life would be different and white Americans would open up the doors to housing, jobs, and education on the basis of equality. But, for the most part, they returned to an America that still treated Blacks as second-class citizens.

In 1946, at least six African Americans were lynched in the South. Restrictive covenants were still legal, barring Blacks (and Jews) from buying homes in many neighborhoods—and not just in the South. Banks refused to grant mortgages to Blacks who wanted to buy homes in white neighborhoods. Likewise, the federal government's mortgage program, created during the Depression to encourage homebuilding and expanded after World War II, refused to insure loans to families that wanted to purchase homes in racially mixed areas. After the war, many white Americans were able to buy homes in the booming suburbs, especially veterans who could use the government's new Veterans Administration mortgage program, while Blacks were prohibited from living in these new housing developments. On the political front, African Americans in the South were prohibited from voting and those in the rest of the country had little voice in either the Republican or Democratic Party. Only two Blacks sat in the US Congress—Chicago's William Dawson (elected in 1942) and Harlem's Adam Clayton Powell (elected in 1944). No big city had a Black mayor.

As a result of these pent-up frustrations, the civil rights movement accelerated during and especially after the war. Led by military veterans, Black Americans participated in a wide variety of civil rights organizations like the National Association for the Advancement of Colored People (NAACP), the Congress of Racial Equality (CORE), the Southern Regional Council, and the Regional Council of Negro Leadership. They engaged in lawsuits, protests, voter registration drives, and other strategies to secure their rights.

CORE was founded in 1942 by University of Chicago students, many of whom were members of the Fellowship of Reconciliation (FOR), a Christian pacifist organization. As early as the 1940s, CORE experimented with nonviolent direct action methods to challenge racial discrimination, such as sit-ins in segregated restaurants and protests against segregated buses.

On July 16, 1944, Irene Morgan refused to surrender her seat to white passengers and move to the back of a Greyhound bus while traveling from Gloucester County, Virginia, to Baltimore, Maryland. She was arrested and convicted in the Virginia courts for violating a state law that required racial segregation on all public transportation. The NAACP appealed her case to the Supreme Court, and on June 3, 1946, by a 6–1 decision, the court ruled in *Morgan v. Virginia* that the Virginia law was unconstitutional when applied to passengers on interstate transportation. To test the Supreme Court's decision, in 1947 Bayard Rustin of the FOR and George Houser of CORE organized the Journey of Reconciliation. Sixteen Black and white men left Washington, DC, on a bus and train trip through the upper South. In North Carolina, three people, including Rustin, were arrested and sentenced to serve on a prison chain gang. From 1949 to 1953, CORE members successfully engaged in pickets and sit-ins to break segregation at lunch counters in St. Louis. The Journey of Reconciliation served as a model for the Montgomery bus boycott in 1955 and the Freedom Rides in 1961.

After the war, A. Philip Randolph led a coalition of civil rights group to lobby Congress to create a permanent Fair Employment Practices Committee (FEPC), which FDR had established to monitor discrimination in wartime defense industries. Southern Senators blocked creation of a permanent FEPC in 1946, 1950, and 1952. In October 1947, W. E. B. DuBois and the NAACP submitted an appeal to the United Nations for redress for American racism entitled *An Appeal to the World: A Statement of Denial of Human Rights to Minorities.*

In 1945, the NAACP took up the cause of J. D. Shelley, a Black man who had purchased a home in St. Louis covered by a restrictive covenant that prohibited sales of homes to African Americans. Louis Kraemer, a white neighbor, obtained an injunction in the Missouri Supreme Court to bar Shelley from occupying his home. In May 1948, the US Supreme Court affirmed in *Shelley v. Kraemer* the right of individuals to make discriminatory restrictive covenants but held that the Fourteenth Amendment's equal protection clause prohibited state courts from enforcing the contracts.

Two months later, on July 26, 1948, President Truman issued two executive orders. Executive Order 9980 instituted fair employment practices in the civilian agencies of the federal government. Executive Order 9981 officially desegregated the military. In October 1948, in *Perez v. Sharp,* the Supreme Court of California ruled that the state law banning interracial marriages violated the Constitution's Fourteenth Amendment. But many states continued to have laws prohibiting Black-white marriages. (It wasn't until 1967 that the US Supreme Court ruled in *Loving v. Virginia* that states could not prohibit interracial marriages.)

Mahatma: Branch Rickey

It was in this atmosphere of growing civil rights militancy that Branch Rickey hatched his plan to integrate the major leagues. In many ways, Rickey was an unlikely candidate to dismantle baseball's apartheid system. Politically and socially, he was quite conservative. He opposed swearing and drinking alcohol; in his youth, he was active in the Anti-Saloon League, a temperance group.

As a baseball executive, he was extremely stingy. *New York Daily Mirror* sportswriter Dan Parker wrote that "Rickey believes in economy in everything except his own salary."[1] After Rickey dumped several older Dodger players who commanded decent salaries, *Daily News* columnist Jimmy Powers gave him the nickname "El Cheapo"—a moniker that stuck.[2] Reflecting the prejudices of his time, Rickey occasionally made anti-Semitic and anti-Catholic comments.

Rickey was born in 1881 to a pious Methodist family that, according to his biographer Lee Lowenfish, endured a "hardscrabble existence" as vegetable farmers in south central Ohio.[3] He dropped out after grade school, but he was an avid reader, and he educated himself well enough to get into Ohio Wesleyan University, where he played baseball and football and later coached the school's baseball team. He had an unspectacular career as a major league catcher and outfielder from 1905 through 1907, which was made even more difficult by his refusal, on religious grounds, to play on Sundays. He returned to college (at the University of Michigan) to get a law degree, while serving as the university's head baseball coach and then as Ohio Wesleyan's athletic director.

In 1911 he moved to Boise, Idaho, to open a law practice, but he was a miserable failure. He was saved from a career in law by Robert Hedges, owner of the St. Louis Browns, who hired Rickey as a scout and general manager, and by 1913 he was the Browns' on-field manager. His method of teaching his players involved lectures, heart-to-heart talks, and drills, all done with a kind of religious fervor. In 1917, the crosstown St. Louis Cardinals hired Rickey as team president, and it was there that his career blossomed, primarily through his success at creating the Cardinals' minor league farm system. He employed scouts to find young talent to populate the Cardinals' chain of minor league teams, and then he signed these players to contracts for little pay and nurtured the best up the ladder toward the major leagues. Rickey was an excellent judge of talent, and the Cardinals became a powerhouse National League team, winning nine pennants and six World Series between 1926 and 1946. The World Series–winning 1942 Cardinals were the product of Rickey's farm system, whose roster included Stan Musial, the greatest player in Cardinals' history. Other teams began to emulate Rickey's farm team strategy, but none were as successful.

But Rickey and Cardinals owner Sam Breadon were constantly battling over the team's finances. So, in 1942, Rickey accepted an offer to become the Brooklyn Dodgers' general manager. During World War II, the number of minor league teams shrank dramatically because so many players were in the military, but Rickey quickly began hiring new talent, eventually turning the Dodgers' farm system into the best in baseball. By the war's end, the Dodgers had over seven hundred players under contract. To provide better and consistent training and easier evaluation of prospects, Rickey made a deal with the town of Vero Beach, Florida, to transform the former Navy training base for pilots into a training complex for the Dodgers—an idea that other teams eventually borrowed. As a result, for more than a decade after 1949, the Dodgers were the only major league team free of Jim Crow housing discrimination during spring training in Florida. All the players lived in the same barracks and ate together.

Soon after he joined the Dodgers, Rickey began strategizing about challenging baseball's color line. The question of *why* he did so has been the subject of much debate. He viewed baseball in almost missionary terms, as a sport that enhanced American democracy and opportunity.

A deeply religious man, Rickey believed that segregation violated Christian principles. Rickey frequently talked about an incident that occurred in 1904 when he was coaching the baseball team at Ohio Wesleyan. One of his best players was Charlie Thomas, a Black first baseman. When the team traveled to South Bend, Indiana, to play Notre Dame, the hotel refused to provide Thomas a room. Rickey persuaded the hotel to put a cot in his own room for Thomas to sleep on. That night, Rickey witnessed Thomas weeping and rubbing his hands. "Black skin. Black skin," he said to Rickey. "If I could only make them white." Rickey recalled, "I never felt so helpless in my life." He explained, "That scene haunted me for many years, and I vowed that I would always do whatever I could to see that other Americans did not have to face the bitter humiliation that was heaped upon Charles Thomas."[4]

But Rickey often denied that he was on a moral crusade to challenge racism. "My only purpose is to be fair to all people and my selfish objective is to win baseball games," he explained. "The greatest untapped reservoir of raw material in the history of the game is the black race. The Negroes will make us winners for years to come."[5]

Rickey was also aware that hiring Black players would boost attendance among the growing number of Black Americans who were moving from the South to the New York area during and after the war. Negro League teams were attracting large crowds when they played at the Giants' Polo Grounds or Yankee Stadium. The Brooklyn Bushwicks, a popular semipro team, had the biggest crowds when they played Negro League teams.

Rickey also knew that breaking the sport's color line would be viewed as a revolutionary move that would reverberate outside the sports world. As a brilliant baseball executive, Rickey had already made his mark on the game, but integrating major league baseball would be a way for him to make his mark on the wider society. His crusade was motivated by a combination of religious belief, idealism, profit, and ego.

Rickey set upon a strategy not only to find the right player to be the pioneer but also to win acceptance for his plan from the wider community. In 1943, Rickey got approval from the Dodgers' board of directors to hire Black players as part of his plan to rebuild the team. Amazingly, the board members kept Rickey's idea secret, even from their own families. In April 1945, Rickey announced that he was creating a new baseball league, the United States League, composed of Black players, using the occasion to criticize the existing Negro Leagues for their financial problems, non-standard contracts, and irregular schedules. This bit of subterfuge gave Rickey an excuse to ask his Dodger scouts to begin looking for top-flight Black players for the "Brown Dodgers," a team he claimed would operate in the new league parallel to the Brooklyn Dodgers. Rickey's goal was to hire several Black players but move one of them to the front of the line to be the pioneer on the Brooklyn team.

Rickey's scouts sent him reports about Negro League players not only evaluating their baseball skills but also their character, ability to handle conflict, and personality. Rickey also sought the advice of Wendell Smith, the *Pittsburgh Courier* sportswriter, about the most suitable Negro League players. Rickey's attention turned to Jackie Robinson, who was playing for the Kansas City Monarchs in the Negro Leagues. He sent his top scout, Clyde Sukeforth, to meet with Robinson and tell him that Rickey wanted to talk with him in Brooklyn as a prospect for his new league. Robinson didn't quite believe Sukeforth but was curious enough to make the trip. After Robinson met Rickey in his office on August 28, 1945—an encounter that has been dramatized in many films and books—Rickey decided that he was the right player to carry out the experiment. Rickey swore Robinson to secrecy until he was ready to make a public announcement.

Rickey wanted to wait until the new year to make the announcement, but his hand was forced by New York City Mayor Fiorello LaGuardia, whose Committee on Baseball was about to issue a report calling on the three New York City teams to hire Black players. LaGuardia was unaware of Rickey's plans. Rickey did not want it to appear that he had signed Black players under pressure. So he arranged for the president of the Montreal Royals, the

Dodgers' top farm team, to introduce Robinson at a press conference in Montreal on October 23, 1945, as the newest member of the Royals. It immediately became national news. Most sportswriters wrote positive stories about the Dodgers' initiative, viewing it as a natural outcome of a country that had just fought a war for freedom and democracy, but some, and not only those in the South, attacked the idea. Some said that baseball wasn't ready for integration. Some argued that it was too big a burden to put on one man's shoulders. Others claimed that even if integration was a good idea, Robinson lacked the skill and experience to take on that task.

None of the other National League team owners supported Rickey's move, but they were helpless to stop him. Had Kenesaw Mountain Landis still been baseball commissioner, he might have tried to thwart the experiment, but he had died in 1944, replaced by Albert "Happy" Chandler, who embraced Rickey's plan despite the opposition from the owners, who were his employers.

In October 1945, as he was getting ready to announce that Robinson had. signed a contract, Rickey visited his friend, the famous radio broadcaster Lowell Thomas. "Branch, all hell will break loose!" Thomas told Rickey, as recounted by Lee Lowenfish in *Branch Rickey: Baseball's Ferocious Gentleman.* "No, Lowell," said Rickey. "All heaven will rejoice."[6]

Pioneer: Jackie Robinson

The grandson of a slave and the son of a sharecropper, Robinson was fourteen months old in 1920 when his mother moved her five children from Cairo, Georgia, to Pasadena, California—a wealthy, conservative Los Angeles suburb—where she worked as a maid. During Robinson's youth, Black residents, who represented a small portion of the city's population, were treated as second-class citizens. Blacks were allowed to swim in the municipal pool only on Wednesdays (before the water was changed) and could use the YMCA only one day a week. Robinson learned at an early age that athletic success did not guarantee social or political acceptance. When his older brother Mack returned from the 1936 Olympics in Berlin with a silver medal in track, he got no hero's welcome. The only job the college-educated Mack would find was as a street sweeper and ditch digger.

Robinson was a star athlete at Pasadena Junior College before enrolling at UCLA, where he became its first four-sport athlete (football, basketball, track, and baseball), twice led basketball's Pacific Coast League in scoring, won the National Collegiate Athletic Association (NCAA) broad jump championship, and became an All-American football player.

In 1942, Robinson was drafted into the wartime Army. He was sent to Fort Riley, Kansas. With the help of boxer Joe Louis, Jackie was accepted to Officer Candidate School and became a second lieutenant in January 1943. Many of the Negro League's finest ballplayers saw military service during the war, but like other African Americans they faced discrimination and humiliation as soldiers. Most Black soldiers with baseball talent were confined to playing on all-Black teams. When Robinson went out for the baseball team at Fort Riley, Kansas, a white player told him that the officer in charge said, "I'll break up the team before I'll have a n–– on it."[7]

He was transferred to Fort Hood, Texas, assigned to the 761st Tank Battalion, an all-Black battalion known as the Black Panthers. There, on July 6, 1944, Robinson—a twenty-five-year-old Army lieutenant—boarded a military bus at Fort Hood with the light-skinned Black wife of another Black officer and sat down next to her in the middle of the vehicle. "Hey you, sittin' beside that woman," the driver yelled. "Get to the back of the bus." Robinson refused, knowing that buses had been officially desegregated on military bases. When the driver threatened to have him arrested, Robinson shook his finger in the driver's face and told him, "Quit fucking with me."[8] Two military policemen soon arrived and escorted Robinson away.

He faced trumped-up charges of insubordination, disturbing the peace, drunkenness, conduct unbecoming an officer, insulting a civilian woman, and refusing to obey the lawful orders of a superior officer. Unlike the routine mistreatment of many Black soldiers in the Jim Crow military, Robinson's court-martial trial, on August 2, 1944, triggered news stories in the Black press and protests by the NAACP because he was already a public figure. Voting by secret ballot, the military judges found Robinson not guilty. By November, he was honorably discharged from the Army.

Describing the ordeal, Robinson later wrote, "It was a small victory, for I had learned that I was in two wars, one against the foreign enemy, the other against prejudice at home."[9]

After his release from the Army, Robinson returned home to California and then joined the Negro League's Kansas City Monarchs on a contract paying $400 a month. Robinson played forty-seven games for the Monarchs during the 1945 season.

Rickey could have chosen other Negro League players with more talent, experience, or name recognition, such as Satchel Paige or Josh Gibson. He picked Robinson not only because of his athletic talent but also because Robinson was young, educated, religious, and had formed friendships with his white neighbors and classmates in Pasadena and at UCLA. He believed that Robinson could help the Dodgers on the field and attract more fans to Ebbets Field. Rickey knew Robinson had a hot temper and strong political views, but he believed that Robinson could handle the emotional pressure. Robinson promised Rickey that, at least during his rookie year, he would not respond to the verbal barbs and physical abuse he would face on a daily basis. Rickey knew that if the experiment failed, it would set back integration for years.

Robinson endured more verbal, psychological, and physical abuse than any professional athlete before or since. By the time he reached the Dodgers, he was twenty-eight years old. He had lost at least five years of major league experience due to baseball's color line.

After signing Robinson to a contract, Rickey assigned him to the Montreal Royals, the Dodgers' top minor league team, for the 1946 season. Rickey figured that Robinson would face less overt racism in Montreal than in most other minor league cities. But he also knew that the Dodgers and the Royals had their pre-training camp (where they gave tryouts to players trying to get a contract) in Sanford, Florida and their spring training camp in nearby Daytona Beach. Like the rest of Florida, these towns were racially segregated and governed by Jim Crow laws.

Robinson arrived in Sanford in March 1946 after he and his new bride, Rachel, experienced their first taste of Southern racism. After flying from Los Angeles to New Orleans, they were bumped from their connecting flight and were stranded in the New Orleans airport, where none of the restaurants would serve them. They took a later flight to Pensacola, Florida, where they were to get on another connecting flight to Jacksonville. Once on board, they were ordered off the plane and replaced with two white passengers. Furious, they boarded a bus for Jacksonville. On the bus, the driver told them to move to the back of the bus, which (unlike the seats up front) had no reclining seats. After a long, bumpy ride they arrived in Jacksonville and switched to a bus to Daytona Beach, where they were picked up by Wendell Smith and Billy Rowe (the *Pittsburgh Courier's* photographer), whom Rickey had asked to serve as the Robinsons' traveling companions. They drove the Robinsons to Sanford.

Robinson and John Wright (a Negro Leagues pitcher whom the Dodgers had also signed) were not permitted to join their white teammates who were staying at the lakefront Mayfair Hotel, which barred Blacks. So Rickey arranged for the two Black players—as well as Rachel Robinson, Smith, and Rowe—to stay at the Sanford home of David Brock, a local Black businessman and doctor.

The Brocks, who lived in a large house, were one of Sanford's few middle-class Black families. In Sanford to cover Robinson's historic moment, Bill Mardo, a white sportswriter for the *Daily Worker*, described the city to his readers. "Sanford's got the smell. The smell of the South, the silent, lazy and ominous smell of a million lynchings that weren't good enough for the pretty palms. Strange Fruit Hangin' on the Poplar Trees," he wrote, referring to the Billie Holiday song about lynching. Mardo visited the city's Black section. "Here's where the Negroes live. Here's where every street is a shanty-town. Here's where you walk by and the Negroes look up at you quickly and then away again. Here's where they live and die, some sooner than others."[10]

Robinson and Wright joined their teammates at the Sanford ballpark for the first two days of spring training. On the evening of the second day, a white man drove to the Brock home and warned Smith, who was sitting on the porch, that a white mob was ready to run the Black players out of town. According to some accounts, the man was delivering a message from a meeting of about one hundred white Sanford residents, including the mayor. The Ku Klux Klan (KKK) had a presence in Sanford, so Smith took the threat seriously.

Anyone living in or familiar with Florida at that time knew of the state's long history of racial lynchings. Between 1882 and 1930, Florida mobs lynched 212 Blacks. The state had the highest number of lynchings per capita in the nation. For every 1,250 Blacks in Florida during that period, one was lynched, a rate even higher than in Mississippi, Alabama, and Georgia. Three lynchings occurred in Florida in the 1940s, including one in 1943, only three years before Robinson's Florida sojourn.

Indeed, white mob violence against African Americans in Florida was widespread during and after World War II. As recounted in Chris Lamb's history of baseball's desegregation, *Conspiracy of Silence*, in September 1945, a sixty-year-old Black man who lived near Live Oak, Florida "was removed from his car, pistol-whipped, lynched, and dumped into a river. The suspects, including a police chief, were not indicted."[11] Two weeks later, a white mob in Raiford, Florida (near Tallahassee), kidnapped Black teenager Jesse Payne from an unlocked and unguarded jail cell in the middle of the night, shot him to death, and left his body on a highway several miles away.

Smith called Rickey and told him about the threat of violence by the Sanford mob. Rickey told Smith to get Robinson and Wright out of town. Smith whisked them out of Sanford at night, taking them to Daytona Beach. There, they were also barred from the all-white hotel where the other Royals were staying, so the two Black players had to stay with a local Black family.

Robinson played his first minor league game, an exhibition between the Royals and the Dodgers, in Daytona Beach on March 17, 1946. To the surprise of some, local officials allowed the teams to play despite the Jim Crow laws. Four thousand spectators—a quarter of them African Americans, confined to a segregated section of the seats—crowded into the ballpark to watch this historic event.

But they had no such luck in Sanford. On April 7, the Royals returned to Sanford to play an exhibition game against the St. Paul Saints. According to Jules Tygiel in *Baseball's Great Experiment,* "City officials asked Rickey to leave the black second baseman at the Dodger camp. Rickey ignored the request and the Royals again boarded their little-used bus for the twenty-mile ride to Sanford."[12]

The Royals put Robinson in the starting lineup. In the first inning, he beat out an infield single, then stole second base. But in the bottom of the second inning, the Sanford police chief walked onto the field and ordered Royals manager Clay Hopper to remove Robinson and Wright from the stadium.

After that incident, Rickey refused to allow the Royals to play in any city that barred his Black players, so the spring training included a few canceled games. Instead, the Royals moved their road games to their home field in Daytona Beach, which was segregated but somewhat more racially tolerant than other Florida locales. Worried that barring Black players from playing there would generate bad publicity and hurt the city's ability to attract northern tourists, local officials negotiated with Rickey to permit Robinson to join his Royals teammates on the field.

Neither Jackie nor Rachel Robinson would ever forget their Florida ordeal. Jackie Robinson wrote about it, his anger still palpable, in his autobiography. Rachel Robinson told Arnold Rampersad, author of *Jackie Robinson: A Biography,* that their experiences in Florida that spring made her "a much stronger, more purposeful human being." She said, "I saw the pointlessness, the vanity, of good looks and clothes when one faced an evil like Jim Crow. I think I was much more ready now to deal with the world we had entered."[13]

When Robinson played for the Royals during the 1946 season, the team traveled to segregated cities like Louisville and Baltimore, where he couldn't stay in the same hotel or eat in the same restaurants as his white teammates. Despite these obstacles, he led the International League with a .349 batting average and 113 runs, finished second with forty stolen bases, and led the team to a 100–54 season and a triumph in the minor league World Series.

During spring training in 1947, some of Robinson's own teammates let it be known that they resented having a Black man on the team. A handful of Dodgers, led by Georgia-born outfielder Dixie Walker, even circulated a petition asking Rickey to keep Robinson off the club. Rickey and manager Leo Durocher quickly squashed the revolt. Even so, Robinson often sat by himself in the clubhouse while his teammates played cards or chatted. Describing Robinson's relationships with his teammates during his rookie year, columnist Jimmy Cannon called him "the loneliest man I have ever seen in sports."[14]

When he played for the Dodgers, the team played in segregated cities like Cincinnati, St. Louis, and Philadelphia. In those cities, too, Robinson could not stay in the same hotels or eat in the same restaurants as his white teammates. He also had to endure segregated buses, trains, public parks, movie theaters, and other facilities. He received a torrent of hate mail and death threats. On the field, he heard constant racist taunts from fans and opposing players. A week after he joined the Dodgers, he was playing a game in Philadelphia. During the game, Phillies manager Ben Chapman called Robinson a "n––" and shouted, "Go back to the cotton field where you belong" and "They're waiting for you in the jungles, black boy" without rebuke from the umpire or National League officials.[15] Throughout his rookie season, opposing pitchers threw fastballs at his head, brushed him back, and occasionally plunked him. Runners on opposing teams went out of their way to spike him when he was covering the bases.

Robinson seethed with anger, but he kept his promise to Rickey, enduring the abuse without retaliating. But it took a toll. He developed stomach pains. His hair turned prematurely gray.

Even so, Robinson had an outstanding rookie season. He hit .297, led the National League with twenty-nine stolen bases (including three steals of home), and led the Dodgers to the National League pennant. *The Sporting News* named him baseball's Rookie of the Year. That year, the Dodgers set road attendance records in every National League park except Cincinnati's Crosley Field. His first appearance at the Chicago Cubs' Wrigley Field set an attendance record of 46,572 fans. He appeared on the cover of *Time* magazine on September 22, 1947. At the end of the season, an Associated Press poll ranked Robinson second only to singer Bing Crosby as America's "most admired man."[16] Despite this, that year Robinson made the major league minimum of $5,000—$58,650 in today's dollars. In 1956, his final year in the majors, he earned $42,500—$428,609 in 2021 dollars, below Major League Baseball's (MLB's) 2021 minimum salary of $570,500.

During his rookie season—and throughout his playing days—Robinson utilized the media to express his views. In 1947, he wrote a column, "Jackie Robinson Says," in the *Pittsburgh Courier* documenting his rookie season. In the off-season after his second year in the majors, he hosted a daily radio program. The following year, he hosted a TV show. Soon after joining the Dodgers, he participated in many charitable and social service activities. He mentored young people at the Harlem YMCA and the Police Athletic League, visited sick children in hospitals and brought toys and baseballs autographed by himself and his teammates, and gave speeches at schools and universities.

During those early years, despite the opposition of baseball's owners and executives, Commissioner Albert "Happy" Chandler had Robinson's back. When Robinson and the Royals traveled to Louisville for the 1946 minor league World Series, Chandler warned the Louisville team, the Colonels, against fomenting any protest. At the start of the 1947 season, when the Phillies taunted Robinson with racist slurs, Chandler threatened them with fines and other disciplinary action if it happened again. When some members of the Cardinals threatened to strike in protest of Robinson's presence on the field, Chandler supported National League President Ford Frick, who pledged to suspend any player who went on strike.

In 1949—a year when Robinson would be named the National League's Most Valuable Player and again lead the Dodgers into the World Series—he made his first major foray into the world of politics, although the circumstances were not of his own making.

That summer, right-wing and segregationist members of Congress orchestrated a confrontation between Robinson and Paul Robeson—the two most well-known and admired African Americans in the country. The media salivated at the opportunity to portray the clash of these larger-than-life figures as a surrogate for the Cold War between capitalism and communism.[17]

In early July, Robinson received a telegram from Congressman John Wood, an arch segregationist and former KKK member from Georgia, who chaired the House Un-American Activities Committee (HUAC). He invited Robinson to address a hearing on "Communist infiltration of minority groups."[18] Specifically, he wanted Robinson to attack Robeson for being a disloyal American who sought to recruit Black Americans to the Communist cause.

The pretext for the hearing was a statement that Robeson had made that April at a left-wing conference in Paris. The media ignored Robeson's main point—that most Americans, including Blacks, did not want to go to war with the Soviet Union. Instead, most news outlets used the Associated Press report, which quoted Robeson saying that if a war broke out between the United States and Russia, "It is unthinkable that American Negroes would go to war on behalf of those who have oppressed us for generations against a country which in one generation has raised our people to the full dignity of mankind."[19]

At the time, Robeson was at the height of his fame. Born in 1898 to a former runaway slave, he had starred in four sports at Rutgers, was twice named to the football All-American team, won Rutgers' oratory award four years in a row, was elected to Phi Beta Kappa, and was valedictorian of his 1919 graduating class. He played professional football to pay his tuition at Columbia University law school but gave up practicing law to pursue a theater career. A highly successful film and stage actor, he could also sing opera, show tunes, Negro spirituals, and international songs in twenty-five languages. His concerts drew huge audiences. His recordings sold well. During World War II, he entertained troops at the front and sang battle songs on the radio.

Robeson was also a defiant activist. He gave free concerts for left-wing unions and progressive causes. He refused to perform in roles that demeaned African Americans. In 1945 he headed an organization that pressured President Truman to support an antilynching law. That year the NAACP awarded Robeson the Spingarn Medal, its highest honor. He was an outspoken critic of European and American imperialism and a strong supporter of nations, in Africa and elsewhere, seeking to unleash themselves from the yoke of colonialism. He embraced the Soviet Union, which he believed had done more than his native country to battle racism and anti-Semitism.

Robeson also played a key role in paving the way for Robinson's breakthrough. In 1943 he was part of a delegation of prominent African Americans, including the owners of major Black newspapers, who met with baseball commissioner Landis and team owners to demand the sport's desegregation.

Robinson was reluctant to testify against Robeson. He didn't agree with Robeson's communist views, but he admired his lifetime of courageous activism. "I didn't want to fall prey to the white man's game and allow myself to be pitted against another black man," he later wrote. "I knew that Robeson was striking out against racial inequality in the way that seemed best to him."[20]

Rickey, a fervent anti-Communist, reminded Robinson that if he refused to testify, HUAC might subpoena him anyway. Robinson also felt a "sense of responsibility" to convey Black Americans' loyalty to America. So on the morning of July 18, Robinson and Rachel flew to Washington, DC, a city where first-class hotels were still racially segregated. On this occasion, HUAC waived its rule against media photographs.

As expected, Robinson criticized Robeson, but it was far from the harsh attack that Wood and his HUAC colleagues were hoping for. Instead, Robinson made an impassioned demand for racial integration and challenged America's hypocrisy around race relations. Regarding Robeson's Paris speech, Robinson said that Robeson "has a right to his personal views, and if he wants to sound silly when he expresses them in public, that is his business and not mine. He's still a famous ex-athlete and a great singer and actor."[21]

Robinson insisted that Blacks were loyal Americans who would "do their best to help their country stay out of war. If unsuccessful, they'd do their best to help their country win the war—against Russia or any other enemy that threatened us."[22]

In contrast to Robinson's testimony, at the time many Americans—and certainly most HUAC members—believed that Communists did not have the right to express their views or hold jobs. Robinson also challenged HUAC's view that Black Americans' anger and activism was the result of communist agitators: "The fact that it is a Communist who denounces injustice in the courts, police brutality, and lynching when it happens doesn't change the truth of his charges. Just because Communists kick up a big fuss over racial discrimination when it suits their purposes, a lot of people try to pretend that the whole issue is a creation of Communist imagination."[23] In fact, Robinson insisted, "Negroes were stirred up long before there was a Communist Party, and they'll stay stirred up long after the party has disappeared—unless Jim Crow has disappeared by then as well."[24]

Robinson's appearance was a major news story, but the press focused on his criticism of Robeson and virtually ignored his condemnation of racism. It was part of a wider campaign to isolate Robeson, who was denounced by the media, politicians, and conservative and liberal groups alike as being a traitor and Soviet shill. Radio stations banned his recordings. Concert halls and colleges cancelled his performances. In 1950, the State Department revoked Robeson's passport so he couldn't perform abroad, where he was still popular. His annual income plummeted from over $150,000 to less than $3,000. His voice was marginalized during the 1960s civil rights movement. His name and photo were even stricken from the college All-America football teams.

By 1949 Robinson was an established star, but he was still subject to America's racist culture, reflected by the controversy triggered by his presence in the Dodgers lineup in Atlanta. Rickey had arranged for the Dodgers to play three exhibition games against the all-white Atlanta Crackers of the Class AA Southern Association before the start of the major league season. With Robinson and catcher Roy Campanella on the Dodgers' roster, it would be the first mixed-race baseball game in a major Southern city and the first interracial sporting event in Atlanta history. The city was in the midst of an upsurge of racist activism, including a resurgence of the KKK. Dr. Samuel Green, an Atlanta obstetrician and head (Grand Dragon) of the Georgia KKK, claimed that an integrated game violated state law and told columnist Jimmy Cannon of the *New York Post* that it would be "breaking down the traditions of Georgia."[25] He threatened to initiate a permanent boycott of Crackers games.

Members of the Georgia state legislature introduced a bill to outlaw interracial athletic events. Embarrassed by the Klan's extremism, Atlanta newspapers editorialized against this proposed law and generally supported the plan for interracial games. Some city leaders, including the mayor, feared that the game would trigger a race riot and sought to prohibit it from taking place, but other leaders encouraged Rickey and Crackers president Earl Mann to proceed with their plans. The CEO of Coca-Cola, the Atlanta-based company that owned the Crackers, worried that the controversy might lead to a white boycott of the profitable soda, but to his credit, he did not interfere. Rickey said, "Nobody can tell me anywhere what players I can or cannot play. If we are not allowed to use the players we want to play or are informed that by using certain players we are violating a law, why, the Dodgers simply won't play there, and that is all there is to that."[26] On his nightly radio program in New York, Robinson insisted, "I will play baseball where my employer, the Brooklyn Dodgers, wants me to play."[27]

Prior to the first game—on the night of Friday, April 8, 1949—Dodgers manager Burt Shotton gathered his players in the clubhouse and read a letter whose author threatened to shoot Robinson if he took the field against the Crackers. Robinson had received many death threats since joining the Dodgers two years earlier, but his teammates were nevertheless shocked by the letter and afraid of what might happen. Then Dodger outfielder Gene Hermanski broke the tension by suggesting that all Dodgers players wear number 42—Robinson's uniform number—so that the assassin wouldn't know whom to target. Robinson and his teammates laughed at Hermanski's joke.

The letter turned out to be a false threat. The games were played without incident and, with 49,309 fans in the stands over the three days, set a record for the Southern Association. Black fans, in particular, came from across the South to watch the contests. Robinson told Associated Press sportswriter Joe Reichler, "Believe me, this is the most thrilling experience of my life. It's the most wonderful thing that ever happened to me. . . . The strain is over now, but I don't mind telling you I was plenty worried. . . . I didn't know what to expect. . . . Deep down in my heart, though, I knew nothing would happen."[28] Robinson played nine innings in each game and stole home in the third game. The contests gained widespread coverage in the country's newspapers and helped encourage other cities to welcome interracial games. Between 1950 and 1954, every city in the Southern Association, including Birmingham and Little Rock, hosted fifty-five integrated baseball games, all without incident. This gave liberal forces in the South a boost of self-confidence that helped propel the civil rights movement over the coming decade.

During the 1949 season, after his initial two years establishing himself as a Dodger, Robinson began to unleash his frustrations and his temper. He argued constantly with umpires and opposing players. He was less willing to stifle his anger at the second-class accommodations and mistreatment that he, and the handful of other Black major leaguers, had to endure. In 1950, for example, he wrote a letter to National League president Ford Frick complaining that umpires treated him differently than white players when calling balls and strikes and ejecting him from games for arguing calls. Robinson also saw a racist double standard when, in 1950, sportswriters chose the Giants' Eddie

Stanky over Robinson as the second baseman for the National League All-Star team, even though Robinson was having a much better season in every category and Stanky was, like Robinson, known as an aggressive player, even a hothead. Appearing on a local TV talk show in 1953, Robinson publicly accused the New York Yankees—the only one of the three New York City teams without a Black player—of racism. He started to speak out more forcefully on social issues, particularly about the persistence of racism in America. He got more directly involved in organizations working for social change.

Freed from Rickey's straitjacket, he participated more in social action. In 1949, he agreed to chair the New York state committee of the United Negro and Allied Veterans of America, which helped returning World War II veterans readjust to life in the United States, including education, jobs, and housing. He also joined the advisory board of Harlem's Solidarity Center, which provided health insurance and medical services. (It was sponsored by the International Workers Order, a left-wing group,) In 1954 and 1955, he chaired the Commission on Community Organizations, a civil rights campaign of the National Conference of Christians and Jews, and toured the country during the off-season on its behalf. In 1955, he became co-chair of New York's Committee of the United Negro College Fund.

In 1949, at the height of the Cold War, Robinson agreed to star in a movie about his life, *The Jackie Robinson Story*, which was released the following year. With Ruby Dee portraying his wife, Rachel, the film depicted some of the racism that Robinson faced growing up and during his first few years with the Dodgers, but its central theme reflected the celebration of America as a land of opportunity where anyone could succeed if he had the talent and will. The movie opens with the narrator saying, "This is a story of a boy and his dream. But more than that, it's a story of an American boy and a dream that is truly American."[29] Robinson recognized that the film skirted the reality of the nation's racial caste system and the denial of equal opportunity for Black Americans.

Robinson had to walk a tightrope between his outrage at racial injustice and his loyalty to his country during the Cold War, when almost any dissent of the status quo was characterized as radical, even communist. Throughout his playing career, Robinson was constantly criticized for being so frank about race relations in baseball and in society. Many sportswriters and many other players—including some of his fellow Black players, content simply to be playing in the majors—considered Robinson too angry, vocal, and ungrateful for the opportunity he was given. Syndicated sports columnist Dick Young of the *New York Daily News* complained that when he talked to Roy Campanella, they always talked solely about baseball, but when he talked with Robinson, "sooner or later we get around to social issues."[30] The same forthright comments or assertive behavior by white players was out of bounds for Robinson. A 1953 article in *Sport* magazine, "Why They Boo Jackie Robinson," described him as "combative," "emotional," and "calculating" as well as a "pop-off," a "whiner," a "showboat," and a "troublemaker."[31] A Cleveland paper called Robinson a "rabble rouser" who was on a "soap box." The *Sporting News* headlined one story, "Robinson Should Be a Player, Not a Crusader." Others called him a "loudmouth," a "sorehead," and worse.[32]

The Dodgers took the lead in hiring other Black players after Robinson. While scouting the Negro Leagues, Rickey had his eye on several top Negro League players. Between 1947 and 1953, the Dodgers signed ten players—including future Hall of Famer Roy Campanella and All-Star Don Newcombe.

On July 17, 1954, in an away game against the Milwaukee Braves, the Dodgers fielded MLB's first majority-Black team, a roster that helped turn the 1950s Dodgers—memorialized in Roger Kahn's book, *The Boys of Summer*—into one of the greatest teams in baseball history, including winning the World Series in 1955.

Forgotten Hero: Larry Doby

Although Bill Veeck's plan to integrate baseball by purchasing the Philadelphia Phillies was blocked by Commissioner Landis, he had another chance when he bought the Cleveland Indians in 1946. He enlisted his friend Bill Killefer to scout the Negro Leagues for Black players to sign. He also consulted with Wendell Smith and Harlem Globetrotters promoter Abe Saperstein.

Anticipating the hiring of Black players, Veeck planned to move the team's spring training season from segregated Florida to Arizona. Although Arizona was hardly a bastion of racial tolerance, it was not officially a Jim Crow state. Prior to buying the Indians, he persuaded New York Giants owner Horace Stoneham to have his team hold its 1947 spring training in Arizona too. Decades later, many other MLB teams would transplant their spring training facilities to Arizona, but Veeck pioneered the Cactus League. As a result, some first-generation Black major leaguers played their preseason games in Phoenix, Tucson, Scottsdale, and other Arizona cities, where they faced racial animosity but not legalized segregation.

Veeck signed outfielder Larry Doby three months after Robinson joined the Dodgers, making Doby the first Black player in the American League. Doby was a three-sport star in high school in Patterson, New Jersey, and then played baseball and basketball in college until he was drafted into the military. After his discharge in 1946, he joined the Newark Bears of the Negro Leagues, where he had an outstanding season. Midway through the 1947 season, Veeck bought his contract from the Eagles, and Doby made his major league debut for the Indians on July 5, 1947. After signing Doby, Veeck received twenty thousand hate letters. According to reports at the time, he answered all of them by hand.

Doby faced the same racist obstacles that Robinson endured, including hostility from some of his white teammates. On his first day with the team, some Cleveland players refused to shake his hand. When he took the field before the game, his teammates ignored him until, after standing alone for five minutes, Jewish second baseman Joe Gordon threw him a ball and warmed up with him. During much of his major league career, he could not stay in the same hotels as his teammates and was denied service in restaurants. Opposing pitchers threw at him, and opposing infielders spat on him when he slid into the base. Like Robinson, he received hate mail from across the country.

Like Robinson, too, Doby dealt with these indignities with quiet stoicism, which fueled his ambition to succeed. In 1948 he was a regular outfielder, batted .301, hit fourteen home runs, and had sixty-six runs batted in (RBI), helping the Indians win the pennant. In the fourth game of the World Series against the Boston Braves, Doby became the first Black player to hit a home run in the fall classic, helping his team to a 2–1 win and eventually to winning the championship. A photo taken after the fourth game of Doby embracing Cleveland pitcher Steve Gromek became an iconic symbol of Doby's acceptance as a member of the Indians. In 1952, he led the American League in slugging percentage (.541), home runs (thirty-two), and runs scored (104). In 1954, he led the team to the American League pennant with thirty-two homers and 126 RBI.

During his thirteen-year major league career, Doby had a .283 batting average, 243 doubles, 253 home runs, and 970 RBI and was selected to seven American League All-Star teams. "I had to take it," Doby said, "but I fought back by hitting the ball as far as I could. That was my answer."[33]

Doby played in Japan in 1962. In 1969, the Montreal Expos hired him as a batting coach. After serving as batting coach for other several teams, he was ready to manage but was passed over several times. Finally, in 1977, Veeck offered him a coaching job with the Chicago White Sox and the following year elevated him to manage the team. But his stint as manager lasted just a year. In 1998, he was elected to the Baseball Hall of Fame by the Veterans Committee.

Satchel: Leroy Paige

In 1948, Veeck signed Satchel Paige, who was certainly the greatest pitcher in the Negro Leagues and may have been the greatest pitcher of all time. We'll never know, because in his prime he didn't play integrated baseball, so the white press ignored his exploits, and the Negro Leagues kept spotty records. He did, however, often play against all-white teams, often composed of major leaguers, and more often than not, he beat them. In barnstorming games in the United States and Caribbean, he pitched and prevailed against Dizzy Dean, Bob Feller, and other great white players. More than any other Black athlete, he showed that Negro League players were on a par with their white major league counterparts.

Born in 1906 in Mobile, Alabama, Leroy "Satchel" Paige began playing pro baseball in 1926 for the Chattanooga White Sox in the Negro Leagues. He played his last game in organized baseball in 1966—forty years later—for a Virginia club called the Peninsula Pilots. As his biographer Larry Tye noted, "In between, the Hall of Famer pitched more baseballs, in more ballparks, for more teams, than any player in history. It also is safe to say that no pitcher ever threw at a higher level, for longer, than the ageless right-hander with the whimsical nickname."[34]

Television and radio didn't cover Negro League games, but Paige's legend grew by word of mouth and reports in the Black newspapers. He pitched for eight different Negro League teams between 1926 and 1947.

Paige recognized that he was a popular gate attraction and often jumped from team to team throughout his career, cutting deals to improve his salary. In 1935, he clashed with Pittsburgh Crawfords owner Gus Greenlee, who he thought was underpaying him. He quit the Crawfords and joined a racially integrated semipro team in Bismarck, North Dakota, for $400 a month and the use of a car. A team photo reveals five white and six Black players, including several other Negro Leaguers. That season, Paige won thirty games against only two losses and led the team to the national semipro championship. In the postseason seven-game tournament, Paige pitched four complete game victories and struck out sixty-four batters in thirty-nine innings.

For over two decades Paige (along with catcher Josh Gibson) was the most popular player in the Negro Leagues. Within the Black community, Paige was a celebrity. He would often start several games per week to draw the crowd, but pitch for only three or four innings and thus not get credited with a win. But he once won three games in the same day. Paige claimed to have pitched in more than 2,500 games and to have won at least two thousand of them. These figures may seem improbable, but Tye explained that Paige played for forty-one years, often all year (in the United States and elsewhere), and pitched several times a week. Many major leaguers who played against him in his prime, in barnstorming games against Negro League teams, said that Paige had pinpoint control, an outstanding fastball, and an ability to outwit batters with his irregular motion.

Despite Paige's extraordinary accomplishments, few white Americans knew about him until he joined the Indians in 1948. By the time he arrived in the majors, he was well past his prime. Reporters focused as much on his eccentricities (including his windup) and colorful comments ("Don't look back. Something might be gaining on you" and "Don't eat fried food, it angries up the blood") as on his pitching prowess.

But even as a forty-two-year-old rookie, Paige excelled on the mound. In 1948 he had a 6–1 record and a 2.48 earned run average (ERA), second best in the American League. His performance helped the Indians capture the pennant. With Doby and Paige on the team, the Indians broke baseball's attendance record, drawing 2.6 million fans that season, a record that endured for fourteen years. Paige became the first African American pitcher to pitch in the World Series when he worked two-thirds of an inning in Game 5. That was his best season in the majors, which included another year with the Indians and then three with the lowly St. Louis Browns. After the 1953 season he pitched in the minors and on barnstorming teams. In 1965, when Paige was fifty-nine, Kansas City A's owner Charles O. Finley hired him to pitch one final game. He threw three innings of shutout ball against the Boston Red Sox, needing just twenty-eight pitches to get nine outs, striking out one, walking none, and allowing only one hit, by All-Star Carl Yastrzemski.

The legendary hitter Ted Williams recognized Paige's greatness. During his Hall of Fame induction speech in 1966, Williams said, "I hope that someday the names of Satchel Paige and Josh Gibson in some way could be added as a symbol of the great Negro players that are not here only because they were not given the chance."[35] That statement provoked the Hall of Fame to begin inducting Negro League players. Paige was the first, elected in 1971.

With Doby and Paige's help, the Indians had won the American League pennant and then the World Series against the Boston Braves. Veeck did not view Doby and Paige as tokens. By the start of the 1949 season, he had fourteen Black players under contract. The team's 1949 major league roster included four Black players—Doby, Paige, Luke Easter, and Orestes "Minnie" Minoso—the most on any big league team and one more than the Dodgers. Some other major league teams simply signed Negro League players without compensating their team owners—a source of much frustration by the Negro League owners—but Veeck purchased the contracts of Doby, Paige, and Easter. Veeck also hired Louis Jones, MLB's first Black front-office executive, as the Indians' assistant director of public relations. In April 1949, the *Sporting News* called Veeck "the real Abe Lincoln of the game."[36]

Veeck's commitment to racial integration extended beyond baseball. Shortly after moving to Cleveland, he joined the NAACP, which in 1948 was considered a radical organization by many Americans and certainly by the baseball establishment. He even appeared, along with Paige and Doby, in a poster designed to recruit new members to the civil rights organization, featuring the phrase, "The NAACP gets the ball for you."[37]

In 1956, Veeck led an investors group seeking to buy the Detroit Tigers. Particularly with the city's large African American population, Veeck wanted to finally break the Tigers' boycott as one of only two teams that hadn't signed a Black ballplayer. Even though Veeck presented the best offer, it was rejected in favor of another group, which didn't hire a Black player, Ossie Virgil, Sr., until two years later. As *Daily Defender* reporter Leslie Matthews wrote, "The reason why Bill Veeck did not latch onto the Tigers is because the AL moguls never forgave him for ending the loop's racial bar [when Veeck owned the Indians]."[38]

Dismantling the Negro Leagues

After Robinson signed his Dodger contract Black baseball fans and players alike were excited about seeing major league baseball erase its color line, but their enthusiasm was mixed with recognition that the opening of the Major Leagues to Black players would devastate the Black-owned Negro Leagues and lead to a loss of jobs for players, stadium workers, and others.

Once Robinson crossed the threshold, many Negro League players had their hopes raised that they might get a chance in the majors. In 1947, about 311 players filled the rosters of the twelve Negro League teams. By the end of the 1953 season, however, only thirty-five former Negro League players had reached the major league level.

Without the same fanfare that greeted Robinson, some former Negro League players signed contracts and served as pioneers, integrating the minors, which was particularly rough in many Southern cities and towns. But many of them languished in the minors for years without ever advancing to the majors. Others—like Paige, Sam Jethroe, Willard Brown, and Artie Wilson—joined major league teams past their prime and didn't last long.

The major leagues treated the Negro Leagues like a colony, poaching their players without providing the teams with adequate compensation, contributing to their financial demise. Those players who crossed into MLB were the Negro League's best players, including young stars like Willie Mays (who played for the Birmingham Black Barons), Hank Aaron (Indianapolis Clowns), Doby (Newark Eagles), and Ernie Banks (Kansas City Monarchs), as well as older stars such as Paige and Jethroe. As a result, the quality of Negro League play suffered, as did attendance.

Negro League teams—especially those that played in the same cities as their MLB counterparts—had a hard time attracting fans. The cost of renting major league ballparks to play games put a severe strain on their operating budgets. The Negro Leagues had to change their business model. Negro League teams played fewer games at home and did more barnstorming— traveling to different cities and towns to play each other as well as local semi-pro teams and, occasionally, teams composed of white major leaguers during the off-season.

In 1948, the Negro National League collapsed. The once-mighty Homestead Grays (based in Pittsburgh) withdrew from the league. It continued as a barnstorming team but lost $30,000 and folded the next year. The New York Black Yankees also folded. The Newark Eagles moved to Houston, Texas. The Negro American League briefly survived.

To attract more fans, a few teams in the Negro American League put women on their rosters, starting with Toni Stone, who joined the Indianapolis Clowns in 1953. The women helped gain attention, but their presence on the field didn't put enough bodies in the stands. The Negro American League collapsed around 1960, but a few all-Black teams hung on. The teams held their last All-Star game in 1962. By 1966, the Indianapolis Clowns was the only former Negro League team still playing, primarily by staging exhibition games against local teams, peppering the games with humorous antics, similar to the Harlem Globetrotters basketball team. The Clowns called it quits in the 1980s.

The Jet: Sam Jethroe

Sam Jethroe has the distinction of being the oldest Rookie of the Year in major league history. He won that honor in 1950, playing for the Boston Braves, at age thirty-three. Because of his race, he lost about ten years of playing in the major leagues in his prime, but he still had enough left to excel during his rookie year.

Jethroe was the Braves' first African American player. Five years earlier—in response to a demand by City Council member Isadore Muchnick—Boston Red Sox general manager Eddie Collins begrudgingly agreed to give Jethroe, Jackie Robinson, and Marvin Williams a sham "tryout" at Fenway Park, but the team didn't bother to follow up with any of them. Had they done so, the Red Sox might not only have been the first team to put a Black player on its roster but also could have become a dominant team from the early 1950s through the mid-1960s. In January 1951, after Jethroe had won the Rookie of the Year Award, he sat next to Collins at the Boston Baseball Writers annual dinner. Collins congratulated Jethroe on his fine season. According to sportswriter Howard Bryant, "Jethroe thanked him and without bitterness replied, 'You had your chance, Mr. Collins. You had your chance.'"[39]

Like many older Negro League players, Jethroe lied about his age when he was being scouted by major league teams, shaving off at least three years. He was born in January 1917 in rural Lowndes County, Mississippi, the son of a farmer and a domestic worker. The family moved to East St. Louis, Illinois, an industrial city, where Jethroe grew up. As a kid he would hitchhike to Sportsman's Park and peek through a knothole in the fence to watch Dizzy Dean and the St. Louis Cardinals. From 1942 to 1948, Jethro played in the Negro Leagues with the Cleveland Buckeyes. He was one of the league's best players, selected to the East-West All Star Game four times. He led the Negro American league in hitting in 1942, 1944, and 1945. In the latter year, he hit .393 and led the Buckeyes to the Negro World Series championship, beating the Homestead Grays. Jethroe played in the Cuban Winter League in 1947–48 and 1948–49, leading the league in stolen bases both times, catching the eye of Rickey's scouts.

In his quest to recruit Black ballplayers, Rickey considered Jethroe, a switch hitter, for the role of racial pathbreaker, but when Jethroe told Rickey that he drank and smoked, Rickey knew that he wasn't the right man. Robinson "had everything Mr. Rickey wanted," Jethroe later recalled. "He was a college man who had experienced the white world, and I wasn't."[40]

In 1948, the Dodgers bought Jethroe's contract from the Buckeyes for a reported $5,000 and assigned him the Montreal Royals, its Triple-A minor league team. He had two outstanding seasons, batting .322 and .326. In his second year, he set a league record with eighty-nine stolen bases and had 207 hits, thirty-four doubles, and nineteen triples. Some referred to him as "the man who made Montreal forget about Jackie Robinson."[41]

But at the end of the 1949 season, Rickey sold Jethroe to the Boston Braves. With the Braves, Jethroe met with the same racist obstacles that other Black players faced—segregated hotels and restaurants during spring training in Florida and in St. Louis during the regular season.

Jethroe was popular with the fans, however, even though Boston had a reputation as a racist city and even though Blacks comprised only 5 percent of its residents in 1950. The Boston newspapers focused primarily on Jethroe's speed, not his race. Looking back on that season, neither reporters nor fans recall any racist incidents or slurs coming from the Boston stands, although this wasn't true during some away games. "I loved the Boston fans," Jethroe recalled in a 1997 interview with the *Boston Globe*. "They used to chant, 'go, go, go,' every time I got on base. Never had a problem in Boston."[42]

On September 15, 1950, the Braves staged a Sam Jethroe Night to honor him. Boston Mayor John Hynes presented him with a check as well as a television, radio, easy chair, luggage set, and a week's hunting trip in Maine. Jethroe donated the money to a college scholarship fund for Black students.

He had an outstanding rookie year. He batted .273 and hit eighteen home runs, with fifty-eight RBI and one hundred runs scored. But what excited the fans and sportswriters most was his speed on the bases. During spring training in 1949, he recorded a 5.9 second sixty-yard sprint—two-tenths of a second faster than the world's record at the time. He helped revive the art of base stealing, garnering thirty-five thefts to lead the league. (The American League leader, Dom DiMaggio, had just fifteen.) The baseball writers selected him as the National League's Rookie of the Year by a wide margin in 1950. He had a very similar sophomore year with impressive offense and blazing speed. Hampered by intestinal surgery and a racist manager, Charlie Grimm, who once called him "Sambo," he still managed to steal twenty-eight bases.

The Braves moved to Milwaukee in 1953, but they left Jethroe off the roster. Instead, they sent him to their minor league franchise in Toledo. He had an outstanding year—batting .309 with twenty-eight home runs, twenty-seven stolen bases, and 137 runs—but the Braves never brought him up to Milwaukee. He was thirty-six years old, and the Braves were nurturing twenty-seven-year-old Bill Bruton as their center fielder. Instead, they traded Jethroe to the Pittsburgh Pirates, and he finished off his career mostly in the minors, retiring in 1958 at age forty-one.

Jethroe's role as a baseball pioneer encompassed more than being the first Black player on the Braves. Near the end of this life, he sued MLB, claiming that the baseball establishment's racism had kept him out of the majors in his prime and thus denied him the playing years needed to be eligible for a major league pension. It was both a courageous and desperate move, and it set the stage for MLB's eventual inclusion of former Negro League players in its pension plan.

After he left pro baseball, Jethroe and his wife, Elsie, owned and operated Jethroe's Bar and Restaurant in Erie, Pennsylvania. The business did well enough to provide a modest lifestyle for the family for thirty years. But in the 1990s the city's redevelopment agency forced him to sell the property. He took out a loan and purchased another restaurant in a tough, high-crime part of the city. The business and Jethroe fell on hard times. He even had to sell his Rookie of the Year trophy to a collector for $3,500. In 1994, he lost his home in a fire. Homeless, he and his wife wound up living in the shuttered restaurant with his grandchildren, aged ten and sixteen.

Jethroe wasn't the only former Negro League player who faced hard times. In 1992, Joe Black, former Negro League pitcher who won the National League's Rookie of the Year award with the Brooklyn Dodgers in 1952 at age twenty-eight, urged MLB to compensate living Negro Leaguers, most of whom never got the opportunity to play in the majors. "These men don't want charity, but they should be included in the Players Association medical plan," said Black, who became a school teacher and then top executive with the Greyhound bus company. "It wouldn't cost much. It only involves about 100 guys." Black helped set up an organization of former Negro League players and pushed the MLB to provide former Negro Leaguers with medical insurance.[43] In response, in 1993 MLB gave thirty-nine Negro League veterans and their spouses lifetime health insurance. But it took a lawsuit to force MLB to deal with the pension problem.

At an event in Cleveland, Jethroe ran into his old Montreal Royals roommate, Don Newcombe, and described his family's hard times. Newcombe introduced him to a lawyer, John Puttock, who urged Jethroe to sue MLB for denying him a pension. Jethroe had three years and seven days of major league service—less than the four full years required to be eligible for a pension. (Players who played after 1980 could earn pension benefits after only one day in the majors.)

Puttock believed that many Negro League players would have reached the majors at a younger age, and qualified for a pension, if MLB hadn't discriminated against Black athletes during their most productive years. In March 1995, he filed a class action lawsuit in US District Court for the Western District of Pennsylvania on behalf of Jethroe and other former Negro League players. In October 1996, the court dismissed the suit—not because the judge didn't think Jethroe had a case but because he had waited too long to sue, after the statute of limitations had expired.

US Senator Carol Moseley-Braun, an Illinois Democrat and the first Black woman in the Senate, heard about Jethroe's plight and mentioned it to Chicago White Sox owner Jerry Reinsdorf. In turn, Reinsdorf convinced other owners to set up a special fund to provide annual payments of $7,500 to $10,000 to eighty-five former Negro League players who had also played at least one day in the majors. National League president Leonard Coleman, who was one of three Black players kicked off the Princeton University football team in 1969 after they filed charges that the university had discriminated against them, formulated the program and appointed Joe Black to chair the committee. The pension program began in 1997. It also bestowed $10,000 annual pension payments to former white players who played before the players' pension fund was established in 1947. Jethroe collected his pension for four years until he died of a heart attack in 2001.

In 2004, US Senator Bill Nelson of Florida persuaded Commissioner Bud Selig to expand eligibility for the program to athletes who played for at least four years in the Negro Leagues but who never played in the majors, arguing that baseball wasn't truly integrated until 1959, when Pumpsie Green joined the Red Sox, the last team to hire a Black player. As a result, twenty-seven other former Negro League players were added on slightly different terms—$40,000 for four years, or $350 per month for life.

The fund can be seen as a form of reparations for the historical injustice of racial exclusion. The amounts were modest, and the fund's existence was due to the owners' voluntary contributions, based on a combination of good-will and efforts to avoid bad publicity, not a matter of the players' rights. Had Jethroe filed his suit before the statute of limitations expired, and had he prevailed, he would have helped set a legal precedent with regard to restorative justice for racial discrimination.

Robinson's Post-Baseball Activism

Robinson was more than a baseball pioneer. He was the first athlete in post–World War II America to use his celebrity as a platform to address social and political injustice, becoming an inspiration to subsequent activist athletes.

Robinson spent his entire major league career (1947 to 1956) with the Brooklyn Dodgers. He was voted Rookie of the Year in 1947 and Most Valuable Player in 1949, when he won the National League batting title with a .342 batting average. An outstanding base runner and base stealer, with a .311 lifetime batting average, he led the Dodgers to six pennants and was elected to the Hall of Fame in 1962.

After he retired from baseball in 1956, no team offered him a position as a coach, manager, or executive. He went to work as an executive with the Chock Full O' Nuts restaurant chain. He wasn't simply a token figure. He was given considerable management responsibilities. The firm's liberal owner allowed Robinson to engage in his community service and civil rights activities, even though much of it was controversial. That gave Robinson an opportunity to spend a great deal of time traveling around the country giving speeches on behalf of civil rights groups, participating in rallies and protests, raising money for civil rights causes, and serving on boards of civil rights and social reform organizations. He wrote a three-times-a-week column in the *New York Post*, then a liberal daily, and then wrote for the New York *Amsterdam News*, a Black weekly. He used these venues to discuss racial injustice, politics, sports, and other topics.

He served as the NAACP's fundraising chair, raising a record amount of money for the nation's premier civil rights organization. His willingness to speak out and his involvement with civil rights and social reform groups led the NAACP to give Robinson its highest award, the Spingarn Medal, in December 1956—making him the first athlete to receive that honor. In his acceptance speech, he explained that although many people had warned him "not to speak up every time I thought there was an injustice," he would continue to do so.[44] For example, in 1957, he publicly urged President Eisenhower to send troops to Little Rock, Arkansas, to protect Black students seeking to desegregate the public schools.

Robinson went beyond making public statements, serving on committees and lending his name to letterheads for good causes. But he did more than lend his name. He was often on the front lines of the civil rights movement. In 1960, he was impressed with the resilience and courage of the college students engaging in sit-ins at Southern lunch counters. Several of the student activists traveled to New York City to meet with Robinson, who agreed to raise bail money for the students lingering in Southern jail cells. Within a few days he raised $20,000 and then organized a fundraiser at his Connecticut home that featured jazz greats Ella Fitzgerald, Sarah Vaughan, and Duke Ellington. This became the first of Robinson's annual "Afternoons of Jazz" at his home to raise money for civil rights causes. He also joined civil rights activists in picketing the Woolworth lunch counters in New York in solidarity with the Southern sit-inners.

In 1961, Robinson used his newspaper column to support the Freedom Riders, even writing a public letter to the chair of the Interstate Commerce Commission demanding that he immediately order the desegregation of interstate bus travel. Robinson drew on his own anticommunist credentials to criticize segregationist Senator James Eastland of Mississippi, who attacked the Freedom Riders as communists. The next year, at Martin Luther King Jr.'s request, Robinson traveled to Albany, Georgia, to draw media attention to three Black churches that had been burned to the ground by segregationists. He then led a fundraising campaign that collected $50,000 to rebuild the churches and returned to Georgia once they were rebuilt to demonstrate the civil rights movement's resilience and resistance to intimidation. In 1963, he devoted considerable time and travel to support King's voter registration efforts in the South. He traveled to Birmingham as part of King's campaign to dismantle segregation in that city. "His presence in the South was very important to us," recalled Wyatt Tee Walker, chief of staff of King's Southern Christian Leadership Conference (SCLC).[45] Although he was personally close to King, he did not confine his fundraising efforts to SCLC. He continued to raise money for the NAACP, the Student Nonviolent Coordinating Committee (SNCC), and other civil rights groups.

Once he retired from baseball, Robinson took a more active interest in partisan politics, but he never wanted to run for office himself. Although he was frequently criticized by liberals for his support for Republicans, his embrace of candidates was based almost entirely on their views and track record on civil rights issues, not party affiliation. In fact, in the 1960 presidential election, he initially supported Hubert Humphrey, a liberal Democratic Senator from Minnesota and a longtime civil rights stalwart, traveling to different cities to speak on Humphrey's behalf during the Democratic primaries. By May, however, Senator John F. Kennedy's primary victories forced Humphrey to drop out. Both JFK and Vice President Richard Nixon, the GOP candidate, actively sought Robinson's endorsement. Robinson met with both candidates. He was not impressed with Kennedy's commitment to civil rights (including his waffling on the 1957 Civil Rights Act) and worried that the Massachusetts senator would be beholden to the segregationist Democrats who controlled Congress. At the time, there were a significant number of liberal Republicans who supported civil rights, and many African Americans still viewed the GOP as the party of Abraham Lincoln. Robinson even used his New York Post column to criticize Kennedy "as long as he continues to play politics at the expense of 18,000,000 Negro Americans."[46]

Nixon had been cultivating Robinson as early as 1952, when they met by accident in Chicago. They occasionally exchanged letters. When they met in 1960, Nixon persuaded him that he would be more forceful on civil rights issues than Eisenhower and that he would appoint Black people in positions of responsibility in his administration. In September 1960, Robinson shocked his liberal fans by endorsing and campaigning for Nixon. He quickly regretted his choice, especially after Nixon refused to make an appearance in Harlem and refused to act after Martin Luther King Jr. was arrested for participating in an Atlanta sit-in and sent to an isolated prison in rural Georgia, where his family and friends feared he would be killed. (In contrast, JFK's aides secured King's release from the jail, which turned many Blacks into Kennedy voters.) Three weeks before Election Day, Robinson said that "Nixon doesn't deserve to win."[47]

In 1962, Robinson endorsed the reelection campaign of New York's Governor Nelson Rockefeller, the last of the high-ranking liberal Republicans who supported activist government and civil rights, even donating money to King's civil rights crusades. After the election, Robinson briefly worked as an aide to Rockefeller and in 1964 supported him for president, but when reactionary Senator Barry Goldwater of Arizona won the nomination, Robinson left the GOP convention commenting that he now had "a better understanding of how it must have felt to be a Jew in Hitler's Germany," and left the Republican Party behind.[48] In 1968, he supported Humphrey over Nixon.

Robinson was not naïve about the realities of racial segregation and white racism. He and his wife, Rachel, had to use a white intermediary in order to buy a home in white, affluent Stamford, Connecticut. His children faced racism in the local public schools. He was rejected for membership in a local country club. Even so, he was a firm believer in racial integration. In his newspaper column and in other public forums, he clashed with Malcolm X, who accused Robinson of being a puppet of "white bosses."[49] Some young Black nationalist militants called Robinson an "Uncle Tom" because of his support for racial integration.[50]

Ironically, Robinson's ventures into the business world reflected some of the ideas of Black nationalists, who believed in the creation of Black-owned businesses as an alternative to Black ghettos being colonized by white corporations. Robinson openly criticized American business for discriminating against Black executives, employees, and consumers. He was particularly angered by white-owned banks and by slumlords. He lent his name to several businesses, including a construction company and a Black-owned bank in Harlem, to help address the affordable housing shortage and white banks' persistent redlining. Both businesses fell on hard times and dimmed Robinson's confidence in Black capitalism as a strategy for racial advancement and integration.

As he grew older, Robinson became more impatient with the slow progress against racism in sports and society. In 1964, he expressed his displeasure with Muhammad Ali when the boxer announced he had joined the Nation of Islam (under the tutelage of Malcolm X) and refused to submit to the draft during the war in Vietnam due to his religious convictions. "He's hurting, I think, the morale of a lot of young Negro soldiers over in Vietnam," said Robinson, whose son was serving (and would later be wounded) in Vietnam.[51] But by 1967, after Ali was convicted, Robinson talked about the "heroism and tragedy" of Ali's situation and said that Ali "has won a battle by standing up for his principle."[52] Even so, he was upset when King came out against the Vietnam War that year. In 1967, Robinson resigned from the NAACP board for its failure to include "younger, more progressive voices."[53] The following year, he publicly supported track stars John Carlos and Tommie Smith's fist-raising protest at the Olympic Games in Mexico City.

In 1970, he was one of three ex-ballplayers (the others were Hank Greenberg and Jim Brosnan) to testify in court in support of Curt Flood's challenge to baseball's reserve clause, which kept players in indentured servitude.

Robinson refused to participate in a 1969 Old Timers Game because he did not yet see "genuine interest in breaking the barriers that deny access to managerial and front office positions."[54] Robinson's statement irked fellow Hall of Famer Bob Feller. He and Robinson happened to be at the same press conference in Washington, DC, to celebrate baseball's alleged hundredth anniversary. Feller, who in 1946 predicted that Robinson was not good enough to make it in the majors, took the opportunity to attack Robinson. "Robinson has always been bush," Feller said. "He's always been a professional agitator more than anything else. He's just ticked off because baseball never rolled out the red carpet when he quit playing and offered him a soft front office job." An angry Robinson responded, "My big thing is I don't believe that the Black players are getting an equal opportunity with the whites after their playing days are through. I think the public is more ready for a Black manager than the owners."[55]

At his final public appearance, throwing the ceremonial first pitch before Game 2 of the 1972 World Series, shortly before he died, Robinson accepted a plaque honoring the twenty-fifth anniversary of his major league debut, then observed, "I'm going to be tremendously more pleased and more proud when I look at that third base coaching line one day and see a black face managing in baseball."[56] No major league team had a Black manager until the Cleveland Indians hired Frank Robinson in 1975. The majors' first Black general manager—the Atlanta Braves's Bill Lucas—wasn't hired until 1977.

"I cannot possibly believe," he wrote in his autobiography, I Never Had It Made, published shortly before he died of a heart attack and complications from diabetes at age fifty-three in October 1972, "that I have it made while so many black brothers and sisters are hungry, inadequately housed, insufficiently clothed, denied their dignity as they live in slums or barely exist on welfare."[57]

He also apologized to Paul Robeson, writing that he would reject HUAC's invitation to testify "if offered now" and further reflecting that "I have grown wiser and closer to the painful truths about America's destructiveness and

I do have an increased respect for Paul Robeson, who, over the span of that 20 years sacrificed himself, his career and the wealth and comfort he once enjoyed because, I believe, he was sincerely trying to help his people."[58]

During his post-baseball years, some Black nationalists called Robinson an "Uncle Tom" because he was a Republican, pro-business, anticommunist, and opposed to Black separatism. But none of these beliefs shielded Robinson from severe criticism for being outspoken and militant on behalf of racial equality. In fact, the FBI kept a file on Robinson because it was concerned about his activism and influence. Robinson was the first well-known professional athlete in post–World War II America to use his celebrity to speak out against social injustice. He set the stage for other athletes to speak out, but no other professional athlete, before or since, has been so deeply involved in social change movements. The scale, depth, and variety of Robinson's activism is so remarkable that it would be almost impossible to replicate. Robinson's engagement with the civil rights movement was a central part of his life, despite the demands of being a full-time athlete under enormous physical and psychological pressure for his pathbreaking role. When his playing days ended, Robinson's involvement deepened further, often at the expense of his health and his livelihood.

Years before Colin Kaepernick was born, Robinson wrote, "I cannot stand and sing the anthem. I cannot salute the flag; I know that I am a black man in a white world."[59]

CHAPTER FIVE

Defending Civil Rights

Major League Baseball integrated at a snail's pace after Robinson broke the color barrier in 1947. By 1951, African Americans held only twenty-one of the four hundred spots on big league rosters. Only six of baseball's sixteen major league teams had a Black player. By the end of the 1954 season, only twelve teams had put a Black player on their rosters. The next three teams to integrate were the New York Yankees (1955), Philadelphia Phillies (1957), and Detroit Tigers (1958). The Boston Red Sox were the final holdout. Elijah "Pumpsie" Green was the first Black player on the Red Sox, joining the team in the middle of the 1959 season, twelve years after Robinson joined the Dodgers.

Green was an outstanding athlete whose opportunity to excel on the diamond was hampered by the slow pace of baseball's racial integration and the racism he encountered in both the minor and major leagues. The 1950s Red Sox featured both a racist owner, Tom Yawkey, and a racist manager, Pinky Higgins. A Texan, Higgins was unwilling to put a Black player on his squad. At one point, he told columnist Al Hirschberg, "There'll be no n—s on this ball club as long as I have anything to say about it."[1] When Boston sportswriter Larry Claflin asked Higgins about Green's prospects for the team, the manager called him a "n— lover" and then spit tobacco juice on him. Green made the team nevertheless, and Higgins was fired halfway into the season.

By 1959, African American ballplayers comprised 10 percent of major league players, reaching 20 percent by the mid-1960s. Black ballplayers who pioneered integration in the 1950s learned that simply making it to the majors didn't mean an end to the racial discrimination and segregation they would continue to face. And merely because MLB began to integrate didn't mean the rest of America automatically did so. Organized baseball deserves some credit for helping to desegregate other aspects of society. As Martin Luther King Jr. claimed, without Jackie Robinson, his work for civil rights would have been immeasurably more difficult. Even so, while baseball integration might have provided an important model for promoting civil rights,

MLB itself, and it frequently acquiesced to, if not facilitated, segregation out-side baseball.

The generation of Black ballplayers who followed Jackie Robinson sought the right to play on the same field as whites. After all sixteen MLB teams inte-grated, however, another generation sought to have Black ballplayers paid the same respect and deference as their white peers. The Black stars sought the same reverence fans and sportswriters extended to white stars, who benefit-ted from racist double standards.

As Black Hall of Famer Henry Aaron recalled, decades after Robinson broke the color barrier, "There wasn't a white person in the South—or in baseball, for that matter—who was going to change things just out of his sense of decency."[2] According to Howard Bryant, Aaron began experiencing a political awakening in 1963, influenced by the Black writer James Baldwin, Malcolm X, and Martin Luther King Jr. When rumors began surfacing that the Braves would be moving from Milwaukee to Atlanta, Aaron was alarmed, having no interest in returning to the Deep South racism of his birth. As the move became more of a reality, it became necessary to cultivate Aaron's sup-port, and he was asked by the NAACP and the National Urban League to give the South a second chance.

Aaron met and played ball with King, who was a big baseball fan. Aaron expressed his embarrassment that he "wasn't publicly visible in the front lines of the movement," but King convinced him that his contribution would be to help bring big league sports to Atlanta. As Jimmy Carter, the former Geor-gia governor who later became president, reflected, "Having sports teams [in Atlanta] legitimized us. It gave us the opportunity to be known for something that wasn't going to be a national embarrassment. Henry Aaron was a big part of that because he integrated pro sports in the Deep South, which was no small thing. He was the first black man that white fans in the South cheered for."[3]

In 1966, Aaron insisted that Fulton County Stadium seating and facilities be desegregated before he would join the move of the Milwaukee Braves to Atlanta. When Atlanta welcomed the Braves with a parade, Andrew Young—a close aide to King who had become executive director of the Southern Chris-tian Leadership Conference, based in Atlanta—watched Aaron riding past in an open convertible and overheard a white spectator comment to his white companion: "If we're going to be a big league city, that man [Aaron] is going to have to have a home anywhere in this city he wants to have it, and . . . we've got to open the doors to this city to people and not worry about their color."[4]

The Trials of Integration

As difficult as it was for Jackie Robinson to be the first ballplayer to break through baseball's segregation, the athletes who followed in the next two decades also had to endure persistent racism, not only in the minor leagues but also after they made it to the majors. Besides facing resistance and resentment from some white teammates, African American ballplayers also encountered discrimination and an endless stream of indignities in every walk of life, especially in (but not entirely limited to) the South. They were either unable to use or were segregated in hotels, motels, buses, trains, bathrooms, restaurants, drinking fountains, swimming pools, lunch counters, movie theaters, ballpark stands, and elsewhere.

Black ballplayers were extremely vulnerable. If they spoke out against their mistreatment, they couldn't be sure they'd be backed by their white teammates, and they risked being labeled as troublemakers by team owners, who could stifle their careers. White players who empathized with their Black teammates were also in a tough situation. If they protested, then they risked being labeled agitators, with no protection (before the players' union ended the reserve clause and won free agency) from being dropped, demoted, or blacklisted.

A few Black ballplayers pushed back in small ways, even using humor to object to their treatment. When the Black Puerto Rican first baseman, Vic Power, was told by a waitress, "We don't serve Negroes here," Power responded, "That's okay, I don't eat Negroes. I just want rice and beans."[5] A few other ballplayers were notable for going further. They pushed for desegregation and better treatment of Blacks not only in baseball but also in the broader society.

In 1960, the Milwaukee Braves held their spring training in Bradenton, Florida, a segregated city. For six weeks, Henry Aaron and his Black teammates had to endure Jim Crow segregation. When local Black leaders demanded that local politicians and Braves' officials put an end to such blatant discrimination, the team's executive vice president, Birdie Tebbetts, assured the media that his Black players were happy with their accommodations. In fact, although the Black players, who couldn't stay in the same hotel as their white teammates, appreciated the home cooking at Mrs. Gibson's garage apartment, they were angered when the Ku Klux Klan marched down Ninth Street, past Mrs. Gibson's house. It was, wrote a local reporter, "A not-so-subtle reminder that they were very much in a Southern town."[6]

Along with his Black teammates, Bill Bruton and Wes Covington, Aaron forcefully contradicted Tebbetts. "It's about time you [the Braves management] all realized we're a team and we need to stay together,"[7] explained Aaron. But both the team and the city resisted change, claiming they'd never had any complaints before from any Negro players. The Braves, Tebbetts argued, had no business trying to change local customs.

The media routinely portrayed MLB as progressive on race relations because of the visibility of Robinson's breakthrough. But as historian Jack Davis observed, this "was not enough to [also] break down segregation barriers" off the field, in spring training and elsewhere, for Black players and Black citizens alike. "In the South," according to Davis, "the white power structure chose not to follow the American pastime's example of racial integration."[8] In 1942, Bill Veeck had challenged local racist customs when his team, the Milwaukee Brewers, held its spring training in Ocala, Florida. Like Veeck, MLB could have exerted pressure but, Davis explained, "Since baseball officials had taken a nonassertive position, the state government was able to minimize its role . . . and safeguard its principal industry [tourism] as well as the traditions of Jim Crow." As Davis further noted, "It required more than a mere example [MLB integration] to affect a fundamental shift in the social patterns in the South. With remarkable success, the white-determined social structure had managed to absorb external pressures that fell short of active opposition."[9]

Hall of Fame outfielder Roberto Clemente played his entire career with the Pittsburgh Pirates, from 1954 to 1972, during the peak of civil rights activism. He closely followed the movement and identified with its struggles. He admired King and became his friend. They met often, including a long visit on Clemente's farm on the outskirts of Carolina, Puerto Rico, where they discussed King's philosophy of nonviolence and racial integration. Clemente voiced these ideas both inside and outside the clubhouse. As teammate Al Oliver recalled, "Our conversations always stemmed around people from all walks of life being able to get along. He had a problem with people who treated you differently because of where you were from, your nationality, your color; also poor people, how they were treated."[10]

Clemente was a proud American (from 1958 to 1964 he served in the Marine Corps Reserves), Puerto Rican, and Black man. Coming from a more racially integrated island of Puerto Rico, he was shocked by the segregation he encountered in mainland America, especially during spring training in the Jim Crow South. He couldn't stay in the same hotels or eat in the same restaurants as his white teammates. Clemente and other Black players were excluded from the Pirates' annual spring golf tournament at a local country club, while their white teammates participated. He bristled over the racist way that sportswriters covered him. They called him "Bobby" or "Bob," instead of his preferred name "Roberto." They made fun of his accent, quoted him in broken English and paid little attention to his powerful intellect and social conscience.

King was assassinated in Memphis on Thursday, April 4, 1968, during the last week of baseball's spring training. His funeral was scheduled for Tuesday, April 9, the day after opening day. Immediately, the National Baseball Association (NBA) and National Hockey League (NHL) suspended their playoff games. Racetracks shut down for the weekend. The North American Soccer League called off games. But Major League Baseball waffled. After many players sat out the last few games of spring training to honor King, several owners insisted that Baseball Commissioner William Eckert, a retired Air Force general, penalize them for refusing to play. But Eckert was more concerned about the start of the regular season.

Clemente was upset that Eckert announced that each team could decide for itself whether it would play games scheduled for opening day and the day of King's funeral. Some team owners, torn over what to do, approached their Black players to feel the pulse of their employees. "If you have to ask Negro players, then we do not have a great country," Clemente told the *Pittsburgh Post-Gazette*.[11]

King's murder triggered rebellions in a number of cities with major league teams. Two teams—the Washington Senators and Cincinnati Reds—postponed their home openers because their stadiums were near the protests. But Houston Astros owner Roy Hofheinz, a businessman and former Houston mayor, insisted that his team would play its opener against the Pirates—the third game scheduled for April 8. "Our fans are counting on it," explained Astros' vice president Bill Giles.[12]

Under baseball rules, as the visiting team, the Pirates were required to play if the Astros wanted the game to go on. But veteran third baseman Maury Wills urged his teammates to refuse to play on Opening Day and the following day, when America would be watching or listening to King's funeral. At the time, the Pirates had eleven Black players (six of them also Latino) on their roster, more than any other major league team.

After Clemente, the team leader, urged his teammates to support Wills' idea, they took a vote. It was unanimous. Clemente and Dave Wickersham, a white pitcher, contacted Pirates general manager Joe L. Brown and asked him to postpone the season's first two games. The two players wrote a public statement on behalf of their teammates: "We are doing this because we white and Black players respect what Dr. King has done for mankind."[13] Pirate players Donn Clendenon and Willie Stargell walked into the Astros' locker room and persuaded the Black players to join the protest. The other players agreed and informed the Houston brass: they would not play the first two games until after King was buried.

St. Louis Cardinals pitcher Bob Gibson and some of his teammates had the same idea. They met in first baseman Orlando Cepeda's apartment and then told Cardinals management that they wouldn't play on April 9, the opening day for most of the teams. Players on other teams followed their lead. The Los Angeles Dodgers' Walter O'Malley was the last owner to hold out, but when the Phillies players refused to take the field against the Dodgers, his hands were tied. Commissioner Eckert, his back against the wall, reluctantly moved all opening day games to April 10. No sportswriter at the time described the players' action as a strike. But that's what it was—a two-day walk-out, not over salaries and pensions, but over social justice.

During the 1960s and 1970s, a few other rebels—including Bill White, Dick Allen, Curt Flood, Jim "Mudcat" Grant, and George Gmelch—challenged racism in baseball and in the larger society in different ways and with different consequences.

Uppity: Bill White

Bill White demanded respect. An African American, White was born in the Florida panhandle, near Alabama, in 1934. He was raised by his mother and grandmother, initially in a shack with no plumbing or electricity. When White was three, his family joined the Great Migration, escaping virulent Southern racism by moving to Warren, Ohio, where he grew up. Black and white residents and laborers lived and worked side by side, even if some racial discrimination persisted. As one of only a few Black students at Warren G. Harding High School, White was elected senior class president. But the school principal canceled the tradition of the top officeholder dancing with the prom queen (who was white) at the annual prom.

An unremarkable athlete in school, White was a strong student who aspired to a medical career. Columbia University and Case Western Reserve University offered him scholarships, but White decided to study closer to home at Hiram College's premed program. His performance on the diamond was undistinguished until he hit two home runs in the championship game, which happened to be seen by Alan Fey, a New York Giants scout. White had no ambitions to become a professional ballplayer, but Fey convinced him to try out for Giants manager, Leo Durocher, in 1953. Despite his strong performance, White was nevertheless surprised when the Giants offered him a contract and bonus to sign with the team. Since he promised his mother he'd finish college, he refused until Durocher offered to pay his tuition.

During 1953 spring training in Arizona, White became Durocher's pet project. The Adams Hotel in Phoenix had only recently agreed to host the Giants Black players after the team threatened to boycott the hotel, but the pool, lobby, and dining room remained off limits to Blacks. Jeff Chandler, a movie actor, knew White and invited him to attend a screening of a film he was starring in. White didn't know that Phoenix's movie theaters were segregated. When he showed up at the theater, he was told the theater had no balcony. It took White a few minutes to realize that balconies were the only place Blacks were allowed to sit. When he returned to the hotel, he yelled and screamed about the incident to his roommate, the future Hall of Famer Monte Irvin, who advised him, "Don't rock the boat."[14] White held off then, but ultimately changed his attitude and became a boat-rocker.

For the 1953 season, the Giants assigned White to their minor league club in Danville, Virginia. There he encountered strict segregation, and endless racist taunts of "n—" and other epithets while playing for the Danville Leafs. Like other northern Black Americans, White had been sheltered from the worst, most blatant, racism until he traveled through the South, encountering repeated discrimination, especially on road trips in Texas and Louisiana. White was the only African American on his team and in the entire Carolina League. In Beaumont, Texas, he couldn't resist giving the finger to the racist crowd, and only narrowly avoided being lynched by a mob of five hundred fans who confronted him after the game. Only his bat-wielding teammates saved him, escorting him to the bus, which pulled away amidst a barrage of rocks from the crowd.

In 1954, White moved to the Sioux City, Iowa team in the Western League, and discovered that racism wasn't limited to the South. On a road trip in Kansas, a restaurant refused him service and he had to eat his dinner on the team bus. Although he rarely cried, this time he put his face in his hands and sobbed. Some white teammates were sympathetic, but White claimed that "Many white players and team owners were indifferent to the restrictions placed on Black players. The prevailing attitude was, 'That's just the way it is. We're not politicians or lawyers. There's nothing we can do.'"[15] The racism continued the following year, when White joined the Giants' Dallas farm team in the Texas League.

White later observed that "In some ways, in the 1950s, Black ballplayers in the Southern minor leagues—guys like Henry Aaron in Jacksonville, Florida; Curt Flood in North Carolina; and Willie McCovey, who followed me in Danville in 1956—were the point men in the fight for racial equality."[16] If they hadn't spoken out, then their ability to tolerate the racism, and succeed with and against white ballplayers, wouldn't have provided inspiration for other Blacks who were otherwise constantly told they were inferior.

In 1956, White was promoted to the Giants. He was one of the few major league players to hit a home run in his first at bat. He had a strong rookie season, swatting twenty-two home runs in 138 games and batting .256 as the team's starting first baseman. He spent the entire 1957 season and part of the 1958 season in the Army, where he played for the Fort Knox, Kentucky baseball team. But he quit the team after he was refused service at a local restaurant and his white teammates went on with their meal, refusing to stand up for him. Instead, he supplemented his Army pay by playing semipro ball for $50 a game.

White returned to the Giants in 1958 after his military service, but two rising stars at first base—Orlando Cepeda and Willie McCovey—stood ahead of him. Seeing no future with the Giants, he did the unprecedented; he demanded a trade. The Giants traded him, but he was disappointed that his new team was the St. Louis Cardinals. St. Louis had a reputation for racism. Moreover, the team already had three first basemen, including Stan Musial, playing at the end of his Hall of Fame career. White played outfield that first year and made the All-Star team, but then Musial retired, and White won the starting first base job. In 1957, he won the first of seven Gold Glove awards for outstanding fielding.

As a major leaguer, White and the other Black ballplayers faced flagrant discrimination in the South. In St. Petersburg, Florida, where the Cardinals and other major league teams held their spring training, segregation remained firmly entrenched. Each spring, the St. Petersburg Chamber of Commerce held a "Salute to Baseball," inviting the ballplayers to an elaborate breakfast at the St. Petersburg Yacht Club. In 1961, as in the past, Blacks were left off the list of invitees. Other African American ballplayers felt powerless to respond, but White spoke up. He told local reporters, "I wanted to go [to the breakfast] very badly. I think I'm a gentleman and can conduct myself properly.... This thing keeps gnawing away at my heart. When will we be made to feel like humans?"[17]

White took a big risk in allowing the reporters to attribute the protest to him. He later reflected, "I saw the list included several rookies who'd never swung a bat in the majors. The idea that the local bigwigs wanted to honor unproven players while ignoring proven players because of the color of their skin rankled me.... No, it more than rankled me. Combined with all the other crap that black players had to take, it made me furious."[18]

Most national media ignored the story, but TV sportscaster Howard Cosell and Associated Press reporter Joe Reichler gave it some publicity. A Black newspaper in St. Louis, the *Argus*, picked up the story and proposed a Black boycott of Busch beer, which was owned by Cardinals president August Busch. With the company's profits at stake, the Cardinals' brass successfully lobbied the Chamber of Commerce to invite the Black ballplayers to the breakfast, creating a new precedent and showing players and others that challenging racism could pay off.

In the end, White refused the invitation, saying, "I hadn't wanted to eat with those bigots anyway. All I had really wanted, what all the black players wanted, was simply the opportunity to say no." Later, White recalled that speaking out "wasn't an easy thing to do. This was before baseball free agency, a time when the 'reserve clause' gave team owners complete control over a player's career. A player who was thought to be too outspoken—the word 'uppity' was sometimes used—ran the risk of being sent down to the minors or released. But we (sic) felt it had to be done."[19] Actually, it became "we" only after White stuck his neck out and a few other Black ballplayers followed suit.

Working with NAACP leaders in the city, White also protested St. Petersburg's segregated restaurants and hotels, and a few other Black ballplayers signed on. White lobbied Busch to convince the other MLB owners to threaten to leave St. Petersburg and Florida if the hotels didn't integrate. In the meantime, Busch leased an entire motel for the Cardinals, where Black and white ballplayers could live, eat, and socialize together. It became a public attraction, as southern whites drove by to watch the unprecedented spectacle of Blacks and whites in the same swimming pool or eating together at outside barbeques.

White leaked instances of segregation to the northern press, which began covering baseball conditions in the South. The following spring, Bill Veeck, by then the owner of the Chicago White Sox, canceled his team's reservations at Miami's McAllister Hotel when it refused to accommodate Black players, moving the entire team to the Biscayne Terrace Hotel. In 1962, White and Milwaukee Braves outfielder Bill Bruton got the players' union, the Major League Baseball Players Association, to vote unanimously not to play in any city requiring Black and white ballplayers to use separate facilities. Florida hotels and restaurants began to accept Black guests. This contributed substantially to desegregating Florida spring training. Jackie Robinson sent White a thank you letter, urging him to "keep fighting."[20]

White never stopped fighting, sometimes publicly, but often behind the scenes. He observed, "Of course, compared with the accomplishments of people like Rosa Parks and the Rev. Martin Luther King and so many others, this [integrating spring training] was a small step. After all, we were just baseball players, not civil rights crusaders. . . . Still, I believe the desegregation of baseball and other professional sports on and off the field helped prepare America for desegregation throughout the country. Looking back on it a half century later, of all the things I did in baseball, being a part of that struggle is the thing of which I am most proud."[21]

White wished that more had been done. He observed that "for some reason the major civil rights organizations didn't make much use of sports figures in the battle for equal rights throughout the 1960s." He noted that "black sports figures across the country were desegregating previously all-white neighborhoods—usually quietly, sometimes publicly."[22] Making his home in St. Louis, White desegregated his own neighborhood, fighting off the resistance of a neighbor and ultimately achieving acceptance for himself and his family.

In 1964, White played in his eighth All-Star game, finished third in the MVP voting, and got the winning hits to clinch the 1964 pennant for the Cardinals, earning his only World Series ring in the postseason. But when the Cardinals fell to seventh place in 1965, they traded White and several teammates to the Phillies. White was wary of Philadelphia's racist reputation and clashed with Phillies manager Gene Mauch, yet he nevertheless had another All-Star season until he was injured. Along the way, he became a mentor to the budding but troubled star Dick Allen. Never fully healed, White limped through subpar seasons in 1967 and 1968, when he was traded back to St. Louis, where he ended his playing career in 1969.

White was highly regarded as a smart player. The Cardinals wanted him to manage the team, suggesting he get a year of experience with their Tulsa farm club. But White didn't want to manage. Instead, he was intrigued by broadcasting. He had already been doing a pregame "Bill White Show" in his earlier years with the Cardinals and then again with the Phillies. The Cardinals asked him to replace the outgoing Harry Caray in the broadcast booth. It was a tempting offer, and White initially accepted. But then he changed his mind, realizing the challenge he'd face replacing the popular and iconic Caray. Instead, he pursued broadcasting in Philadelphia where, among other things, he became WFIL-TV's full-time sports anchor.

White rekindled his friendship with broadcaster Howard Cosell, who was outspoken in his coverage of sports' racism. In 1971, Cosell recommended White for the Yankees play-by-play job, and White became the first, full-time African American broadcaster in MLB history. This began an eighteen-year-long partnership and friendship with Phil Rizzuto, where White routinely played the straight man for the former Yankee's antics.

While working for the Yankees, White pursued other broadcasting assignments, including a short stint on NBC-TV's *Today Show*. But when he produced and ran a favorable program on the radical Black actor and activist Paul Robeson, the network fired him after the segment generated controversy. Near the end of his Yankee broadcasting tenure, White impressed George Steinbrenner enough to be offered the job of general manager, but he rejected the offer, realizing the nightmare it would be working for the authoritarian owner. In 1989, White left the Yankee broadcast booth for an unexpected opportunity.

Two years earlier, in 1987, a bombshell exploded in MLB. In an interview with host Ted Koppel on NBC-TV's popular *Nightline* program, Al Campanis, the Los Angeles Dodgers general manager, was asked why so few Blacks held positions at the managing, coaching, and front-office level in baseball, forty years after Jackie Robinson broke the color line. Remarkably, Campanis responded, "They [African Americans] may not have some of the necessities to be a field manager or perhaps a General Manager." When Koppel claimed that sounded like the "kind of garbage" we heard before Robinson's signing, Campanis made it worse: "It's not garbage, Mr. Koppel. It just might be that—why are black men or black people not good swimmers? Because they don't have the buoyancy."[23]

Although many condemned his comments, others defended Campanis, claiming that as a player and Dodger official he never engaged in racist behavior. Campanis had been Jackie Robinson's teammate and friend on the Montreal Royals. But the public outcry forced the Dodgers to fire Campanis. MLB was faced with an enormous public relations problem, especially since it had no Black managers or general managers, much less any Black owners. Observing this, White claimed, "In the end I had to conclude that while Al Campanis was a basically decent man, he had said not only what he believed but what many other baseball executives of the time believed—that blacks in general lacked the ability to work in high-profile front office and managerial positions."[24]

In this context, when National League president Bart Giamatti became MLB commissioner in 1989, White was one of several African Americans proposed as candidates for the vacant position. MLB denied it wanted to fill the job with a Black person simply to diffuse the Campanis controversy, but that perception was difficult to avoid. White observed, "Obviously, there was a considerable effort to get a black man into this job," and he initially shunned it.[25] He was persuaded, however, to at least be interviewed for the position. The National League owners unanimously selected him. Hall of Fame pitcher Bob Gibson, White's former teammate, observed, "Bill had no choice but to accept that job. Not for himself, but for other people."[26]

Predictably, White had a roller coaster ride after he became the first Black league president not only in baseball, but in any major sport. Outspoken all his previous career, White felt he had to take a different approach now that he was on the inside, in the seat of power. When Giamatti died soon after assuming the commissionership, Fay Vincent succeeded him and repeatedly compromised White's independence. White had to resist Vincent's pressure to fire longtime National League attorney Lou Hoynes. Then, Vincent vowed to break the umpire's union, having White do the dirty work of bringing an injunction, rather than negotiating with the union when they went on strike during spring training. Then, Vincent abruptly dropped the suit, circumventing White and taking credit for settling the strike.

White made few friends in his role as enforcer, in charge of fines and suspensions. He also had to deal with Cincinnati Reds owner Marge Schott and her periodic racist outbursts, ultimately leading the other owners to expel her from her ownership position.

White pushed back against the business incentives he believed were ruining the sport. And he resisted the rule changes that he believed watered down the competition: the ban on pitching inside and breaking up double plays, the hypersensitivity of umpires to player complaints, and the threat of the designated hitter entering his league. As White observed, "We're probably not asking [any longer] for things that black players brought to this game. You don't have to play that way anymore, apparently."[27] The commissioner, the owners, and the umpires all constrained his ability to resist.

White could not ignore the persistent problem of racism within the sport, but he didn't want to be known as the baseball executive who focused mostly on that topic. Even so, he brought about important reforms. He condemned the Colorado Rockies in 1990 for persistently breaking their promise to interview minorities for front-office jobs, and they conceded. He insisted that Arizona wouldn't get an expansion team until the state endorsed a Martin Luther King Jr. national holiday. As only one of two states that hadn't done so, Arizona finally relented.

For the most part, however, White worked behind the scenes. To show his independence, he didn't join the Baseball Network, a group of Black ballplayers who organized after the Campanis interview. He reminded the younger players, "When I fought [against racism], they [Southern racists] could have cut my throat. I said things that weren't supposed to be said and I said them in Florida, Georgia, Alabama. Today, there's no sense of history, no sense of responsibility among most of the black players. . . . I've fought my battles. It's someone else's turn." Reflecting on his position, White noted that "I'm not your average diplomat. I don't have to be. I wasn't as a player."[28]

White worked to get more Blacks hired in organized baseball, but he did most of his work quietly, refusing to be a vocal cheerleader. He claimed that "if I spend my time doing that alone and not do my job, bang, I'm gone. If that happens, I'm not sure anyone else [another Black] would get that opportunity. So my job, first, is to do the best job I can. Whatever I do that is positive for minorities, I will try to do at the same time."[29]

After a long interview with White two years into his National League presidency, *New York Times* baseball writer Claire Smith wondered, "But can White override his ultimate caution not to foul the waters for those who follow the first black to attain such a lofty position? Can he continue to suppress his raging emotions for the rest of his term?"[30] White claimed that the owners "could get a black man they could control or they could get a black man who's been around this game as long, if not longer, than they have. I think that's what they got. What they didn't get was a puppet."[31]

In the end, White admitted that he accomplished far less for Blacks in baseball than he had wanted. But he was proud of the progress he had catalyzed. When he left the presidency, he had built up enough confidence in that position that the team owners hired another African American, Leonard Coleman, to succeed him. As White got closer to the end of his term, he got more vocal. In 1992, he told the Black Coaches Association audience that "I deal with people now who I know are racists and bigots. . . . I'm bitter, I'm mad. I've gone through things none of you have gone through. If I said what I really feel, no one [Black] would follow me into that chair."[32]

For White, it wasn't just the continuing absence of Blacks in baseball but also the treatment of those (including himself) who were in the game and the disturbing direction he saw the sport taking. From White's perspective, the owners cared only about the bottom line and not about the game. "No longer," he observed, "is there even the pretense that an objective 'outside baseball' authority was watching over the best interests of the game." Instead, in 1992 the owners made one of their own, Milwaukee Brewers owner Bud Selig, the acting commissioner and appointed him the official commissioner six years later. According to White, "They [the owners] understand the business of baseball. But I don't think they ever truly understood the game." Responding to the weakening, and ultimately (a few years later) the elimination, of the National and American league presidents, White resigned in 1994. Realizing his disgruntlement, the owners tried to give him a farewell dinner, but instead, White told his successor Leonard Coleman, "You can tell the owners I said the hell with them."[33]

White had a standout baseball career for three major league teams. He played in six All-Star Games, won seven Gold Gloves, and ended with a .286 lifetime batting average and 202 home runs. He followed this with a distinguished baseball broadcasting career, breaking barriers for African Americans as a New York Yankee play-by-play announcer. And he became the first Black president of the National League. Through all of this, beginning with his time in the minor leagues and his role in desegregating Florida spring training, White refused to accept the status quo, often vocally, sometimes quietly, during the harsh and difficult years after Jackie Robinson broke the color line.

Referring to the title of his autobiography, *Uppity*, White explained that "I use 'uppity' as a point of pride. I demanded to be recognized for what I accomplished, nothing more. If people thought I was uppity—and many did—so be it." White never finished college or pursued the medical career he once sought, but he always had those options. His advantage was that he didn't need baseball: "I didn't love baseball. Because I knew that baseball would never love me back."[34] And yet he spent almost all of his professional career in the game, making a difference.

Agitator: Curt Flood

In 1969, White's former Cardinals teammate, Curt Flood, refused a trade to Philadelphia, and filed suit against MLB and the reserve clause. White spoke out in support of Flood's efforts when even most of Curt's closest friends thought he was crazy. More than any other player in baseball history, Flood sacrificed his career for a principle. In doing so, he changed baseball forever.

For years, ballplayers accepted the idea that every one of their contracts included a reserve clause that restricted the right of players to move from club to club. The clause undermined their bargaining power to improve their pay and working conditions. A player could only negotiate with the team that had him on its reserve list. He could not talk with other clubs for a better contract. A team could sell, trade, or terminate his contract without his consent. Players remained the property of the team until they retired.

The players formed the Major League Baseball Players Association (MLBPA) in 1953, primarily to push the teams to provide pensions, but the union was ineffective—without any full-time staff or an adequate budget— for its first thirteen years. In 1966, All-Star pitchers Jim Bunning and Robin Roberts convinced their fellow players that the union needed a full-time executive director. That year they hired Marvin Miller, a veteran union activist who had served as the United Steelworkers union's chief economist and negotiator.[35] Miller began to discuss with players ways that the union could overturn the reserve clause, baseball's version of indentured servitude. Most players, even most union leaders, thought the cause was hopeless. But Flood was willing to try. He was only thirty-one when he stood up to baseball's establishment by challenging this feudal system. He was in his prime—an outstanding hitter, runner, and centerfielder. His protest destroyed his career.

Flood, an African American, was born in Houston on January 18, 1938 and moved with his family to Oakland, California, when he was a toddler. During World War II, his father worked in various defense-related jobs while his mother ran a small café and mended parachutes to help the family make ends meet. After the war, both parents found menial jobs at Fairmont Hospital.

Growing up, Flood pursued two passions. He was a talented artist and an outstanding athlete. As a teen, he created the artistic backgrounds for school proms and plays and earned extra money designing storefront window displays and advertising signs for a local furniture store. From the time he was nine, local baseball coaches recognized that Flood was a gifted player. He played at Oakland Technical High School and led his local American Legion team to the 1955 state championship, hitting .620 in twenty-seven games. After graduating in 1956, he signed a $4,000 contract, with no bonus, with the Cincinnati Redlegs (the name they used for several years to avoid being called the "Reds" during the height of the Cold War). When he showed up at spring training in Tampa, Florida, he was ushered out of a side door of the Redlegs' hotel and sent across town to a boarding house where the Black players stayed.

The team sent Flood to its High Point-Thomasville team in the Class B Carolina League for the 1956 season. He was prohibited from staying in the same hotels or eating in the same restaurants as his white teammates. He couldn't use the bathrooms when the team bus stopped at gas stations. Many southern fans were not happy with Flood's presence on the diamond.

"One of my first and most enduring memories is of a large, loud cracker who installed himself and his four little boys in a front-row box and started yelling 'black bastard' at me," Flood recalled. "I noticed that he eyed the boys narrowly, as if to make sure that they were learning the correct intonation."[36]

Flood had difficulty adjusting to the segregation and hostility, not only from fans but also from his white manager and teammates. He frequently returned to his hotel and cried. But, as he explained, "I solved my problem by playing my guts out."[37] He led the league in batting with a .340 average, set a league record with 133 runs scored, led the league with 388 putouts, and set a team record with twenty-nine home runs. He was named the league's Player of the Year.

The Redlegs called him up at the end of the 1956 and 1957 seasons. After playing winter ball in Venezuela, he got a telegram informing him that he'd been traded to the St. Louis Cardinals, the most southern team in the major leagues. He began the 1958 season with the Cardinals' Double-A team in Omaha, but after hitting .340 in thirteen games he was called up and became the Cardinal's starting center fielder.

Between 1958 and 1969, Flood was one of the best players in major league baseball. He didn't play in 1970 and played only thirteen games in 1971. Overall, he played in 1,759 games, had a .293 lifetime average, won seven Gold Gloves, and was a three-time All Star (1964, 1966, and 1968). He hit over .300 six times. He had 1,861 hits, but had he been able to remain in baseball, he would have certainly reached 2,000 hits and perhaps 2,500 hits. He was a catalyst for the Cardinals' three National League pennants and two World Series victories in 1964 and 1967. His teammates selected him as their cocaptain (with Tim McCarver) each year between 1965 and 1969. *Sports Illustrated* put a photo of Flood making a leaping catch on the cover of its August 19, 1968, issue, with the headline "Baseball's Best Center Fielder."[38]

Flood was one of the first ballplayers to get involved with the burgeoning civil rights movement. In February 1962, at the invitation of his hero, Jackie Robinson, the twenty-four-year-old Flood traveled to Jackson, Mississippi, to speak, along with Robinson and African American boxers Floyd Patterson and Archie Moore, at a protest rally against segregation organized by civil rights leader Medgar Evers. He told the crowd of 3,800 at the Masonic Temple that the rally helped him realize that he had a personal responsibility to fight racial injustice.

Flood knew that bigotry wasn't confined to the South, but he was shocked by his experience trying to move into an all-white neighborhood in the Oakland suburb of Alamo. In October 1963, Flood put down a deposit to rent a three-bedroom house for himself, his pregnant wife, and their four kids. Once the property owner learned that Flood and his family were Black, he threatened to shoot them if they arrived to integrate the all-white neighborhood. Flood filed suit in Contra Costa County and won a temporary restraining order allowing his family to occupy the home. They arrived accompanied by eleven sheriff's deputies, several highway patrolmen, and two representatives from the state Fair Employment Practices Commission, along with many print and TV reporters. About a dozen white supporters—local women and their children—showed up to welcome the Floods to their neighborhood.

After the law enforcement officials determined that the house was safe to enter, Flood addressed the crowd: "It doesn't make any difference whether I'm a professional athlete or a Negro or whatever. I'm a human being. If I have enough money to rent the house, I think I ought to have it."[39] He told the *Baltimore Afro-American* newspaper, "You don't do these things if you scare easily, and this time I knew I was legally and morally right."[40] After the Floods moved in, white neighbors brought them meals, took them shopping, and invited Flood to play golf and bridge, but they continued to get racist phone calls, and the Flood children confronted racist taunts.

Experiencing racial injustice made Flood more sensitive to other forms of injustice. "For Curt, players' rights and civil rights were part of the same idea," recalled his widow, actress Judy Pace Flood. Even before the MLBPA had any influence, Flood was an eager trade unionist. "On our first date, over dinner in 1964, he quizzed me about the Screen Actors Guild," Pace Flood remembered. He was particularly interested in the fact that SAG members had their own agents and lawyers, could negotiate with film studios over salaries, and could move to different studios—all things prohibited in Major League Baseball at the time."[41]

Flood played for the Cardinals for twelve seasons. After the 1969 season, the Cardinals traded him to the Philadelphia Phillies, but Flood didn't want to move to Philadelphia, which he called "the nation's northernmost southern city."[42] The Phillies offered him a $100,000 salary for the 1970 season, a $10,000 boost from his Cardinals salary. But for Flood, it was a matter of principle. He objected to being treated like a piece of property and to the reserve clause's restriction on his (and other players') freedom.

Flood talked with Miller about the possibility of suing Major League Baseball in order to overturn the reserve clause. In 1922, in a case called *Federal Baseball Club v. National League*, the US Supreme Court ruled that the Sherman Antitrust Act, which was intended to prevent collusion and monopolistic practices by business, did not apply to baseball. The court claimed that baseball was an "amusement" rather than a business engaged in interstate commerce and thus was exempt from the federal antitrust law. The ruling allowed major league baseball owners to operate as a monopoly, with teams colluding to deny players their right to bargain with prospective employers. Many scholars believed that this was one of the high court's worst decisions, but it remained in force a half century later.[43] It was as if, as Miller once observed, "The courts were saying, 'Yes, you're an American and have the right to seek employment anywhere you like, but this right does not apply to baseball players.'"[44]

Miller warned Flood that the odds were against him. He pointed out that a lawsuit would be expensive and could take two or more years. Moreover, Miller said, even if he won the lawsuit, he'd probably be unemployable in major league baseball; the owners would blacklist him as a player and as a future coach or manager.

Miller recalled, "I said to Curt, 'Unless some miracle takes place and the Supreme Court reverses itself, you're not going to win,' and Curt, to his everlasting credit, said, 'But would it benefit all the other players and future players?' And I said, 'Yes.' And he said, 'That's good enough for me.'"[45]

Miller invited Flood to the Major League Baseball Players Association executive committee meeting in San Juan, Puerto Rico, in early December to seek the union's financial and moral support. Many of the players were skeptical of Flood's idea to sue. After all, two previous legal challenges—by New York Giant outfielder Danny Gardella in 1949 and Yankees minor leaguer George Toolson in 1953—had failed. Tom Haller, the Dodgers All-Star catcher, bluntly asked Flood if his decision to challenge his trade was based on race. "I didn't want it to be just a black thing," Haller recounted in *A Well-Paid Slave*. "I wanted it to be a baseball thing."[46] Flood responded that while being Black no doubt made him more sensitive to injustice, he was doing this for all ballplayers, regardless of color.

The tide turned after the Pirates' Roberto Clemente—a superstar and union leader who had challenged baseball's establishment in the past—spoke out on Flood's behalf. Clemente explained how as a minor leaguer he'd been traded by the Brooklyn Dodgers to the Pittsburgh Pirates without any say in the matter because of the reserve clause. He would have preferred to play in New York, with its large Puerto Rican population, rather than Pittsburgh, a more racist city for Latinos. He also estimated that playing in Pittsburgh had already cost him $300,000 because of the shortage of endorsement opportunities in the smaller and whiter region. After Clemente spoke, Miller repeated his recommendation that the MLBPA support the lawsuit of their fellow player and union member.

The players voted unanimously to back the lawsuit. Miller recruited Arthur Goldberg—his former colleague in the steelworker's union, President John F. Kennedy's secretary of labor, a former associate justice of the US Supreme Court, and former US ambassador to the United Nations—to represent Flood.

On December 24, 1969, Flood sent a letter to Commissioner Bowie Kuhn. Flood wrote,

> After twelve years in the major leagues, I do not feel I am a piece of property to be bought and sold irrespective of my wishes. I believe that any system which produces that result violates my basic rights as a citizen and is inconsistent with the laws of the United States and of the several States.

It is my desire to play baseball in 1970, and I am capable of playing. I have received a contract offer from the Philadelphia club, but I believe I have the right to consider offers from other clubs before making any decision. I, therefore, request that you make known to all Major League clubs my feelings in this matter and advise them of my availability for the 1970 season.[47]

Kuhn immediately rejected Flood's request, so Flood made the letter public and sued Major League Baseball.

Most baseball writers opposed Flood's suit. They viewed him as a whining spoiled brat, making $90,000 a year. He alienated many baseball fans when, during an interview with Howard Cosell on ABC's *Wide World of Sports*, in January 1970, Flood said that "a well-paid slave is, nonetheless, a slave."[48]

Flood became the plaintiff in the case known as *Flood v. Kuhn*, which began on May 19, 1970, in federal court in New York City. Flood's lawyers recruited four prominent baseball figures to testify on Flood's behalf—Jackie Robinson, Hank Greenberg, Bill Veeck, and Jim Brosnan. Both Robinson and Greenberg had been traded by their longtime teams (the Dodgers and Tigers, respectively) against their will. Robinson chose to retire rather than play for the Giants. Greenberg played for the Pirates for a year, then retired as a player, eventually becoming the White Sox general manager. He knew that testifying at Flood's trial meant he'd never work in organized baseball again. Veeck, the maverick owner, had always battled his fellow owners to democratize professional baseball. Brosnan had been a major league relief pitcher from 1954 through 1963. In 1959, he wrote *The Long Season* based on his baseball diary followed by *The Pennant Race*, based on his 1962 diary. Both the Reds and White Sox told him he could no longer write about his experiences without their permission. Brosnan complained to Commissioner Ford Frick, who didn't bother to respond. By the time of Flood's trial, Brosnan had become a full-time writer and sports commentator.

On the witness stand, Robinson testified that "anything that is one-sided in this country is wrong, and I think the reserve clause is a one-sided thing in favor of the owners, and I think certainly should at least be modified to give a player an opportunity to have some control over his destiny." He predicted that unless the reserve clause was changed "it is going to lead to a serious strike in terms of the ballplayers."[49]

Flood later said that Robinson's statements at the trial on his behalf "sent chills up and down my spine."[50] Robinson was his hero whose courage in the face of adversity had inspired him. After three weeks, the judges nevertheless ruled in favor of the owners. Flood's lawyers appealed to the US Court of Appeals, which in April 1971 also ruled against Flood. The Supreme Court agreed to hear the case and heard oral arguments on March 20, 1972.

Goldberg was not well-prepared and made several mistakes during his oral argument before his former Supreme Court colleagues. He lost his place, repeated himself, failed to answer the justices questions, went past his allotted time, and recited Flood's year-by-year batting averages for no apparent reason. His friend Justice William Brennan cringed from the bench watching Goldberg struggle to make the case. But, given the makeup of the court, it is unlikely that Goldberg would have prevailed, even if he had been at the top of his game.

On June 19, 1972, the Supreme Court ruled against Flood by a 5–3 vote. Writing the majority decision, Justice Harry Blackmun admitted that baseball's exemption from federal antitrust laws was an "aberration" but declared that it was up to Congress, not the court, to fix the situation. Miller found another way to dismantle the reserve clause. At the close of the 1975 season, he persuaded Los Angeles Dodgers pitcher Andy Messersmith and Montreal Expos pitcher Dave McNally to refuse to sign contracts with their teams, claiming that they were free agents. Miller viewed this as a way to challenge the clause that gave owners the right to renew a player's contract without his consent.

The union had already won the right to a three-person board to hear all grievances. In the case of the two pitchers, Miller represented the union, John Gaherin (MLB's chief negotiator) represented the owners, and both sides agreed to hire Peter Seitz, an experienced arbitrator, as the third member. Everyone knew that Seitz would be the deciding vote. Seitz tried to convince the union and the owners to resolve the matter without his intervention, but the stakes were too high for either side to concede.

Miller pointed out something he had believed from his first day on the job—that, based on the contract language, the reserve clause allowed a team to renew a player's contract "on the same terms" for "one year." To Miller, "one year" meant "only one year."[51] On December 23, 1975, Seitz ruled in favor of Messersmith and McNally, agreeing with Miller that owners didn't have the right to perpetually renew contracts, that renewals could only be a one-time thing, and that players should be free to negotiate with another team.

This was a momentous decision, revising almost a century of labor-management relations in major league baseball. It led to a dramatic increase in ballplayers' salaries. In 1975, the starting MLB salary was $16,000, while the average salary was $44,676. By 1990, the figures had skyrocketed to $100,000 and $597,537. By 2000, they had jumped to $200,000 and $1.9 million.

But Flood never benefitted from the end of the reserve clause. In fact, he paid a huge financial and emotional price for his crusade. Not only did he give up his 1970 salary of $100,000, but—as Miller warned him—he was blacklisted by major league owners, despite his talent. Instead, he spent years traveling to Europe, devoting himself to painting and writing, including his autobiography, *The Way It Is*. When he returned to the United States, he briefly found a job overseeing baseball programs for the Parks and Recreation Department in Oakland, his hometown, and later worked briefly as a baseball broadcaster.

Looking back, Flood explained,

> I guess you really have to understand who that person, who that Curt Flood was. I'm a child of the sixties, I'm a man of the sixties. During that period this country was coming apart at the seams. We were in Southeast Asia. Good men were dying for America and for the Constitution. In the southern part of the United States we were marching for civil rights and Dr. King had been assassinated, and we lost the Kennedys. And to think that merely because I was a professional baseball player, I could ignore what was going on outside the walls of Busch Stadium was truly hypocrisy and now I found that all of those rights that these great Americans were dying for, I didn't have in my own profession.[52]

Flood died of throat cancer in 1997 at age fifty-nine. The following year, with the support of Jim Bunning—by then a Republican senator from Kentucky—Congress passed the Curt Flood Act, which overturned, for labor issues, baseball's antitrust exemption, which the Supreme Court had three times upheld, although the new law included many loopholes. "All that exemption has done is allow a controlled monopoly to dictate for years to the fans, players, and taxpayers," Bunning told *Lords of the Realm* author John Helyar.[53]

Although he didn't win his lawsuit, Flood's case educated Major League players about the unfairness of the reserve clause, opening their eyes to the reality that something they took for granted could be overcome. Flood's legal battle also persuaded many skeptical members of the press about the injustice of the reserve clause. Many influential sports writers and editorial writers attacked the court's decision.

In 1999, *Time* magazine named Flood one of the ten most influential people in sports in the twentieth century. Upon Flood's untimely death, Miller said,

> At the time Curt Flood decided to challenge baseball's reserve clause, he was perhaps the sport's premier center fielder. And yet he chose to fight an injustice, knowing that even if by some miracle he won, his career as a professional player would be over. At no time did he waver in his commitment and determination. He had experienced something that was inherently unfair and was determined to right the wrong, not so much for himself, but for those who would come after him. Few praised him for this, then or now. There is no Hall of Fame for people like Curt.[54]

Mudcat: Jim Grant

The All-Star pitcher Don Newcombe once observed that the earliest Black players in the major leagues after Jackie Robinson were "part of a revolution." Jim "Mudcat" Grant claimed he was "thrilled to have been part of that revolution, not for the fame, but for the pure joy of pursuing that dream, and helping to open the door for others, of all colors, to realize a similar dream."[55] Amidst the joy, however, harsh conditions and persistent discrimination prevailed.

Born in 1935, Grant grew up in the poor, mostly African American town of Lacoochee, Florida. His father, a log cutter, died from pneumonia when Grant was a baby, and he was raised by his mother, whose moral and religious convictions strongly influenced him. Early in his life, Grant learned the hazards of being Black. "From the very minute you walked out of your house," Grant recalled in his 2006 book, *The Black Aces*, "There were incidents . . . you had water fountains you couldn't drink from . . . restaurants you couldn't go into. You had to always watch where you were and know what you were going to do, because something was going to happen to you every day. You knew of the lynchings. You would hear it in the night, and if you didn't, word came through the next town that somebody was hanged or castrated."[56]

Reminiscent of the 1955 Emmett Till incident where a fourteen-year old Black teenager was lynched in Mississippi for allegedly whistling at a white woman, Grant remembered the unwritten Florida law against Black men "reckless eyeballing" white women. "And sometimes whites, including the Ku Klux Klan, would get drunk, go riding through town, and fire guns into your house. . . . That was called 'n—-shooting time.'" His mother would put him down by the fireplace in a wooden box to keep the bullets from hitting him. Grant continued, "If you were born black in the South, no matter where you were, you were subject to violence, especially if you went to another section of town, they would have the right to harm you. We had to run like hell in many circumstances."[57]

From a young age, Grant showed talent at baseball. Local Black stars mentored him at almost every position. As a poor Black kid in the segregated South, however, Grant felt that dreaming he "was going to the majors was like dreaming you were going to win the lottery." But when Jim was twelve, word came that Jackie Robinson had been signed by the Brooklyn Dodgers, soon to be followed by Larry Doby by the Cleveland Indians. This was enormous news, even in a remote outpost such as Lacoochee. It gave Blacks, and not merely budding ballplayers, some hope for the future, although Grant remembered that "it didn't change things in our day-to-day life. . . . It was a limited great thing that happened, but a great thing nonetheless."[58]

At age fourteen, Grant was pitching for the Lacoochee Nine Devils against the Sylvester Bulldogs in a road game in Georgia. By the eighth inning, he had struck out sixteen batters and held the lead by a run. Before the ninth inning, however, a white man called Grant and his manager over. Showing them a shotgun under his overcoat, he said they better lose because he had money on the game. Grant struck out the first two batters. Then the manager called a team meeting on the mound, ordered his players to run for the bus after the final out, and told Grant to walk the next three hitters to allow the equipment to be packed and put on the bus. Grant walked three batters, then struck out the next hitter on three pitches. The entire team raced for the bus, its engine already running. They sped off, fleeing racist curses and buckshot through the back window.

In high school, Grant excelled not only in baseball (as a pitcher and position player) but was also named to the All-State football team as a quarterback and to the All-State basketball team as a forward. The Boston Braves offered him a contract until the scout realized that Grant was only sixteen. Instead, Grant attended Florida A&M University in Tallahassee, hoping to become an English teacher. When he learned about the miserably low salaries Black teachers earned, he left college to relocate closer to the Florida spring training sites. He worked at a lumber mill and played again for the Lacoochee team, hoping he'd get another look from the pros. Fred Merkle, a Cleveland Indians scout, had noticed Grant during his high school days and saw him again pitching for the Lacoochee team. He invited Grant to an Indians tryout in 1954.

Cleveland offered Grant a contract to report to the Class D Georgia-Florida League, but the Indians farm team was in Tifton, Georgia, which enforced its Jim Crow segregation laws. Instead, the Indians sent Grant to its Class C team in Fargo, North Dakota. As one of only a handful of African Americans in the town, Grant drew considerable attention, more wonderment than discrimination. For the first time, Grant experienced desegregated public facilities. Escaping any serious incidents in Fargo, he was nevertheless confronted by a white fan during a road game in Eau Claire, Wisconsin, who hysterically screamed "you, n—." But Grant didn't let racist incidents disrupt his ambitions to make the majors. He won seventeen games and the league's Rookie of the Year Award for 1954. When he returned home to Florida after the season, he visited a nearby white town and failed to follow the local custom of addressing whites with "Yes sir, no sir"—something he didn't have to do while playing in the North. He was beaten and arrested by a sheriff for not paying the proper respect.

Reflecting on this and other incidents, Grant observed,

> When you sign a contract you think that baseball is going to be the savior from all the humiliation you normally face. It gives you a sense of false security that now you can eat regardless of your race. . . . So, we anticipated everybody would say, 'Okay, you're a ballplayer. Come on in!' You think that for a minute, but you're hurt that you can't go in [to a restaurant] with your [white] teammates. What are they going to think once they get inside and you're sitting on the bus and they have to bring you a sandwich? It's a hurtful feeling.[59]

Even Grant's nickname carried some vaguely racist origins, coming from a white teammate who mistook Jim's home state and said his face looked like a Mississippi mudcat.

During the 1955 season, Grant won nineteen games for the Keokuk Kernels in Iowa—a team later voted as one of the top thirty minor league teams of all time. But Grant again encountered segregation in housing and restaurants. That continued in 1956 when he moved up to the Indians farm team in Reading, Pennsylvania. One night, he went into a bar and was refused service. He decided to keep trying. He went to the same bar night after night, and finally a white teammate came over to him and said, "Mudcat, I don't know why you keep coming. They don't want you in here. They are not going to serve you. Why don't you just leave?" Grant responded, "But you are my teammate. Why wouldn't you come over and sit at my table with me?"[60]

Some of his white teammates were more sensitive than this, recognizing the difficulty that Grant faced, but few of them believed that it was their responsibility to stand up for him. Grant observed, "We've been taking it for so long that they just thought we could keep on taking it." On the other hand, "On every team there was always one or two or three or four or five ballplayers that were glad you weren't allowed to go inside a restaurant," yet you couldn't "afford to let this stuff keep you from your accomplishments." As Grant explained, "You were always aware that you were black . . . because there were stares. People that took your money at the counter that didn't want to touch your hand. People when you sat next to them on the airplane who sat sideways, away from you."[61]

Grant was promoted to the Indians' Triple-A team in San Diego for the 1957 season. He was an outstanding hitter and often played shortstop or outfield when he wasn't pitching. In San Diego, Grant dated a white woman named Trudy and they wanted to get married. According to Grant, the Indians front office called and told him, "We understand that you are dating this white lady. . . . Well, that don't happen in the big leagues."[62] Not wanting to ruin his professional career, the couple broke up and went their separate ways. In 1960, Grant's future teammate Maury Wills was a rising star when he got the same treatment from the Los Angeles Dodgers. General manager Buzzie Bavasi told Wills to stop dating white actress Doris Day, otherwise it would ruin both of their careers and embarrass the team. Like Grant, Wills complied with the team's demand. (The US Supreme Court didn't outlaw state bans on interracial marriage until 1967 with its *Loving v. Virginia* decision.) Years later, when Grant married and then divorced, and after Trudy's husband died, they got back together and married in 1984.

In 1958, Grant made the Indians roster. Before one of the first games he pitched, a large crowd of African Americans in the bleachers began rooting for the Indians, even though they were playing on the road in Detroit. When his teammate Larry Doby told Grant they were cheering for him, it brought him to tears. He and Doby mingled with the crowd, and even though he was pitching against their team, Grant realized how much they were counting on him to promote the race.

Most of Grant's coaches and teammates did not help him deal with the steady racism he faced on and off the diamond. "In the 1950s and 1960s," Grant observed, "there were coaches who felt blacks were inferior, that we didn't have it in us, that we couldn't be quarterbacks or pitchers. Blacks and whites could be absolutely equal but the coach would see them differently."[63]

Grant began to push back against some of the abuses. Most white Texans he met were racist, but he quickly became close friends with his teammate from San Antonio, Gary Bell. Having them pal around together both on and off the field raised some eyebrows but also showed it was possible. In 1958, Grant and Bell decided to room together and became the first Black and white roommates in the major leagues.

After several good seasons, 1960 became a tumultuous year for Grant. While pitching against Baltimore, he threw a ball that nearly hit a batter, and the Orioles manager, Paul Richards, yelled out, "Damn n—." When Grant came to bat, the Orioles pitcher threw at him, but he got a single instead. At first base, the Orioles Jim Gentile apologized profusely to Grant for his manager's racism. While Grant had learned to control his reactions to the endless racist onslaughts, that day he couldn't hold back, and after backing up a play the next inning he shot the ball at the Orioles dugout right over the head of Richards.

On Labor Day that year, Grant was with the Indians at the Sheraton Cadillac Hotel in Detroit when he got an unexpected invitation to breakfast from Senator John F. Kennedy, who was the Democratic Party's presidential candidate. Kennedy was in the city campaigning, and Grant was surprised to learn that the senator had been closely following the careers of both Grant and his former roommate Larry Doby (who had recently retired). JFK, who had sought and failed to get Jackie Robinson's endorsement, told Grant that he admired the Black ballplayers who pioneered integration. At an hour-long breakfast, Grant described for Kennedy the harsh poverty, poor education, and virulent racism he and other Blacks had experienced. Kennedy was jolted by what he heard. When he addressed workers and labor leaders later that day, he inserted a call to end racial discrimination as a campaign pledge in addition to his prolabor pitch. After he was elected president, Kennedy invited Grant to another breakfast, this time at the White House. After the meeting, the President arranged for federal assistance to Grant's hometown, which brought running water to Lacoochee for the first time, as well as a park, a school, and new housing.

Between the Richards incident and his encounters with Kennedy, Grant may have wondered what more he could do to make a difference. Amidst the emerging lunch counter sit-ins, Freedom Rides, and other civil rights fervor, Grant's white teammates Gary Bell, Frank Funk, and Barry Latman encouraged him to make some statement about southern segregation—a dangerous thing for the pitcher to contemplate.

Late in the 1960 season, the Indians were playing the Yankees in Cleveland. Grant sat in the bullpen with the other pitchers before the game. As usual, when the national anthem was played, Grant sang along. However, instead of the normal closing words of the song, "O'er the land of the free and the home of the brave," Grant sang, "This land is not free. I can't even go to Mississippi and sit down at a counter."[64]

The white teammates who had been encouraging Grant to speak out applauded his commentary, but the Indians' pitching coach, Ted Wilks, a Texan, got in Grant's face and said, "If you don't like our country, then why the hell don't you get out?" Grant answered, "If I wanted to leave the country, all I'd have to do is go to Texas, which is worse than Russia." Wilks snapped, "If we catch your n— ass in Texas, we're going to hang you from the nearest tree."[65] Wilks and Grant engaged in a fist fight. The other players had to separate the two men. Upset, Grant headed for the clubhouse and then left the ballpark.

To reporters, Wilks claimed he caught himself before completing his racial epithet and apologized to Grant. Others, however, confirmed Wilks' lynching comment and his history of racist remarks. Grant claimed he was sick of hearing "derogatory remarks about colored people. I don't have to stand there and take it." Indians manager Jimmy Dykes suspended Grant for the rest of the season (one week), explaining, "I had no alternative but to suspend the boy," using another derogatory word.[66]

Officially, Cleveland disciplined Grant for making negative comments about the United States during the national anthem and for leaving the game before it was over. The team made no public comment about Wilks's racist insults but, to the Indians' credit, he was quickly reassigned to the minor leagues. Grant received a great deal of hate mail as a result of the incident.

The slights and the challenges would continue. In 1961, as the fastest player on the Indians, Grant was asked to pinch run in a game. At first base,

Indians coach Ray Katt told him, "If this guy hits a 'tweener [a batted ball that splits the fielders], I want you to act like you've got two watermelons and a man's after you with a shotgun." Grant answered, "So you mean to tell me you want to talk to me about some watermelons?" and then let loose on Katt to protest his racist instructions.[67]

Then Grant called time-out and walked slowly off the field into the dugout in disgust. When his manager ordered him back on the field, Grant took off for the clubhouse. While the incident wasn't funny, his African American teammate, Willie Kirkland, joked about it anyway, and his white teammates joined in. Grant played along and decided to have a civil conversation about what happened. Generously, Grant suspected that as a southerner, Katt was just used to talking that way to Black people and may not have realized what he was saying. Grant felt that letting Katt know how his words hurt would do some good.

This approach began to define Grant's response to racist insults and segregation. Grant had met and become friendly with Martin Luther King Jr., whose philosophy and his mother's guidance convinced Grant that "you can't act like them . . . you can't be like them." No matter how badly you were treated by another, you couldn't treat them that way. Grant said, "Martin Luther King's passion for humanity enhanced my passion for humanity . . . to improve humanity, for everybody. Even though he was black and worked so hard for black people, his idea was to encompass everybody."[68] Grant pursued this philosophy of engagement with his white teammates and others, and it changed people. His longtime teammate Jim Perry was from North Carolina and held many racist attitudes. One day, when the team was on the road, he called Grant to his hotel room and said, "I just want you to know that the way I was [racist], I'm not going to be that way anymore."[69]

After President Kennedy was assassinated in November 1963, Grant tried to overcome his shock and gather his thoughts about the president who had befriended him. He held the wheel of his car and wept. Like other African Americans, Grant had pinned great hopes on the president for dealing seriously with America's racism. "What now?" he asked himself.

In 1964, the Indians traded Grant to the Minnesota Twins. Although he was pleased to go to the Twin Cities where the fans were less racist, he braced himself for working for Calvin Griffith, the team owner who had a well-deserved reputation as a racist. When Griffith brought the Senators from Washington, DC to the Minneapolis-St. Paul suburb of Bloomington to become the Minnesota Twins, he told a local group that he was drawn to the area because it had so few African Americans: "Black people don't go to ball games, but they'll fill up a rasslin' ring and put up such a chant it'll scare you to death. It's unbelievable. We came here because you've got good, hardworking, white people here."[70]

To their credit, Twin Cities white fans and leaders lambasted Griffith for these and other racist comments. Eventually, Griffith softened his tone in public. But as Grant recounted in *The Black Aces*, Griffith treated "all blacks differently. He paid you less. He thought of your value as less . . . he had to be convinced that he had to have black ballplayers."[71] It wasn't until June 2020 that the Twins removed a statue of Griffith in front of Target Field, not long after a Minneapolis police officer's murder of George Floyd triggered a nationwide uprising against racial injustice.

In the 1950s and 1960s, some major league managers tried to prevent Black pitchers from becoming twenty-game winners. Birdie Tebbetts made it difficult for Cincinnati's Brooks Lawrence, and Pinky Higgins stood in the way of Boston's Earl Wilson. "Not only managers," according to Grant, "but catchers [conspired against Black pitchers]. Some catchers would tell the hitters, the opposing player, what was coming because they didn't want you to do well as a pitcher." You had to win the game anyway, "But now you're not only pitching against the opposing team, you're pitching against your own catcher."[72]

On the Twins, however, Grant joined with Earl Battey to form an all-Black battery, and he credited his catcher for helping him become, in 1965, the first African American to win twenty games in the American League. Minnesota won the pennant that year, and Grant also became the first Black American League pitcher to start a World Series game. The Dodgers narrowly beat the Twins in seven games. Grant had gone 2–1, the same as the Dodgers' Sandy Koufax. But while Koufax enjoyed a wide array of gifts and accolades, as well as a long list of commercial endorsements, Grant got little more than his World Series bonus.

Several reporters recognized the discrepancy. In *Newsday*, Steve Jacobson wrote that Grant "won twenty-one games, pitched two complete game victories in the Series and wears clothes as well as anybody around. But nobody has been around yet to ask him to endorse a product."[73] As a Black man, Jacobson wrote, "Being the biggest winner in the American League won't get those fringe benefits for him." In the *New York World Telegram & Sun*, Phil

Pepe observed, "The world is not quite ready for Negro heroes, and so Jim must struggle because nobody is breaking his neck to sign him for movies and endorsements. He is handsome and he is famous, but he is black. . . . Sandy [Koufax] could get $100,000 just for demonstrating the way he soaks his arm in a bucket of ice after he pitches. Jim Grant has the kind of pleasant face that would look good in a television commercial . . . if television was ready for his kind of face."[74]

At the very least, Grant expected the Twins to give him a significant raise after his sterling season and World Series. He asked for an increase from $21,500 to $50,000 to put himself closer to the pay level of other top pitchers. But Griffith only offered him a $2,000 raise, reminding Grant that he had also received a $4,000 World Series bonus. In the end, Grant managed to get $35,000, but he became more outspoken about his owner after 1965. To make up in income some of what he should have received in salary and endorsements, Grant organized a singing group, Mudcat and the Kittens, which toured the country during the off season, including appearances on Johnny Carson's and Mike Douglas's TV shows. "I made way more money in music than I did in baseball," Grant recalled.[75] The Twins traded Grant to the Los Angeles Dodgers, where he transitioned into a successful relief pitcher. He pitched four more seasons with the Dodgers, Expos, Cardinals, and Athletics and retired from MLB in 1972 with 145 wins, 54 saves, and a 3.63 ERA.

Before Jackie Robinson died in 1972, he urged Grant to do more in his retirement than just pursue a singing career. In his hometown of Lacoochee, Grant helped start a Boys and Girls Club, a Food for Thought program, a Wounded Warriors chapter (to support military veterans), and a benefit golf tournament. He continued working in baseball as a broadcaster, doing public relations, and as a pitching coach for the minor league Durham Bulls. But Robinson—who was disappointed about lingering barriers to Blacks in baseball, especially in coaching, managing, and the front office—encouraged Grant to speak out about the sport's persistent discrimination.

Grant put that advice into practice. He was inspired by the words of the early twentieth century Black leader Marcus Garvey, who claimed that "a people without the knowledge of their history is like a tree without roots." In 2006, Grant published a book, *The Black Aces*, about the great African American pitchers, part of his project to educate Americans about the history of baseball integration after Jackie Robinson. "We need to change," Grant wrote, "the commonly held, but totally distorted, notion that baseball and America integrated instantly in 1947, resulting in a steady march forward toward a successfully integrated society and a harmonious racial co-existence ever since."[76]

Grant hoped that his book and his frequent speeches would "stir people to action: the people who run major league baseball . . . who own teams . . . who run universities . . . who run youth sports leagues, the parents and the children." As he explained, "The great game of baseball, so often used by so many as a metaphor for life and the American dream, will only maintain its exalted status as America's game if it truly reflects America, and all of its many and varied constituent groups."[77]

Echoing the scholar W. E. B. DuBois, Grant wrote that the Black aces "were not only successful black pitchers, they were successful pitchers, period. . . . They lived with a separate and similar 'twoness' as both a ballplayer and a black ballplayer. . . . Their great accomplishments are part of the history of both the game and America itself. The context in which that history unfolded and in which they attained their success makes their accomplishments that much greater."[78]

Grant also pledged to help "re-energize the interest of today's black youth in baseball." In 2020, African Americans composed only eight percent of all major league players, down from a high of twenty-seven percent in the mid-1970s. Through his Black Aces Foundation, Grant recruited other African American major leaguers to tour the nation's big cities and small towns, encouraging local officials to provide the playgrounds, equipment, and other resources to expand the participation of young Blacks in organized baseball. "We bring out our love of the game," Grant explained, "our desire to share the rich heritage of blacks in baseball, and our hope that young black kids will embrace the game and grow from it, just as we did. We're following the advice of Jackie Robinson, defining the importance of our lives by the impact we have on the lives of others."[79] Grant died in June 2021 at age eighty-five.

Crash: Dick Allen

To paraphrase the poet Dylan Thomas, Richard Anthony Allen would "not go gentle into that good night." For this, he paid a price: despite his Hall of Famer credentials, he was shunned by Cooperstown for speaking out. Allen died in December 2020 in his hometown, Wampum, Pennsylvania at age seventy-eight. As the *New York Times* observed in its obituary, "With better health and no coronavirus pandemic, he might have instead spent the day at baseball's winter meetings, reveling in his status as a newly elected member of the Hall of Fame. The Golden Days committee would have considered his candidacy on Sunday, but the vote was canceled, as were the meetings, because the group could not gather in person."[80]

Dick Allen was born in Wampum in 1942. He was one of nine children raised by his mother. At Wampum High School he starred in baseball and was also an All-American basketball guard. The nearby Philadelphia Phillies finally integrated in 1957, ten years after Jackie Robinson broke the color barrier. But even then, the Phillies were slow to overcome racism and develop African American players. When the Phillies signed Allen in 1960, it was their first attempt to cultivate a potential Black superstar to help rebuild their terrible team.

Allen began his minor league career as a shortstop for the Elmira club in the New York-Penn League. He moved to second base in 1961 to play for Idaho's Magic Valley club in the Pioneer League. The next year he played for the Phillies' Double-A Williamsport team in the Eastern League. In those first three seasons he hit forty-nine home runs and had 245 runs batted in (RBIs).

Growing up in Pennsylvania, Allen hadn't yet encountered the level of flagrant Jim Crow racism that he would face after he was sent to the Phillies Triple-A affiliate in Little Rock, the Arkansas Travelers, for the 1963 season, in the midst of an upsurge of civil rights activism across the South, including local protests and the famous March on Washington. He was not only that club's first Black minor leaguer but also the first African American to play professional baseball in the entire state of Arkansas. Allen wasn't prepared for the challenges he would encounter. As he recalled, "I didn't know anything about the racial issue in Arkansas. . . . Maybe if the Phillies had called me in, man to man, like the Dodgers had done with Jackie Robinson [Allen's hero], at least I would have been prepared. Instead, I was on my own."[81]

Organized baseball has long used Robinson's barrier breaking to congratulate itself for its enlightened racial policies. When Allen joined the Travelers, *The Sporting News* lauded Little Rock for welcoming its first Black player and credited baseball for continuing the healing process: "Baseball provided the means for making [integration] work in Little Rock as it has in almost every section of the country since integration became a reality after World War II," the newspaper noted.[82]

Reading this, most Blacks—including Allen—would have rubbed their eyes in disbelief. Only a few years earlier, Arkansas' staunch segregationist Governor Orville Faubus had tried to bar Black students from Little Rock Central High School, while local white citizens protested against the integration of its public schools. Allen was on the field in a Traveler's uniform when Faubus threw out the Opening Day first pitch before a capacity crowd at Ray Winder Stadium. That would only begin what Allen soon described as a nightmare experience in Little Rock, where he was called "darkie" and "monkey," got sucker punched, was harassed by police and local merchants, suffered attacks on his home, received threatening phone calls and hate mail, and couldn't get served in a restaurant unless accompanied by a white player. Little Rock residents staged protest parades opposing Allen playing for their minor league team. His car windshield was plastered with signs saying, "N— Go Home" and "Don't Negroize our Baseball." According to Allen, "There might be something more terrifying than being black and holding a note that says, 'N—' in an empty parking lot in Little Rock, Arkansas in 1963, but if there is, it hasn't crossed my path yet."[83]

Nevertheless, Allen performed well on the field, leading the International League with thirty-three home runs and ninety-seven RBIs. Although he was voted the Travelers' MVP, off the field he was a second-class citizen. While Allen's experience was typical for Black ballplayers in the South, he was angry, confused, and alienated by this mistreatment and by the Phillies' indifference to his situation. This intensified when the Phillies treated Allen's request for a small $50 raise as an ungrateful demand.

After his great 1963 Little Rock season, the Phillies brought Allen up to the majors in September. He appeared in ten games, hitting .292, with two doubles and a triple. He had a strong 1964 spring training and made the Phillies roster, providing them the right-handed power hitter they badly needed. But manager Gene Mauch put him at third base, a position he had never played before. He made forty-one errors and had a .921 fielding average, far below average.

Even so, Allen made an immediate impact with his bat. After a game in May, *Philadelphia Daily News* reporter Larry Merchant wrote, "The rumors are that [rookie] Allen is not returning with the Phillies to Connie Mack Stadium on Wednesday. He's going directly to the Hall of Fame."[84] By August, Allen was batting over .300 and leading the Phillies atop the National League standings. In September, local African American and Jewish merchants organized a

"Richie Allen Night" to honor his sensational rookie season. Allen observed, "I won't say, like Cassius Clay, that I'm the greatest. But if a pitcher makes a mistake against me I might drop one out of the park."[85]

On September 20, with a six and a half game lead in the National League, the Phillies seemed destined for the World Series. Then the team went into a nosedive, losing ten straight games and their first-place lead, ultimately registering the most infamous collapse in baseball history. Yet Allen remained red hot, with an eleven-game hitting streak during which he batted .429. It wasn't enough. The Phillies finished in second place. Allen, however, ended the season hitting .318, with twenty-nine home runs, ninety-one RBIs, and a league-leading 125 runs scored, playing in all 162 games, en route to National League Rookie of the Year honors.

Despite being a rookie, Allen told sportswriters at the *New York Times* and other newspapers about the racism he endured in Little Rock and how it made him feel less than human. Trouble was brewing with the Philadelphia sportswriters when they inexplicably started calling him Richie. In news articles and on rosters, scorecards, and press releases, he was Richie Allen instead of Dick, which he preferred. "I don't know how Richie started," Allen said. "My first name is Richard and they called me Dick in the minor leagues. [Richie] makes me sound like I'm ten years old. I'm 22. Anyone who knows me well calls me Dick. I don't know why as soon as I put on a uniform, it's Richie."[86] Despite his complaints, the reporters kept calling him Richie until 1966, when they switched to Rich, which Allen wasn't happy with either. It wasn't until 1972, during his first season with the White Sox, that he recovered his preferred name. His new team's management called him Dick in its press book and told their public address announcer to do the same.

This might not seem like a huge issue, except that white ballplayers (especially stars) had no trouble getting reporters and team officials to use their preferred names. It was a matter of respect. Growing concerns about Black identity and history also contributed. As Allen recalled years later, "Racial tensions were at the boiling point [summer 1964]. The neighborhood around Connie Mack [stadium] looked like a bomb had just hit it. The streets were empty. People stayed indoors. Police cars patrolled the streets. Stores were boarded up. And whites blamed blacks for that. I guess being the star black player for the Phillies also made me a threat to white people, especially since I said what was on my mind. They weren't used to a black athlete like that."[87] A clause in the MLB contract forbid players from participating in protest marches, but Allen couldn't resist registering his resistance. And the Phillies didn't help. Despite his stellar rookie season, the team refused to raise his salary to $25,000. He sat out the 1965 spring training, hoping the Phillies brass would give him his due, but he ultimately signed for less.

The situation didn't get better. Midseason, during batting practice at Connie Mack Stadium, Johnny Callison razzed his teammate Frank Thomas about his missed bunt attempt the night before. Thomas thought Allen was voicing the taunts and he lashed out, "Who are you trying to be, another Muhammad Clay?" referring to the boxing champion who had actually changed his name from Cassius Clay to Muhammad Ali.[88] Allen objected to the comment, Thomas hit him in the shoulder with a bat, and Allen hit Thomas in the jaw. It wasn't clear who struck first.

After the incident, the Phillies released Thomas, and manager Mauch threatened to heavily fine any player—including Allen—who discussed the fight publicly. The press blamed Allen, intensified by the public relations campaign that Thomas launched on the radio and in the newspapers. Sportswriter Larry Merchant, who had been an Allen ally, claimed that the incident "only exposes Allen as a kid who caused a veteran to lose his job."[89]

Since Allen couldn't and wouldn't tell his side of the story, the truth was buried. As the last National League team to integrate, racial tensions still ran high on the Phillies. Thomas was notorious for exploiting this environment, repeatedly taunting young Black ballplayers, including outfielder Johnny Briggs, whom Thomas ordered, "Hey boy, get over here and shine my shoes." Allen warned Thomas to "knock it off, knock off that crap,"[90] but the situation kept escalating. The batting-cage incident was the last straw. The Phillies actually released Thomas for not hitting, but Allen became the scapegoat.

Philadelphia Inquirer reporter Allen Lewis claimed that Allen hadn't really been treated badly by the Phillies, but simply wasn't ready for the responsibility of being a star. He wasn't willing, according to Lewis, to make the sacrifices that came with fame, even though he expected to be paid like a superstar. Many fans sided with Thomas, including those who brought pro-Thomas signs to the ballpark. Allen said, "I stuck my head out of the dugout and I'd never heard such booing. People yelled, 'N—,' and 'Go back to South Street with the monkeys.'" When Allen observed that "the people in this town like to boo, but I just play as hard as I can and don't listen," fans rode him even harder.[91]

Despite his stellar play as one of the National League's most feared hitters, Allen endured taunting by fans and the press throughout his seven years

(1963–1969) in Philadelphia. According to teammate Bill White, "Baseball should never forget the Allen-Thomas fiasco. There's an important lesson here. When Dick Allen came to the big leagues he was a kid in love with the game. Baseball was all that mattered. After the Thomas incident, the love was taken right out of him. There's historical significance in how that was handled."[92]

After blowing the pennant in 1964, the Phillies kept above .500 but never finished higher than fourth place in the National League until 1974. Many fans blamed Allen for the team's mediocrity, despite his excellent play. Allen was expected to "play by the rules," yet as a Black ballplayer he was treated differently. Allen still couldn't get the sportswriters to call him by his correct name. In frustration, he began drinking and making demands for more money, thus cultivating an "uppity" reputation. The backlash created a downward spiral.

In 1967, when Allen was pushing his stalled car, he accidently put his hand through the headlight, suffering serious cuts, requiring a five-hour surgery to reconnect the tendons. Given only a 50–50 chance of playing again, Allen wore a shoulder-fingertip cast most of the winter. While the pain never went away, he recovered by spring training 1968 without missing any games.

Despite Allen's resilience in getting back into playing shape, many doubted his story about the car, some believing he got knifed in a bar fight, others claiming he cut himself on a bedroom window, fleeing after being caught with a teammate's wife. Neither was true, but it illustrated how Allen was subjected to racist stereotypes.

Allen's alienation escalated. Sportswriters criticized him for not hustling or talking to them. For speaking out about adverse treatment, the media labeled Allen as militant, arrogant, and radical. Fan abuse continued, and Allen was assaulted with ice, fruit, refuse, smoke bombs, and flashlight batteries. To protect himself from flying objects, he began wearing his batting helmet out in the field. For this, baseball announcer Bob Uecker nicknamed him "Crash."

In response to the abuse, Allen began committing minor transgressions, sometimes calling out the racist treatment he was subjected to, hoping to induce a trade. In *September Swoon*, William Kashatus claimed that "Allen's rebelliousness mirrored the social and moral conventions of the time period, which stressed individuality, personal expression, and open defiance at the expense of conformity and deference to authority. Philadelphia, like the rest of urban America, found itself caught in the crosscurrents of social unrest spawned by the Vietnam War and the civil rights and youth movements of the 1960s."[93] The poverty, unemployment, and police abuse in the areas surrounding Connie Mack Stadium reminded Allen of the nation's racial double standard.

In 1968, with the Phillies still ignoring his demand to be traded, Allen got more rebellious. He left spring training early, sat out games claiming he injured himself horseback riding, and arrived late for several games. Although the Phillies fined Allen for his lapses, reporters claimed he was being pampered, never acknowledging the team's and the city's racist environment. During the season, manager Mauch removed Allen from the lineup, but owner Bob Carpenter ordered him reinstated. When Mauch was fired, Allen was blamed again.

After Mauch's departure, Allen had an excellent month. Bob Skinner, the Phillies new manager, praised him as a team player. Things begin to sour, however, when Allen got into an altercation with a racist bartender. After the charges were dropped, Allen again requested a trade, but Carpenter told him he needed to grow up. Allen answered, "I did grow up. Black and poor. You grew up white and rich."[94] Although Allen had another great season (thirty-three home runs and ninety RBIs), the fans jeered him again, and Carpenter complained that Allen should have had a higher batting average and more RBIs.

During the 1969 season, Allen was at a New Jersey racetrack—he owned and followed horses—and hadn't gotten the word that a Phillies doubleheader at Shea Stadium in New York had been moved to earlier in the day. When he turned on his radio, he realized his mistake, but was shocked to hear that he had been fined and suspended by Skinner without being given a chance to tell his side of the story. Instead of continuing to New York, he returned to Philadelphia. Furious, Allen turned his suspension into a boycott, explaining that "I made up my mind that no fine—no matter how stiff—would ever dictate my behavior again." After twenty-six days, he finally met with Carpenter, who promised he would trade Allen in the off-season if he returned to the field. When he did go back, he hit a double in his first at bat, and observed, "They could do a lot to this ol' country boy. They could take my money, take my freedom, take my self-esteem, but they couldn't take my stroke."[95]

But Allen received a new round of abuse, and he responded by writing messages in the dirt at his first-base position. When fans taunted him with catcalls and insults, he wrote "Boo." Another time he wrote "Coke," later claiming he planned to stifle hecklers by hitting a home run over the Coca Cola sign behind the Connie Mack Stadium outfield stands. In August, Baseball

Commissioner Bowie Kuhn attended a game in Philadelphia and saw Allen writing words in the dirt. He ordered the Phillies to make him stop. Instead, Allen began sending messages to Kuhn, such as "Why?" and "No." When an umpire erased the words, he wrote "Mom," later explaining that his mother "was the only one who could tell him what to do."[96] The incident turned into a *Life Magazine* feature story in August 1969, the same month that Allen— with permission from Carpenter—sat out an exhibition game in Reading, Pennsylvania. Skinner soon resigned as manager.

Even Allen's hair became an issue. "In Philly," Allen claimed, "white barbers won't even let you in their shops, and whites were hollering from the stands, 'Get your hair cut.' My hair is my business. It's neat and clean, and that's what matters to me. I wouldn't say I hate Whitey, but deep down in my heart, I just can't stand Whitey's ways. . . . Philly taught me that people can be the cruelest things in the world."[97]

The Sporting News claimed that Allen needed professional guidance and counseling, and of course, another manager's departure was blamed on Allen. Interim manager George Myatt claimed that "I believe that God Almighty Hisself would have trouble handling Richie Allen."[98] Most sportswriters remained unsympathetic. *Philadelphia Daily News* reporter Bill Conlin claimed he "kept veering from one viewpoint to another [about Allen]: awe, empathy, and finally disgust. The awe was for his huge talent, the empathy was for his rebellious streak and his endurance for needless racial hassles—many inflicted by his own ball club. The disgust was for his self-regard and indifference to the team, which became total by 1969. That year I called him the Maharishi of Mope."[99]

Los Angeles Times columnist Jim Murray issued a rare dissent in "The Case of the City of Philadelphia vs. Richard Anthony Allen," writing,

> Together with the cross-complaint of the defendant, it might go as follows: "He drinks" (Does he now? Well, that makes him unique in baseball. Think what it might have done to Babe Ruth's career. Or General Grant's.) "He forced the trade of Frank Thomas after they got into a fight" (Frank Who?! Oh, you mean the guy who's playing slow-pitch softball now? Is that Richie Allen's fault too?) "He feuds with the fans" (You mean those lovely people who call his wife at all hours of the night, throw bricks through his windows, insult his kids? This time, Richie Allen, you've gone too far! I mean, those people pay for the privilege. Always remember who pays your salary, boy!).[100]

Allen stuck his neck out to complain in the Black press about the absence of African American managers and the double standards and racism clubs used to evaluate candidates. The Black newspapers were more sympathetic to this situation. *Ebony*, a magazine targeted to Black readers, observed that "Richie says he's his own man and he's going to live his own life no matter what, and that should cause little commotion. But Richie Allen is black and he's proud and he has the gumption to be a proud, black man in one of America's most conservative sports. He sports a lush Afro that's anchored with long and wide sideburns."[101]

In October, Allen got his wish when the Phillies traded him to the St. Louis Cardinals. It turned out to be one of major league baseball's most controversial deals. In exchange for getting Allen and two other players, the Cardinals sent Curt Flood, veteran catcher Tim McCarver, Byron Browne, and Joe Hoerner to the Phillies. But, as described earlier, Flood refused to report to the Phillies in part because of the city's racist reputation. Referring to Flood's lawsuit against major league baseball over the reserve clause, Allen observed, "Flood is doing a marvelous thing for baseball and many people don't know it . . . but my hat's off to him. I'm for him. I hope he wins."[102]

But Allen welcomed the trade. By then the Cardinals had nine Latino and three other Black players, including Bob Gibson and Lou Brock. Allen thought he would fit in better there. He observed, "You don't know how good it feels to get out of Philadelphia. They treat you like cattle. It was a form of slavery. Once you step out of bounds they do everything possible to destroy your soul."[103]

In 1970, Allen produced another All-Star season, slugging thirty-four home runs and 101 RBIs for the Cardinals. Nevertheless, after only one season St. Louis traded Allen to Los Angeles, where he hit .295 for the Dodgers in 1971, with twenty-three home runs and ninety RBIs. Traded again in 1972 to the Chicago White Sox for pitcher Tommy John, Allen had a sensational season—with a league-leading thirty-seven homers and 113 RBIs as well as a .308 batting average—raising the lowly White Sox to second place and earning an MVP award. When Chicago reporters, at long last, began calling him "Dick," Allen claimed that "I made up my mind then and there that Dick Allen was going to pay back Chicago for the respect they were giving me."[104]

Instead of being shuttled between several positions, Allen became the White Sox's regular first baseman. His defense improved, and he hit his way to three more All-Star seasons, highlighted by mammoth and memorable home runs at Comiskey Park, as well as two inside-the-park home runs in one game in 1972.

With the White Sox headed for the playoffs in 1973, Allen fractured his tibia, losing five weeks in the season. The next season he led the league in home runs, slugging, and on-base plus slugging (OPS), but he was playing in pain and left the team two weeks before the season's end. Unsure of his future status, the White Sox sold Allen's contract to the Atlanta Braves, but he refused to play in the South and announced his retirement.

Most big league teams weren't interested in Allen. He was considered too toxic. But in 1975, at the urging of broadcaster and former outfielder Richie Ashburn, the Phillies—of all teams—coaxed Allen out of retirement. Phillies fans welcomed Allen back to Philadelphia's Veteran's Stadium with a standing ovation. His skills had clearly declined; in 119 games he hit just .233 with twelve homers. The next season, Allen played in only eighty-five games, although his hitting improved (he had fifteen home runs and batted .268).

Toward the end of the season, the Phillies were in first place, but Allen was playing poorly and continued to generate controversy. Allen criticized manager Danny Ozark for not using Black players Bobby Tolan and Ollie Brown as often as they deserved to play, accusing the manager of "working a quota system."[105] When the team rebounded, Allen then discovered that Tony Taylor, his Phillies teammate in the 1960s, would be left off the postseason roster. Although Taylor was, by then, a bench player, it bothered Allen that Taylor would be denied his only postseason appearance in his long career with the team. Allen said that he wouldn't play in the League Championship or World Series if Taylor was excluded, even refusing to celebrate when the team clinched its playoff berth. Taylor was ultimately added to the roster, although as a coach, but the Phillies were swept in the first round. In March 1977, Allen signed on as a free agent with the Oakland Athletics. He played poorly for the first half of the season and then retired for good.

In September 2020, two months before he died, the Phillies sought to make amends for the abuse Allen endured by retiring his uniform number, 15. But the baseball establishment has refused to bestow on Allen the honor he really deserves: induction into the Hall of Fame.

During his fourteen-year (1963–77) major league career, Allen posted Hall of Fame–worthy statistics. He batted over .300 seven times, had lifetime averages of .292 batting, .534 slugging, and .378 on base, with 351 home runs and 1119 RBIs, even though he played in pitcher-friendly ballparks and in a pitching-dominant period, sometimes described as the "second dead-ball era."[106] Allen's OPS average is the second highest of any retired player who is not in the Hall of Fame. His massive hitting power ranks in a league with Mickey Mantle, Barry Bonds, Jimmy Foxx, Henry Aaron, and Babe Ruth. He played multiple positions and was a Rookie of the Year, MVP, and a seven-time All Star. His numbers outpace many Hall of Famers, including inductees Tony Perez and Jim Rice. Despite this track record, in the fourteen years he was on the Hall of Fame ballot, he never received more than 18.9 percent of the vote—far short of the 75 percent required for induction. In 2014, he missed induction by the Golden Age Committee by a single vote.

Why isn't Allen in the Hall of Fame? Rather than his numbers, he's been kept out because of "character issues," according to his biographer Mitchell Nathanson.[107] Allen's rebellious attitude has thus far disqualified him. Historian and baseball statistician Bill James reinforced this impression in 1985 when he wrote in his historical baseball abstract that Allen "did more to *keep* his teams from winning than anyone else who ever played major league baseball."[108] James reached this conclusion without any proof or any historical context for Allen's behavior. People simply "know" Allen was a clubhouse headache. If they understood the backstory, they might view him differently. As Allen said, "Baseball quit on me, I didn't quit on baseball."[109]

Allen's managers and fellow players had a different view than James. While White Sox teammate Carlos May acknowledged that "[Allen] danced by his own song," Phillies teammate Don Lock and White Sox teammate Wilbur Wood said Allen had no clubhouse enemies on those teams.[110] Another fellow White Sox, Stan Bahnsen, said that "Dick was better than his stats. Every time we needed a clutch hit, he got it. He got along great with his teammates and was very knowledgeable about the game. He was the ultimate team guy."[111] Hall of Fame teammate Mike Schmidt called Allen his mentor, including a lecture Allen gave him about relaxing and having fun prior to the 1976 game when Schmidt hit four home runs. "The baseball writers," Schmidt observed, "used to claim that Dick would divide the clubhouse along racial lines. That was a lie . . . but he did get guys thinking."[112] At a 2020 event honoring Allen, Schmidt said that "Dick was a sensitive Black man who refused to be treated as a second-class citizen. He played in front of home fans that were products of that racist era," alongside "racist teammates" at a time when there were "different rules for whites and Blacks."[113]

Asked whether Dick was a "clubhouse lawyer" who had a negative influence on team chemistry, Phillies manager Gene Mauch responded, "Never. His teammates always liked him. I'd take him back in a minute."[114] Cardinals manager Red Schoendienst said, "Allen did a fine job for us, and we never had any problems with him."[115] According to White Sox manager Chuck Tanner, "Dick was the leader of our team, the captain, the manager on the field. He took care of the young kids, took them under his wing. And he played every game as if it was his last day on earth."[116]

Hall of Famer Rich Gossage, who was Allen's teammate, echoed Tanner's view: "I've been around the game for a long time, and he's the greatest player I've ever seen. . . . He's the smartest baseball man I've ever been around. . . . He taught me how to pitch from a hitter's perspective, and how to play the game right. . . . The guy belongs in the Hall of Fame."[117] Orlando Cepeda, another Hall of Famer, said that "Dick Allen played with fire in his eyes."[118] Former Phillies groundskeeper, Mark Carfagno, watched how Allen was treated early in his career: "Allen is the most misunderstood player, and person, I've met in my life. . . . I saw how he was abused. They called him every name in the book. Every racial epithet. I couldn't believe he could play with all that pressure on him. . . . He would hang out with us on the grounds crew after the games. We understood him. Nobody else did."[119]

Allen astutely assessed the inequalities in contract negotiations and was one of the first players to interject an agent into the process. "A lot of people who run baseball," Allen observed, "still don't think of us, really, as human beings."[120]

Allen was a rebel, but he wasn't a protester in the sense that he joined organized campaigns. In his biography of Allen, *God Almighty Hisself*, Mitchell Nathanson claims that Allen spoke through acts of refusal to "bring a measure of dignity to what might otherwise be a situation devoid of any." He developed an oppositional identity for self-protection. But he was also willing to "speak out often on racial issues at a time when most others didn't . . . open[ing] up and say[ing] things you'd never hear other people (particularly black major leaguers) say."[121]

Dick Allen was both a symbol and catalyst for change in 1960s America and a hero for rebellious youth. As Hall of Famer Willie Stargell put it, "Allen played the game in the most conservative era in baseball history. It was a time of change and protest in the country, and baseball reacted against all that. They saw it as a threat to the game. The sportswriters were reactionary too.

They didn't like seeing a man of such extraordinary skills doing it his way. It made them nervous. Dick Allen was ahead of his time."[122]

Allen remembered Branch Rickey's famous instruction to Jackie Robinson to bury his anger in exchange for white praise and not talk about death threats, racist taunts, and other forms of intolerance. Most other Black players after Robinson took the abuse without public protest. But Allen refused. By the 1960s, as Nathanson observed, Allen rebelled "by simply refusing to go along with it all. And the game would never be the same."[123] As Philadelphia mayor Jim Kenney observed, Allen "was our Jackie Robinson . . . Robinson was under orders not to respond to the taunts. Allen came along later and spoke his mind."[124]

"I wonder how good I could have been," Allen wrote in his 1989 memoir, *Crash: The Life and Times of Dick Allen*. "It could have been a joy, a celebration. Instead, I played angry. In baseball, if a couple things go wrong for you, and those things get misperceived, or distorted, you get a label. I was labeled an outlaw, and after a while that's what I became. . . . I could have handled things a little better but I wouldn't have changed a thing. I said what I said, did what I did, meant what I meant—and I'll stand behind every word of it."[125]

As writer Roy Blount Jr. has observed, Allen was "the first black man, and indeed the only contemporary man of any color, to assert himself in baseball with something like the unaccommodating force of Muhammad Ali in boxing, Kareem Abdul-Jabbar in basketball, and Jim Brown in football."[126]

Professor: George Gmelch

Black players endured bigotry in baseball and in the wider society long after Jackie Robinson broke the color line in 1947 and for decades after the Red Sox became the last team to hire a Black player in 1959. While a few white ballplayers endorsed segregation, most others simply had no comment. They ignored the obvious racial double standard. Some white players resisted in ways large and small, including reaching out to Black teammates to show support, but only a few publicly challenged racism among fans, sportswriters, and team management. Those who thought that segregation was wrong often just assumed it was inevitable in the South, and speaking up might jeopardize their baseball futures. The Black ballplayers talked about it among themselves but not with the white ballplayers, and while some Blacks complained, most of them coped with the racism as something they abhorred but could not change.

George Gmelch, a white first baseman, was one of the exceptions. His minor league career ended prematurely because he spoke out against the racism he witnessed. Born in 1944, Gmelch grew up in the sheltered, white San Francisco suburb of Hillsdale. His father was a shipping business executive. The six-foot-two Gmelch was a standout slugger at Hillsdale High School and then at the College of San Mateo. In April 1965, after his sophomore year in college, the Detroit Tigers signed him to a contract for a modest bonus. That season he played for the Tigers' Jamestown, New York, affiliate in the New York-Penn League and the Duluth-Superior Minnesota Dukes of the Northern League. In the off-season of 1965, Gmelch had a job working on the Oakland docks with longshoremen, most of whom were Black. He became friends with some of them and learned much about Black life. Later, he befriended Black and Latino teammates in the minors. He saw the myriad ways they were discriminated against, and what he didn't see first-hand, his friends told him about.

In 1966, the Tigers sent Gmelch to the Daytona Beach Islanders in the Florida State League, then the Rocky Mount Leafs of the Carolina League. Combined, he hit .267 that season and in the off-season he enrolled at Stanford University. During spring training in 1966, while taking correspondence courses to keep his deferment and avoid the military draft, the Tigers allowed him to study at night in the Tigertown front office. One night he wandered into a nearby office and noticed on corkboards spread across the wall the names of all 120 ballplayers in the Tigers organization, including those on their minor league teams. On the boards, each player's name was followed by a color-coded star indicating his military draft status. President Lyndon Johnson had escalated the Vietnam War, increasing the number of American combat troops. Some writers had accused major league teams of intervening with local draft boards or accused members of Congress of sheltering their players in the National Guard or Reserves or avoiding the draft completely. The corkboard showed Gmelch, if nothing else, that the Tigers were closely monitoring the draft status of all their minor and major league players.

Because he was a student at Stanford, read books, and regularly used the local Rocky Mount library (in part because it was air conditioned), his teammates sometimes called him the "professor." Other players called him "Moonbeam." As a college student, Gmelch was supposed to have a student deferment from the wartime draft. He was surprised and upset when it was taken away and he got called for a military physical in Jacksonville.

Aside from risking death or ending one's baseball career if one was drafted, Gmelch opposed the Vietnam War as an illegal and immoral conflict. Most of his teammates hadn't attended college and hadn't been exposed to the growing antiwar sentiment on many campuses. Most players didn't follow the news. But on campus Gmelch had learned about US foreign policy and knew something about American aggression abroad. He wrote his brother, "Our foreign policy is a bad joke—the Bay of Pigs, CIA scandal, U2 incident, Vietnam. . . . We must develop our intellects . . . and time is running out." Attending Stanford in the off-season, Gmelch observed antiwar activism and antiwar resisters. "I no longer believe," Gmelch wrote in his journal that winter of 1966, "in the 'domino theory'—that if Vietnam was communist, it would set off a chain reaction in which other countries would likewise become communist." He wasn't sure how, but he was determined that he would not go to Vietnam. Even if it meant fleeing to Canada.[127]

Many Americans, including many MLB managers and coaches, viewed protesting the war as unpatriotic and disloyal to US soldiers. Gmelch didn't lobby his mostly conservative teammates, but as the war escalated and was the subject of TV news segments and public debate, they increasingly talked about the war. Gmelch never held back his views and his opposition to fighting in Vietnam.

Even if they opposed the war, players believed that expressing opposition to US involvement in Vietnam, much less attending antiwar rallies, could sink their baseball prospects. Few players spoke out on the issue, so MLB teams had little occasion to sanction baseball players. But Gmelch became more upset with the war after a month-long trip to Europe during the off-season. The Europeans he met "saw the world much differently than Americans . . . [They] viewed the Vietnam War more as a nationalist struggle and America's involvement as an anticommunist crusade. . . .," he wrote in his journal. "No one . . . believes in the domino theory."[128]

His increasing outspokenness about Vietnam may have planted the seed of resistance among some of his teammates. Accompanying Gmelch on the bus to their draft physical, two teammates schemed with him on how to fail. Gmelch tried to fail the hearing test, although an audiologist later told him it was almost impossible to rig. Even so, Gmelch failed his overall physical, as did both of his complicit teammates. Here were three healthy professional athletes, all turned down by the military. Remembering how the Tigers had been closely monitoring their draft status, Gmelch asked the Tigers farm director years later if the team had intervened. He responded, unconvincingly in Gmelch's eyes, that his failure to pass the physical exam had just been the "luck of the draw."

When he arrived in Rocky Mount, North Carolina, to play for the Leafs in the Single-A Carolina League, he was shocked by the segregation and blatant racism. Gmelch had seen anti-Black discrimination before, but coming from California he never witnessed anything like the rigid self-righteous racism aimed at Blacks every minute of the day in the South. On the edge of Rocky Mount's downtown, Gmelch saw a large statue of a Confederate soldier and monument to the Confederate States of America. The town's movie theaters, restaurants, bowling alley, library, and other public venues were all racially segregated, in clear violation of the 1964 federal Civil Rights Act.

On road trips, the Tigers made sure that when the team stayed in hotels, white and Black players never shared a room. The Black players would be subject to felony convictions for interracial sex or marriage. Segregation was also the norm when they got to the ballpark. "What really struck me about Municipal Stadium [in Rocky Mount]," he recalled years later, "was seeing blacks and whites sitting in different sections, ordering food from different concessions, drinking from separate fountains, and relieving themselves in separate restrooms." One local white fan nicknamed "Country" repeatedly taunted Black players with, "N—, you couldn't hit a hog in a ditch."[129]

Unlike most other ballplayers, Gmelch rose early and explored each town where he was based or traveling before going to the ballpark in the late afternoon. In the Carolina League, every town had its Confederate monuments and flags. Gmelch became interested in Southern culture and cultural differences generally, and often tried to engage with the townspeople wherever the team was playing. On a walk one Saturday in Rocky Mount, he stopped to watch a Little League game. He got into a friendly conversation with the father of one of the players. "When I asked him why there were no black kids on the field considering that nearly half the town's population was black," Gmelch recalled, "he explained matter-of-factly, 'We don't let n—s play in our Little League. They have their own league across town.'"[130]

Gmelch recounted a conversation that "I had accidentally overheard outside our general manager Joe Summrel's office. Members of the Chamber of Commerce had been there reminding Joe that the town would not support the team if there were too many 'colored boys' in the starting lineup."[131] During the 1967 season, one of Gmelch's Rocky Mount teammates was injured and forced to remain behind during the team's road trip. He went out to the Rocky Mount ballpark to workout, expecting it to be empty. Instead, he discovered the field being used for an event run by the local Ku Klux Klan, which would have required the permission of the club and the ballpark owners. Obviously, some level of cooperation existed between the Klan and the town.

One of Gmelch's white teammates, who had been born and raised in Rocky Mount, told him that the town's police chief, DC Hooker, was a member of the Ku Klux Klan and that his brother was the leader (Grand Dragon) of the local Klan. Since 1965, Gmelch had kept a journal about his baseball experiences and had been writing monthly articles on life in the minor leagues for the *Burlingame Advance Star*, a newspaper near his California hometown. The Tigers' brass had asked him to stop publishing these pieces, since they objected to some of his characterizations of minor league baseball. But he kept doing so, believing the team had no right to tell him he couldn't write articles for a local paper on the other side of the country. His relationship with the Leafs' management only worsened after he wrote an article about segregation in Rocky Mount, including what he'd learned about the local police chief and his brother. The paper's editor headlined Gmelch's story, "Life in Rocky Mount with the Klan."[132]

In those pre-Internet days of limited communications across long distances, Gmelch never imagined that an article published in a small California paper would get back to North Carolina. But soon he realized his mistake. A reader took offense to the article and sent a copy to Rocky Mount's police chief and the head of the local Chamber of Commerce. Two weeks later, Gmelch was with the team in Winston-Salem when Al Federoff, the Leafs' manager, pulled him aside and said that he'd just received a telegram from the Tigers' headquarters in Detroit saying they wanted him to immediately get on a bus back to Rocky Mount.

The twenty-two-year-old ballplayer was told to report to city hall the next morning, where he found himself in a windowless room in a meeting with the police chief, the city attorney, the Chamber of Commerce head, the Rocky Mount Leafs team president, and the mayor. An angry town official had a copy of Gmelch's article and read out loud several damning sentences, including, "The police chief is a Klansman and his brother is the area Grand Dragon" and "Klan meetings are the only entertainment locals have."[133] They said that Gmelch had no right to publish his claims, although they offered no denials about Klan memberships, which were not uncommon among

Southern police chiefs at the time. They threatened Gmelch with a libel suit and possibly prison. They demanded to see everything else Gmelch had published that season. Instead of coming to Gmelch's defense, the team president apologized to the local officials for Gmelch's behavior. Gmelch apologized, too, realizing that the article was a big error in judgment.

Like most minor league teams located in small towns and cities, the Leafs were concerned about maintaining good relations with local officials and didn't challenge the racist laws and customs. Joe Summrel, the Leafs' general manager, told Gmelch that the police chief agreed to drop his threatened libel suit if the team removed him from the roster.

Gmelch should have seen it coming when, during his last ten days on the team, the Leafs played both a catcher and outfielder at his first base position. Even when Gmelch was put back in the lineup and went five for five in a game (including two triples and five RBI), he was benched again the next day. As soon as the team acquired another first baseman, Gmelch was dropped from the roster in June 1967.

The Tigers declined Gmelch's offer to take a demotion to another Tigers minor league team. The Leafs' general manager claimed he tried to shop Gmelch around to other teams but said he got no takers. It didn't help that in sixty-two games and 218 plate appearances, Gmelch was only hitting .218, although he was still the team's home run and RBI leader. Evidently blacklisted by major league organizations, Gmelch extended his career only by accepting an offer to play for the Drummondville Royals in the independent Quebec Provincial League (QPL) in Canada.

In the 1940s, the QPL had previously been a refuge for major leaguers, such as Sal Maglie, Max Lanier, and Danny Gardella, who had jumped to the Mexican League to escape the depressed wages caused by the reserve clause in every MLB ballplayer's contract. More than twenty blacklisted players landed in the QPL, extending their careers until the MLB ban was lifted. For Gmelch, the QPL was also a refuge, two decades later, to continue playing professionally. After Rocky Mount released him midseason, he finished the season with the Royals, hitting well. Another good season followed with the Royals in 1968. But after entering graduate school in anthropology that fall, he decided to leave organized baseball.

Gmelch's minor league experience in the South and his encounter with Jim Crow awakened him to different cultures, piquing his curiosity about the diversity of human behaviors and beliefs. When he returned to Stanford, he changed his major from biology to anthropology. "I had become far more interested in understanding people and culture than invertebrates," he recalled.[134] His concerns about poverty and discrimination, which first emerged in towns such as Rocky Mount and Statesville, North Carolina, and Daytona Beach, Florida, where he played minor league ball, evolved into his post-baseball career as an anthropologist.

Missing baseball, Gmelch returned to Drummondville in 1970, but a few weeks into the season he again left the professional game, this time for good. Anthropologists explore the similarities and differences in human societies, including the lives of marginalized peoples. While his experiences in those minor league towns initially planted the seeds, months of fieldwork living in a poor Mexican village further radicalized Gmelch about how societies often mistreat different groups based on stereotypes. Already alienated toward US foreign policy by the Vietnam War, he began to see how bigotry and exploitation promote inequality and poverty among large segments of some societies and in some cases entire societies. During his fieldwork in Mexico, he was particularly repulsed by a local priest whose church dripped with riches and who drove the village's only car, while the town's people were starving. Gmelch recalls emerging from that experience "pretty much on a crusade."[135]

Gmelch earned his BA from Stanford in 1968 and completed his PhD in anthropology at the University of California at Santa Barbara in 1975, then taught at McGill University, Union College, and the University of San Francisco. Much of his research and writing has focused on marginalized communities around the world, including nomadic Irish Travellers, subsistence fishermen in Alaska, farmers in Tanzania, displaced fishermen in Newfoundland, rural villagers in Barbados, and urban refugees in Tasmania. He has also used his baseball experience to focus an anthropological lens on the sport. His first article, "Baseball Magic," published in 1978, looked at baseball players' rituals and superstitions. Among his fifteen books are four about baseball, including *In the Ballpark: The Working Lives of Baseball People* (1998), *Inside Pitch: Life in Professional Baseball* (2001), *Baseball without Borders: The International Pastime* (2006), and *Playing with Tigers: A Minor League Chronicle of the Sixties* (2016), an account of his years in the minors.

Gmelch has spoken out against minor league players' deplorable pay and working conditions. He noted that "the pay structure of modern day baseball may be the most glaring example of income inequality in the American workplace,"[136] pointing out that major league stars like the Tigers' Miguel Cabrera and the Los Angeles Angels' Albert Pujols earn more for one game than the entire roster of a Class A minor league team over an entire season. He served on the board of directors of More Than Baseball, the nonprofit organization working to improve conditions for minor league ballplayers, and received the Minor League Baseball Association's Lifetime Achievement Award.

1. Octavius Catto.
Library of Congress

2. Moses Fleetwood Walker.
Baseball Hall of Fame

3. Andrew "Rube" Foster. Baseball Hall of Fame

4. Willie Wells. Portrait
by Graig Kreindler
(www.graigkreindler.com)

5. Frank Sykes. Portrait
by Graig Kreindler
(www.graigkreindler.com)

6. Lester Rodney.
Photo by Bryon LaGoy

7. Wendell Smith.
Baseball Hall of Fame

8. Bill Veeck.
Baseball Hall of Fame

9. Sam Nahem.
Baseball Hall of Fame

10. Branch Rickey. *Sporting News*

11. Jackie Robinson.
Bob Sandberg, *Look Magazine*

12. Larry Doby.
Baseball Hall of Fame

13. Satchel Paige.
Baseball Hall of Fame

14. Sam Jethroe. Baseball Hall of Fame

15. Bill White. Baseball Hall of Fame

16. Curt Flood.
Baseball Hall of Fame

17. Mudcat Grant.
Credit: Sergei Scurfield

18. Dick Allen.
Baseball Hall of Fame

19. George Gmelch.
Courtesy of George Gmelch

20. Alta Weiss.
Baseball Hall of Fame

21. Helen Callaghan.
Courtesy of Kelly Candaele

22. Toni Stone. Negro Leagues Baseball Museum Inc.

23. Mamie Johnson.
Negro Leagues
Baseball Museum Inc.

24. Connie Morgan
with Jackie Robinson.
Negro Leagues
Baseball Museum Inc.

25. Pam Postema.
Baseball Hall of Fame

26. Ila Borders.
 Courtesy of Ila Borders

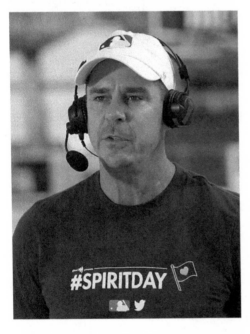

27. Billy Bean.
Photo by Arturo Pardavilla

28. Glenn Burke.
Baseball Hall of Fame

29. Tyler Dunnington.
Photo by Shelly Dunnington

30. Ian Desmond. Photo by Keith Allison

31. Keynan Middleton.
Photo by Keith Allison

32. Gabe Kapler.
Photo by Keith Allison

33. Sean Doolittle. Photo by Keith Allison

34. Bruce Maxwell. Photo by Keith Allison

35. Dexter Fowler.
Photo by Arturo Pardavilla

36. Terry Cannon.
Credit: Jon Leonoudakis

PART TWO

Challenging Sexism and Homophobia

Women in Baseball

O n Mother's Day in 2017, Casey Candaele, then a coach with the Seattle Mariners, described how his mother, Helen, instilled her love of baseball when he was young. "She would go out and play catch and hit me ground balls and pitch me batting practice," recalled Candaele. "I thought everyone's mom was doing that."[1]

When Candaele and his four brothers were growing up in Lompoc, California, their mother didn't talk much about her days as a player in the All-American Girls Professional Baseball League (AAGPBL). She and Candaele are the only mother-son combination to have played professional baseball. Candaele ranked fourth for the National League's Rookie of the Year in 1987 and played in the major leagues for eleven years with the Houston Astros, Cleveland Indians, and Montreal Expos, but he always claimed that his mother was the better player. As Helen Callaghan, she played pro baseball for four seasons (1944–48), batting .257 and stealing 354 bases in 388 games.

The world of women's baseball had almost been forgotten until Candaele's brother Kelly made a documentary film, *A League of Their Own*, for public television in 1987. That documentary inspired director Penny Marshall to make a Hollywood version of the story in 1992, with the same title, starring Geena Davis, Tom Hanks, Madonna, and Rosie O'Donnell. It is the highest-grossing baseball movie of all time, outpacing *Moneyball, Bull Durham, 42,* and *Field of Dreams.*

Since the demise of the AAGPBL in 1954, professional women's basketball, soccer, golf, and tennis have become well-established, but it is still almost impossible for exceptionally talented female baseball players to earn a living playing the game in all-women's leagues. But thanks in part to the federal Title IX law, which Congress passed in 1972, and in part to the popularity of *A League of Their Own,* an upsurge of women's participation in baseball and softball has occurred among all age groups and at the professional and amateur levels.

Women have played baseball since the sport was invented. They have played in all-women leagues and on teams with men, in amateur and professional leagues, with softballs and hardballs. They have also owned teams, worked as sportswriters, and called balls-and-strikes as umpires. But the closest a woman has come to making a major league team was in the 2016 ten-episode television drama, *Pitch*, about a woman who pitched for the San Diego Padres.

Since its inception in the early 1800s, baseball has been known as a sport for boys and men. "Baseball is war," wrote Albert Spalding in *America's National Game*, the first major history of the sport, published in 1911. As a star pitcher, manager, owner, sporting goods entrepreneur, founder of the National League, and author of the first official set of rules, Spalding believed that as the "national pastime," baseball should reflect America's growing economic dynamism and military power on the world's stage, which he associated with masculinity. "A woman may take part in the grandstand, with applause for the brilliant play, with waving kerchief to the hero . . . loyal partisan of the home team, with smiles of derision for the umpire when he gives us the worst of it. . . . But neither our wives, our sisters, our daughters, nor our sweethearts, may play Base Ball on the field. . . . Baseball is too strenuous for womankind."[2]

Spalding's words reflected the dominant views of the 1800s and early 1900s. American women were expected to conform to very narrow roles in society. Victorian values, reflecting the views of the white upper class, stressed that women should be submissive, focus on domesticity, and dress modestly (including tight-fitting corsets, petticoats, hoop skirts, long dresses, and high button shoes), all of which limited their pursuit of vigorous physical activity, exercise, and athletic competition, like riding bicycles or playing tennis. Playing baseball wasn't considered a respectable thing for women to do, and they faced ostracism and derision—including the fear of becoming unmarried "spinsters"—if they dared violate social norms about engaging in sports.

The cause of equal rights for women, led by the women's suffrage movement, began in the 1840s and challenged the dominant culture and women's second-class citizenship, but it evolved slowly and unevenly around the country. Although women won the right to vote in some states as early as the late 1800s, it wasn't until 1920, with the passage of the Nineteenth Amendment, that women gained the franchise at the national level. The next wave of modern feminism emerged in the late 1960s and catalyzed activist efforts around equal pay, reproductive rights, domestic violence, narrow definitions of "women's work," family responsibilities, and women's participation in politics.

Baseball's Women Pioneers

As baseball became more popular after the Civil War, Americans in both rural areas and cities played and watched the game. Rural areas had plenty of room to lay out baseball fields. The influx of immigrants to the burgeoning cities in the late 1800s and early 1900s led social reformers to demand that local governments build school playgrounds and parks so that children could exercise and participate in sports. The settlement house reformers—who were essentially the first generation of community organizers, most of them women—organized baseball games for male and female children alike. In 1919, the New York City school system incorporated baseball as one of the physical education activities for girls. Most young girls played what eventually became known as softball, but some insisted on playing with men's rules and baseball equipment. Gladys Palmer's 1929 book, *Baseball for Girls and Women*, included a variety of rules for indoor and outdoor games.

To participate in baseball, women had to break barriers, and they did. Soon after the first women's colleges were established in the 1860s, some of them—including Vassar, Smith, Wellesley, and Mount Holyoke—fielded baseball teams. Vassar students organized teams as early as 1866 and by the 1870s it had seven or eight teams on campus. Vassar graduate Sophia Foster Richardson (class of 1879) recalled, "The public, so far as it knew of our playing, was shocked, but in our retired grounds, and protected from observation even in those grounds by sheltering trees, we continued to play in spite of a censorious public."[3] Some women's teams played by the same rules as men, but others experimented with different length base paths, different distances between the pitcher's mound and home plate, different size balls, pitching overhand and underhand, and different kinds of gloves and bats.

Regardless of how they played the game, women faced widespread scorn, as reflected in a *St. Louis Post-Dispatch* editorial in 1885, which proclaimed that "the female has no place in base ball, except to the degradation of the game."[4] A 1911 article in the *Reach Official American League Guide* argued that making baseball an official sport at women's colleges was "one more indictment against the modern unsexing system of female education and training."[5] Women who wanted to play baseball were not confined to the relatively affluent set of those who could afford to attend private women's colleges. Some girls and women simply got together to play pickup games, to form their own leagues, and even to earn money playing baseball.

In 1867, a year after Octavius Catto formed one of the first professional baseball teams in the country, Philadelphia's all-Black Excelsior Club, African American women formed a team called the Dolly Vardens in the same city. By the 1870s, some enterprising businessmen in Illinois organized two all-women teams—the "Blondes" and "Brunettes"—confident that the novelty and spectacle would draw a crowd of paying customers. A newspaper account described them as "a selected troupe of girls of reputable character."[6] In dress and demeanor, they were expected to be feminine so as not to be seen as acting like men. In the 1880s, another male entrepreneur organized an all-women barnstorming team of players whom a New Orleans newspaper called "buxom beauties" and "short-skirted ball tossers." New Orleans officials then arrested the owner "on the charge of being a dangerous and suspicious character."[7] In 1886, women in Gilmore, Pennsylvania, organized themselves into two teams—the "Singles" and the "Marrieds"—and played before a large crowd, with a woman even serving as umpire. In the late 1890s and early 1900s, businessmen formed teams of women ballplayers—called "Bloomer Girls"—who traveled around the country playing exhibitions against men's amateur and semiprofessional teams before shocked and gawking spectators. (Bloomers were loose-fitting pants that some young women had begun to wear instead of long skirts.) Some teams included one or two boys or men dressed with women's wigs. And in some towns, a few women players joined the men's teams.

Some women were recruited to play on men's semipro and professional teams. One of the best known was pitcher Alta Weiss, who was born in rural Ohio in 1890. Her father, a physician, encouraged her to play baseball. He even built a gymnasium attached to the barn. It included body-building equipment so she could practice her pitching and stay in shape during the winter. By fourteen she was pitching for boys' teams, and at seventeen she joined the Vermillion Independents, a men's semipro team, and was soon its star pitcher and a media sensation. In her debut outing, attended by a large crowd of 1,200 spectators, she gave up only four hits and one run in five innings. For her next game, a local railroad company scheduled a special train from Cleveland to Vermillion, twenty miles away, to accommodate the fans eager to see what local papers called the "Girl Wonder." When her team played in Cleveland, more than three thousand people paid to watch her pitch.

Like other women athletes, she had to battle with the taboos, prejudices, and compromises that men didn't face. She once told reporters, "I found that you can't play ball in skirts. I tried. I wore a skirt over my bloomers—and nearly broke my neck. Finally I was forced to discard it, and now I always wear bloomers, but made so wide that the fullness gives a skirt-like effect."[8]

Her father bought a part interest in the team and changed the name to the Weiss All-Stars. She continued to play while attending medical school, where she was the only female in her 1914 graduating class, and played for several years while starting her medical practice. Her baseball career lasted from 1907 to 1922. Then she quit to devote herself to medicine full time.

Lizzie Murphy was another outstanding athlete from a very different social background. Born in 1894 in Warren, Rhode Island, like many working-class girls she left school at age twelve to work in the same woolen mill where her father worked. While working on the looms she was also "dreaming of the outdoors and baseball."[9] By the time she was fifteen she was playing first base and infield positions with teams of adult men in her spare time. She was also an outstanding long-distance runner, skater, and swimmer, but she gained the most notoriety for her impressive skills on the diamond. In her first semi-pro game, the team manager divided the gate receipts ($85) among the male players but not her. Before the next game, she refused to board the team bus unless the manager paid her. Knowing that many of the fans were coming to watch Murphy play, he agreed to pay her $5 a game plus a share of the gate receipts. She supplemented her salary by selling postcards of herself to her fans. Eventually, she was able to earn a living as a professional ballplayer, partly as a novelty but also because she was a star-quality player with great drawing power, referred to as the "Queen of Baseball."

Murphy's professional baseball career spanned from 1918 to 1935, playing for local teams as well as touring with teams on which she was the star attraction, even though they included some former major league players. In the 1920s she was paid $300 a week, more than most minor league players at the time, and sportswriters opined that she had as much or more talent than many male minor leaguers. In 1922 her team beat the Boston Red Sox in a charity exhibition game at Fenway Park. Later in her career she got a hit off Satchel Paige in an exhibition game with a Negro League team. She married in 1937, but two years later her husband died and she had to return to working in the woolen mills and on oyster boats to make ends meet. Even local residents soon forgot her baseball exploits.

In 1928, an American Legion team from Blanford, Indiana, defeated a team from nearby Clinton in the first game of the county tournament on a twelfth inning hit by fourteen-year-old Margaret Gisolo. The Clinton team protested that a girl wasn't eligible to play American Legion ball, which was created for teenage boys, but their appeals were denied. As her team advanced in the American Legion tournament, Gisolo was the main attraction. She was big news around the country, including a story in one newspaper headlined, "Girl Babe Ruth Made Eligible in Legion Tourney."[10] Gisolo helped her team win the county, district, sectional, and state championships. In the seven-game tournament, she hit .429, scored ten put-outs and twenty-eight assists without any errors. That year, another girl in Indiana made her boys' high school baseball team, and a New York girl made a local amateur team.

To some, these girls' successes were viewed as a threat, reflected in one headline, "Girls Usurping National Sport: Suffrage Now Extends from Ballot Box to Baseball Diamonds."[11] In 1929, the American Legion barred girls from playing. Instead, over the next six years, Gisolo played for several all-girls barnstorming teams based in Chicago and Los Angeles. Her college, Indiana State Teachers College, didn't field any intercollegiate sports teams, but Gisolo played during the summer to help pay for her education. She eventually earned a master's degree and became a professor of physical education at Arizona State University, retiring in 1980.

Jackie Mitchell may be the most legendary woman baseball player of all time, but her fame rests on her accomplishment pitching to two batters. She was born into a middle-class family in 1913 in Chattanooga, Tennessee. Her father taught her to play baseball, and their neighbor Dazzy Vance (a major league pitcher and future Hall of Famer) showed her how to pitch, including how to throw a sinker, then called a "drop ball." She was her school's star pitcher. In 1931, hoping to boost attendance for the Chattanooga Lookouts, a double-A minor league team, owner Joe Engel signed the seventeen-year-old, 130-pound Mitchell to a contract. Engel announced that Mitchell would pitch in an exhibition game against the New York Yankees. The day before the game, Mitchell told reporters, "Yes, I think I can strike him out,"[12] referring to Babe Ruth, who had said that women were "too delicate" to play baseball every day.[13]

On April 2, a crowd of between 3,500 and 4,000 fans showed up at Engel Stadium. After starting pitcher Clyde Barfoot, a former major leaguer, gave up hits to the first two Yankee batters, Lookouts manager Bert Niehof brought Mitchell to the mound to pitch to Ruth. "The Babe performed his role very ably," wrote New York Times reporter William E. Brandt. "He swung hard at

two pitches then demanded that Umpire Owens inspect the ball, just as batters do when utterly baffled by a pitcher's delivery."[14]

Mitchell's next two pitches were off the plate. With the count two and two,
Ruth struck out looking on a pitch on the outside corner of the plate. He
gave an angry stare to the umpire and walked back to the dugout. According
to one news account, Ruth threw his bat against the dugout in disgust over
being called out on strikes. Next, slugger Lou Gehrig, another future Hall
of Famer, struck out on three pitches. The Lookouts manager took Mitchell
out of the game after she walked the third batter, Tony Lazzeri. The Yankees
won the game 14–4, but the news around the country was about Mitchell's
performance.

Mitchell hoped to remain on the Lookouts roster and perhaps even make
the major leagues. But MLB Commissioner Kenesaw Mountain Landis put
an end to that dream when he announced that women were banned from
playing pro baseball and that Mitchell's contract was null and void. Mitchell
returned to the Englettes, an all-girls team sponsored by Engel and managed
by her father, which played against men's semipro teams. The next year, she
disobeyed Landis's dictate and joined a Piedmont League minor league team
in Greensboro, North Carolina, but only for road trips, not home games.
Her infraction probably never came to Landis's attention because she hadn't
signed an official contract. Between 1933 and 1937, she barnstormed with
the House of David, a traveling all-men's team whose players wore beards and
long hair and claimed to be part of a religious sect. During the off-season, she
toured with an all-men's basketball team, then returned to Chattanooga to
work for her father, an optometrist.

In the first half of the 1900s, Americans got used to seeing women excel
at individual sports like tennis and golf, but it took longer for the public to
accept women as baseball, or softball, players. The number of organized
women's baseball and softball teams and leagues expanded, accelerating in
the 1920s. Most were local amateur teams, sponsored by local companies,
community recreation programs, YWCAs, churches, and high schools, disproportionately in rural areas and urban working-class neighborhoods.

Like men's baseball, many women's teams—like the Johnson's Wax team in
Racine, Wisconsin and the Wells Lamont Glovers (Wells Lamont manufac-
tured gloves) in Louisiana, Missouri—were sponsored by local businesses as
a way to promote worker loyalty and expand companies' good will in the community, especially during the Depression, a time of rising labor-management

conflict. Some employers recruited first-rate athletes to work for them primarily so they could join their company teams, which paid for the equipment and uniforms and rented local ball fields. These industrial leagues were popular, well-organized, and exhibited a high caliber of talent. Men played both baseball and softball, but most women played softball. The game was so popular that the Amateur Softball Association was founded in 1933 and began sponsoring regional and national tournaments for men and women. In 1935, an estimated two million Americans were playing softball in organized leagues. By 1943, there were at least forty thousand women's softball teams— one quarter of all the softball teams in the country.

The All-American Girls Professional Baseball League Players

The big increase in the number of women playing softball and baseball during the 1930s and early 1940s provided the talent pool for the AAGPBL, which operated from 1943 to 1954.[15] Like previous all-women's teams and leagues, the AAGPBL was started by male businessmen who thought that fans would pay to see the unusual spectacle of women in skirts on a baseball field. But the AAGPBL surpassed all expectations in its popularity and the quality of play. It played an important role in providing jobs and morale-boosting entertainment for a country at war.

When the United States entered World War II at the end of 1941, about five million women entered the workforce, demonstrating that they could do "men's" jobs, including welders, taxi drivers, lumberjacks, coal mine checkers, crane operators, bus drivers, and train conductors. The fictional "Rosie the Riveter" became a national heroine.

The war threw professional baseball into turmoil. President Franklin Roosevelt even considered prohibiting professional baseball during the war, but he ultimately decided that continuing it would help lift the nation's spirits. Even so, professional baseball faced a labor shortage. Men over eighteen years old were being drafted or enlisted into the armed services or put to work in defense plants. Eventually, over five hundred major leaguers served in the military during the war. The war depleted the rosters of many minor league teams; many were disbanded. Owners of major league teams feared that they, too, could find themselves without an adequate supply of qualified players to fill their rosters.

Some major league owners worried that fans would stop paying to watch teams whose best players were in the military and not on the field. Philip K. Wrigley, the multimillionaire chewing gum magnate who owned the Chicago Cubs, decided to establish a women's softball league that would play in major league stadiums. He hoped to schedule the women's games while the major league teams were on the road.

By the spring of 1943, Wrigley was ready to carry out his plan. He used his fortune to bankroll the league and recruited Midwestern businessmen to sponsor local teams. The league was set up as a nonprofit organization, as were the individual teams. Wrigley failed to persuade other major league owners and executives to sponsor women's teams. So rather than play in big cities and in major league parks, the league's teams were located primarily in midsize industrial Midwestern towns within a one-hundred-mile radius of Chicago. The league started with four teams—the Racine Belles and Kenosha Comets in Wisconsin, the Rockford Peaches in Illinois, and the South Bend Blue Sox in Indiana—and grew to ten teams before it folded in 1954. Throughout its history, the league's board of directors, team sponsors, and managers were all men; not a single woman was in any decision-making position.

Over six hundred players participated in the league. Wrigley insisted that their contracts be with the league, not the individual teams, so league executives could move players around to guarantee a relatively competitive balance. League executives constantly changed the rules, often in midseason. The AAGPBL began as an underhand-pitching softball league then allowed pitchers to throw sidearm, and then switched to an overhand-pitching hardball game. The league changed the rules regarding the length of the base paths, the distance from the pitching mound to home plate, and the size of the ball. The players had to make the appropriate adjustments.

Wrigley hired scouts to find players from the United States and Canada. Most of them were in their late teens and early twenties and came from the existing women's softball leagues around the country. Before its first season, the league held tryouts in different cities and invited 280 players to the final tryouts at Wrigley Field in Chicago. They were tested on their fielding, catching, throwing, running, sliding, and hitting abilities. Sixty women were selected to fill the initial four teams. The ranged in age from sixteen to twenty-eight. The managers were men, three of them with major league experience, which Wrigley thought would provide the league with instant credibility.

As a teenager, Lois Youngen played for a softball team in Ashland, Ohio. In 1950, the sixteen-year-old Youngen traveled to Fort Wayne, Indiana, to visit her cousin, who invited her to attend a Fort Wayne Daisies game. While sitting in the stands, Youngen recalled, "I turned to my cousin and said, 'You know, I can do that,' just like that, right out of the blue. That surprised even me because I don't think the majority of women in that generation were terribly aggressive and I surprised myself by saying that."[16] The next day, Youngen was on the field trying out for Daisies manager Max Carey, a Hall of Famer. At the end of her senior year in high school, she traveled to Alexandria, Virginia, where the AAGPBL teams held spring training. Although she had to miss three weeks of school, her teachers told her, "Go with our blessing, and make the team," except one teacher who insisted that she send back her homework.[17] She spent four years in the AAGPBL as a catcher and outfielder with the Kenosha Comets, Fort Wayne Daisies, and South Bend Blue Sox from 1951 through 1954.

The league signed the women to professional contracts that stipulated that they could not have other jobs during the baseball season. Most of the players were from working class families. Their salaries—which initially ranged from $45 to $85 a week—were considerably higher than those of most other jobs available to women, including jobs in defense plants. In fact, their pay exceeded what most men were making at the time. Even so, most had to work during the off-season, a majority in factories or in clerical and office jobs.

The AAGPBL was a liberating experience for the players. Not only did they earn good salaries, but many were away from home and on their own for the first time. They enjoyed the camaraderie of their teammates. "It was just a chance of a lifetime for someone who loved to play baseball as much as I did to get involved with this league," recalled player Gloria Cordes Elliot.[18]

Although the experience was liberating for many players, the league perpetuated sexist stereotypes and imposed constraints on their behavior that annoyed many of them. Wrigley and the team owners wanted to differentiate the AAGPBL from existing amateur women's softball leagues, where players were often viewed as rough and masculine, including wearing regular male-style uniforms or pants on the field. The AAGPBL handbook spelled out the message: "The more feminine the appearance of the performer, the more dramatic the performance." Wrigley insisted that the ballplayers radiate femininity and the "highest ideals of womanhood." The league required players to "dress, act, and carry themselves as befits the feminine sex."[19]

Wrigley wanted the public to think of the players as the "girl next door." The league expected the players to "look like Betty Grable and play ball like Joe DiMaggio," recalled Lois Youngen.[20] They particularly wanted to avoid any suspicion—with regard to clothes, hairstyles, and physiques—that AAGPBL teams had lesbians on their rosters.

Each team had a female chaperone who was expected to enforce the league's strict code of conduct. After daily practices, players were required to attend classes run by Helena Rubenstein's charm school and beauty salon. The instruction included makeup tips, etiquette, language, posture, social skills, and personal hygiene, plus the league's strict dress code. Each player was given a guide with specific instructions on how to look and behave and came with a kit that included cleansing cream, lipstick, hair remover, and other feminine products. On the field, they played in flared skirts similar to those worn by women involved in figure skating, field hockey, and tennis, even though they were expected to slide, which led to many bruises. "We played tough, even when we were hurt," Helen Callaghan remembered.[21] The chaperones taped them up and they'd continue to play.

Off the field, they were prohibited from smoking or drinking in public, had to be in their rooms by a curfew hour, and were required to get the permission of their chaperones for "all social engagements."[22] The league sent local newspapers profiles of the players, which not only focused on their playing skills but also their domestic skills and hobbies, such as cooking and sewing. In local ads and publicity events, the league promoted the most traditionally feminine-looking players. As Callaghan recalled, "That was basically what the league was based on—femininity. Play like a guy and act like a woman. To me, it was just funny."[23]

In the first season, the four teams played 108 regular games from mid-May to early September, drawing 176,612 fans, then competed in a championship series. Sportswriters and league officials were impressed with the high caliber of play and the enthusiasm of the hometown fans. In those pre-TV days, the games were a major source of entertainment, especially since gasoline was rationed and few Americans could take vacations during the war. Local radio stations broadcast the AAGPBL games, and newspapers featured stories about the players. The athletes (many of whom had fathers, brothers, husbands, and friends in the military) played exhibition games for the Red Cross, visited wounded soldiers at military hospitals, and, at the start of each game, formed a "V" for Victory by lining up from home plate down the first and third baselines, followed by the playing of the "Star Spangled Banner." The teams were so popular in their small Midwestern cities that the communities sponsored "junior" leagues for girls fourteen years and older.

By 1944 it was clear that the war wouldn't force Major League Baseball to shut down and Wrigley lost interest in the AAGPBL. He sold the league to his advertising agent, Arthur Meyerhoff, who enthusiastically promoted, advertised, and expanded it to new cities. The 1945 season included teams in Grand Rapids, Michigan, and Fort Wayne, Indiana.

World War II ended in August 1945. At season's end, more than 450,000 fans had attended AAGPBL games. In 1946, the league added new teams in Peoria, Illinois, and Muskegon, Michigan. In 1950, the league still had eight teams, but the Muskegon franchise moved to Kalamazoo. The next year, the Racine team relocated to Battle Creek, Michigan. Some teams drew three thousand or more fans per game. At its peak, in 1948, the league attracted 910,000 fans, with ten teams. To promote the league, teams traveled to Mississippi, Cuba, and Florida for spring training during the 1946 to 1948 seasons and made postseason tours to Cuba and South America. They played some exhibition games in Yankee Stadium in New York and Griffith Park in Washington, DC. A *Movietone News* crew made a newsreel called "Diamond Gals" about the league during its 1947 spring training in Havana that was shown in movie theaters around the country. Major national magazines, like *Colliers* and the *Saturday Evening Post*, published stories about the league and its players. Within a year, after the players demonstrated their athletic skills, local papers in cities with AAGPBL teams routinely covered their games as athletic events rather than as novelty entertainment.

Attendance began to decline after 1948 for several reasons. Many major leaguers returned from the war to resume their baseball careers, reigniting enthusiasm among fans. The rise of television provided postwar families with a new form of entertainment. Local stations televised major league games, reducing the appeal of local minor league franchises as well as AAGPBL games. Much of America reverted to prewar attitudes toward women in the workplace. As male soldiers returned from the war, the heroic image of Rosie the Riveter was replaced with the stereotype of women as primarily housewives and mothers. Exacerbating these problems, in 1951 Meyerhoff sold the teams to individual owners, who lacked the resources to adequately recruit players, balance the caliber of talent on the different teams, and publicize the league. By 1954, only five teams remained. Teams were losing money and at the end of the season the executives decided to terminate the league. It had lasted nine years beyond the end of the war.

In 1944, businessmen started a rival professional league, the National Girls Baseball League. It began with four semipro teams and added two more teams, all in the Chicago area. They played under softball rules and occasionally played against men's teams in exhibition games. The NGBL never got the national attention of its rival, but it competed for players, which pushed the AAGPBL to increase salaries. Both leagues folded after the 1954 season.

Helen Callaghan

Helen and Marge Callaghan reflected the pioneering spirit of many AAGPBL players. They were two of six children in a working-class family from Vancouver, Canada. (Over 15 percent of AAGPBL players were Canadians.) Marge was born in 1921 and Helen arrived two years later. Their mother died of cancer when Helen was in kindergarten, and their father Albert remarried. Growing up during the Depression, the family experienced hard times, especially when Albert, a factory foreman, lost his job and the Callaghans lost their home and their car.

Sports were a diversion for the struggling family. "We were from an athletic family, and there wasn't a lot of money," Helen recalled. "There wasn't anything else to do. We didn't have money to go to the shows so we grew up playing baseball."[24] Even in a family of sports-minded children, Helen and Marge stood out. They grew up excelling in softball, soccer, roller hockey, basketball, lacrosse, and track and field. They played in their neighborhood streets (mostly with boys) and at school. Marge graduated from high school in 1939, but Helen dropped out to help with family expenses. They both found jobs at a Boeing aircraft factory and played on a traveling semipro softball team, the Mutuals. When their team traveled to Detroit, Michigan, in 1943 for the World Championship Tournament, AAGPBL scouts took notice, particularly of Helen, who was invited to spring training in Illinois in May 1944.

"I loved to play ball, and the thought of getting paid to play it really excited me," Helen recalled. "Plus, I'd be independent. At that time you were expected to stay in the kitchen and raise kids. It wasn't that I didn't want to do that. But this meant I was going to do something else, too." When she returned from Detroit, she "pleaded with my father to let me go. He didn't want me going all that way. But I just kept at him. I wore him down."[25]

Helen signed a contract for $75 a week and was assigned to the Minneapolis Millerettes, one of two new AAGPBL teams. Worried about sending his daughter far away on her own, their father urged Marge to look out for her. She received permission from Boeing to leave her wartime job and joined the Millerettes. The team played at Nicollet Park, home of the Minneapolis Millers, a top Double-A minor league team. But unlike the teams in small cities that didn't have to compete with men's minor league franchises, the Millerettes drew few spectators. By midseason they abandoned their home field and operated as a traveling "orphan" team, playing all their games at other AAGPBL teams' home parks.

"We were on the road all the time, living out of suitcases, traveling on old buses. We'd sing and play cards. Some of the girls would gamble a bit. And we'd sleep," Helen remembered. "Often we'd play a doubleheader in 110 degree heat and travel to another town and just have time to shower and play another doubleheader."[26] The following year, the team moved to Fort Wayne, Indiana, and changed its name to the Daisies. As Helen recalled, "I looked feminine. But I played tough. I was real serious about it. Before the game I wouldn't talk to anyone. I wanted to be left alone. That was just my personality. I practiced as hard as I played."[27]

Throughout AAGPBL history, the average batting average was around .200, but Callaghan—an outfielder who was five foot one and threw and batted left-handed—was an outstanding hitter, using the heaviest bat in the league, a thirty-six-ounce Louisville Slugger. In her rookie season, she hit .287, the second-best batting average in the league.

With shorter distances between bases, AAGPBL players stole more bases than their male counterparts. Helen, who had excellent speed, stole 112 bases in 111 games, which ranked her seventh in the league. After her exceptional rookie season, the league increased her pay to $125 per week, one of the highest salaries in the AAGPBL. The next year she more than earned her pay boost. Playing in all of the team's 111 games, she led the league in hitting with a .299 average and in total bases (156), extra-base hits (24), hits (122), doubles (17), and home runs (3), all inside the park, and ranked second in stolen bases (92) and runs scored (77). One newspaper called her "the Babe Ruth of the league," observing that "she's a Vancouver secretary during the offseason, but at the plate she has the timing and co-ordination of Ted Williams."[28]

After the 1945 season, Helen married Bobby Candaele, who ran a taxi business in Vancouver. She returned to Fort Wayne for the 1946 season, still playing under her maiden name. She played in all 112 games. Her hitting declined, but she continued tearing up the basepaths. She missed the 1947 season to deliver her first son, Rick. She returned to Fort Wayne for the 1948 season but played in only fifty-one games due to a tubal pregnancy that required surgery. For the 1949 season, the league assigned Helen to the Kenosha Comets. She played in 106 games and batted .251, seventh best in the league.

During the 1948 and 1949 seasons, Bobby spent part of the baseball season driving a cab while taking care of the baby, a rare sharing of responsibilities for married couples at the time. But after the 1949 season, Helen had had enough. "It wasn't fun anymore. I finally figured out that baseball wasn't everything, and it was time to hang it up and get on with life. A lot of girls played for ten years. Not me. I got out, and I never looked back."[29]

Although Helen rarely talked about her AAGPBL days to her friends and family, she instilled a deep love of sports, and a strong competitive drive, in her five sons. Rick was a baseball and football star at the College of Idaho and later coached high school and college football for over fifty years, including stints as head coach at the University of California-Santa Barbara and the Claremont Colleges. Casey was a multisport star in high school, played shortstop at the University of Arizona, and played in the majors for eleven years with the Montreal Expos, Houston Astros, and Cleveland Indians, finishing with a .250 lifetime batting average. Short in stature at five foot nine, Casey was respected for his hustle and enthusiasm, as well as his sense of humor.

"I tried to motivate him [Casey] to always be aggressive," Helen said in an interview.[30] "I didn't get her athletic ability," said Casey, who has coached with the Toronto Blue Jays, Texas Rangers, and Seattle Mariners and during the 2021 season was manager of the Blue Jay's triple-AAA team in Buffalo. "She was a better player than me." Throughout his playing days in the majors, "She lived it with me. She wanted me to do so well. It was like she was playing me. It was in her soul. She told me that you don't have to have any talent to hustle and play the game the right way. I always lived with that."[31]

After a long battle with breast cancer, Helen Callaghan died in Santa Barbara on December 8, 1992, at age sixty-nine. Marge, who originally joined the AAGPBL to look after Helen, stuck with the league for eight years, retiring after the 1951 season. She died on January 11, 2019, at age ninety-seven.

Traveling around the country to make his documentary, *A League of Their Own*, Kelly Candaele listened to the women—by then in their sixties and seventies—tell their stories about the AAGPBL. He discovered that for many players, their AAGPBL experience forged lifetime friendships and a sense of pride.

Candaele's documentary inspired director Penny Marshall to make a Hollywood version of the story in 1992, with the same title. Many people believe that the fictional siblings in the film are based on Helen and Marge Callaghan, but Candaele insists that the characters in the movie are composites drawn from many different players, including the Callaghan sisters.

In the 1980s the AAGPBL alumni association initiated talks with the Baseball Hall of Fame in Cooperstown to recognize the athletes of the AAGPBL, and in November 1988 the Hall opened a permanent exhibit dedicated to the league. Many former players traveled to Cooperstown for the opening ceremony. The exhibit celebrates the league and the athletes, but none of the women who played in the AAGPBL were actually inducted into the Cooperstown shrine as individuals.

There's been no poll to determine which women would deserve entry into the hall, but there's a general agreement among experts that any list of the AAGPBL's greatest players would include Helen Callaghan, Faye Dancer, Jean Faut, Betty Foss, Dorothy "Snookie" Harrell, Betsy Jochum, Dorothy "Dottie" Kamenshek, Helen Nicol, Doris Sams, Dorothy Schroeder, Audrey Wagner, Joanne Weaver, and Connie Wisniewski.

For some players, their experience in the AAGPBL opened doors to careers that they might not otherwise have had. They gained self-confidence that helped them when their playing days ended. While only 8.2 percent of the women of their generation earned college degrees—and an even smaller number for working-class women—35 percent of AAGPBL players secured a college degree, with 14 percent gaining graduate degrees.[32]

Despite the demise of the AAGPBL, amateur and semipro softball continued to thrive around the country. AAGPBL players continued to play baseball or softball with local leagues, and a few became well-known for their prowess in golf, bowling, and other sports. Many became high school teachers and college professors of physical education, promoting and encouraging more young women to become involved in sports, which catalyzed the dramatic increase in participation in women's sports that began in the 1970s.

Mabel Holle, one of the original players in the AAGPBL, played for the South Bend Blue Sox in 1943, then went to college and taught physical education for forty-five years at Waukegan High School in Illinois, where she also coached softball, basketball, and volleyball. According to the *Chicago Tribune*, she was "instrumental in getting girls involved in sports before Title IX legislation paved the way for equality in school athletic programs."[33]

Margaret Wigiser, who played for the Minneapolis Millerettes and Rockford Peaches from 1944 to 1946, earned her degree at Hunter College and became a high school physical education teacher in New York City. In 1969 she became the school district's first director of interscholastic women's sports. The passage of Title IX three years later provided Wigiser with the resources to expand the program. By the time she retired in 1982, the citywide program had twelve sports, 450 coaches, ten thousand athletes, and a budget over $1 million.

After playing in the AAGPBL for four years, Lois Youngen earned a bachelor's degree in physical education from Michigan State University. In 1960 she joined the University of Oregon faculty, where she taught women's physical education, coached the women's track and field and tennis teams, and became director of physical activities and recreation services. She earned a PhD from Ohio State University in 1971. During her thirty-six years at Oregon, she helped expand the university's program in women's sports, especially after Congress passed Title IX, despite resistance from male administrators, coaches, and athletes. One of her key achievements was persuading both male and female professors to teach coeducational classes. She led by example, which included playing in pickup recreational games with men. She retired in 1996.

A Lavender League: Lesbians in the AAGPBL

The Hollywood version of *A League of Their Own* made no mention of the fact that many AAGPBL athletes were lesbians. During the AAGPBL's days—the 1940s and early 1950s—none of the players were open about their sexuality except to close friends and some teammates.

According to Kelly Candaele, his mother, Helen Callaghan, "told me that she didn't even know about lesbianism until she joined the Minneapolis Millerettes. She said that all the players knew that gay relationships in the league were common, but also that nobody seemed to make much of it." Candaele said that among his mother and her fellow players: "Their attitude seemed to be that what happens within the team stays within the team."[34]

The story of lesbians in baseball parallels the struggles of women and gay people to gain more equality in all walks of life. In the 1940s and 1950s, lesbianism was a taboo topic, especially in the world of sports, and thus the AAGPBL did everything it could to avoid that stigma. The rise of modern feminism in the 1970s, especially after the passage of Title IX in 1972, significantly increased the number of women participating in organized sports at all levels, from preteens through the professional ranks. As the gay rights movement also burgeoned in the 1970s, a growing number of lesbian athletes came out of the closet. In 1981, when tennis star Billie Jean King acknowledged she was gay, it was big news.

Because so many of the best female ballplayers were lesbian, it was impossible for the league to exclude them. But they had to keep their sexuality secret through a code of silence. Local newspapers that covered the AAGPBL helped them maintain the code.

The reason for insisting that the players dress in a skirt or dress, take etiquette classes, wear makeup, and attend charm school was to avoid the perception that AAGPBL rosters included lesbians. They weren't allowed to appear unfeminine or mannish. One magazine article from 1943 expressed concern that the players in the new AAGPBL would turn women's baseball into an "uncouth Amazonian spectacle," codewords for lower class and lesbian.[35] Connie Wisniewski—a five-time All-Star who played from 1944 to 1952—was told that she would be released if she got a close-cropped haircut called a "bob." Dottie Ferguson. an outstanding player between 1945 and 1954, was warned by her team chaperone not to wear women's Oxford shoes, because they were too masculine-looking.

Many AAGPBL players were married, engaged, or had boyfriends back home or in the military. Like many pro athletes, some had affairs during the baseball season. Some of those affairs were with men, while others were with women, including teammates. Nobody really knows how many lesbians played in the league because they were all in the closet. But league officials did their best to monitor the players' personal behavior and to punish those who engaged in same-sex relationships or even had the appearance of being lesbian, based on the stereotypes of the period.

If a league official or manager suspected that two players were part of a lesbian couple or having an affair, they would refuse to let the women room together. One AAGPBL manager released two players whom he suspected of being lesbians, worried that they would "contaminate" other players on the team.[36] A team chaperone discovered that a married player was having an affair with another woman who was not connected to the team. She confronted the player, who insisted that she would continue the relationship. So Fred Leo, the AAGPBL publicity director and later its president, contacted her husband, who came and took her home and out of the league.

A Secret Love, a documentary film that debuted on Netflix in 2020, reflects the changing attitudes. It focuses on Terry Donahue and Pat Henschel, who met and fell in love in 1947, when Donahue, then twenty-two, was playing for the AAGPBL and Henschel, then eighteen, was a long-distance phone operator. The couple kept their true relationship secret for over six decades.

Both women grew up on Canadian farms. A topflight softball player in Moose Jaw, Donahue joined the AAGPBL's Peoria Red Wings in 1946 and remained until 1949. After Donahue left the AAGPBL, the couple moved to the Chicago area, where Donahue played part time for professional women's softball teams.

Donahue rarely talked about her baseball-playing days. But after the release of *A League of Their Own*, she gained some notoriety. In 2010, she was invited to be grand marshal of the St. Patrick's Day parade in St. Charles, Illinois. An article about Donahue in the local newspaper described Henschel as her "cousin and roommate."[37] In an oral history interview conducted that year, Donahue didn't even mention Henschel.[38] Chris Bolan, Donahue's great-nephew, decided to make the film after the couple came out to him in 2009. Although they lived clandestine lives, they nevertheless documented their relationship in dozens of audiocassette tapes and photo albums, some of which are shown in the film.

During the AAGPBL season, Henschel often traveled to the small Midwestern cities where Donahue's team was playing to attend her games and to have private moments together. While apart, they wrote long love letters to each other but tore off their signatures to keep their relationship secret from family, friends, and team officials in case the letters were ever found.

In the 1950s and 1960s, they avoided gay bars, which were often raided by the police. They feared that they could get arrested, be fired from their jobs, or be deported to Canada. They had a small coterie of gay friends who socialized in each other's homes, where they could be safer. When the gay rights movement erupted in the 1970s, they remained on the sidelines. They worked for the same Chicago interior design firm but hid their relationship from fellow employees.

The film also recounts their later years dealing with declining health, moving to an assisted living facility, and coping with Donahue's Parkinson's disease. *A Secret Love* also depicts their decision to come out to family and friends, to live openly as a couple, and to get married in 2015, the first year that same-sex marriage was legalized, on Donahue's ninetieth birthday. American culture had changed enough by the time Donahue died in 2019, at age ninety-three, that the AAGPBL posted a photo of the couple on its Twitter page, describing Henschel as her "partner of 71 years."[39]

Many lesbians in the AAGPBL had long-lasting relationships during and after their playing days but remained closeted, even years after many of them had hung up their spikes. It was only after they, or their partners, died that they came out of the closet, usually through phrases in their obituaries like "long-term partner" or "long-term companion." Even into their eighties, however, many refused to come out.

Mildred "Millie" Deegan, born in Brooklyn in 1919, was an outstanding high school athlete. At fifteen she came in second (to Babe Didrikson) in the women's javelin throw and would have made the US Olympic team in 1936 except she was too young. Her prowess on the softball field led to her nickname, "the Babe Ruth of women's softball." She pitched and played second base for six teams during her nine years (1943–51) in the AAGPBL. In 1944, the Brooklyn Dodgers brought Deegan and two other women players to the team's spring training camp at Bear Mountain, New York. After watching her play, manager Leo Durocher said, "If we run out of men, Millie will be the first on the team. . . . If she were a man, she no doubt would have been a Dodger."[40] In the off-season and after she left the AAGPBL, she worked as a secretary and as a portrait photographer.

When her playing days were over, she coached a women's softball team from 1958 to 1979 in Linden, New Jersey, where she met Margaret Nusse, the team manager and star pitcher. Nusse played for the Linden Arians beginning in the late 1930s. She pitched through the early 1960s, threw at least thirty no-hitters and batted .537 during that period. In 1968 Nusse was named commissioner, and Deegan secretary-treasurer, of the Eastern Major Softball League. Deegan and Nusse were lifelong partners. They moved to Florida in 1976. A 1993 profile of Nusse in the *Tampa Bay Times* described Deegan as her "cousin" and "roommate."[41] But the *New York Times* obituary for Deegan on July 28, 2002, described Nusse as her "companion and her only survivor."[42] Nusse died the following January.

Born in 1920, Mabel Holle grew up in Jacksonville, Illinois. Her father had been a semiprofessional ballplayer, and Holle played on sports teams with local boys. She even played on the boys' football team in her freshman and sophomore years in high school. In 1942 she earned a bachelor's degree in physical education from MacMurray College, where she played field hockey, volleyball, and basketball. She was one of the original sixty players in the AAGPBL in 1943, playing for Kenosha and South Bend, but the league did not renew her contract after one season. For the next two seasons she played for the Chicago Chicks in the rival National Girls Baseball League. She then taught physical education and coached softball, basketball, and volleyball for forty-five years at Waukegan High School, and she earned a master's degree in 1955 from MacMurray. When she died in 2011 at ninety-one, obituaries in the *Chicago Tribune* and *State Journal-Register*, and on a family website, described Linda Hoffman as her "longtime partner."[43]

Josephine "Jo" D'Angelo began playing baseball as a little girl and, as a young woman, devoted her evenings to playing the sport in her hometown of Chicago while working in a steel mill during the day. She played outfield for the AAGPBL's South Bend Blue Sox during 1943 and 1944, batting a respectable .200. D'Angelo was a lesbian, but she made a point of wearing feminine-style clothes and avoiding hanging around with the league's "gay crowd" in order to keep her sexuality a secret.[44] Despite this, during her second year with the Blue Sox, she was released from her contract. Years later, D'Angelo said that she knew the reason: "a butchy haircut," which a hairstylist had given her without her permission.[45]

D'Angelo used the money she made playing pro ball to help pay tuition at DePaul University, where she earned a degree in physical education. She later got her master's in counseling, and spent her career working at Chicago-area high schools as a gym teacher and school counselor. She died in 2013 at eighty-eight. Her obituary in the *Chicago Sun-Times* noted that as early as her teenage years, D'Angelo identified as a lesbian.

As a teenager in Rockford, Illinois, Jean Cione played for industrial league women's softball teams. While in high school in 1945, she joined the AAGB-PL's Rockford Peaches and played for three other league teams through 1954. She was one of the AABPL's greatest pitchers, throwing two no-hitters in 1950 and winning twenty or more games in three seasons. After the league folded, she earned a bachelor's degree from Eastern Michigan University and a master's degree at the University of Illinois. For a decade she taught physical education in elementary school. She returned to Eastern Michigan University in 1963 as a professor of sports medicine, coached women's track and basketball, and in 1973 became the university's first director of women's athletics. After retiring from Eastern Michigan University in 1992, she and her partner, Ginny Hunt, moved to Bozeman, Montana, where she died in 2010 at age eighty-two. Her obituary in the *Bozeman Daily Chronicle*, and her profile on the Society for American Baseball Research website, described Hunt as "her partner."[46]

June Peppas, born in 1929, played on local women's softball teams in Fort Wayne, Indiana, while in high school before being recruited to the AAGPBL. She pitched and played first base for four teams between 1948 and 1954. After the league folded, she played amateur softball and basketball. Her softball team won the Michigan state championship in 1955. She earned her bachelor's and master's degrees from Western Michigan University and taught school. According to the obituary for Polly Huitt in the *Palm Beach Post* in 2007, "Polly and her partner of forty-five years June Peppas began the PJ Printing Company in Allegan, Michigan in 1975. After selling the business and retiring, Polly and June moved to Jensen Beach, Florida in 1990."[47]

Eunice Taylor was born in 1934 and grew up in Kenosha, Wisconsin. In 1950, at sixteen, she played for an AAGPBL barnstorming team, the Chicago Colleens. She played one season as a catcher for the AAGPBL's Kenosha Comets. In the mid-1950s, she moved to Florida. When she died in 2009, the *Orlando Sentinel* described Diana Walega as her "partner in life for 45 years," reporting that they had owned and operated Hobscot Pet Supply for forty of those years and owned their house together.[48]

Some outstanding lesbian athletes refused to play in the AAGPBL when they heard about the strict rules and constant surveillance. Dot Wilkinson was only eleven when she joined the Phoenix Ramblers of the fast-pitch American Softball Association (ASA) in 1933 and was soon considered one of the best players in the country. A decade later, the AAGPBL eagerly recruited Wilkinson, offering her $85 a week (the equivalent of over $1,300 today), but she refused. She didn't want to put up with the AAGPBL's curfews, charm school, chaperones, and dress code. She remained with the Ramblers—who allowed her to play in Levi's or shiny satin shorts—until 1965. She earned nineteen All-American awards and led the Ramblers to three world championships. Many consider Wilkinson one of the great women softball players—and the greatest catcher—of all time. While traveling around the country with the Ramblers, she also had a full-time job, because her pay wasn't sufficient to make ends meet. As a professional bowler, she won Women's International Bowling Queen's Tournament events in 1962 and 1963.

In 1963, Estelle "Ricki" Caito joined the Ramblers as a second baseman. Wilkinson and Caito only played together on the Ramblers for two seasons, but they began a lifelong relationship that lasted forty-eight years, until Caito died in 2011. "We were born at a time when we were all in the closet and that was just the name of the game," Wilkinson explained. "And you have to live with it and that's what we did."[49] Caito's obituary in the *Arizona Republic* identified Wilkinson as her "longtime companion."[50]

Today, many of the most prominent professional female athletes—such as soccer star Megan Rapinoe and WNBA basketball standout Chelsea Gray—publicly identify as lesbians. They, in turn, are role models for the many young lesbian athletes in high school, college, and semipro sports. Unlike the lesbians in the AAGPBL, today's lesbian athletes, including baseball and softball players, no longer have to hide their sexuality on or off the diamond. One indication of how things have changed can be seen in the Amazon TV series based on *A League of Their Own*, which was scheduled to debut in 2021 but was delayed by the COVID-19 pandemic. The series, also called *A League of Their Own*, will include a more diverse group of female athletes, including lesbian characters, according to the show's cocreators. Rosie O'Donnell, who starred in the original film, will be part of the cast.

Women and Black Baseball: Toni Stone, Mamie "Peanut" Johnson, Connie Morgan

A brief scene in the Hollywood film *A League of Their Own* shows a ball rolling away from the playing field during an AAGPBL team practice. A Black woman picks it up and fires it back to the Rockford Peaches catcher played by Geena Davis. The throw is so hard that the Davis character has to rub her hand to ease the pain. She stares at the Black woman, who smiles back knowingly, as if to say, "I belong on that field, too," before walking away.

Like American society in general, and Major League Baseball until Jackie Robinson joined the Brooklyn Dodgers in 1947, the AAGPBL was racially segregated. In fact, the league never had an African American player, even after Robinson broke the color barrier. Barred from playing in the AAGPBL, three African American women—Toni Stone, Mamie "Peanut" Johnson, Connie Morgan—played in the otherwise all-male Negro Leagues.[51]

After 1947, as major and minor league teams slowly but steadily hired African American players, Black fans began to lose interest in the Negro Leagues. The Negro National League (NNL) folded in 1948. Its rival, the National American League (NAL) continued but struggled with low attendance. By 1953, only four teams remained. NAL team owners began looking for ways to rejuvenate the league's appeal.

Syd Pollack, owner of the Indianapolis Clowns, was a brilliant promoter. The Clowns played first-rate baseball, but they also engaged in various theatrics in order to draw paying customers to games. The games included comic acts that fed on racist stereotypes, similar to the play of the Harlem Globetrotters basketball team. Some players found it demeaning, but they put up with it because they needed the jobs and the theatrics brought in the fans. Not only did the Clowns win the Negro American League pennant in 1950, 1951, 1952, and 1954, but it was also the most profitable club.

Despite that success, Pollack knew that the future of the league was in doubt and so he hit on the idea of hiring a woman to play for the Clowns. His scouts found Marcenia Lyle Stone—known as Toni—playing second base for the New Orleans Creoles, a Negro minor league team. She played softball because most women played that version of the sport, but she preferred baseball.

Born in 1921, Stone grew up in St. Paul, Minnesota. Her parents emphasized education, not sports, but she was determined to excel in athletics. She played on her Catholic school's boys baseball team, then played softball on an all-girl high school team. At fifteen, inspired by her exposure to barnstorming Negro League teams, she was playing for a men's semiprofessional team, the St. Paul Giants, and then joined an all-male American Legion team in San Francisco. She began her professional baseball career in 1949 playing for the San Francisco Sea Lions and then joined the Creoles between 1949 and 1952.

After the Clowns' star player, Henry Aaron, signed a contract with the Boston Braves in 1952, Pollack signed Stone to a contract. Pollack claimed that "this is no publicity stunt," but he clearly recruited Stone to help boost attendance.[52] Pollack tried to get Stone to wear a skirt like the AAGPBL players, but she refused. She wore the regular men's uniform. Pollack heavily publicized her arrival. Her image was included on scorecards, flyers, and other materials to promote the games. Pollack's strategy worked. With Stone in the lineup, the Clowns began drawing crowds larger than at any time since the late 1940s, including an opening game against the Kansas City Monarchs that brought 17,205 fans to the ballpark. Some exhibition games drew even larger numbers, including an increasing number of female fans.[53]

The records of Negro League games are incomplete, so it is impossible to say how well Stone, and the two other women players who followed her, performed on the field. Stone was a good ballplayer, but most observers at the time said she was not up to Negro League standards. The Clowns typically put her in the game for the first two or three innings before replacing her. Many opposing pitchers gave her a break by only throwing fastballs.

In response to the publicity surrounding Stone, the Clowns received many letters from coaches and athletes promoting the talents of other Black females seeking a chance to play in the Negro Leagues. Pollack was open to adding one or two more women, but he wasn't interested in fielding an all-women's team or even having too many women on the Clowns. The owners of other Negro League teams showed even less interest, despite the Clowns' success with Stone.

Mamie "Peanut" Johnson, a South Carolina native born in 1935, began playing baseball after her family moved to Long Branch, New Jersey. She was the only girl, and the only Black person, on the Police Athletic League team, helping them win two division championships. When she was twelve her family moved to Washington, DC, and she began playing for a local Black, all-male team, the St. Cyprian's. After graduating from high school, she sought a tryout with the AAGPBL but was rebuffed because of her race, so she continued to play for the St. Cyprians on weekends while working at an ice cream shop. At the end of the 1953 season, on the advice of a scout, Pollack hired Johnson—a five-foot-four, 120-pound pitcher—to play in the Clowns' off-season exhibition games and then added her to the roster for the 1954 season. She had a 33–8 win-loss record during her years with the Clowns and was a solid hitter as well with a .270 batting average.

Connie Morgan, a nineteen-year-old from Philadelphia, wrote a letter to the Clowns seeking a tryout. She excelled in several sports in high school and in 1949, at age fourteen, joined an all-Black women's softball team, the North Philadelphia Honey Drippers. Pollack and his coaches were impressed with Morgan's athletic skills but also impressed with her appearance. She had light skin, a curvy figure, and curled hair, which seemed more "feminine" than Stone's muscular build and darker skin. Pollack viewed her as more marketable, hired her in 1954, and made sure that she, more than Stone, was included in publicity events, including a photo of Morgan with Jackie Robinson. Pollack put that image on the team's official scorecard.

Angered by the Clowns' favoritism toward Morgan—who also played second base—Stone asked Pollack to trade her to another NAL team. He sold her contract to the Kansas City Monarchs before the beginning of the 1954 season.

As result, three women played on Negro League rosters that year. They each had to endure catcalls, physical harassment, sexual advances, pitches thrown at them when they batted, and ridicule from their male players on their own and opposing teams. Pollack and the team's business manager reminded the male players that the women were a drawing card that put fans in the seats and helped pay their salaries. Occasionally the women exacted revenge. Johnson threw fastballs at opposing players who ridiculed her. Stone once swung a bat at a teammate who sexually harassed her.

Ironically, Sam Lacy, Doc Young, and Wendell Smith, three prominent Black sportswriters for Negro newspapers who had actively pushed for the racial integration of Major League Baseball, opposed the entry of women in the Negro Leagues. "Negro baseball has collapsed to the extent it must tie itself to a woman's apron strings in order to survive," wrote Smith soon after Stone joined the Clowns.[54]

By 1954, however, attendance declined; perhaps as the novelty wore off and more Negro League stars embarked for minor and major league teams. The Clowns and Monarchs operated primarily as barnstorming teams, traveling around the country playing local semipro teams and occasional exhibition games against teams composed of white major leaguers during the off-season.

At the end of the 1954 season, Stone left the Negro Leagues. She took care of her ailing husband (who was thirty years older) and worked as a personal care assistant in San Francisco, but she was eager to stay connected to the sport she loved. She coached a Little League team sponsored by St. Francis Cathedral, played in pickup games with local men's teams, and joined a league of lesbian teams in the Bay Area. Morgan quit the Clowns around the same time and returned to business school in Philadelphia, eventually working for the AFL-CIO, the labor union federation, in her hometown. Johnson quit in 1955, obtained a nursing degree from North Carolina State A&T University, and worked at Sibley Memorial Hospital in Washington, DC, for several decades.

During their brief careers in the Negro Leagues, the Negro press covered their activities, but the white media—which generally ignored the Negro Leagues anyway—paid almost no attention to these three Black female sports pioneers. The 1980s witnessed increased interest in Negro League history, and the following decade saw an upsurge of interest in women's role in baseball, drawing renewed attention to Stone, Johnson, and Morgan. Stone was elected to the Women's Sports Hall of Fame in 1993, and St. Paul dedicated a baseball field to her four years later. Martha Ackmann's biography of Stone, *Curveball*, was published in 2010, and an off-Broadway play based on her life, *Toni Stone*, opened in June 2019. Morgan was elected to the Pennsylvania Sports Hall of Fame in 1995. Stone and Morgan both died in 1996.

After retiring from her nursing career, Johnson coached youth baseball and helped run a store of Negro League memorabilia. In 1996, President Bill Clinton and Hillary Clinton honored Johnson at a White House ceremony. In 1999, Columbia, South Carolina, Mayor Bob Coble presented Johnson with a proclamation. In 2002, Michelle Green published a children's book about Johnson, *A Strong Right Arm*. In 2005, Washington, DC, Mayor Anthony Williams invited her to join him at the first game of the Washington Nationals. That year, Brown University premiered a one-woman play about her life, called *Change Up*.

In 2012, Johnson was introduced to eleven-year-old Mo'ne Davis, a pitcher for a Philadelphia-based team, the Anderson Monarchs, who were in Virginia as part of a nationwide bus tour to visit civil rights and baseball sites. Two years later, the seventy-eight-year-old Johnson was invited to attend the opening game of the Little League World Series in Williamsport, Pennsylvania, where she watched Davis, by then thirteen years old, pitch the first shutout by a girl in a championship game. "That's me when I was her age—the size, the way she throws, everything," Johnson said at the time. "I never, ever thought I would witness this."[55] Johnson died in 2017 at eighty-two.

Little League, Title IX, and Upsurge of Women's Sports

Like Jackie Robinson and other sports rebels and pioneers, Mo'ne Davis's accomplishments—including being the first female baseball player to appear on the cover of *Sports Illustrated*—were the result of both her individual talents and commitment and the efforts of a broader movement that opened new doors. Davis's feats and fame reflected a resurgence of girls' and women's participation in baseball and softball after a long hiatus.

Since it began in 1939, the Little League tried to keep girls out.[56] Few girls even bothered to sign up, but when they did, they were rebuffed. In 1950, twelve-year-old Kathryn ("Tubby") Johnston wanted to play in the Corning, New York, Little League like her younger brother was doing.

Knowing that girls were barred, her mother cut off Kathryn's braids, gave her some of her brother's clothes to wear, and told the coaches that she was a boy who went by the nickname Tubby. She made the team, played first base, and didn't reveal her secret to her coach for a week. Even after she revealed her gender, the coach thought she was good enough to play and kept her on the team. Once the national Little League office learned about this breach of custom, however, it adopted what became known as the "Tubby rule," prohibiting girls from trying out or playing on Little League teams.[57] During the 1950s and 1960s, several other girls—some pretending to be boys—joined Little League teams but were quickly forced to quit.

By 1972, the Tubby rule was in full force. Over two million boys, but no girls, played Little League baseball. That year, however, a Little League coach in Hoboken, New Jersey, made an exception for Maria Pepe. After she pitched three games, the national Little League insisted on enforcing the rules, forced her off the team, and revoked the charter held by all ten Hoboken Little League teams. The National Organization of Women (NOW) filed a gender discrimination claim on Maria's behalf with the New Jersey Division on Civil Rights. At the hearing, Little League executive Creighton J. Hale testified about the "physiological differences" between boys and girls. Girls had weaker bones and muscles, and slower reaction times, than boys, he said, adding that "a blow to the breast of a female, as by a batted or thrown ball, could cause cancer." (On another occasion, he explained that "it wouldn't be proper for coaches to pat girls on the rear end the way they naturally do boys.")[58]

Sylvia Pressler, a New Jersey Division of Civil Rights hearing officer, didn't buy the argument and ruled in favor of Pepe. Little League's national office appealed the ruling, but the New Jersey Supreme Court upheld the decision. By 1974, New Jersey Little League told its local chapters that they must allow girls to play.

The ruling had a significant ripple effect. That year, Little League faced more than twenty lawsuits around the country, and some local leagues relented. That same year, twelve-year-old Ambra Offutt from Hillsboro Village, Tennessee, found a local Little League coach, Harold Huggins, who welcomed her on his team, but the national Little League told him he couldn't let her play. "I was better than most of the guys out there," Offutt recalled. "I remember thinking, 'This is the dumbest thing ever.'"[59]

On May 11, 1974, the Offutts sued Little League in federal court for its boys-only policy. Huggins testified on Ambra's behalf, explaining that she was capable of competing with boys her age. By June 12, Little League revised its national "boys-only" policy, citing "the changing social climate."[60] On July 1, the court deemed the suit "moot" because Ambra already was able to play. With Ambra on the team, they won four of their next six games.

Another lawsuit was on behalf of Kim Green, a nine-year-old from Delaware. Green grew up in a baseball-loving family. Her father, Dallas Green, had pitched for the Phillies, Senators, and Mets between 1960 and 1967 and then worked for the Phillies as a minor league manager and farm system director. Green attended lots of Phillies games, played stick ball at the local playground, and served as the bat girl for her older brother's Little League team. By 1974, she was ready to sign up for Little League herself, but when she went to register, a middle-aged man told her, "I'm sorry. Little girls can't play baseball."[61] Green went back home in tears. Her mother mentioned the incident to one of Green's elementary school teachers, who was a member of NOW and knew about the New Jersey lawsuit. When reporters asked her father about the lawsuit, Dallas said that if a girl was good enough to compete with the boys, she should be allowed to play.

TV talk show host Mike Douglas heard about Green's plight and invited her to appear on his nationally syndicated program that aired on June 3, 1974, along with Miami Dolphins fullback Larry Csonka and actress Marlo Thomas, a prominent feminist and author of a new book, *Free to Be You and Me*. On the stage, Csonka tossed tennis balls to Green, who missed the first pitch but hit all the rest. The audience applauded. Csonka asked the crowd, "See, don't you think this girl should be allowed to play ball?"[62] Nine days later, in the face of Green's TV exploits and growing lawsuits by Maria Pepe, Amber Offutt, and others, Little League announced it had revised its charter to allow girls to play.

Back home in Delaware, however, the local Little League told Green that they had already selected the teams and she'd have to wait until the following year to sign up. Rather than give up, Green and her mother plastered flyers at her school and in the area advertising tryouts for an all-girls Little League team for eight and nine-year-old players. About one hundred girls showed up. The Midway Little League agreed to allow the all-girls team, the Angels, to compete against the other all-boys teams.

The Angels won their first eight games of the 1974 season and finished second in the league. The next year, Green and more than thirty thousand other girls played in Little League. The number of girls playing Little

League has escalated since then. "We changed a lot of reactions," recalled Green, who became a firefighter, breaking another gender barrier. "Parents thinking if a little girl can hit like this, she can play. Nobody was purposely mean about it, but I think it was an educational thing."[63] Girls' participation in Little League got a boost in 1976, when actress Tatum O'Neal starred as pitcher Amanda Whurlitzer, the only girl on her team, in the film *The Bad News Bears*.

In 2004, thirty years after Maria Pepe's legal victory, Little League's national office invited her to throw out the ceremonial first pitch at the Little League World Series in Williamsport, Pennsylvania. The Little League explained that it was honoring her "for helping to blaze the way for millions of girls—not only in Little League, but in other aspects of life for which girls and women were previously thought to be unsuitable."[64]

The rise of modern feminism, changing attitudes, and lawsuits like those by Little League girls clearly opened doors for female athletes. But the most important catalyst was the passage of Title IX, a 1972 amendment to the federal Education Act designed to provide everyone with equal access to any program or activity that receives federal financial assistance. The sponsors of the bill didn't focus on sports, but the law is often associated with the dramatic increase in the number of girls and women who participate in athletics. Many of the girls' and women's teams that are common at high schools and universities today didn't exist in 1972. Title IX didn't apply to Little League, a private organization, but it helped change the climate that influenced how parents, coaches, and judges felt about girls playing sports.

Between 1972 and 2018, the number of boys participating in high school sports grew from 3.6 million to 4.5 million, a 25 percent increase, while girls' participation grew from 294,000 to 3.4 million, a spike of over 1,000 percent.[65] By 2018, about 100,000 girls played pre–high school youth baseball each year, but only 1,284 girls played baseball in high school during that season. Girls get channeled into fast-pitch softball, particularly since that's where the college scholarships are. Since 1973, the number of high school girls playing fast-pitch softball rose from 110,140 to 362,038.[66]

Systematic information about participation in intercollegiate sports wasn't available until 1982. Participation for men increased, but it grew even more dramatically for women. The number of women participating in intercollegiate sports increased from 64,390 in 1982 to 216,378 in 2018—from 28 percent to 44 percent of all intercollegiate athletes.

Women's fast-pitch softball at the college level has seen a major increase. In 1982, only 752 colleges and universities (55 percent of all NCAA member institutions) offered the sport, and 7,465 women participated. By 2018, 1,114 colleges and universities (90 percent of NCAA members) offered intercollegiate women's fast-pitch softball, attracting 20,316 female athletes.[67] These numbers don't even include the growing number of women's teams and athletes participating in club sports on college campuses.

For decades after the demise of the AAGPBL, it was almost impossible for exceptionally talented female athletes to earn a living playing softball or baseball, but there has recently been a renaissance, in large part due to the growing number of girls and women who played the sport in Little League, high school, and college, and the growing acceptance of women in professional sports—a trend discussed in chapter 9.

Ila Borders

Ila Borders was the first woman to play in an otherwise all-male professional baseball league with the exception of the three women who played in the Negro Leagues. Borders was a beneficiary of the Title IX revolution—in high school, college, and eventually the minor leagues. She was the first female pitcher to start a men's NCAA or National Association of Intercollegiate Athletics (NAIA) college baseball game, the first woman to receive a baseball scholarship to play men's collegiate baseball, the first woman to win a game in men's collegiate baseball, and (with the exception of the three women who played in the Negro Leagues) the second woman to integrate an all-male professional baseball, breaking that barrier on May 31, 1997. (Susan Perabo, who played second base for Webster University in 1985, was the first woman to play on an NCAA baseball team. Kendra Hanes played ten games for the Kentucky Rifles in the independent Frontier League in 1994.)

Although Borders was well aware of these and other milestones, she did not seek notoriety as the "first woman ever." She loved baseball and wanted to play at the highest level her talent and determination would allow. Borders was born on February 18, 1975, and grew up in the Los Angeles suburb of La Miranda. Her father had played semiprofessional baseball and earned a living painting cars. Her mother ran a preschool. "Every Saturday and Sunday, from the time I was 5, my whole family would play ball," Borders recalled. "My dad basically taught me everything: the mental part, the control, how to call a game, how to take care of my arm."[68]

Borders' father encouraged her to pursue her passion for baseball. At six she began playing in an all-girls Little Miss Softball League and excelled. But she told her father that she wanted to pitch overhand, with a real baseball, and so at ten, she signed up for Little League, despite efforts by league officials to dissuade her. Her father wanted her to be proud of her gender and insisted that she wear her hair long, "so everyone knows you're a girl."[69] In her first game, the young left-handed pitcher struck out the first six batters. In high school, she faced hostility from opposing teams. Some opposing pitchers threw hardballs at her, while some opposing spectators (particularly parents) threw rocks. "Go back to Barbie dolls," some shouted at her.[70] For the most part, her male teammates and coaches considered her a valuable asset with her strong pitching and hitting. Upon reading an article about Borders' breakthrough, San Francisco Giants manager Dusty Baker sent her a letter of encouragement. With her father's support, she learned to steel herself against slurs and face adversity with discipline and resolve. In 1989, when she was fourteen, her father forged an ID for her so she could play on a local semipro team with men in their 20s and older, and learn to pitch sixty feet six inches, the mound-to-home plate distance used in college and professional baseball.

Borders was the only girl on the baseball teams at Whittier Christian Junior High School and then at Whittier Christian High School. The coaches at both schools recognized her talents and encouraged her. "For that age, her speed was above average, and she had a really good curve ball," said her junior high coach, Rolland Esslinger. "She spotted her pitches well, and her slow pitches were wicked—hard for hitters to hit. She was smart and knew where to throw the ball and what would get hitters out."[71] She continued to improve in high school. She posted a 16–7 win-loss record, with a 2.31 earned run average (ERA) and 165 strikeouts in 147 innings over four years of high school. She won the Most Valuable Player award her senior year.

Borders' performance attracted the attention of college scouts. She chose to attend Southern California College, a small Christian college in Costa Mesa, becoming the first woman to win a college baseball scholarship (and the first in her family to attend college). Like other women in baseball, she faced criticism that her presence on the diamond was merely a publicity stunt. But her college coach, Charlie Phillips, stood up for her. "I don't sign anybody who cannot pitch. I'm not in the game for publicity," he said. "If she can get outs, who cares if she's male or female?" He told his players, "If you can't put up with this, you won't be here."[72]

She won her first game by a 12–1 score before an unusually large crowd (for Southern California College) of five hundred spectators and lots of national media, becoming the first woman to pitch, and to win, in a NAIA game. Borders—who was five-foot-ten and 165 pounds—had a seventy-mile-per-hour fastball, slightly slower than other college pitchers' speed, but she compensated with changeups, curves, and excellent control, and she eventually learned to throw a screwball. During the baseball season, opposing players hurled abuse at her and she also faced ostracism and abuse from some teammates, who resented the media attention she was getting. Some threw balls at her back during workouts. Her own catcher tipped off her pitches to opposing batters.

The college fired Phillips after Borders' freshman year, and the new coach was not as enthusiastic about her place on the team. She was no longer a starting pitcher and spent much time on the bench. She transferred to Whittier College for her senior year and was part of the starting rotation on the otherwise all-male team. At Whittier she became the first woman to pitch in NCAA Division III baseball. Although she increased her fastball speed to seventy-five miles per hour, she struggled on the mound, finishing the season with a 4–5 win-loss record and a 5.22 ERA.

In 1997, Mike Veeck—owner of the Saint Paul Saints, a professional team in the independent Northern League—offered her a place on the roster for $750 a month. It was understandable that some accused Veeck—the son of Bill Veeck—of inviting Borders to play for the Saints as a public relations gimmick. One manager of another Northern League team warned that he'd boycott a game if Borders was on the mound, but he never carried out the threat.

Borders only pitched in seven games for the Saints, mainly as a reliever. One month into the regular season, she was traded to the Duluth-Superior Dukes, who also used her in relief. She was popular among fans, especially young girls who emailed her and wrote her fan letters. But she also received disturbing letters, including death threats. She finished the 1997 season with a 7.53 ERA, fifteen appearances, fourteen innings, allowing twenty-four hits and nine walks while striking out eleven, and no decisions.

On July 24, 1998, Borders became the first woman (outside the Negro Leagues) to officially win a game in a men's regular season professional league. She threw six scoreless innings against the Sioux Falls Canaries, giving up only three hits and two walks. She had a streak of twelve scoreless innings, but she pitched poorly for most of the season, which included a severe bout of food poisoning. She returned to the Dukes in 1999. A new manager used her in relief. In three games, she posted a disastrous 30.86 ERA, giving up ten hits and four walks in less than three innings. She was traded to the Madison (Wisconsin) Black Wolf, where, in fifteen games, she posted good numbers: a 1–0 record and a 1.67 ERA in thirty-three innings. The following year she played for the Zion Pioneerzz in Utah, part of the Western Baseball League. Halfway into the season, she had a disappointing 8.31 ERA in five games and eight innings, giving up seventeen hits. Convinced that no minor league team affiliated with the major leagues would offer her a contract, she retired from professional baseball at age twenty-five.

In four years of playing in the low minor leagues, Borders pitched 101 innings in fifty-two games, twenty of them as a starter. She gave up 149 hits, walked thirty-nine, and struck out thirty-six batters. She compiled a 2–4 win-loss record and a 6.75 ERA.

Being a pathbreaker took a toll on Borders. Throughout her career, starting in Little League, she faced isolation and rejection from male teammates, with some important exceptions, and hostility from opposing teams and fans. This persisted during her four years as a professional in the minor leagues. As Marilyn Cohen recounts in *No Girls in the Clubhouse,*

> Several factors contributed to Borders' difficulties fitting in with and being accepted by her teammates: their resistance to her presence as a player; her exclusion from bonding in the dugout, locker room and bus; her own inclination to keep to herself; and her Christian faith. Locker rooms are key settings for social interactions among players. As a woman, Borders obviously changed and showered elsewhere, rarely entering the locker room. . . . She knocked on the locker room door and called out "housekeeping" to forewarn her teammates before team meetings, read on the bus, and avoided partying. When invited by the manager to watch television in the locker room with her teammates she refused. In the bullpen, where she spent most of her time, she listened to endless stories about sexual encounters. During her second season she began to join in for post-game beer and pizza and she became friends with men who had also experienced marginality: a Jew, an African American and a closeted gay man.[73]

During her playing days, Borders often brought with her a copy of a biography of Jackie Robinson, which she read for inspiration. "It made me just feel not as alone," Borders remembered. "We obviously had different circumstances completely. But just hearing his experiences impacted me so much."[74]

Borders proved she could play at the professional level, but not well enough to advance beyond the bottom rung of the minors. Her performance on the field was hindered by the constant stress caused by the abuse she endured. As the only woman on every team, she could not share housing costs with her minor league teammates. During the 1999 season, playing for the Madison Black Wolf, earning only $750 a month, she was often broke and could not afford to eat a diet of healthy food. During her pro playing days, she often couldn't afford a car, so she biked or walked from the stadium to wherever she was staying. One time, walking home following a game, she was beaten and robbed. She refused to tell her teammates or team executives about these incidents for fear that they would view her presence on the team as a problem and release her.

"I've been spit on, had beer thrown on me and been sworn at and was hit 11 times out of 11 at-bats while in college," Borders recalled, "But the memories I have are the ovations when I would run in from the bullpen." "I'll look back and say I did something nobody ever did," she told a reporter. "I'm proud of that. I wasn't out to prove women's rights or anything. I love baseball."[75]

Despite this attitude, the additional pressure took its toll. "If it were just me pitching out there, it would have been fine. But because everyone was [weighing] in saying if I mess up, I'm messing up for women. . . . Oh my gosh, I thought, I can't mess this up. I've always been fine failing on my own and owning it. But then failing for everybody, when they are not going to recover, that takes on a whole different meaning."[76]

Borders recognized that she was gay in elementary school, when she had her first crush on another girl. Through high school, college, and her professional baseball career, she kept her sexuality secret. "I tried everything in my power to make my feelings for girls go away. I prayed, and when that didn't work, I prayed harder," she wrote in her autobiography, *Making My Pitch*, published in 2017.[77]

Borders' sexuality conflicted with the strict values of the fundamentalist Christian junior high school, high school, and college she attended, which gave her opportunities to excel in sports, even allowing her to play on teams with boys, but condemned homosexuality. Although she was a star athlete, she felt like a misfit and was lonely, with few close friends. She occasionally dated boys "because it made me seem straight," but eventually "I decided I would rather be alone than a miserable phony." Had it not been for sports, she wrote, "I could have ended up somewhere bad."[78]

"If a woman plays hardball, people figure she's likely gay," Borders wrote. "In the closet as I was, I unconsciously accepted the message that I must look feminine. So I only did cardio workouts," rather than lift weights and gain visible muscle mass. With her long hair, Borders did not fit the stereotype of a lesbian, so reporters rarely probed about her sexuality. Throughout her baseball career, however, she was frequently asked if she had a boyfriend. She would sometimes lie and say that she dated men, but more often she simply said that she was too busy to date because she was concentrating on her athletic career. "When people tried to set me up [with men], it was easy to say, 'No thanks, too busy.'"[79] She had her first secret, platonic romance with a woman in college, but they avoided being seen together in public.

Borders began dating women during her minor league days but did so secretly. "When I dated in the off-season, I would avoid being seen in public twice with the same person. I would say, 'I cannot hold your hand in public, you cannot go to special events with me, and if we go out to a banquet, you cannot sit with me.'"[80]

The fear of being outed—especially given all the media attention she received as a woman trying to make it in men's baseball—put extra pressure on Borders. The psychological toll, as well as the very low pay, hampered her performance on the field. Like other gay athletes, Borders found it emotionally exhausting to live a double life: "It's why I quit. It's the worst thing on Earth to hide who you are. . . . I remain certain that my professional career would not have been possible had I come out," she wrote in her autobiography. Even so, in retrospect she realized that her greatest regret about her baseball career "wasn't not making it into Organized Baseball; it was living the Great Lie of who I was."[81]

After retiring from pro baseball, Borders, who had finished her college degree during the off-season, worked as a firefighter and emergency medical technician in California, Arizona, and Oregon. Her college and professional baseball gear are on display at the Baseball Hall of Fame in Cooperstown.

In 2005, Borders met Shannon Chesnos, "my soul mate," and they moved in together the following year, intending to get married. Borders hit bottom in 2007 when Shannon was killed by a drunk driver. But when she told her colleagues at the Gilbert, Arizona, fire department that she was depressed because she had just lost her fiancée in a head-on collision, "I dared not mention her gender. Arizona is not an anti-discrimination state, and I could be let go for no cause."[82] She contemplated suicide but came through the ordeal because of her Christian faith. She began to date again. When she eventually decided to come out to her fire department colleagues, it "made barely a ripple. Were times changing or just me?"[83]

In 2016, Borders married Jenni Westphal, a shoe designer for Nike. They later divorced. She came out publicly in 2017 when she published her memoir. Borders frequently does clinics and coaches young women and men. During the 2021 All-Star Week in Denver, she participated in a pitching clinic for MLB.

Following in Borders' Footsteps

In the past two decades, a small but growing number of women have played on all-men's teams at the high school and college levels.[84] In 2021, at least six women played baseball on otherwise all-men's college teams.[85]

Borders is one of several women who have played for all-male professional baseball teams.[86] In 2009, Eri Yoshida, a seventeen-year-old knuckleball-throwing pitcher, played for a professional team in the Japanese minor leagues in a country where the glass ceiling for women is more elusive. Yoshida taught herself to throw the knuckleball from a book after watching knuckleballer Tim Wakefield on TV when she was fourteen. "I could tell Wakefield's pitches were very slow and they struck out a lot," she recalled. "That's when I started to get interested in the knuckleball. I didn't know whether or not I could do it, but I just wanted to try it."[87] Her success in high school earned her the nickname "Knuckle Princess." In 2010, Yoshida signed a contract and pitched for the Chico Outlaws, a team in the independent Golden Baseball League, and was traded the following season to a team in the same league based in Hawaii. In her three years playing in the minor leagues in the United States, she compiled a 5–10 win-loss record and a 7.62 ERA. Yoshida played five more seasons of pro baseball in Japan.

In 2016, the Sonoma Stompers, in the independent league, the Pacific Association of Professional Baseball Clubs, signed two women who had won gold medals playing for the US Women's National Baseball Team in the 2015 Pan American Games. One was twenty-six-year-old Stacy Piagno, a five-foot-nine, right-handed pitcher and infielder, who played softball at the

University of Tampa. In two years, she compiled a 1–2 win-loss record and a 6.33 ERA. The other was seventeen-year-old outfielder-pitcher Kelsie Whitmore, who had just graduated from high school and was headed for California State University-Fullerton on a softball scholarship. Over two seasons she batted .077, striking out seventeen times in twenty-six at bats. She pitched in two games and was 0–1, with a 21.00 ERA.

Most women who play baseball or softball, whether amateur or professional, now do so in all-women leagues. As the number of women participating in softball and baseball teams at the college, semipro, and professional levels have grown in the past two decades, the number of out-of-the-closet lesbians has increased as well, like their counterparts in other sports. Local amateur softball leagues are often a gathering place for lesbians. Most straight women on those teams recognize but don't mind the stereotype, while others try to distance themselves from it. "Softball being a euphemism for homosexual is pretty funny," said Rosalyn Bugg, an official in a Los Angeles women's softball league. "But not so funny to a lot of the women I play with who are not homosexual."[88]

In 2010, President Barack Obama nominated Elena Kagan, the solicitor general and former dean of the Harvard Law School, to serve on the Supreme Court. The *New York Post* ran a seventeen-year-old black and white photograph of Kagan smiling and getting ready to swing a bat in a softball game under the headline, "Does This Photo Suggest High Court Nominee Elena Kagan Is a Lesbian?"[89] Other news outlets quickly raised the same question, stirring a controversy over Kagan's sexuality, which was no doubt what those opposed to Kagan's nomination intended.[90] The controversy reflected both the persistent stigma against lesbianism and the persistent stereotype that links women athletes—and particularly baseball and softball players—to lesbianism.

Zoe Donaldson's story reveals that for many women the link between lesbianism and baseball is no longer as big a stigma. In fact, it can be a badge of pride. Donaldson, a first-rate athlete from middle school through college, participated in volleyball, field hockey, lacrosse, and softball. Her first love was softball, but in seventh grade she abandoned the sport. In 2019, at thirty years old, she acknowledged, "I feared softball would out me before I even knew what that meant." She explained, "What ridicule would I face when I threw harder and faster than my male peers?"[91]

Eventually her girlfriend goaded her into joining a women's softball team.

I was also ready to witness various cross-sections of queer life. I didn't know this, but the league is a smorgasbord of LGBTQ experiences. While not exclusively for queer women, many participants identify as such—and we cover various points on a beautiful scatterplot: We're old and young, white, Latinx, and Black, teachers and lawyers and public servants, parents and spouses, veteran athletes and total newbies, born-and-bred New Yorkers and transplants. The fulfilling, possibly happy queer future I couldn't dream of as a kid? I now find proof of it every single week when I run onto a dusty field.[92]

Some baseball fans hope that, just as Jackie Robinson broke the color line in 1947, a female athlete will someday break MLB's gender line. The first women to play on an MLB team may have just been born. Or she may currently be playing in Little League, or have participated in MLB's Trailblazer training program for girls, or be one of the few girls playing on coed high school baseball teams. In addition, like several other countries (including Japan, Australia, and Canada) have already done, the United States may be able to support an all-women's professional baseball league, similar to all-women's professional leagues in basketball, tennis, and soccer.

Pam Postema and Women Umpires

Women have played other roles throughout baseball history, and in each case faced a variety of obstacles. Women umpired in semiprofessional games as early as 1905. Bernice Gera was the first woman to attend the Fort Lauderdale umpire training school and the first woman to umpire a professional game. She won a lengthy court battle with Major League Baseball and umpired her first pro game in the minor league New York-Penn league in June 1972 but soon resigned.

In 1975, after attending umpiring school, Christine Wren was hired to umpire in the Single-A minor leagues. She spent four years in the low minors, but Barney Deary—the administrator of the MLB Umpire Development Program—refused to promote her to Double-A. He explained, "For a girl, she's made of sturdy stuff. But you see, that's what we're worried about, whether she can take the physical punishment. You never hear the men complaining, because the pain is second nature, just part of the job. And I doubt very seriously any of the players tried to set her up to get hurt. If anything, I think they were more prone to protect her."[93] Realizing that such attitudes would likely impair her umpiring career, she quit.

Pam Postema had to apply three times to umpiring school in Florida before she was finally admitted. She graduated seventeenth in her class of one hundred students (and another thirty had dropped out), but she still had a difficult time finding a job. In 1977, she umpired her first pro game in the rookie Gulf Coast League, then spent the next thirteen years in the minors, including six years at the Triple-A level. During those years, she faced constant abuse from players, fans, and even other umpires beyond that which male umpires confront. In 1988 Baseball Commissioner Bart Giamatti offered her a contract to umpire at the major league level during spring training. Later that year, he invited her to umpire at the Hall of Fame Game in Cooperstown between the New York Yankees and the Atlanta Braves. She impressed major league managers in both instances. But instead of promoting her to the majors, MLB canceled her contract the next year, so she never got to umpire in the major leagues. Postema filed a federal sex-discrimination lawsuit, which was settled out of court. She brought the suit because, she said, "I believe I belong in the major leagues. If it weren't for the fact that I'm a woman, I would be there right now."[94]

After her umpiring career ended, she worked as a truck driver, factory worker, and welder and wrote a book about her experiences, *You've Gotta Have Balls to Make It in This League*, published in 1992. It took eighteen more years—until 2007—before another woman, Ria Cortesio, got to work as an umpire in a major league spring training game. In 2016, Emma Charlesworth-Seiler and Jen Pawol (who had been umpiring Division 1 college baseball for a decade) were hired by the Gulf Coast minor league, a rookie league. In 2018, Pawol umpired an exhibition game between the Detroit Tigers and Florida Southern University. Perry Barber, who began her professional umpire career in 1981, was still umpiring in 2021. She's umpired more than 6,300 games in her career at all levels, including major league spring training, and has also worked games in Japan, the Caribbean, and other countries.[95] As of 2021, at least eight women have umpired in professional baseball, but still no women have worked as major league umpires.[96]

Women Owners, Executives, Managers, and Coaches

In November 2020, the Miami Marlins announced that they had hired Kim Ng as the team's general manager, making her the first woman to become a

GM of a men's team in the history of major American sports, as well as the first female Asian American GM in MLB history. Born in 1968, Ng is the eldest of five daughters born to parents of Chinese descent. Her father, an accountant, died when she was eleven. Her mother was a banker. She was inspired by tennis greats Billie Jean King, who battled for equality for women, and Martina Navratilova, who changed the idea of what it looked like to be a female athlete.[97]

Ng played tennis and softball in high school in Ridgewood, New Jersey. At the University of Chicago, she played softball for four years, serving as team captain in her senior year. She wrote her senior thesis on the impact of Title IX and earned a BA in public policy in 1990. After college she worked as an intern with the Chicago White Sox and was hired full time in 1991, eventually being promoted to assistant director of baseball operations under then-GM Ron Schueler in 1995. Two years later she went to work for the American League as director of waivers and records, responsible for approving all transactions. In 1998, Brian Cashman, the New York Yankees' GM, recruited Ng to work as assistant GM. Only twenty-nine, she was the youngest person, and only the second women, to hold that position in MLB. In 2001, she joined the Dodgers as vice president and assistant GM, overseeing player development and scouting. After being interviewed but turned down for GM jobs with several other teams, in 2011 MLB hired her to be senior vice president of baseball operations, working for Joe Torre, the Hall of Fame manager who was then MLB's executive vice president for player operations.

"Women were always looked at as intruders into a supposedly man's sport," Torre told the New York Times after the Marlins announced Ng would be their next GM. "That change evolved over the years when they started opening the clubhouse to female writers, which obviously was the right thing to do. I came from a family with two sisters, and they were such loyal baseball fans. The female could know as much about the game as the male fan, that's for sure."[98]

Derek Jeter, the Hall of Fame infielder for the Yankees who became the Marlins' part owner and CEO in 2017, knew Ng when she worked for the Yankees. He took the initiative to hire her as the team's GM. (Jeter also hired Caroline O'Connor as the team's chief operating officer.) "I was not the kid that was always going to follow the rest of the group," Ng said at the news conference announcing her appointment. "That was not me. I was going to do my own thing and I didn't care what people said. I was just going to do it."[99]

In January 2021, Ng participated in the events celebrating the inauguration of President Joe Biden and Vice President Kamala Harris, the first woman and person of color to hold that office. Ng, NBA Hall of Famer Kareem Abdul-Jabbar, labor leader Dolores Huerta, and Brayden Harrington (a thirteen-year-old boy whom Biden bonded with during his campaign over their shared challenge of stuttering), recited portions of famous inaugural addresses from past presidents.

Ng stands on the shoulders of a handful of other women who have ascended into baseball's executive suites. Helene Hathaway Britton, who owned the St. Louis Cardinals from 1911 to 1916, was the first woman to own a professional baseball team. But Effa Manley, who owned the Negro League's Newark Bears with her husband Abe Manley from 1935 to 1948, was the most prominent woman in baseball for many years.[100] Born in 1897 in Philadelphia to a mixed-race mother and white father, she grew up in a predominantly Black neighborhood. After high school she moved to New York City. She was light-skinned enough to pass as white and she frequently did so in order to secure better jobs working in the millinery industry. But she lived her life as a member of the Black community. All four of her husbands were African Americans.

Manley met Abe, her second husband, at a World Series game in Yankee Stadium in 1932, and they married the following year. Already an activist, she continued her involvement after her marriage to Manley. In 1934, for example, she walked a picket line as part of a campaign called "Don't Buy Where You Can't Work" to pressure local white-owned businesses in New York City to hire Black employees. (One target of the protests, a department store located in Harlem, agreed to hire Black women as sales clerks.) Manley was active in the NAACP and hosted an antilynching rally at the Eagles' stadium, during which ushers wore "Stop Lynching" sashes.

By 1941, she was in charge of the Eagle's day-to-day operations, including marketing, finances, press interviews, schedules, hotel and travel plans, purchasing equipment, and negotiating player contracts. She also sought, with mixed success, to oversee the players' personal lives, including how to dress and what kind of people to avoid associating with. Like most other Negro League teams, the Eagles were never on solid financial footing, and things got harder after MLB teams began hiring Negro League players.

In 1946, when the Eagles had a 56–24 win-loss record, beat the Kansas City Monarchs for the Negro League championship, and had their best year in attendance (120,292), the Manleys' profit for the season was only $25,000. Negro League owners particularly resented how Dodgers owner Branch Rickey signed Jackie Robinson without compensating the Kansas City Monarchs. Manley fought hard to get the MLB teams to purchase, rather than steal, their players' contracts—a great irony that accepted the idea that players were "owned" by their teams and couldn't decide for themselves which team to play for. In 1947, the Cleveland Indians agreed to compensate Manley's Newark Eagles $15,000 to sign Larry Doby, the first African American in the American league. That set a precedent that other MLB teams followed reluctantly and sporadically. In 2006 Manley was the first woman elected to the Baseball Hall of Fame.

Like Manley, most of the woman who have owned MLB teams co-owned them with their husbands or inherited them from their husbands or parents. They included Grace Comiskey (Chicago White Sox, 1939–56), Dorothy Comiskey (Chicago White Sox, 1956–59), Louise Nippert (Cincinnati Reds, 1973–81), Jean Yawkey (Boston Red Sox, 1976–88), Joan Kroc (San Diego Padres, 1984–90), Jamie McCourt (Los Angeles Dodgers, 2004–2009), and Sue Burns (San Francisco Giants 2006–2009). The exceptions include Joan Whitney Payson (an original owner of the New York Mets from 1961 until her death in 1975), Marge Schott (who owned the Cincinnati Reds from 1984 to 1999), and Billie Jean King (who purchased a minority share of the Los Angeles Dodgers in 2018).

Margaret Donahue was probably the first woman in a top management capacity on a major league team. She was responsible for marketing (such as season tickets and reduced prices for children) for the Chicago Cubs between 1919 and 1958. Since the 1980s, many women have been hired as executives, and even GMs, for minor league teams, but few have climbed the ladder into the majors. Some women, however, have ascended to top management positions on major league teams. In 2020, women filled 29 percent of senior administrative positions—and 20 percent of vice president (executive vice president, senior vice president, and other vice president)—positions on MLB teams.

Most female executives work in communications, marketing, community relations, and finance. Few have dealt with player development or personnel, but there have been some exceptions. In 1988 the Boston Red Sox hired Elaine Weddington-Steward, who had a law degree from St. John's University, as its associate counsel and promoted her to assistant GM in 1990, becoming the first African American woman to hold an executive position in Major League Baseball. In 1991, Priscilla Oppenheimer became the first woman hired as a director of a Major League team's minor league operations.

In 2001, when Ng left her assistant GM position with the Yankees, the team replaced her with Jean Afterman. An attorney, Afterman caught the attention of Yankees owner George Steinbrenner and GM Cashman for her aggressive negotiating tactics on behalf of her clients, Japanese ballplayers, when she worked for a San Francisco-based sports management firm. Other executives have included Eve Rosenbaum (the Baltimore Orioles' director of baseball development) and Melissa Lambert (the Kansas City Royals' assistant director of behavioral science).

In January 2020, the San Francisco Giants hired Alyssa Nakken as an assistant coach, working for manager Gabe Kapler. In July, she coached first base during an exhibition game between the Giants and Oakland Athletics, becoming the first woman to coach on the field during a major league game. Nakken, a four-time Academic All American softball player (and lifetime .304 hitter) for Sacramento State University, earned her BS in 2012 and then received her master's degree in sport management from the University of San Francisco in 2015. She joined the Giants as an intern in 2014 and was quickly hired full time and given responsibility for the team's health and wellness initiatives. Her coaching responsibilities also included scouting opponents, analytics, and even throwing batting practice.

Other women have coached in all-male professional leagues. Baseball for All founder Justine Siegal, who earned an MA in sports studies and a PhD in sports and exercise psychology, was assistant coach for the Springfield College men's baseball team from 2008 to 2010. In 2009 she became the first female coach of a professional men's baseball team, when she served as first base coach for the Brockton Rox in the independent Canadian American Association of Professional Baseball. In 2011, at thirty-six, she threw batting practice for the Cleveland Indians during spring training and subsequently threw batting practice for several other MLB teams. In 2015, the Oakland Athletics hired Siegal for a two-week stint as a coach in its instructional league in Arizona, making her the first female coach employed by an MLB team. In May 2019, the Fukushima Hopes, a minor league team in Japan, hired Siegal as a coach.

In 2019 the Chicago Cubs named Rachel Folden as their lead hitting lab tech and fourth coach of their Arizona Rookie League team. Folden was a star hitter for Marshall University's women's softball team and then played professional baseball for the Chicago Bandits in the National Pro Fastpitch League. She founded Folden Fastpitch—a company that provides baseball and softball instruction based on biomechanics, technology, and data—and worked as a hitting consultant for Elite Baseball Training, run by Justin Stone, a seasoned batting instructor. When the Cubs hired Stone as their top hitting instructor, he asked Folden to work for him. "If (Folden) were a guy . . . she would already be a big-league hitting coach. That's how good she is," said Stone, unwittingly exposing the persistence of stereotypes and discrimination.[101]

The Yankees recruited Rachel Balkovec (who has two master's degrees in the science of human movement) as a minor league hitting coach. The Brewers promoted Sarah Goodrum as its minor league hitting coordinator. The Cardinals hired Christina Whitlock as a minor league coach. In 2019, the Oakland Athletics hired Veronica Alvarez—a star catcher for the Villanova University women's softball team who also played for the United States Women's National Baseball Team, which won a gold medal at the 2015 Pan American Games—as a coach during spring training.

In December 2020, Bianca Smith became the first Black woman to coach in professional baseball. She originally thought she wanted to work as a baseball executive but later decided she preferred working on the field. In high school in Dallas, she played softball and was a cocaptain in her senior year. At Dartmouth College, Smith played on the women's softball team and was also the only woman on the college's club baseball team. After graduating in 2012 with a sociology degree, she earned an MBA in sports management and a JD with an emphasis in sports law at Cleveland's Case Western Reserve University, with a goal of becoming a GM in Major League Baseball. She served as the university's director of baseball operations. According to a profile in the *New York Times*, "Smith didn't miss a practice or game. She pitched to players at batting practice, scheduled team travel and meals, helped coach circuit training, watched videos of hitters and sent [coach Matt] Englander her critiques."[102]

Smith interned with the Texas Rangers in 2017 and with the baseball commissioner's office in 2018. During that year's winter meetings, she participated in MLB's Take the Field program, designed to bring more women into jobs in baseball operations. In 2019 she did another internship with the Cincinnati Reds and decided that her passion was for coaching, not the front office. Reds manager David Bell encouraged her. At practices, she warmed up the players and, on game days, analyzed hitters' swing decisions. In August 2019 Carroll University in Wisconsin hired her as assistant athletic director for compliance and administration as well as assistant baseball coach and hitting coordinator. Molly Harris, the Boston Red Sox executive responsible for identifying diverse candidates for executive and on-field management jobs, heard about Smith and recommended her to the team's brass. Her first assignment was to work with the Sox's minor league position players at the team's facility in Fort Myers, Florida.

In 2015 the Seattle Mariners hired Amanda Hopkins as the first full-time woman scout since the 1950s. She had been captain of her Central Washington University softball team during her junior and senior years, then spent three summers interning for the Mariners.

Jennie Finch grew up in the same town as and became friends with women's baseball icon Ila Borders, who was five years older and a role model. Finch went on to become one of the greatest softball players in history—a college All-American at the University of Arizona, a gold medal winner at the 2004 Olympics, and a silver medal winner four years later. *Time* magazine described her as the most famous softball player in history. In 2011, ESPN hired her as a color commentator for women's professional and college softball games. For one day in May 2016, Finch was guest manager for the Atlanta League's Bridgeport Bluefish, thus becoming the first woman to manage a professional baseball team. (The Bluefish won the game.)

Women Baseball Writers and Broadcasters

Until the 1970s, there were few female reporters or editors in the nation's news media, particularly its largest and most prestigious newspapers and TV networks. The handful of women reporters were typically consigned to write about fashion, cooking, gossip, religion, women's clubs, and other so-called women's concerns. The rise of modern feminism helped integrate newsrooms and broaden the kinds of assignments they were given, but even today there is a significant gender gap in American journalism in the number of women and their ascendency to top management jobs. Despite serious barriers, women have been gaining influence in mainstream print and broadcast journalism, but sports journalism has lagged behind in opening opportunities for women.[103] Throughout the twentieth and early twenty-first centuries, the sports beat, especially baseball, was particularly off-limits to women. But there were exceptions, journalists who overcame enormous obstacles and eventually opened doors for more women in the press box and broadcast booth. Since the 1970s, women have made significant progress gaining access to what were once overwhelmingly male occupations, including baseball writing. Even so, in 2017 men composed 90 percent of sports editors, 83 percent of sports columnists, and 88 percent of sports reporters.

In 1890, Ella Black sent stories about baseball for *Sporting Life* from her home in Pittsburgh, a city with a strong labor movement and a robust baseball culture. She was sympathetic to the Players League, which challenged the American Association and the National League. Her columns revealed her deep knowledge of the game, but the editors insisted on topping stories with headlines that focused on her gender, such as "The Base Ball Situation Considered and Commented Upon from a Female Standpoint."[104] Her male colleagues made certain that she didn't have as much direct access to players, managers, and executives. She nevertheless filed stories filled with fascinating insights and details, drawn from close observation and from informal conservations with fans and by eavesdropping.

In the early 1900s, Ina Eloise Young covered baseball for the *Trinidad Chronicle-News* in Colorado, a baseball-crazy mining town; for *Baseball Magazine*, a national publication based in Boston; and for the *Fort Worth Record* and *Denver Post*. She mostly wrote about local semipro teams for the *Chronicle-News*, but she had wider horizons. Although it was a small paper and a town without a major league team, she was allowed to cover the 1908 World Series between the Chicago Cubs and Detroit Tigers. Her articles for *Baseball Magazine* were mostly human-interest stories, including glimpses into players' lives. Her colleagues on the bigger papers respected her sufficiently to elect her as an honorary member of the Sporting Writers Association.

The Depression and World War II opened up more opportunities for women baseball writers. One was Jeane Hoffman, who began her career in 1937 covering Pacific Coast League games for the *Hollywood Citizen-News* and was the first woman permitted to sit in the press box at Los Angeles' Wrigley Field, home of the Triple-A Los Angeles Angels. She later covered Major League Baseball for the *Philadelphia Evening Bulletin* and the *New York Journal-American*. But she faced demeaning treatment from some male colleagues, including one who described her in his own column as a "tall willowy blond" whose "favorite athletes are ball players, and she believes they make excellent husbands."[105] In 1938, after *Time* magazine's sports reporter unexpectedly resigned, the publication promoted thirty-nine-year-old Pearl Kroll from researcher to sports editor. In 1941 she traveled to Florida to cover spring training, but her male colleagues barred her from the press box; she even had to pay for her tickets to the games. Mary Garber began her forty-two-year career as a sportswriter in 1944 covering the popular Winston-Salem minor league team for the *Sentinel* in North Carolina. For much of her career she was barred from membership in the sportswriters' association. It wasn't until her thirty-first year as a baseball writer that she was allowed into locker rooms to interview players, a custom male writers took for granted. She persisted in her career because, she explained, sports people are "fascinating" and "sportswriting was loads of fun."[106]

From the 1920s through the 1950s, newspapers catering to Black readers hired several women to cover Negro League baseball, including Marion Foster Downer of the *Chicago Defender*, Nell Dodson of the *Baltimore Afro-American*, and Willa Harmon of the *Kansas City Call*, who was promoted to sports editor.

In 1957, when *Cleveland News* assigned Dorothy O'Donnell to cover the Indians, major league press boxes still posted signs saying, "No Women or Children." Eventually, the writers in several major league cities allowed her into the press box. But throughout her career she had to overcome obstacles, such as being denied access to locker rooms and facing sexual advances and insults from other writers.

Canadian Alison Gordon became the first female baseball beat writer when she began covering the Toronto Blue Jays for the *Toronto Star* in 1979. Some players weren't pleased having a women reporter covering the team. Outfielder Barry Bonnell, a devout Mormon who played for the Jays from 1980 to 1983, protested against having women in the clubhouse on religious grounds. Star outfielder George Bell simply believed that the locker room should be restricted to men.[107] Gordon faced sexist insults while simply trying to do her job. As she recalled in *Foul Balls*, her memoir of her days covering the team, during her first few weeks on the beat a Blue Jays pitcher offered her $200 for sex to settle a bet. A male baseball writer told her that a requirement for the job was being able to "piss in a urinal."[108]

In 1977, while covering the World Series for *Sports Illustrated*, Melissa Ludtke was barred from the Yankees locker room. Ludtke and the magazine filed suit against MLB, charging sexual discrimination. Federal judge Constance Baker ruled in Ludtke's favor, telling the Yankees to figure out another way to protect players' privacy. She suggested that they wear towels. The Yankees' intemperate response was to limit reporters to only ten minutes to interview players in the locker room, then requiring them to leave for half an hour so the athletes could take showers. Some male reporters were upset with Ludtke for starting the controversy leading to their reduced access, but Ludtke recalled that for many of them, "It really opened their eyes to what we'd [women reporters] been dealing with."[109] After Ludtke and her employer went back to court, Commissioner Bowie Kuhn announced a cowardly, wishy-washy policy of allowing each team to set up their own rules with regard to locker room access.

The issue of equal access still wasn't resolved when Claire Smith started covering baseball for the *Hartford Courant* in the 1980s. She was still one of a handful of women covering baseball for major publications. Like her predecessors, some teams refused to let her into the clubhouse to conduct post-game interviews, a privilege granted to all male reporters. After the first game of the 1984 World Series between the Padres and Tigers, security personnel threw Smith out of the Padres' locker room while some players swore at her. While she stood outside, wondering how she'd file her story, Padres star Steve Garvey came out and told her, "You've got a job to do. I'll stand here until you have whatever you need." (That incident is recounted in a 2013 ESPN documentary, *Let Them Wear Towels*, about the battles that female sports writers have had to endure.) The next season, Commissioner Peter Uebuerroth changed the rules, requiring all teams to give women reporters full and equal access.

Smith persevered, becoming a well-regarded baseball writer for the *New York Times* and ESPN. In 2017, she became the first woman, and the fourth African American, voted into the writers' wing of the Baseball Hall of Fame. She received the J. G. Taylor Spink Award, presented annually since 1962 for meritorious contributions to baseball writing. In 2012, the Baseball Writers Association of America elected its first female president, Susan Slusser, a reporter for the *San Francisco Chronicle*, a sign that the number of women covering baseball for major papers and websites had increased considerably, as had the respect given women writers by players, managers, and male journalists. In 1987, four women sports writers founded the Association for Women in Sports Media, with the slogan "We Are AWSM." Sixty women showed up at its first convention the following year. By 2019 it had more than a thousand members.

Red Barber, the Hall of Fame broadcaster, once claimed that "the feminine voice just doesn't connote what people expect in the broadcasting of sports events."[110] But that taboo was broken in 1971, when KSFO, which broadcast the San Francisco Giants games, hired Wendie Regalia as the first women to conduct interviews and provide commentary before games and in-between doubleheaders. She wasn't permitted to do the play-by-play and quit after a year to become an agent for professional football players, but other women eventually filled the more prestigious positions. In 1990, CBS Sports' Lesley Visser became the first woman to cover the World Series, serving as their lead field reporter, and covered subsequent World Series for CBS and ABC through 1995. In 1993, Gayle Gardner became the first woman play-by-play announcer on a telecast for a major league team when she called a Rockies-Reds game. It took another twenty-five years for another woman, Jenny Cavnar, to join the play-by-play ranks in the majors, when she called a Rockies-Padres game in 2018. In 2005, the New York Yankees hired Suzyn Waldman as the team's regular play-by-play radio announcer. Four years later, she became the first woman to work a World Series game from the broadcast booth. Jessica Mendoza was an All-American outfielder for Stanford University's women's softball team, a member of the US women's national softball team from 2004 to 2010, winning a gold medal at the 2004 Olympics in Athens and a silver medal at the 2008 Olympics in Beijing, and 2011 Player of the Year in National Pro Fastpitch. In 2016 she joined ESPN's Sunday Night Baseball broadcast team, doing color commentary.

On July 20, 2021, five women served as the on-air crew for the Baltimore Orioles game against the Tampa Bay Rays in Florida. Melanie Newman, the Orioles' regular play-by-play announcer, called the balls and strikes, with Sarah Langs providing the color commentary. Alanna Rizzo handled the on-field reporting and Heidi Watney and Lauren Gardner anchored the pre- and postgame shows. This was the first time that an all-woman team broadcast a major league game.[111]

CHAPTER SEVEN

Gay Men in Baseball

I n his 1990 autobiography, *Behind the Mask: My Double Life in Baseball*, Dave Pallone—a gay major league umpire who was quietly fired in 1988 after rumors about his sexual orientation circulated in the baseball world—claimed there were enough gay major league players to create an All-Star team.

It's been three decades since Peter Lefcourt published his 1992 novel, *The Dreyfus Affairs: A Love Story*, about major league shortstop Randy Dreyfus, a married father of two who falls in love with his second baseman in the middle of a pennant race. In 2021 Universal Television optioned the novel for a TV series to be directed and cowritten by Oscar- and Emmy-winner David Frankel (*The Devil Wears Prada, Marley & Me*).

In 2003, Richard Greenberg's *Take Me Out*, which tells the story of a celebrated New York City baseball hero who announces that he's gay, won the Tony award for best Broadway play. In 2021, Broadway's Second Stage Theater announced that it was staging a revival, directed by Scott Ellis, the following year.

Since Pallone wrote his book, Lefcourt penned his novel, and Greenberg wrote his play, attitudes and laws about homosexuality have changed. High profile figures, including athletes, have come out of the closet. But major league baseball still awaits its gay Jackie Robinson.[1] Since major league baseball began in 1871, over twenty thousand men have played the game, but no gay player has ever publicly acknowledged his homosexuality while still in uniform.

Sports and the Gay Rights Movement

The gay rights movement has influenced every aspect of American society, including sports. Gay men started the first gay rights organization, the Mattachine Society, in 1950 at a time when homosexuality was considered a mental illness and gay people were routinely discriminated against in employment, housing, and other aspects of everyday life. Police routinely arrested homosexuals—at bars and other meeting places, including private homes—for the simple fact of being gay. In 1953 President Dwight Eisenhower barred homosexuals from all federal employment, including the military, on the grounds that they were susceptible to blackmail by communists. Neither the Mattachine Society nor its lesbian counterpart, Daughters of Bilitis, formed in 1955, were visible to the general public. But these organizations nurtured a generation of activists who laid the groundwork for the later gay rights movement. A milestone occurred on June 28, 1969, when patrons of the Stonewall Inn, a gay bar in New York City, defiantly resisted efforts by police to arrest them when they raided the bar. The "Stonewall riot" was the opening act of the modern gay rights movement, which challenged stereotypes, battled discrimination, and urged gay people to come out of the closet.

As the movement burgeoned in the 1970s, public opinion and public policy began to shift. As activism accelerated, attitudes changed. Public support grew for allowing openly gay teachers in public schools, health benefits for gay partners, gay couples to adopt children and marry, ending antisodomy laws, outlawing job and housing discrimination, funding research to combat AIDS, and imposing penalties on people who commit hate crimes against gays and lesbians. In 1973 the American Psychiatric Association removed homosexuality from its list of mental disorders.

More public figures—politicians, entertainers, teachers, judges, journalists, businesspersons, athletes, and clergy—publicly acknowledged their homosexuality. In 1997, comedian Ellen DeGeneres came out as a lesbian on the cover of *Time* magazine. In 2014, Apple's Tim Cook became the first gay CEO of a Fortune 500 corporation to come out of the closet. In 2002, the *New York Times* began including gay couples in wedding announcements, and other papers followed its lead. Since the 1970s, the number of films, plays, and TV shows with openly gay characters has grown dramatically. In 2015, the Boy Scouts of America removed its national restriction on gay leaders and employees.

In 2003, in the case of *Lawrence v. Texas*, the US Supreme Court decriminalized same-sex sexual relations. In 2010, President Barack Obama signed legislation ending the seventeen-year "don't ask, don't tell" policy so that homosexuals could serve openly in the US military. In 2013, in *United States v. Windsor*, the US Supreme Court ruled that states cannot prohibit same-sex marriage.

Between 1991 and 2019, the number of openly gay elected officials increased from 49 to 728.[2] When Representative Gerry Studds of Massachusetts came out of the closet in 1983, he was the first member of Congress to do so. In 2012, Representative Tammy Baldwin of Wisconsin became the first openly gay person elected to the US Senate. By 2021, there were nine LGBTQ members of the US House and two in the Senate.[3] LBGTQ Americans have served as mayors and city council members, school board members, district attorneys, and state legislators as well as two governors, Jared Polis of Colorado and Kate Brown of Oregon.

Americans have become more open-minded about LGBTQ rights. The proportion of Americans who said they knew somebody who was gay or lesbian increased from 61 percent in 1993 to 87 percent in 2013. Between 1993 and 2008, the proportion of Americans who believed that gays should be allowed to openly serve in the military grew from 44 percent to 75 percent. The proportion of Americans who believed that same-sex marriage should be legalized increased from 27 percent in 1996 to 67 percent in 2018, with 83 percent of Americans age eighteen to twenty-nine, compared with 47 percent of Americans over sixty-five years of age, in support.[4] One consequence of changing attitudes and laws is that LGBTQ athletes have become increasingly visible. Since 1999 a website called *OutSports* has been identifying LGBTQ athletes and chronicling the dramatic increase in out-of-the-closet sports figures.

It has been easier for athletes in individual sports—like tennis stars Billie Jean King and Martina Navratilova, diver Greg Louganis, and figure skater Adam Rippon—to come out of the closet than it has been for players on team sports. In team sports, gay women have been more likely than men to assert their sexual orientation publicly. Many athletes in women's professional basketball, softball, and soccer have come out of the closet. When the US women's national soccer team won the World Cup championship in July 2019, Megan Rapinoe—a charismatic thirty-four-year-old midfielder—became the public face of women's soccer and perhaps the most well-known athlete, gay or straight, in the world. "You can't win a championship without gays on your team. It's never been done before, ever," she told the media.[5]

At least 185 publicly out gay, lesbian, bisexual, transgender, queer, and nonbinary athletes participated in the 2021 summer Olympic Games in Tokyo, more than triple the number in the 2016 Rio games and more than all the out-of-the-closet LGBTQ athletes who have participated in all of the previous summer Olympic Games combined, according to *OutSports* magazine. Gay women outnumbered men by a 9–1 margin. *OutSports* identified eight women's softball players—four from the United States—as lesbians, but did not include any gay men among the rosters of Olympic baseball teams.[6] According to conventional wisdom and stereotypes, a gay male teammate would threaten the macho camaraderie that involves constant butt-slapping and the close physical proximity of the locker room.

Only fourteen players in major professional team sports—eleven of them former NFL players—have come out as gay or bisexual after their careers were over. Dave Kopay, who hid his homosexuality while playing as an NFL running back for nine years in the 1960s and 1970s, came out in 1975. He was the first former athlete in a major team sport to do so. Roy Simmons, an offensive guard for the Giants and the Redskins from 1979 to 1983, revealed his sexual orientation during an appearance on *The Phil Donahue Show* in 1992. Esera Tuaolo, a 280-pound defensive lineman who played nine years in the NFL, came out in 2002, three years after he retired. Revealing his secret on HBO's *Real Sports* and in *ESPN Magazine*, he acknowledged that while playing in the NFL he lived with his partner, with whom he later adopted children, but felt compelled to keep it a secret. His teammates routinely told gay jokes in the locker room. Other NFLers who came out included Wade Davis (in 2012), Kwame Harris and Dorien Bryant (2013), Ryan O'Callaghan (2017), Jeff Rohrer (2018), Ryan Russell (2019), Martin Jenkins (2020), and Colton Underwood (2021). Two former NFL players, Jerry Smith and Ray McDonald, kept their homosexuality a secret until others outed them after they died of AIDS.[7]

John Amaechi—who played for the Cleveland Cavaliers, Orlando Magic, and Utah Jazz between 1995 and 2003—became the first former NBA player to come out publicly, doing so in his memoir *Man in the Middle*, published in 2007. Two former major league baseball players—Glenn Burke (1982) and Billy Bean (1999)—came out after they'd hung up their spikes. Among athletes in America's major male team sports—the NFL, NBA, NHL, MLS, and MLB—only five have come out of the closet while still actively playing.

In February 2013, Robbie Rogers, an American professional soccer player then playing in England, posted a statement on social media announcing that he was gay. At that point in his life, the twenty-five-year-old Rogers considered quitting the sport but was persuaded by friends to keep playing. He joined the Los Angeles Galaxy, a Major League Soccer team, and became the first openly gay man to compete in one of America's five top male professional team sports leagues.[8]

Jason Collins, a thirteen-year veteran in the National Basketball Association, announced his homosexuality through a cover story in the May 6, 2013, issue of *Sports Illustrated*. He became a free agent and did not play again until February 2014, when he signed with the Brooklyn Nets. The following year, Michael Sam, an All-American football player for the University of Missouri, publicly came out of the closet before he was picked by the St. Louis Rams in the 2014 draft, making him the first publicly gay player to be drafted in the league. President Barack Obama congratulated Sam, the Rams, and the NFL, "For taking an important step forward today in our Nation's journey." He added, "From the playing field to the corporate boardroom, LGBT Americans prove every day that you should be judged by what you do and not who you are."[9] The Rams cut Sam before the regular season began, but the following year he played with the Montreal Alouettes, becoming the first publicly gay player in the Canadian Football League.

In 2021, two more athletes joined the list of out players in uniform. In June, Las Vegas Raiders defensive lineman Carl Nassib came out of the closet by posting a video to his Instagram account. "Sadly, I have agonized over this moment for the last 15 years," wrote Nassib, a five-year NFL veteran, noting that he was finally "comfortable getting it off my chest." He announced that he was donating $100,000 to The Trevor Project, a nonprofit group that focuses on suicide prevention efforts among LGBTQ youth.[10] Nassib's Raiders jersey quickly became the top seller in the NFL. When Nassib took the field on September 13 for the Raiders' first game after he came out, his teammates, opposing players, fans, and the media took it in stride. "I think the fact that it wasn't a distraction is a very positive sign," Richard Lapchick, director of the Institute for Diversity and Ethics in Sport, told the *New York Times*. "This is a sign of how much this has been accepted and that there was not a big fuss being made."[11]

A few weeks later, nineteen-year-old Luke Prokop, a third-round 2020 draft pick by the Nashville Predators, became the first player with a National Hockey League contract to publicly announce that he is gay. "From a young age I have dreamed of being an N.H.L. player," he wrote on Instagram, "and I believe that living my authentic life will allow me to bring my whole self to the rink and improve my chances of fulfilling my dreams," adding "I am no longer scared to hide who I am."[12]

Glenn Burke

Glenn Burke—who played for the Los Angeles Dodgers and Oakland Athletics between 1976 and 1979—was famous for two things. He invented the high five. On October 2, 1977, Burke ran onto the field to congratulate his Dodgers teammate Dusty Baker after Baker slugged his thirtieth home run in the last game of the regular season. As Baker jogged home from third base, Burke raised his hand over his head and Baker slapped it. It wasn't too long afterward that the gesture became widespread and known as the high five.

Burke was also the first major league baseball player to come out of the closet. Many of his teammates and club owners knew he was gay and he didn't try to hide it, but he didn't come out publicly until 1982, after his playing days were over. "They can't ever say now that a gay man can't play in the majors, because I'm a gay man and I made it."[13] After Burke retired from baseball, he continued to use the high five with other residents of San Francisco's Castro District, the heart of the gay community. It became a symbol of gay pride.

Burke came out publicly in an *Inside Sports* magazine profile called "The Double Life of a Gay Dodger" in 1982, two years after he left professional baseball. "It's harder to be gay in sports than anywhere else, except maybe president," Burke said in that article. "Baseball is probably the hardest sport of all."[14] That week he also appeared on NBC's *Today* show, interviewed by host Bryant Gumbel. He told more about his life in his autobiography, *Out at Home*, which was published a few weeks after he died of AIDS in 1995.

Burke grew up in Oakland, one of eight kids raised by a single mother. At Berkeley High School he was an outstanding baseball star, but his first love was basketball. In his senior year he was named Northern California's Basketball Player of the Year and led his team to a 32–0 record and the state championship.[15] At Merritt College in Oakland, he starred in both sports.

The Los Angeles Dodgers drafted him, and he signed a contract in June 1972. After four years in the minors, the Dodgers called him up to the major league club in 1976.[16] The Dodgers had high hopes for Burke. Coach Jim Gilliam said that given Burke's combination of strength and speed, he could be the next Willie Mays.[17]

"I never knew I was gay growing up," Burke wrote in his autobiography, *Out at Home*. "I didn't truly know I was a homosexual until I was twenty-three," just before the Dodgers brought him up from the minors.[18] Burke worried that his Dodger teammates and executives, as well as opposing players and sportswriters, would discover his homosexuality, At the same time, he didn't go to great lengths to hide it among his friends and family. Having grown up in Oakland, he had gay friends who lived in the Bay Area, including gay athletes. To celebrate his Dodger debut, his friends gave him a party at the Pendulum, a gay bar in the Castro, the center of San Francisco's gay community.

Playing in the majors, Burke lived what he described as a "double life." "When we were on the road, I would wait until my teammates were either in their rooms for the night or out on the town before heading out to gay bars and parties," he recalled. "I would anxiously flag down a taxicab while practically covering my head so no one would notice me. If someone did, I never acknowledged them."[19]

Burke was popular among his teammates. He kept the locker room loose with his loud music, dancing, and impression of comedian Richard Pryor. "No one would say anything to me. And I got used to the 'fag' jokes. You heard them everywhere then," Burke explained. "I knew who I was. I wasn't no sissy, I was a man. It just so happened that I lived in a different world."[20] Burke didn't come out to his teammates, but at least some of them figured out that he was gay, in part because he rarely went out drinking and partying with them after games.

"I'm sure he played in fear—the fear of the fact that it's going to get out that he's gay and once it comes out, you're going to take abuse," recalled Davey Lopes, one of his Dodger teammates, in 1994. "Face it, society isn't ready for that. If there are any gay players, even today, and you would think that there probably are, that's why they choose not to come out, because they know their careers are going to be ruined."[21]

Another one of Burke's Dodger teammates, Reggie Smith, remembered, "Homosexuality was taboo. I'm not going to sit here and say it was anything different. I'm sure it would have ruined his career. He would have not only been ostracized by his teammates, but management would have looked for ways to get him off the team, and the public would not have tolerated it."[22]

Burke's relationship with Dodgers manager Tommy Lasorda was strained by his friendship with Lasorda's openly gay son, Tommy Jr., who was a fixture of Los Angeles' gay scene, although his father denied that his son was gay.[23] Clearly the Dodgers' executives knew about Burke's homosexuality. According to Burke, Al Campanis, the team's general manager, once called Burke into his office before the start of the 1978 season and offered him a $75,000 bonus to get married. "I guess you mean to a woman," Burke responded, refusing the offer.[24]

Living a double life affected his on-the-field play. With his speed, strong throwing arm, and power, he showed flashes of brilliance, but he did not play up to early expectations and was used as a utility player to relieve the starting outfield stars Dusty Baker, Rick Monday, and Reggie Smith. In 1976 he appeared in twenty-five games and batted .239. The following year he appeared in eighty-three games and batted .254 with thirteen stolen bases and played in three games in the World Series against the Yankees. Two months into the 1978 season he had appeared in only sixteen games and was batting .211 when the Dodgers announced that they were trading Burke to the Oakland Athletics for Billy North, a onetime base-stealing whiz whose career was on a downhill arc and was batting .212 when the teams made the switch. Burke's teammates were upset by the trade, and suspected that it had more to do with his homosexuality than his hitting and fielding. "He was the life of the team, on the buses, in the clubhouse, everywhere," teammate Davey Lopes said the next day.[25]

Returning to his hometown of Oakland was a double-edged sword. He had many friends and family in the area, but it would become harder to hide his homosexuality. Herb Caen, a popular columnist for the *San Francisco Chronicle*, wrote a story that a local ballplayer was a frequent visitor to San Francisco's gay Castro district. He didn't mention Burke by name, but suspicions increased. When some fans in the bleachers began calling him "fag" when he was playing in the outfield, he knew his secret was out.

"He was absolutely a hero," said Jack McGowan, onetime sports editor of the *San Francisco Sentinel*, a gay newspaper. "It was not so much that he was masculine, but that he was superbly athletic, and we were proud because he showed the world that we could be gay and be gifted athletes."[26]

The Athletics made Burke their regular outfielder. In seventy-eight games he hit .235 with fifteen stolen bases. A pinched nerve in his neck kept him sidelined for most of the 1979 season. He refused to take cortisone shots to ease the pain so he could play. Instead, he left the team in midseason. At twenty-six, it appeared his major league career was over. "I probably wouldn't have left if there hadn't been the other problem, the gay thing," Burke said in the *Inside Sports* article in 1982 where he came out of the closet. "But put it all together, and it was too much."[27]

Nevertheless, he returned to the Athletics the next spring training. The A's had hired Billy Martin as their new manager. A's outfielder Claudell

Washington recalled a team meeting at which Martin introduced the new players to the veterans: "Then he got to Glenn and said, 'Oh, by the way, this is Glenn Burke and he's a faggot.'"[28]

The atmosphere on the A's was worse than with the Dodgers. Some teammates were uncomfortable around him and even avoided taking a shower while Burke was in the clubhouse. "I liked Glenn, but if I'd seen him walking around making it obvious, I wouldn't have had anything to do with him," A's outfielder Mitchell Page told *Inside Sports* in 1982. "I don't want to be labeled and have my career damaged. You make sure you point out that I'm not gay, okay?"[29]

"I roomed with him," A's pitcher Mike Norris told *Inside Sports*. "Sure, I was worried at first. You came back to your hotel room at midnight, sat around and listened to music, and you wondered if he'd make a move. After a while you realized he wouldn't, and it wasn't a big problem. Guys would watch out for him but it wasn't a completely uncomfortable feeling. If it had been out in the open, though, there would have been all kinds of problems. We're all macho, we're all men. Just make sure you put in there that I ain't gay, man."[30]

Burke suffered a knee injury during spring training and was assigned to the A's Triple-A team in Ogden, Utah. He got into only twenty-five games and batted .226. He retired for good at the end of the season. "I had finally gotten to the point," Burke told *Inside Sports*, "where it was more important to be myself than a baseball player."[31] Burke told the *New York Times* that "Prejudice drove me out of baseball sooner than I should have. But I wasn't changing."[32]

"Glenn was comfortable with who he was," said Burke's childhood friend Abdul-Jalili al-Hakim. "Baseball was not comfortable with who he was."[33] In his four seasons and 225 games in the majors, Burke had 523 at bats, batted .237, hit two home runs, and stole thirty-five bases.

Burke left pro baseball, but he remained an active athlete. Many considered him the greatest openly gay athlete in the country. He won medals in the one-hundred- and two-hundred-meter sprints in the first Gay Games in 1982. He was the star third baseman on a team in the San Francisco Gay Softball League and in 1982 led his team to winning the North American Amateur Athletic Gay Association World Series. He played basketball in the Gay Games in 1986. Berkeley High School retired his uniform number in his honor. He was a celebrity in San Francisco's gay community.

But he was often broke and depended on friends and hangers-on for money and emotional support. His life became consumed by sex, drugs, and parties. He became addicted to cocaine, which destroyed him physically and depleted what little money he had. His situation worsened after he was hit by a car in San Francisco in 1987, crushing his leg and foot, which destroyed his athletic ability, his major source of pride. In 1991, he pleaded guilty to grand theft and possession of a controlled substance. He served six months of a sixteen-month sentence in San Quentin prison. He was briefly jailed two more times for violating parole. He became so desperate that he resorted to panhandling to survive. He even pawned his 1977 National League Championship ring for cash.

Burke lost many of his friends to AIDS, and in 1994 he was diagnosed with the disease himself. He shrunk to 145 pounds, 75 pounds less than his playing weight in the majors. After the local media reported that he was broke, living on the streets, and had AIDS, friends pressured the A's organization to help him with food and medical care. He spent his final months living with his sister Lutha in Oakland. He died on May 30, 1995, at age forty-two. His autobiography *Out at Home* was published a few weeks later.

In 2013, Burke was one of the first class of inductees in the National Gay and Lesbian Sports Hall of Fame. In 2014, Major League Baseball honored Burke at the annual All-Star game. At a press conference before the game, Commissioner Bud Selig told Burke's sister Lutha, "We remember him to this day, and we want to tell his story." The following year, the Oakland Athletics honored Burke as part of Pride Night, inviting his brother Sydney to throw out the ceremonial first pitch.[34] In 2021, the A's announced that its annual Pride Night celebration would be known as Glenn Burke Pride Night.

Billy Bean

At the same 2014 All-Star game that honored Burke, Commissioner Bud Selig appointed former outfielder Billy Bean as MLB's first vice president for inclusion. In that new role, Bean was tasked with being baseball's link with the LGBTQ community, to encourage baseball teams to hire LGBTQ employees at all levels, and to provide education and training for ballplayers and team executives against sexism, homophobia, and other forms of prejudice.

Bean played for the Detroit Tigers, Los Angeles Dodgers, and San Diego Padres for parts of six seasons (1987–89 and 1993–95), hiding his homosexuality from his friends, fans, and teammates. In 1999, he became the second former major leaguer to come out of the closet. He told his story through interviews with the *Miami Herald*, the *New York Times*, and CBS TV's *60 Minutes*, then wrote a book, *Going the Other Way: Lessons from a Life In and Out of Major League Baseball*, published in 2003, describing the joys and anguish of being a closeted ball player.

"I wish that our game had someone in place to whom Billy and Glenn [Burke] could have turned when they played; a friend, listener, a source of support," Selig said when appointing Bean to the newly created position. "That's why I am so delighted to make this announcement today."[35]

Bean was born in 1964 in Santa Ana, California. His parents separated when he was six months old. His mother married a police officer, who raised Billy along with their five other children. He was an outstanding player in Little League. At thirteen, he won the state free throw shooting championship. At Santa Ana High School he played quarterback on the football team, point guard on the basketball team, and led the baseball team to the state championship in his senior year. He was also class valedictorian, with a 3.95 grade point average. He attended Loyola Marymount University in Los Angeles on an athletic scholarship. In 1985, after his junior year, the Yankees selected Bean in the twenty-fourth round of the draft, offering him a $55,000 signing bonus, but he kept his promise to his college coach to return for his senior year. He hit .355 with eight homers and sixty-eight runs batted in (RBI), was a second-team All-American selection, helped lead his team to the College World Series, and graduated with a degree in business administration.

The Detroit Tigers picked Bean in the fourth round of the 1986 draft, and he signed a contract the following April for a $12,000 bonus. He spent the 1986 season with the Toledo Mud Hens. He made his big league debut on April 24, 1987, three weeks before his twenty-fourth birthday. As the leadoff hitter in the Tigers' line-up against the Kansas City Royals, he got a double his first time at the plate and finished the game with four hits (another double and two singles) in six at bats, with two RBI and three runs scored—tying the major league record for most hits by a player in his first game. The next day he got two hits off Bret Saberhagen in four at bats. But after appearing in twenty-five games, he was sent back to Toledo.

Bean spent nine years in professional baseball, bouncing between the majors, minors, winter leagues, and Japanese leagues. His teammates and team executives admired his hustle and enthusiasm and his defensive skills in the outfield and at first base, but he wasn't fast or powerful enough to be a starting player. In six partial seasons in the big leagues with the Tigers,

Dodgers, and Padres, he played in 272 games, batted .226, and had five home runs. He spent most of the 1995 season with the Padres' Triple-A team in Las Vegas, batting .290. It appeared that Bean would soon be back in the majors, but he decided to retire after that season. He was only thirty-one. He felt he could no longer live the double life he was leading.

Bean suspected that he was gay in high school, which led him to try to appear even more heterosexual among his friends. During his high school and college years, Bean dated women, but, according to the *New York Times*, "He was nagged by the feeling that something was missing, that there was an emotional hole at the center of his life." His mother later described it as "a sadness in him I couldn't reach."[36]

The Tigers suggested that after the 1987 season he gain more experience by playing in the winter league in Venezuela, where he finished second to Cecil Fielder for the batting title. While in Venezuela, he felt sexual stirrings for men, which he sublimated with longer and harder workouts.

In July 1989, while playing for the Tigers' Toledo affiliate, Bean's agent called him with the news that he had been traded to the Los Angeles Dodgers. Without Bean's knowledge, the agent had already invested his client's money in an apartment building in Los Angeles. Bean moved into the building with his girlfriend, Anna Maria Amato, whom he had met at Loyola Marymount. The building turned out to be located in West Hollywood, the heart of LA's gay community. Amato signed them both up for membership at a local gym a few blocks from their apartment. The gay men at the gym constantly looked at and flirted with Bean. "I pretended I wasn't participating in these flirtatious games, rationalizing that I was just a 'straight' guy who just happened to be working out in a predominantly gay gym. As long as I didn't touch anyone else, I assured myself, I was still hetero." As Bean observed, "It took me quite some time to get the nerve up to check out the steam room, where I 'learned the definition of 'homoeroticism.'" He began to spend more time at the gym without Anna. [37]

Although still in denial, Bean took some tentative steps to acknowledge his homosexuality. During the 1989 season, when the Dodgers were playing in San Francisco, he took a cab to the Castro district but hid in the back seat. He was "amazed to find a place where men walked hand in hand." The next time the Dodgers visited San Francisco, he entered a bookstore, intending to look at the section on homosexuality. When a Dodger teammate walked into the store, Bean ducked into a video booth and waited for his fellow Dodger to leave. Bean wrote that he felt "wracked with shame" and without "the slightest idea how to reconcile my desires with my life inside or outside of the game. My emotional turmoil was obviously contributing to my inability to concentrate on the field. My self-confidence, the foundation of any player, was shot."[38]

Bean had to endure the homophobic jokes made by Dodgers manager Tommy Lasorda. Unlike Lasorda's dealings with Glenn Burke, the jokes weren't aimed at Bean since Lasorda was not aware of his sexual orientation. Despite his feelings, Bean felt pressure from his teammates to be "one of the boys." Bean married Anna in November 1989, hoping that it would help "fix" the "problem" of his attraction to men.[39] He often used the excuse that he was married to fend off the women, but occasionally, when the team was on the road, he would join teammates on dates with women—or parties in their hotel rooms—after games. "I played along," he recalled, even gaining a reputation as "one of the biggest lover boys."[40]

In 1991, after playing a game with Dodgers' Triple-A team in Albuquerque, Bean hailed a cab and asked the driver to take him to a "nice" gay bar. Nervous and shaking, Bean sat at the bar until a man approached him, engaged in brief conversation, and invited him back to his home. That night, Bean had his first sexual experience with a man.

Visiting gay bars and having sex soon became "a sporadic part of my post-game ritual," Bean recounted in his autobiography. He told his partners that he was in town on a business trip, using the name "Bobby." He never spent the night. He'd return to his hotel room and try to "get my head ready for the next day's game."[41]

In 1993, while playing for the San Diego Padres, Bean met a man with whom he quickly fell in love—Sam Madani, an Iranian whose family had fled their native country. Bean and his wife divorced. He and Madani purchased a house in Del Mar, near San Diego. He kept their relationship a secret from his family, friends, and teammates, as well as the media and fans. Madani rarely went to games to watch Bean play; when he did, he sat in the bleachers. In July 1993, when Bean hit his first major league home run, he didn't stay around to celebrate with his teammates in the clubhouse but hurried home, where Madani had prepared a special meal to honor the occasion. Two of Bean's best friends on the Padres, Brad Ausmus and Trevor Hoffman, wanted to celebrate with Bean, so they showed up, unannounced, at his house with six-packs of beer. Bean quickly hid the dinner plates in the kitchen, while Madani went out the back door into the garage, staying in his car for three hours. "My proudest individual accomplishment on a baseball diamond had turned into an occasion of sadness and shame," Bean recalled.[42]

Madani, who had been diagnosed as HIV-positive, died in 1995. (Bean tested negative.) Bean was unable to talk with anyone about the loss he had just suffered. He was even afraid to ask for personal time off to attend Madani's funeral. Later that year, while visiting Miami in-between Padres games, Bean met Efrain Veiga, who owned a restaurant there, and they began a long-distance relationship. He approached the Florida Marlins about joining its team, based in Miami, but they only offered a minor league contract. He decided to quit baseball and remained in Miami with Veiga. "I regret that I felt I had to walk away from playing to live the life that I'm most comfortable living," he later said.[43]

Later that year he visited his family in California and came out to his mother, stepfather, and siblings, who expressed their affection and acceptance. In 1999, still in the closet publicly, Bean was scheduled to do an interview with *Miami Herald* writer Lydia Martin about the new restaurant that he and Viega had opened. Martin asked Bean if she could report that he and Veiga were both professional and personal partners. He reluctantly agreed and thus became the second former major leaguer to acknowledge his homosexuality, and he did additional interviews with the *New York Times* and ABC's *20/20*.

Bean was pleased by the positive reaction from these stories, including from his former baseball friends.[44] Catcher Brad Ausmus said, "If Billy is happy being gay, then I'm happy for him."[45] But as news of Bean's disclosure became fodder for news stories, other players, including Chad Curtis and Andy Pettitte, said publicly that they would not be comfortable having a gay teammate.

Bean soon became a public figure for LGBTQ rights. He spoke at events sponsored by the Human Rights Campaign, the leading gay rights organization. He joined the board of the Gay and Lesbian Athletics Foundation. He became a spokesman for the Democratic National Committee. In his 2003 autobiography, he declared that "baseball is ready" for an active player to come out of the closet, but he also wrote that "there still isn't a single openly gay scout, front office exec, coach, or even umpire."[46]

When their restaurant failed, Bean and Viega opened a successful business redeveloping residential properties. Bean also did some acting on several TV shows, including *Frasier* and *Arliss*. In 2006 Bean joined the all-gay and lesbian panel of the Game Show Network's revival of *I've Got a Secret*. Ironically, he was only able to appear on the show because he no longer had a secret regarding his sexuality.

Bean always wanted to get back into baseball, so when Commissioner Bud Selig asked him to serve as MLB's first ambassador for inclusion in 2014, he jumped at the opportunity. As discussed in chapter 9, MLB has made significant progress in making the sport more welcoming for LGBTQ fans and staff. Bean and team executives, as well as players, believe that baseball is ready for openly gay players.

John Dillinger

John Dillinger spent thirteen years playing professional baseball, retired in 2005, but didn't come out publicly until 2012. Dillinger was aware of his attraction to males by the time he was ten, but he pushed it aside in order to concentrate on sports. "It really didn't bother me that much," Dillinger recalled. "I was so busy playing sports and I didn't have a whole lot of time to think about it."[47]

In high school in Connellsville, Pennsylvania, he was a star athlete and dated girls. In 1992, at eighteen, while attending junior college in Florida, he was drafted by the Pirates. He spent the next thirteen years bouncing around minor leagues and independent league teams throughout the country and Canada.

During his baseball career, Dillinger occasionally heard antigay slurs in locker rooms or at ballparks, which persuaded him to stay in the closet. "The scariest things are what you can't see or predict," he said. Afraid of exposing his sexuality, he never dated men or told his teammates. In fact, to avoid any suspicions, he partied with his teammates and dated women. "At one point I thought maybe I could get rid of it," he said about his same-sex attraction. "Being gay was a constant thought with me, but it just kind of stood there in a stalemate."[48]

After the 2005 season, at age thirty-two, realizing that his dream of playing in the majors wasn't going to happen, he retired from baseball. He didn't have his first sexual experience with a man until the following year, and the year after that he finally told his family that he was gay. He moved to Nashville, pursued a career as an account executive for a healthcare firm, and began his first long-term relationship with a man. Once he left baseball, he felt safe telling some of his friends and former teammates about his sexuality, but he didn't officially come out of the closet until 2012, inspired by Kevin McClatchy, a former Pittsburgh Pirates owner who came out that year through a story in the *New York Times*, five years after he'd left his position with the Pirates, Dillinger made the announcement through an article in *Outsports*.

Tyler Dunnington

Tyler Dunnington was a promising right-handed pitcher whose experience with homophobia in college and in the minors led him to quit the sport after only one year in the pro ranks in 2014. Dunnington played baseball at Shelton (Washington) High School, then at Skagit Valley College, College of Southern Idaho, and Colorado Mesa University. He was a twenty-eighth-round draft pick by the St. Louis Cardinals in 2014 and played that season for the team's minor league affiliates in the Gulf Coast League and New York-Pennsylvania League, garnering a 4–2 record and a 3.09 earned run average (ERA) with twenty-nine strikeouts in thirty-two innings. He quit before the next spring training without explaining why to his teammates or Cardinal officials.

More than a year later, in March 2016, Dunnington came out of the closet through an article in *Outsports*. He described being "one of the unfortunate closeted gay athletes who experienced years of homophobia in the sport I loved. I was able to take most of it with a grain of salt but towards the end of my career I could tell it was affecting my relationships with people, my performance, and my overall happiness."[49]

Dunnington wrote that one of his coaches at Colorado Mesa talked about Matthew Shepard, the twenty-one-year-old gay man who was tortured and killed in Wyoming in 1998. "We kill gay people in Wyoming," the coach said.[50] When he reached the minor leagues, Dunnington overheard one of his teammates mention that his brother was gay, and two other players asked him how he could possibly be friends with a gay person, even his brother. The two players then mentioned ways to kill gay people. Dunnington recalled that "each comment felt like a knife to my heart. I was miserable in a sport that used to give me life, and ultimately I decided I needed to hang up my cleats for my own sanity."[51]

Soon after the *Outsports* article appeared, the president of Colorado Mesa issued a statement promising to reach out to Dunnington, "learn more about the situation," and "use this situation to promote more education, awareness, and changed attitudes and behaviors." The college's investigation revealed that Sean McKinney, the assistant baseball coach, made the remark about Matthew Shepherd. He issued a statement and called Dunnington to apologize. The college pledged to create programs to "further deepen the acceptance of queer people at the university." John Mozeliak, the Cardinals general manager, issued a statement saying, "This is very disappointing and our hope is that every player, staff member and employee feels that they are treated equally and fairly. Given the nature of these allegations, I will certainly look into this further."[52]

Jason Burch

Jason Burch grew up in a Christian religious and military family in Nebraska and pitched for the University of Nebraska. From 2003 to 2008, he played for nine minor league teams affiliated with the St. Louis Cardinals and Colorado Rockies, compiling a 21–21 record and a 3.72 ERA.[53] He didn't publicly reveal his sexuality until 2015. While in the minors, he quietly dated men, typically meeting them through internet dating services. He wasn't a well-known star, so he could date men without revealing that he was a ballplayer.

He kept his sexuality a secret from his teammates until 2008. While playing for the Bowie (Maryland) Baysox, Burch was sitting in the bullpen with a teammate from Latin America, who asked him if he had a girlfriend to spend the upcoming break with. "I'm not interested in girls. I'm gay," Burch responded. "And I don't have a boyfriend."[54] Burch eventually told some of his other teammates, who supported him and kept his secret. But he had few close friends in baseball, due in part to the peripatetic nature of the sport.

Burch left baseball after the 2008 season. His public explanation was that he had sustained an injury, but he also was unhappy, feeling that baseball "seemed insular and isolated from the rest of the world. The lifestyle didn't change where you were." He went to Northwestern University Law School and pursued a career in law. He waited until 2015 to publicly reveal his sexuality, in an interview with *Outsports*. "Looking back, I wish I had told the whole world that I'm gay from day one," he said. He also acknowledged, "I miss pitching. . . . I miss that agonizing attempt to throw the pitch exactly where I want to throw it. I loved that."[55]

Coming Out in Uniform

The LGBTQ movement changed Americans' attitudes, with colleges and universities in the forefront. But as of 2021, only a few college baseball players have come out. None of them played on the top-tier Division I schools. Three gay professional ballplayers have come out, although none of them were of major league caliber.

Sean Conroy

On June 25, 2015, Sean Conroy pitched his first game for the Sonoma Stompers, a pro team in the independent Pacific Association, making him the first openly gay male player to appear in a professional baseball game.[56]

Conroy, who was born in 1992 and grew up in Clifton Park, New York, came out to friends and family at the age of sixteen. He didn't try to hide his sexuality with his baseball teammates in high school or college. "I always made friends first and then continued to be myself after I came out to them. It's like, 'OK, I was friends with them before, and then I came out, and nothing's changed.'"[57]

Conroy was an outstanding pitcher at Rensselaer Polytechnic Institute (RPI) in Troy, New York. At the Division III school, he had a 21–7 record over four seasons with a 2.05 ERA. He struck out 223 batters and walked only 49 in 259 innings. In his year senior, Conroy was named Liberty League Pitcher of the Year and was a second-team Division III All-American.

He recalled only one ugly moment during his college career, when an opposing batter said, "I can't believe that faggot struck me out."[58] Otherwise, his amateur career passed without incident.

Ben Lindberg and Sam Miller, one-time baseball writers who ran the Stompers' operations, signed Conroy as a result of his impressive statistics at RPI.[59] The Stompers, like the other Pacific Association teams, aren't affiliated with any major league team. Players in the league and other independent leagues, where competition is roughly equivalent to Single-A minor leagues, hope that if they perform well, major league scouts will notice them. To pursue that dream, they settle for extremely modest salaries—a few hundred dollars a month for a three-month season.

Lindberg and Miller didn't know that Conroy was gay when they signed him to a Stompers contract. When he arrived in Sonoma, in northern California wine country, he told his teammates, and eventually the team's owners and executives, about his sexuality. "It's kind of a respect thing," Conroy explained. "I told my teammates I was gay because as we were becoming friends, I didn't want to feel like I was hiding or have to lie when they start to comment on girls. If a teammate tells me about how he met a girl at a bar, I tell him about how I met this guy at a bar. I try to keep it one-to-one as much as possible."[60]

Although his teammates accepted Conroy's sexuality, it initially created an awkward climate in the clubhouse, where players typically tell jokes at each other's expense. "We understood that, you know, maybe making a gay joke or two could be taken the wrong way. Sean never did," explained Isaac Wenrich, a Stompers teammate.[61]

The team's irreverent owners embraced Conroy's sexuality. He agreed to come out publicly during the team's home field gay "pride" night and was given his first starting assignment for that game.[62] The team sent out press releases announcing Conroy's status as a baseball trailblazer, generating national media attention. "I didn't expect it to be a big deal," Conroy admitted. "After I found out from an MLB historian (John Thorn) that I was making history, then it kind of hit me."[63]

A few Stompers season ticket holders and host families boycotted the game. Some nasty comments appeared on Facebook. But overall, the team and the fans embraced Conroy's announcement. In front of a crowd of 478—a good turnout by Stompers' standards—most of Conroy's teammates took the field wearing rainbow socks in solidarity. Conroy pitched a complete game shutout, striking out eleven batters. He finished the season with a 5–3 record and a 2.70 ERA, while also earning ten saves. He struck out fifty-two hitters in sixty innings. During the 2016 season, Conroy went 4–2 with a 5.02 ERA, striking out forty batters in sixty innings.

Conroy hoped to play in the majors, but after two years with the Stompers, he left pro baseball. His eighty-plus-mile-an-hour fastball wasn't powerful enough to advance to a higher level of pro ball. But his June 2015 feat was recognized by the Baseball Hall of Fame, which put the scorecard from his first start in an exhibit marked "Today's Game."

David Denson

A month after Conroy took the mound for the Stompers, David Denson, a twenty-year-old first baseman for the Helena, Montana, team in the

Milwaukee Brewers' farm system, told his teammates that he was gay. A month later, in August 2015, he came out to the rest of the world through a story in the *Milwaukee Journal Sentinel*. Denson thus became the first openly gay active player on an MLB-affiliated team.[64]

Before revealing his secret to the team, Denson told his family. "It was harder on my dad than my mom. He's a very hard-core Christian and he goes off the Bible and all that, which I completely understand, growing up in the church. I'm a Christian myself."[65] Denson didn't know he was gay until he was eighteen. "When I was younger, I knew there were gay people. But I had seen so much hatred toward the community that I didn't really understand that's what I was going through as well," he recalled.[66]

Denson, who is African American, was a fifteenth-round draft pick out of South Hills High School in West Covina, California, a Los Angeles suburb, in 2013. Over the next three seasons, the Brewers shuffled Denson between their rookie league franchise in Phoenix, Arizona, and their Single-A team in Appleton, Wisconsin. He struggled on the field in both leagues. During spring training of 2015, his third year as a pro player, he suffered a serious bout of depression. "I wasn't being myself. It was visible in my body language. I didn't know if I should still stay in the sport," Denson recalled.[67]

He sought advice from a professional counselor that the Brewers had hired to provide mental health assistance to players. He concluded that he had to let the Brewers know he was gay or risk even more emotional and professional turmoil. He scheduled a meeting with the Brewers minor league director Reid Nichols, who was accompanied by the Appleton Timber Rattlers manager Matt Erickson and hitting coordinator Jeremy Reed. "I was shaking and crying, and just very scared," recalled Denson. "I didn't know if it would go good or bad, or if they'd look at me any different."[68]

Their response was accepting. "When I finally told them about my sexuality, Reid said, 'To me, it doesn't matter. You're still a ballplayer. My goal for you, as well as anybody else in the organization, is to get you to the big leagues. You are who you are. That doesn't make a difference. Just go out and play the game. This is a very brave thing for you to do.'"[69] "They said if there was anything they could do to help, let them know. It was a huge relief," Denson recalled.[70]

After spring training, the Brewers assigned Denson to their Single-A franchise in Wisconsin, where he continued to struggle. In midseason, they sent him to their minor league team in Helena, Montana, in the rookie Pioneer

League. Denson wanted to tell his teammates he was gay, but he didn't have a plan or a timetable. "It started to affect my game because I was so caught up in trying to hide it. I was so concerned about how they would feel. I was pushing my feelings aside. Finally, I came to terms with this is who I am and not everybody is going to accept it. Once you do that, it's a blessing in itself."[71]

In June, Denson entered the Helena Brewers' clubhouse when a teammate jokingly referred to him using a derogatory term for a gay man. Denson viewed the comment as locker room banter, not a direct assault on his own sexuality. He doubted that his teammate had any inkling that he was gay. But he seized the opportunity. "Be careful what you say. You never know," Denson cautioned the player with a smile.[72] Without any preparation, Denson told his teammate, and the other players in the vicinity, that he was gay. To his relief, his teammates were supportive.

"Talking with my teammates, they gave me the confidence I needed, coming out to them," recalled Denson. "They said, 'You're still our teammate. You're still our brother. . . . We've got your back.'"[73] "That was a giant relief for me," Denson said. "I never wanted to feel like I was forcing it on them. It just happened. The outcome was amazing. It was nice to know my teammates see me for who I am, not my sexuality."[74]

At Denson's request, his teammates kept his secret among themselves. But Denson felt he had to come out more publicly to relieve the emotional burden and to realize his full potential as both an individual and a ballplayer. Before he did so, he spoke with Bean and Conroy to understand what he'd be facing. Bean encouraged Denson to reach out to the *Milwaukee Journal Sentinel* and to prepare to tell his story. "The beauty of what could come from this is he can be an example that can help change that perception and change the stereotype that there would never be a gay person on a men's professional sports team," Bean told the *Sentinel Journal*.[75]

Brewers general manager Doug Melvin issued a statement supporting Denson: "David is a highly respected member of the Milwaukee Brewers family, and he is a very courageous young man. Our goal for David is to help develop him into a major-league player, just as it is for any player in our system, and we will continue to support him in every way as he chases that dream."[76] Asked if Denson would be accepted in the Brewers' clubhouse, manager Craig Counsell said, "I do. I hope it happens. He's a talented young man and hopefully that happens."[77]

"I think everybody is supportive," said Brewers' All-Star right fielder Ryan Braun, one of the few Jews in MLB. "Overall, we realize it's a courageous decision by him, to come out and embrace his true self. I've never met him, but I hope baseball as a whole is at a point where we judge people by their ability and not their race, religion, ethnicity, or sexuality. I can't speak for everybody on our team, but he would be accepted and supported by me. And I would hope all of my teammates feel the same way."[78]

Helena Brewers manager Tony Diggs said, "We are professional baseball players first, and I think that's the way they've [his teammates] taken it. . . . This is a new chapter as he decides to say it publicly. Now, there will be more people that know and they'll have their opinions as to what they feel about it. At least, he's being himself."[79] "It's a release for me to finally be able to give all of myself to the game, without having to be afraid or hide or worry about the next person who might find out," Denson said.[80]

Playing in the lower rungs of the Brewers' minor league system, Denson compiled a .229 batting average with twenty-nine home runs and 135 runs batted in 318 games—not the statistics likely to lead to the major leagues. During spring training of 2017—his fourth season in pro baseball—Denson announced (on his Facebook page) he was retiring from baseball. He said he wanted to pursue a career as a personal/athletic trainer. "Walking away from it is one of the hardest decisions I've had to make. But I had to do it for myself," Denson said. "I think I opened the door. I showed just because I'm gay doesn't make me any different or less of a person. If there are others who want to come out, hopefully they have my story to fall back on and see it's OK."[81]

Ryan Santana

Ryan Jordan Santana first realized he was attracted to men at fifteen but kept it secret. After starring for St. Mary's Catholic High School team in Phoenix, he played for Azusa Pacific University (APU), an evangelical Christian school outside Los Angeles, earning Player of the Week honors in the PacWest Conference his senior year. Playing at APU "was a tough spot for me because I do believe in God. It was challenging time for sure," especially since the school had a policy prohibiting gay relationships.[82] No major league team offered him a contract, so Santana moved to Adelaide, Australia, to play for the Golden Grove Dodgers, a professional team there.

All through high school and college, Santana was unable to say the words "I'm gay" out loud. "I lived a lie my whole life," he recalled. "I was always too afraid to even tell my teammates. I don't want to have to lie to them about this part of me anymore."[83] So in 2017, while playing in Australia, he agreed to come out of the closet as part of a TLC documentary series called *This Is Life* in April, at the start of the baseball season. "I feel like I struggled with it, and I know there are others struggling with their sexuality as well," Santana said. "And I feel like I don't want them to feel alone or by themselves. And I want to let them know they are not alone. I want to be some kind of outlet, a light."[84]

"I always felt . . . I couldn't come out and play baseball. I thought as soon as I came out, I'm done playing baseball. But it shouldn't be that way. They should be able to know that and judge me off of my athletic ability."[85] Once he came out, his teammates expressed their support. His roommate broke down in tears about the pain Santana must have been feeling. "It doesn't change anything between our friendship," he said.[86]

Soon after coming out, Santana returned to Phoenix, got involved in several LGBTQ projects, and joined a gay softball team that plays around the country. The Arizona Diamondbacks invited him to speak at a Pride Night event. Athletes who were still in the closet or had just come out contacted him through email and social media and thank him for being a role model. In an article for *Outsports*, Santana wrote, "It has been a crazy but amazing year. I am truly the happiest I have ever been in my life. Not having to hide this part of my life and just being able to live without second guessing what I do, say or wear is such a liberating feeling."[87]

Umpires: Dave Pallone and Dale Scott

Dave Pallone was a major league umpire between 1979 and 1988 and was in the closet the entire time. Dale Scott umped in the majors from 1986 to 2017 but came out of the closet in 2014, making him the first (and so far only) major league umpire to be openly gay and the first male game official in the four major sports to come out publicly while still officiating games.

Pallone began his umpiring career in the New York-Penn League in 1971. He gradually moved up the ranks, reaching the Triple-A International League in 1976. In 1979, at age twenty-seven, he was one of eight umpires hired during that year's strike by major league umpires. Being a strikebreaker didn't make him popular with other umpires or players, who had gone through their own strike in 1972 and would do so again in 1981, 1985, and 1994. After Cardinals catcher Ted Simmons, first baseman Keith Hernandez, and manager Ken Boyer insulted Pallone for being a strikebreaker (Simmons called him a "scab"), Pallone threw them out of the game. Pallone had a reputation for getting into confrontations with players and managers.

In January 1988, eight men were arrested in Saratoga Springs, New York, for participating in a sex ring with teenage boys. Five men were found guilty. Pallone was brought in for questioning and cleared of any involvement. But a story in the *New York Post* about the scandal mentioned Pallone, who was thus outed involuntarily. Nevertheless, National League President Bart Giamatti used the incident to justify firing Pallone at the end of the 1988 season. Pallone sued and settled out of court with MLB. He was fired, he wrote in his 1990 book, *Behind the Mask: My Double Life in Baseball,* because MLB "didn't want the publicity surrounding that to tarnish baseball's macho image."[88]

Pallone described his double life. He lied to fellow umpires and others, pretending to have girlfriends. "You lived in daily fear that you'd be found out," he said.[89] He began his first long-term relationship with a man in 1979, his first year umpiring in the majors. Three years later, his lover was killed by a drunk driver, but Pallone had to keep his grief secret. He eventually began dating again but always furtively. He and Keith Humble, a hospital financial analyst, began a relationship in 1996 that was still going strong in 2021.

Pallone contended that he knew gay major leaguers and was even sexually involved with a few of them. They sometimes discussed going public about their sexuality but, Pallone explained, the players "told me their biggest concerns were about losing money, mostly endorsements, and maybe they wouldn't have gotten the contract they should have gotten."[90] After his book was published, Pallone received tens of thousands of letters from people who expressed their support. He began a new career as an LGBTQ activist who does diversity training for corporations, colleges, universities, and athletes with the NCAA. Pallone was part of the first class of inductees to the National Gay and Lesbian Sports Hall of Fame in 2013.

Born in 1959, Dale Scott began umpiring at age fifteen, was hired to officiate in the minor leagues in 1981, and became a regular major league umpire in 1986, officiating until 2017. He came out of the closet in 2014, the first openly gay male official in professional baseball, football, basketball and hockey to come out while still working games.

Scott quietly revealed he was gay in a profile in *Referee Magazine*, a subscription-only publication with a 45,000 circulation. The article included a photo of Michael Rausch, his partner of twenty-eight years, whom he had dated since his first year in the big leagues and married in November 2013.[91] Scott said that MLB executives and his fellow umpires knew he was gay. In fact, when the umpires union signed its 2010 contract, Scott added Rausch as his domestic partner, which made his relationship official in the eyes of the league.

"The first 10 years of my Major League umpire career, I would have been horrified if a story had come out that I was gay," Scott said. "But guys unprovoked started to approach me and say, 'I just want you to know that I would walk on the field with you any day, you're a great guy, a great umpire and I couldn't care less about your personal life.' Basically what they were saying without me provoking it was 'I know and I don't care.' That meant a lot to me because it surprised me since I had not brought it up."[92]

"I am extremely grateful that Major League Baseball has always judged me on my work and nothing else," Scott said. "And that's the way it should be."[93] In 2015, he was inducted into the National Gay and Lesbian Hall of Fame. On April 14, 2017, he was struck in the mask and taken off the field with a concussion and whiplash. It was his fourth concussion in five years and his second in nine months. At the recommendation of his physicians, he didn't return to umpiring.

PART THREE

Today's Activists and an Agenda for Change

CHAPTER EIGHT

Modern-Day Rebels

W hether they seek or acknowledge it, professional athletes are public figures and celebrities. Their celebrity status provides them with a public platform, although many choose not to use it when it comes to social and political issues. Throughout American history, however, a relatively small group of athletes have challenged injustices in sports and America generally. The names of some baseball rebels—such as Jackie Robinson, Curt Flood, Jim Bouton, Roberto Clemente, Bill Lee, Dick Allen, and Mudcat Grant—are familiar to most baseball fans and the wider public. Others—including Octavius Catto, John Montgomery Ward, Mark Baldwin, Rube Foster, Alta Weiss, Sam Nahem, Danny Gardella, Glenn Burke, and Ila Borders—are not as well-known but should be. Like their counterparts in other sports, their activism has typically paralleled the wider social movements of each era, and it has continued into the twenty-first century.

After World War II, Jackie Robinson laid the groundwork for each subsequent generation of activist athletes, among them Bill Russell, Elgin Baylor, Kareem Abdul-Jabbar Bill Walton, Craig Hodges, Steve Nash, Sue Bird, and LeBron James in basketball; Jim Brown, Dave Meggysey, Dave Kopay, and Colin Kaepernick in football; Arthur Ashe, Billie Jean King, Serena Williams, and Madison Keys in tennis; Muhammad Ali in boxing; John Carlos, Tommie Smith, Gwen Berry, and Aly Raisman in track and field; and Megan Rapinoe in soccer. Like Robinson, they used their sports celebrity as a platform to speak out about social injustice. Athletes who are both outspoken and progressive are routinely criticized by sportswriters, politicians, fans, and team owners. For professional athletes, participating in controversial causes—including taking sides in political contests—poses risks and dilemmas. They are often met with derision and contempt.

For example, on the morning of the first game of the 1969 World Series, the *New York Times* ran a story headlined "Tom Seaver Says U.S. Should Leave Vietnam," in which Seaver expressed his opposition to the Vietnam War. "I think it's perfectly ridiculous what we're doing about the Vietnam situation," he told the

Times. "If the Mets can win the World Series, then we can get out of Vietnam." Seaver added, "I feel very strongly about this."[1] Seaver was slated to pitch the fourth game at Shea Stadium in New York. That day, October 15, hundreds of thousands of protesters gathered in cities around the country under the auspices of the Moratorium to End the War in Vietnam. Antiwar protesters under the banner "Mets Fans for Peace" picketed outside the ballpark.

When the public address announcer identified Seaver as the starting pitcher, the fan response was less enthusiastic than usual. Some fans even booed the team's best pitcher, who had been 25–7 during the regular season and won the Cy Young Award as the National League's best pitcher. According to sportswriter Ray Robinson, there were "too many [prowar] hawks fluttering around in their expensive seats at Shea."[2]

Carlos Delgado was an exceptional slugger for the Toronto Blue Jays, Florida Marlins and New York Mets. During his major league career, which spanned 1993 to 2009, Delgado hit .280, with 2038 hits, 473 home runs, and 1512 RBI, as well as earning two All Star selections and a World Series ring. His hero was Roberto Clemente, a fellow Puerto Rican, who had used his baseball celebrity to express his views on social and political issues. Delgado always viewed himself as a patriotic American. Soon after the bombing of the World Trade Center on September 11, 2001, Delgado provided support for first-responders, donating $25,000 to New York City firefighters and another $25,000 to the police.

Delgado publicly opposed the US Navy's use of the Puerto Rican island of Vieques as a weapons-testing ground. Remembering older residents telling horror stories about uranium-depleted shells and the bomb explosions, Delgado viewed the military as waging a kind of war on the tiny island, using the nine-hundred-acre site for bombing exercises. After a civilian was killed by an errant bomb in 1999, Delgado joined Puerto Rican Socialist Party leader Ismael Guadalupe in demonstrations against the Navy. The Navy finally ended the bombing exercises in 2003 but left behind poverty, unemployment, and pollution. "It's still in the environment, it's still in the ground, it's still in the water," Delgado said. "That's why we've got the highest cancer rate of any place in Puerto Rico."[3] Delgado and other protesters wanted the United States to clean up its mess. Rallying other celebrities, including actor Martin Sheen and the Dalai Lama, Delgado contributed hundreds of thousands of dollars to the campaign. He joined singer Ricky Martin and boxer Felix Trinidad in taking out full-page ads about Vieques in the *New York Times* and *Washington Post* and persuaded fellow major leaguers Roberto Alomar, Juan Gonzalez, and Ivan Rodriguez to sign on.

In the aftermath of bombing of the World Trade Center and the Pentagon on September 11, 2001, Commissioner Bud Selig ordered all teams to play "God Bless America." During the 2004 season, a year after the United States invaded Iraq, Delgado sat in the dugouts while the song was played during the seventh-inning stretch.[4] He explained that he was protesting American militarism because he didn't like "the way they tied 'God Bless America' and 9-11 to the war in Iraq, in baseball."[5] When the Blue Jays played in Yankee Stadium, Yankees owner George Steinbrenner required ushers to string up chains during each seventh-inning stretch to keep people standing and secured— and blocked from leaving for the bathroom or concessions—until "God Bless America" was finished playing. During each of Delgado's at bats, fans greeted him with boos and then derisive shouts during each game's seventh-inning stretch. When he was at the plate and made an out, chants of "USA! USA!" went up in the crowd. Predictable howls also came from conservative sports fans and commentators who labeled him "un-American" and unfit to collect his paycheck. One critic said Delgado turned his back on the country that made him rich and that he ought to be paid in "Cuban pesos or Iraqi Dinars until he starts singing along." Another claimed that Delgado's protest "makes him a terrorist and he should be jailed."[6]

Some sportswriters defended Delgado. Associated Press sportswriter Steve Wilstein claimed that "the Puerto Rican slugger is not being anti-American by showing his disagreement with President Bush's policy. He is not disrespecting the soldiers or . . . slapping every New Yorker and American in the face." Instead, Wilstein wrote, Delgado is "exercising the most fundamental of our rights, freedom of speech, or . . . in this case, freedom to sit silently while his teammates stand on the dugout steps."[7]

After being traded to the Mets in 2006, the team insisted that Delgado end his protest. As Dave Zirin reported, "The team made it clear that freedom of speech stops once the blue and orange uniform—their brand—is affixed to his body" and that standing for "God Bless America" wasn't optional.[8] Mets manager Willie Randolph claimed, "I'd rather have a man who's going to stand up and say what he believes. We have a right as Americans to voice that opinion." But Randolph was overruled by Mets Chief Operating Officer Jeff Wilpon, who said that Delgado was entitled to his political views but "he's going to keep them to himself."[9]

While Delgado backed off about "God Bless America," he did not stop speaking out on social issues, including MLB's poor record in hiring Latino managers. "It's really sad," he observed in 2016. "With all the players that come from Latin American countries, you'd want to see more managers."[10]

There is an obvious double standard when it comes to sports and politics. Most professional sports team owners regard political involvement as essential to doing business. They make large campaign contributions to both Republicans and Democrats. They lobby city, state, and federal officeholders on legislation to protect baseball's monopoly and to get tax breaks for new stadiums. They participate in the same social and business circles as the nation's corporate and political power structures. Politicians often try to align themselves with athletes. They appear at professional sports events, where the American flag is ubiquitous, patriotic songs are played, and Air Force jets sometimes fly overhead.

Athletes who speak out on contentious issues face the potential loss of commercial endorsements and, in some cases, the loss of their livelihoods. Their business advisors and agents typically warn them about the consequences of injecting themselves into controversy. In 1981, when Billie Jean King acknowledged that she was a lesbian, she lost commercial endorsements. "Those all went away in 24 hours," she recalled.[11]

In 1990, Michael Jordan, who had a multimillion-dollar contract with Nike, was criticized for his refusal to endorse his fellow black North Carolinian Harvey Gantt, then running for the US Senate against right-wing segregationist Jesse Helm. "Republicans buy sneakers, too," Jordan explained at the time. The resulting criticism must have stung. Six years later he contributed $2,000 to Gantt's second unsuccessful effort to unseat Helms. He also contributed $10,000 to Barack Obama's campaign for the US Senate seat from Illinois. But human rights activists tried and failed to enlist Jordan in their crusade to improve the sweatshop conditions in Nike's overseas factories.[12]

Early in his professional career, golfer Tiger Woods stirred political controversy with one of his first commercials for Nike after signing a $40 million endorsement contract. It displayed images of Woods golfing as these words scrolled down the screen: "There are still courses in the United States I am not allowed to play because of the color of my skin. I've heard I'm not ready for you. Are you ready for me?"[13] At the time Woods told Sports Illustrated, "Some clubs have brought in tokens, but nothing has really changed. I hope what I'm doing can change that."[14]

According to Richard Lapchick, director of the Institute for Diversity & Ethics in Sports at the University of Central Florida, Woods was "crucified" by some sportswriters for the commercial and his comments. Nike quickly realized that confrontational politics wasn't the best way to sell shoes. "Tiger seemed to learn a lesson," Lapchick explained in a 2004 interview. "It is one that I wish he and other athletes had not learned: no more political issues. He has been silent since then because of what happened early in his career."[15] For example, Woods remained on the sidelines during the 2002 controversy over the intransigence of the Augusta National Golf Club, host of the annual Masters tournament, on permitting women to join.

In 2018, Cleveland Cavaliers superstar LeBron James released a video in which he criticized President Trump. "The climate is hot," James said in the video. "The No. 1 job in America, the appointed person (Trump), is someone who doesn't understand the people—and really don't give a (expletive) about the people."[16] Fox News host Laura Ingraham attacked James for "talking politics." She dismissed James' comments as "unintelligible" and "ungrammatical," and said she wasn't interested in the political views of "someone who gets paid $100 million a year to bounce a ball." She said that James should just "shut up and dribble."[17]

Two years later, after New Orleans Saints quarterback Drew Brees said he was staunchly opposed to players kneeling during the national anthem to protest racism, Ingraham said "He's allowed to have his view about what kneeling and the flag means to him."[18] James quickly denounced Ingraham's hypocrisy to his 46.3 million Twitter followers.[19] He probably didn't need to point out that Ingraham had attacked a Black athlete, while defending a white athlete, for exercising their First Amendment rights.

Challenging Trump

The election of Donald Trump triggered a new wave of activism among professional athletes, including major league baseball players. In 2016, to protest police brutality toward Black Americans, San Francisco 49ers quarterback Colin Kaepernick decided to kneel, rather than stand, during the national anthem before his team's preseason games. Throughout that season, other NFL players followed Kaepernick's example of silent protest. Their crusade widened after Trump launched an attack on the players' protest during a political rally in Alabama in September 2017. "Wouldn't you love to see one of these NFL owners, when somebody disrespects our flag, to say, 'Get that son of a bitch off the field right now. Out! He's fired. He's fired!'" Trump bellowed.[20] The next weekend, more than two hundred players sat or kneeled in defiance of Trump. After his protest, Kaepernick was blacklisted by NFL teams, who refused to hire him, even though he was more talented than many NFL quarterbacks.

Kaepernick's act inspired many other professional and amateur athletes to follow his example. In May 2018, NFL owners capitulated to Trump by voting to require players to stand on the field for the national anthem or be subject to a fine. The next day, Trump applauded the owners for doing "the right thing." Players who refuse to stand for the anthem, Trump declared, "shouldn't be in this country." Many NFL players reacted with anger over the league's policy and Trump's comments. "It's disgusting because of our First Amendment rights," said Denver Broncos linebacker Brandon Marshall.[21] A month after Kaepernick's take-a-knee protest in 2016, US soccer star Megan Rapinoe knelt during the national anthem in solidarity with the NFL star. After the US Soccer Federation revised its rules to require all players to "stand respectfully" when the anthem is played, Rapinoe refused to sing the anthem and stood with her hand at her side instead of over her heart.[22] In 2019, as cocaptain of the US women's national soccer team, she announced that she would refuse an invitation to visit Trump at the White House if her team won the World Cup. After Trump scolded Rapinoe on Twitter, her teammates voiced their support for her. Teammate Ali Krieger tweeted, "In regards to the 'President's' tweet today, I know women who you cannot control or grope anger you, but I stand by @mPinoe & will sit this one out as well. I don't support this administration nor their fight against LGBTQ+ citizens, immigrants & our most vulnerable."[23]

Trump, some sportswriters, and some fans criticized them for injecting politics into the sport. But Alex Morgan, the team's cocaptain and women's soccer Player of the Year in 2018, told *Time* magazine, "We don't have to be put in this little box. There's the narrative that's been said hundreds of times about any sort of athlete who's spoken out politically. 'Stick to sports.' We're much more than that, O.K.?"[24] Responding to overwhelming public support for Rapinoe and other athletes, the Soccer Federation repealed its "stand respectfully" policy in 2021, as did the NFL.[25]

In 2017, Trump withdrew his White House invitation to the NBA champion Golden State Warriors after players criticized him. The next year, after the Warriors' Steph Curry and the Cleveland Cavaliers' LeBron James said they wouldn't go to the White House if they won the championship, Trump didn't even bother extending an invitation to the victorious Warriors. (In January 2019, the Warriors met with former president Barack Obama at his Washington office when they were in town to play the Wizards.) After most of the 2018 NFL Super Bowl Champion Philadelphia Eagles players announced that they were skipping the White House victory celebration in protest, Trump proclaimed that they were no longer invited.

Major league baseball players have generally been more cautious, and more conservative, than their counterparts in other sports, particularly football and basketball. But ballplayers were nevertheless part of the wave of activism that emerged in the wake of the Trump administration's racism, sexism, homophobia, and immigrant bashing.

During the 2016 presidential election, Dodgers first baseman Adrian Gonzalez refused to stay at a Trump hotel. Asked to explain his action, Gonzalez told reporters, "You can draw your own conclusions. They're probably right."[26] On election night, 2016, Dodgers pitcher Brandon McCarthy tweeted, "Tonight's result affects me none because I'm rich, white and male. Yet, it'll be a long time until I'm able to sleep peacefully."[27] Two months after Trump's inauguration, McCarthy returned to Twitter to poke fun at Trump's campaign pledge to "drain the swamp" of corporate and Wall Street influence-peddlers. "Was the 'swamp' Goldman Sachs itself?" McCarthy tweeted, referring to the powerful investment bank that provided top officials in Trump's administration.[28]

St. Louis Cardinals outfielder Dexter Fowler, whose wife emigrated from Iran, told ESPN that he opposed Trump's anti-Muslim executive order. In response to angry comments from fans, Fowler tweeted, "For the record. I know this is going to sound absolutely crazy, but athletes are humans, and not properties of the team they work for."[29]

In September 2017, after Trump attacked Kaepernick, Oakland A's African American rookie catcher, Bruce Maxwell, bashed Trump on Instagram: "Our president speaks of inequality of man because players are protesting the anthem! F- this man!"[30] Later that day, Maxwell, the son of an Army veteran, became the first major league player to kneel for the national anthem before a game against the visiting Texas Rangers. A's Outfielder Mark Canha, who is white, stood behind Maxwell and placed his right hand on his teammate's shoulder. "My decision had been coming for a long time," Maxwell told the media, citing his own experiences with racism growing up in Huntsville, Texas, where Trump made his derogatory remarks about NFL players.[31]

In May 2018, Houston Astro players Carlos Beltrán and Carlos Correa, both Puerto Rican, skipped the team's visit to the White House to celebrate their 2017 World Series victory to express their dismay with Trump's bungled recovery efforts after a hurricane devastated the island. In 2019, nine African American and Latino members of the 2018 World Series winners Boston Red Sox—Mookie Betts, Jackie Bradley Jr., Rafael Devers, Hector Velazquez, Xander Bogaerts, Sandy Leon, Christian Vazquez, Eduardo Nunez, David Price, and manager Alex Cora—refused to join Trump at a White House celebration for the same reason.[32]

Every president has tossed the first pitch on opening day at least once during their presidencies since William Howard Taft inaugurated the practice in 1910. (There was no major league team in Washington, DC, when Jimmy Carter was president, so he threw out the first ball in the 1979 World Series.)

During his first three years in office, President Trump declined to follow that tradition. He feared that he would be met with a chorus of boos from the fans, since over three-quarters of Washington, DC, area voters (and 91 percent in the capitol city) supported Hillary Clinton in 2016. In 2019, however, he promised to attend the fifth game of the World Series between the Washington Nationals and Houston Astros, at Nationals Park in DC. Nationals owner Mark Lerner was diplomatic about the president's potential visit to the Nationals-Astros World Series game. "Well, he has every right to come," Lerner told the *Washington Post.* "He's the president of the United States whether you like him or not. It's a special event. He should be at it."[33]

Lerner had already invited chef and humanitarian José Andrés, who was admired for founding World Central Kitchen, a nonprofit that serves meals to victims of natural disasters, to throw out the first ball. Trump arrived at the stadium during the third inning but did not venture onto the field. He sat in a luxury suite along the third base line with several loyal Republican members of Congress. Soon after his arrival was announced over the public address system Trump was greeted with loud and sustained boos, a large "Impeach Trump" banner, and chants of "Lock Him Up!"

Cops and COVID-19

The police violence against two black men in 2020—the death of George Floyd in May in Minneapolis, Minnesota, and the shooting of Jacob Blake in August in Kenosha, Wisconsin—catalyzed an upsurge of protest around the country. Athletes joined the national chorus of frustration and outrage. After Floyd's murder, major league players began wearing jerseys in support of Black Lives Matter and racial equality.

The shootings occurred as the COVID-19 pandemic emerged, raising questions about whether it would even be possible for MLB to start the 2020 season. As the owners and players union negotiated over the options, Colorado Rockies infielder Ian Desmond decided to opt out of his $5.5 million contract to stay at home with his wife and four children during the pandemic. Another factor in making that decision was his growing frustration about the nation's racial climate. "The image of officer Derek Chauvin's knee on the neck of George Floyd, the gruesome murder of a Black man in the street at the hands of a police officer, broke my coping mechanisms. Suppressing my emotions became impossible," Desmond told the *Washington Post*.[34]

The police shootings forced Desmond, who is biracial, to recall the racist taunts he was subjected to while growing up in Florida, including teammates who shouted, "White Power!" He was angered by the conditions he encountered in the Washington, DC ghettoes during the five years he played for the Nationals and volunteered for its Youth Baseball Academy. "Meanwhile, my kids fly all over the country watching their dad play," Desmond observed. "They attend private schools, and get extra curriculum from learning centers. They have safe places to learn, grow, develop. But . . . the only thing dividing us from Antwuan [one of the young people he met] is money."[35]

"It just doesn't make any sense. Why isn't society's No. 1 priority giving all kids the best education possible?" Desmond said.[36] He wanted to take a break from baseball and think about these larger issues, including how to make the sport more inclusive, and working to help revive baseball for low-income and minorities in his hometown of Sarasota. "Think about it: right now in baseball we've got a labor war. We've got rampant individualism on the field. In clubhouses we've got racist, sexist, homophobic jokes or flat-out problems. We've got cheating," Desmond wrote. "We've got a minority issue from the top down. One African American [general manager]. Two African American managers. Less than 8% Black players. No Black majority team owners."[37]

Chicago White Sox pitcher Lucas Giolito, who is white, issued a statement in support of the protests against police abuse: "I don't know what it is to grow up black in the USA because it was not my experience," he wrote on Twitter. "I do know that my parents never had to worry about me being pulled over and maybe never making it home. It's time to do better. It's time for true equality and justice for all Americans. In fact, it's way overdue."

Giolito added, "Stop turning a blind eye, stop refusing to talk about it because it's 'uncomfortable.' Complacency will only allow the scourge of racism to survive. It's been 400 years. Enough is enough. Black men and women like Trayvon Martin, Ahmaud Arbery, George Floyd, and Breonna Taylor will continue to die on the streets and in their homes if we don't stand alongside of them, echoing their voices loud and clear and demand real change and accountability. . . . Please join me and let your voice be heard."[38]

The baseball protests continued in July 2020, when MLB teams played several exhibition games after the COVID-19 outbreak and before the shortened regular season began. Before an exhibition game with the Oakland Athletics, San Francisco Giants manager Gabe Kapler, who is white, told his players that he intended to take a knee during the anthem:

> I wanted them to know that I wasn't pleased with the way our country has handled police brutality. I told them that I wanted to amplify their voices and I wanted to amplify the voice of the black community and marginalized communities as well. I wanted to demonstrate my dissatisfaction with our clear, systemic racism in our country. I wanted them to know they've got to make their own decisions. And we would respect and support those decisions. I wanted them to feel safe in speaking up. We've had these discussions the last several days, and we will continue to have them.[39]

Players Jaylin Davis, Mike Yastrzemski, Austin Slater, Trevor Gott, Chadwick Tromp, and Tyler Cyr and coaches Antoan Richardson, Justin Viele, and Ethan Katz joined Kapler in the protest. The following night, more Giants players, including Hunter Pence, Pablo Sandoval, Mauricio Dubon, and Abiatal Avelino, took a knee.[40]

After the first night of protest, Trump tweeted, "Looking forward to live sports, but anytime I witness a player kneeling during the National Anthem, a sign of great disrespect for our Country and our Flag, the game is over for me!"[41] In response, Kapler told USA Today, "I don't see it as disrespect at all. I see nothing more American than standing up for what you believe in. I see nothing more patriotic than peaceful protests when things are frustrating and upsetting."[42]

On the same night, in a game at Petco Park against the San Diego Padres, Los Angeles Angels reliever Keynan Middleton took a knee and raised a fist during the national anthem. In a social media post, he explained,

> Racism is something I've dealt with my whole life. As a Black man in this country, it is my obligation to want to better the future for generations to come. Over the past few months, I've been out in the community taking part in peaceful protests and having the difficult conversations that are needed for change. Before, pioneers like Jackie Robinson, a Black man, didn't have a voice in the game of baseball. The foundation laid down and sacrifices made by Jackie and others is the reason why I have the platform I do. I will not allow that to go to waste.[43]

The protests backed MLB into a corner. MLB issued a statement that "The players and coaches are using their platforms to peacefully protest. Supporting human rights is not political. Supporting our players and supporting equality is not political."[44]

At an NBA game against the Orlando Magic in Florida in August, a few days after several cops shot Jacob Blake in the back in nearby Kenosha, the Milwaukee Bucks refused to take the court. Even as the buzzer sounded to begin the game, the Bucks were still in the locker room. Guards George Hill and Sterling Brown, both African American, were leading a team meeting, where players crafted a statement, which they issued at a team press conference that evening, explaining why they refused to play: "We are expected to play at a high level. Give maximum effort and hold each other accountable. We hold ourselves to that standard, and in this moment we are demanding the same from lawmakers and law enforcement," Brown said.[45] He called on the Wisconsin legislature to reconvene for a special session called by Governor Tony Evers, to take action and address police accountability, brutality and reform, "And remember to vote on November 3." [46]

The Bucks' defiance started a wave of similar actions by athletes in other sports. Soon after the Bucks refused to play, the NBA and the players association announced that all three playoff games that had been scheduled for Wednesday would be postponed and rescheduled. The WNBA also postponed three games scheduled for Wednesday when players made it clear that they wouldn't take the court.

Later that day, while waiting to host the Cincinnati Reds at Miller Park, the Milwaukee Brewers learned about the Bucks decision. "As soon as we got in the locker room, we started having discussions as a team," explained Brewers outfielder Christian Yelich. "We had a team meeting shortly after and came to the decision" to cancel their game.[47]

"We've been wearing these [Black Lives Matters] shirts throughout the year, but there comes a time where you have to live it, you have to step up," Yelich told the *Wisconsin State Journal*. "That's what you saw here today, us coming here collectively as a group and making a stand, making a statement for change, for making the world a better place, for equality, for doing the right thing and we did that as a group. It was a unanimous vote. Everyone was in favor of not playing, and sending a message and making a statement."[48]

"We wanted to be united with them in what [the Bucks] started," explained Yelich, who is white. "Coming together for the city and we just wanted to provide a better place, a better environment for everybody to be included, and for change."[49] "This is about us supporting our community and our country that's in pain," said another white Brewers outfielder, Ryan Braun. "I think that being that Kenosha is essentially an extension of Milwaukee, this one hits close to home and I think that it obviously impacted (the Bucks) deeply just as it has us."[50]

In New York, the Mets and Marlins initially took the field, but left after a planned forty-two-second moment of silence honoring Jackie Robinson's retired uniform number. After the players left the field, all that remained was a Black Lives Matter shirt covering home plate.

After the Los Angeles Dodgers outfielder Mookie Betts, the team's only African American player, told his teammates that he was going to sit out a game against the San Francisco Giants out of respect for the victims of police killings, the other twenty-seven men in the clubhouse (including six Latino players) decided to join him in the protest. The Seattle Mariners and San Diego Padres did the same. Some players—including the Cubs' Jason Heyward, the Cardinals' Dexter Fowler and Jack Flaherty, and the Rockies' Matt Kemp—refused to play even though their teams took the field. Altogether, players had forced the cancellation of seven games.

Players took the lead, but some coaches and managers expressed their solidarity, too. "The Bucks led here," said Brewers manager Craig Counsell, wearing a Black Lives Matter shirt. "The NBA led here. But our players, they went first in Major League Baseball and I'm still very proud of them for that."[51]

The athletes' protest had an impact. In September 2020, a *Washington Post* poll found that 59 percent of Americans, including a majority of football fans, said it is acceptable for professional athletes to kneel during the national anthem. An even larger proportion of Americans (62 percent) believed that athletes should express their views about social issues.[52]

Rebel for All Seasons: Sean Doolittle

Sean Doolittle has become the most outspoken professional baseball player of the twenty-first century, even before Trump began running for president. *Sports Illustrated* called him the "conscience of baseball."[53] He explained to the *New York Times*, "When I was a kid, I remember my parents would say, 'Baseball is what you do, but that's not who you are'—like that might be my job, but that's not the end-all, be-all. I feel like I might even be able to use it to help other people or open some doors or explore more opportunities."[54]

Doolittle is clear about his priorities. "Sports are like the reward of a functioning society," Doolittle said when the COVID-19 pandemic hit in early 2020. He was upset that the owners and players union were negotiating about salaries, not health and safety, and that the billionaire owners were ignoring the needs of stadium workers and other low-wage employees.[55]

Doolittle comes from a military family. His father served in the Air Force for twenty-six years, including deployment to the Middle East after 9/11. He teaches aerospace science to high school ROTC students in New Jersey. His stepmother is an active duty member of the Air National Guard. A distant cousin, Jimmy Doolittle, was an aviation pioneer who led the first attack against Japan after it bombed Pearl Harbor in December 1941.

Born in 1986, Doolittle grew up in suburban Tabernacle Township, New Jersey, led Shawnee High School to a state championship as an outstanding pitcher, and was named New Jersey's high school Player of the Year by *Baseball America* in 2004. His family emphasized the importance of education. "I could never go to practice or to a game unless I'd finished my homework," he recalled.[56] The Atlanta Braves drafted him in 2004, but he chose to attend the University of Virginia, where he was recruited as a slugging first baseman as well as a pitcher.

In his freshman year he hit .313 and went 3–2 with a 1.64 ERA, and *Baseball America* named him a freshman All-American at first base. The next year he made the All-Atlantic Coast Conference team as a starting pitcher and was the Conference Player of the Year, with a 11–2 win-loss record and a 2.38 ERA, while batting .324. In his junior year he hit .301 at the plate and went 8–3 with a 2.40 ERA on the mound, and was again first-team All-Conference. After three years he was the University of Virginia's all-time leader in both wins (twenty-two) and RBIs (167).

Drafted in 2007 by the Oakland Athletics in the first round as a first baseman, Doolittle left college after his junior year. He spent three years in the minors, then missed the next three seasons to injuries and surgery. Doolittle began his comeback in 2012 as a full-time relief pitcher. The A's called him up to Oakland in June and he soon became the team's top lefty closer, despite frequent injuries that landed him on the injured list. In 2014 he was one of MLB's best relievers, making the All-Star team. In 2016, he pitched in forty-four games and had forty-five strikeouts and only eight walks in thirty-nine innings, but he missed part of the season with various injuries.

In July 2017, Doolittle was traded to the Washington Nationals. The next year, he made the All-Star team again, but injuries limited him to pitching in only forty-three games, going 3–3 with twenty-five saves and a 1.60 ERA. In 2019 Doolittle got off to a spectacular start with twenty-three saves by the end of July, adding five more in August, but then went back on the injured list with right-knee tendinitis. He returned in time to help the Nationals win the AL pennant, finishing the regular season with twenty-nine saves, sixty-six strike outs, and only fifteen walks in sixty innings. Doolittle allowed just two runs in 10⅓ innings in the postseason and didn't allow a run in three World Series appearances against the Houston Astros. His 2020 season was a disaster not only because of the COVID-19–shortened season but because injuries limited him to eleven games and seven innings.

Among fans in both Oakland and Washington, Doolittle was one of the most popular players. A huge Star Wars fan, Doolittle calls himself "Obi-Sean Kenobi Doolittle." His Twitter handle is @whatwouldDOOdo. He and his wife Eireann Dolan, whom he met while she was a reporter covering the Oakland A's for Comcast SportsNet and married in October 2017 (eloping the day after the Washington Nationals' last game of the regular season), approach life with a sense of humor, often poking fun at each other and themselves in their constant tweets.

Doolittle worked with veterans' groups and the Washington Nationals Youth Baseball Academy. In addition to participating in a variety of community activities, both Doolittle and Dolan (who earned her master's degree in theology and religious studies from Fordham University) have been consistently outspoken about their progressive political views.

In 2015, Doolittle and Dolan organized a Thanksgiving dinner for seventeen Syrian refugee families in Chicago, Dolan's hometown. They got Chicago Mayor Rahm Emmanuel and several City Council members to serve as greeters and waiters to get publicity for the refugee cause. "We just felt it was a way we could welcome them to America, to let them know there are people who are glad they're here," Doolittle recalled.[57]

That year, the A's hosted their first Pride Night to support the LGBTQ community. Some social media trolls threatened to boycott the event. In response, Doolittle and Dolan (whose mother is gay) hatched a plan to buy tickets from season ticket holders. They raised almost $40,000 from over one thousand contributors through a GoFundMe campaign, which provided tickets and buses for nine hundred LGBTQ youth to attend the game. "There should be no discrimination or hate in the game or a stadium," Doolittle told a local newspaper. [58]

In 2018, when the media exposed antigay slurs tweeted by several major ballplayers, Doolittle responded with a series of tweets:

> It can be tough for athletes to understand why these words are so hurtful. Most of us have been at the top of the food chain since HS, immune to insults. When all you've known is success and triumph it can be difficult to empathize with feeling vulnerable or marginalized. Homophobic slurs are still used to make people feel soft or weak or otherwise inferior—which is bullshit. Some of the strongest people I know are from the LGBTQIA community. It takes courage to be your true self when your identity has been used as an insult or a pejorative.[59]

In June 2019, Doolittle, then pitching for the Nationals, celebrated Pride Day in Cincinnati by having a trans flag on his right baseball shoe and the rainbow flag on his left shoe. Three days later, at Nationals Park, Doolittle again wore his gay pride cleats as well as a Nationals-branded rainbow shirt under his uniform. "I have received compliments on them from my Nats teammates and they have asked about the trans flag. It's a small thing, but representation matters." Doolittle told the media.[60] "Everyone deserves to feel safe and free to be who they are and to love who they love. Love is love," he tweeted.[61] According to *OutSports,* "There may not be a bigger advocate for LGBTQ rights among Major League Baseball players" than Doolittle.[62]

In 2016, after Trump, then a presidential candidate, dismissed his vulgar "grab them by the pussy" comment as just "locker room talk," a dozen pro athletes—from football, basketball, and soccer—denounced Trump, mostly on Twitter.[63] Doolittle was the only baseball player to record his disgust, writing, "As an athlete, I've been in locker rooms my entire adult life and uh, that's not locker room talk."[64]

In January 2017, a week after Trump's inauguration, the president signed his first travel ban against Muslims, sparking nationwide protests. Doolittle tweeted, "These refugees are fleeing civil wars, terrorism, religious persecution, and are thoroughly vetted for 2yrs. A refugee ban is a bad idea. . . . It feels un-American. And also immoral."[65] Doolittle further observed, "I think America is the best country in the world because we've been able to attract the best and brightest people from all over the world. . . . Refugees aren't stealing a slice of the pie from Americans. But if we include them, we can make the pie that much bigger, thus ensuring more opportunities for everyone."[66]

In an interview with *Time* magazine, Doolittle said that the Trump administration "is relying on stereotypes and Islamophobia, using false information to support its immigration reforms. The facts tell a different story: Crime rates are lower for refugees and immigrants than for American citizens, and net illegal immigration from Mexico is thought to be at or less than zero."[67]

In July 2017, neo-Nazis and white supremacists held a rally in Charlottesville, Virginia, and one of them, driving a car, killed an anti-Nazi protester. In a series of tweets, Doolittle, who attended college there, condemned them. "The C'Ville I knew from my time at @UVA is a diverse and accepting community. It's no place for Nazis," he wrote. "People say 'if we don't give them attention they'll go away.' Maybe. But if we don't condemn this evil, it might continue to spread. This kind of hatred was never gone, but now it's been normalized. They didn't even wear hoods. It's on us to condemn it and drive it out."[68] "It's just white fear," Doolittle told the *Washington Post.* "It's the worst kind of hatred. It's disgusting."[69]

Doolittle has also been an advocate for workers, especially those with ties to organized baseball. In early 2019, New Era Cap Company, which makes caps for all major league teams, announced it was closing its union factory in Derby, New York, to move its production to nonunion facilities in Florida. In a *Washington Post* op-ed, Doolittle expressed his concern that he and other players "will be wearing caps made by people who don't enjoy the same labor protections and safeguards that we do."[70] He told *ThinkProgress*, "It's basically union-busting, plain and simple. The only people wearing (the New Era caps made in Derby) are the players, and these are the players in the union, so we want to make sure they're wearing caps that are made by people earning a union wage."[71]

In October 2019, Doolittle's friend and fellow Nationals reliever Daniel Hudson faced criticism from—among others—former Miami Marlins president David Samson when Hudson missed the first game of the National League Championship Series to be with his wife for the birth of their child. Doolittle defended his teammate on Twitter: "If your reaction to someone having a baby is anything other than, 'Congratulations, I hope everybody is healthy,' you're an (expletive)."[72]

A few weeks later, after the Nationals won the World Series, Doolittle announced that he would not join his teammates at the White House celebration with Trump. He had a problem with Trump's "divisive rhetoric and the enabling of conspiracy theories and widening the divide in this country," he told the *Washington Post*. "I don't want to hang out with somebody who talks like that.'"[73] All-star third baseman Anthony Rendon, outfielders Victor Robles and Michael A. Taylor, and pitchers Javy Guerra, Joe Ross, and Wander Suero also boycotted the event.[74] Doolittle said, "At the end of the day, as much as I wanted to be there with my teammates and share that experience with my teammates, I can't do it. I just can't do it."[75]

The *New York Times* praised Doolittle's "willingness to embrace publicly the kinds of causes rarely discussed, let alone endorsed, in the strongly right-leaning culture of the baseball clubhouse."[76] The *Washington Post* reported that "in a sport with a conservative culture defined by tradition and a near-dogmatic acceptance of the social status quo, they [Doolittle and Dolan] have been unafraid to be different, while determined not to be different for different's sake."[77]

When MLB put its season on indefinite hold in response to the COVID-19 pandemic in March 2020, Doolittle and Dolan hunkered down in a Florida house, where he could exercise and stay in shape. They also hosted a podcast about their daily lives, discussing the books they were reading during the lockdown. No player was more eager to return to play than Doolittle, but he was the first ballplayer to publicly oppose MLB's plans to restore play without adequate guarantees that the players and support staff would be safe and that stadium workers would be compensated during the long layoff.

When MLB proposed to save money during the pandemic by shaving $100 off every minor leaguer's $400 weekly paycheck, Doolittle and several Nationals teammates pledged to cover the lost income of players on the Nationals farm teams. Doolittle tweeted, "Minor leaguers are an essential part of our organization and they are bearing the heaviest burden of this situation as their season is likely to be cancelled. We recognize that and want to stand with them in support."[78] Players on other teams did the same. Embarrassed, the owners withdrew the plan.

Doolittle said that major league players need to demonstrate "solidarity with those workers who are in those supporting roles." Dolan tweeted, "OK now, what about the non-millionaire hotel workers, security staff, grounds crews, media members, team traveling staffs, clubhouse attendants, janitorial workers, food service workers, and the billion other people required to make that 3.5-hour game happen every night?" Doolittle wondered if these workers would "have access to testing and health care if god forbid they got sick."[79]

He quoted epidemic expert Dr. Anthony Fauci's call for daily testing for NFL players and wondered whether baseball players would receive the same treatment. "So how many tests do we need to safely play during a pandemic? And not just tests for players" but also to protect the sport's massive support workforce. What "level of risk [are we] willing to assume? 80% of the cases are considered mild," but what happens if someone in baseball experiences a serious case? How do we protect people who "have pre-existing conditions . . . and seriously consider the increased health concerns of [those] who are at higher risk?"[80]

Insisting that "we want to play. And we want everyone to stay safe," Doolittle's final tweet that day could be described as a baseball rebel's manifesto: "Sorry, I had to get that out of my system. Stay safe. Keep washing your hands and wearing your masks. I hope we get to play baseball for you again soon."[81]

In late May 2020, amid the medical and economic devastation already inflicted by the pandemic, more Black men were murdered by US law enforcement officials. The killing of George Floyd by a Minneapolis police officer provoked nationwide protests, looting, and demonstrations. With American cities on fire, Doolittle again spoke out, tweeting,

> Race is America's original sin . . . passed down from generation to generation. And we struggle to acknowledge that it even exists, much

less to atone for it. . . . Racism and violence are killing black men and women before our eyes. We are told it is done in the name of "law and order," but there is nothing lawful nor orderly about these murders. We must take action and call it for what it is. We must recognize our shared humanity and atone for our Original Sin or else we will continue to curse future generations with it. RIP George Floyd.[82]

Doolittle talked to his teammates about protesting during the national anthem but said he thought the decision should be made by Black players. "The goal should be to amplify the voices, not to be louder than them and steal the spotlight away from what the movement is trying to accomplish—trying to end police brutality and end racism and injustice," Doolittle explained. "Sometimes you got to be Peter Norman," he said, referring to the Australian sprinter who placed third behind Black Americans Tommie Smith and John Carlos at the 1968 Olympics in Mexico City.[83] While Smith and Carlos raised their fists in a Black Power salute on the victory stand, Norman demonstrated his solidarity by wearing an "Olympic Project for Human Rights" badge on his chest.

Long an admirer of civil rights activist and Congressman John Lewis, Doolittle was thrilled to meet him at a Nationals game in 2018. "I've been trying to raise some good trouble around here," Doolittle told him, invoking the phrase that Lewis frequently used to describe his activism.[84]

Doolittle is an avid reader. During the baseball season, he reads for an hour or two after each game—at home or in his hotel room. "Reading is just a way for my brain to focus on something else. And that's why I chose fiction. That's why I like sci-fi," Doolittle explained to *Sports Illustrated*. "It's very much an escape, an alternate reality that has nothing to do with baseball or sports or anything going on."[85]

He is well-known for visiting locally owned independent bookstores on every road trip during the baseball season and documenting his visits on Twitter. Many independent bookstores have disappeared since Amazon arrived on the scene. "I want to support local businesses. I want to support these places that are active in their communities," Doolittle explained. The big online chains like Amazon, he said, "might be a little bit cheaper, but they're not furthering anything as far as author's careers or supporting their workers."[86]

During a *CBS This Morning* interview, Doolittle claimed, "There's a lot of really kind of alarming statistics when it comes to literacy rates in kids in the United States. Over half of kids who are in fourth grade read below basic level—that's a really crucial time for them because there's so many indicators about where they're at in fourth grade can determine where they go in their education level down the road."[87]

Doolittle has made it a point to participate in a reading program for the children of soldiers. In June 2019, for example, he read the children's book *Where the Wild Things Are* to children from military bases in the Washington, DC, area. Reflecting on the event, Doolittle observed, "I hope they came and saw a professional athlete in a major league baseball player that reads books. It shows that maybe reading is not something that's just a part of their homework. It can be something that you enjoy as much as being outside and playing sports."[88]

Considering his left-wing views, some baseball fans can't understand Doolittle's support of American soldiers, but for him it's entirely consistent. His baseball career, he said, "gives you [the perspective] on how fortunate I am to be able to do what I do when there's teenagers leaving the country with M-16s and they're going to the Middle East. And I get to play baseball every day. You start to look at things a little bit differently and you really appreciate the opportunities you have and some of these things other people do for you getting little or no recognition for it."[89]

Doolittle and Dolan have long been strong advocates for military veterans. They supported Operation Finally Home, which builds houses for wounded veterans and their families. They started a registry to help furnish two such houses in Northern California and offered signed A's gear to those who donated. Within weeks, fans had filled every cabinet and drawer with the necessities for the recipients. The couple have worked with Human Rights Watch and wrote an op-ed column in *Sports Illustrated* urging the Veterans Administration to provide adequate mental health services to military vets with less than honorable discharges, or "bad paper."[90] They've also supported Swords to Ploughshares, a Bay Area organization that helps veterans with housing and employment. In 2018, Doolittle received the Bob Feller Act of Valor Award in recognition of his work with military veterans and their families.

Doolittle has criticized ostentatious displays of patriotism at ballparks. He claimed it wasn't enough to "just capitalize on people's patriotism, and sell hats and shirts with your team's logo and camouflage on it." Instead, it was important to "use your platform as a sports league to shine a light on some of the issues facing veterans and military families."[91] He once tweeted that "as long as we have an all-volunteer military, it's on us—the civilians at home—to advocate for our military families. To make sure they are deployed responsibly and that they get the care they were promised when they signed up."[92]

Doolittle's former A's teammate, Bruce Maxwell, also comes from a military family. When Maxwell was criticized for refusing to stand for the national anthem, in solidarity with Colin Kaepernick and other athletes, Doolittle came to his defense: "I came from a military family, so there are a lot of things I think about when the anthem is playing," he told ESPN. "One thing that bothers me is the way people use veterans and troops almost as a shield. They say that's the reason they stand and that veterans deserve to be honored and respected during the anthem. But where is that outrage in taking better care of veterans? The most recent statistics say that we still lose 20 veterans to suicide every day."[93]

Doolittle elaborated, "I worry sometimes in this country that we conflate patriotism exclusively with love of the military and militarism and the strength of our armed forces. That's not the only way that you can be patriotic. People draw a direct line between the national anthem and the military, or patriotism and the military. But there are a lot of things that we're not doing for veterans."[94]

Doolittle was injured for much of the shortened 2020 season. In February 2021, he signed a free-agent contract to pitch for the Cincinnati Reds. Doolittle appeared in forty-five games for the Reds, posting a 3–1 record, a 4.46 ERA with forty-one strikeouts in thirty-eight innings. In August, the Seattle Mariners claimed Doolittle off waivers. He pitched eleven games.

Reliquary Rebel: Terry Cannon

Every year for two decades on a Saturday afternoon in July, Terry Cannon, the founder and guiding spirit of the Baseball Reliquary, would kick off the organization's annual gathering by raising an oversized cowbell and clanging it over his head. At least half of the two hundred people in the audience would join in with their own bells, disrupting the quiet outside the Pasadena Central Library auditorium. The annual cowbell ceremony was a tribute to Hilda Chester, the raspy-voiced Brooklyn Dodgers fan who clanged her own cowbell at Ebbets Field from the 1930s until 1957, when the Dodgers moved to Los Angeles.

Once the cowbell rite of passage ended and the crowd had sung the national anthem (accompanied over the years by a four-piece string band, a trombone ensemble, and musicians playing a saw, water-filled glasses, a tuba, a harp, a ukulele, and a pedal steel guitar), Cannon would bestow the Hilda Award to a fan who had demonstrated dedication to the national pastime. These have included the author of the song "Meet the Mets," a fan who has played his bass drum in the bleacher seats during every Cleveland Indians home game since 1973, a Detroit Tigers enthusiast who organized a volunteer group that restored a vacant ten acre site where the team once played before it build a new stadium, a Catholic nun who bakes cookies for her beloved Cleveland Indians team, actor Bill Murray (part owner of four minor league teams), and a twenty-two-year-old college student who, beginning at the age of twelve, began writing letters to former Negro League players and then organized several Negro League reunions for athletes who hadn't seen each other in decades. Another winner was a retired college professor who had attended at least one regular-season game in all sixty-six stadiums used for major league play since 1950 and had been present for every three thousandth hit recorded in the major leagues since 1959—seventeen in all—as well as Hank Aaron's record-breaking 715th home run and Pete Rose's 4000th career hit.

Cannon, a librarian by trade, founded the Baseball Reliquary in 1996 to celebrate the sport's rebels, mavericks, eccentrics, outcasts, and oddities. He loved the game, but not the business, of baseball and understood that there were many other fans like him around the country. The Reliquary's best-known attraction is its Shrine of the Eternals, which Jim Bouton, the pitcher who scandalized baseball with his 1970 book *Ball Four*, called "the people's Hall of Fame."[95] Cannon launched the annual induction ceremony in 1999. Since then, sixty-six people have been installed into the Shrine.

Unlike the Cooperstown sanctuary, the Shrine election process is democratic. Any Reliquary dues-paying member (there are about three hundred around the country, and another ten thousand fans on social media) can nominate and vote for the candidates. Each year, two or three people are inducted, most of whom travel to Pasadena to accept the award and give a speech about themselves and the game they love.

Not surprisingly, the first induction class included Curt Flood, the All-Star outfielder who sacrificed his career and paved the way for free agency by challenging baseball's reserve clause before the Supreme Court. Flood died in 1997, but his widow, Judy Pace Flood, accepted the award on his behalf. The inaugural class also included Dock Ellis, an All-Star pitcher who spoke out about racial injustice but is perhaps best known for claiming to have pitched a no-hitter under the influence of LSD, and Bill Veeck, the maverick and radical owner of three major league teams. Cannon considered Veeck the Reliquary's "spiritual guru."[96]In 2003, the Reliquary inducted eighty-six-year-old Marvin Miller—the transformational leader of the players' union—who at the time had been rejected by the corporate-dominated Hall of Fame several times. After getting a standing ovation, Miller reminded the crowd about baseball's working conditions in the mid-1960s, when players first began talking about forming a union and asked Miller to join their movement. (Cooperstown finally elected him in 2019.)

Other inductees have included Bouton, Emmett Ashford (MLB's first Black umpire), Pam Postema (the minor league umpire thwarted in her quest to reach the big leagues), Billy Beane (the Oakland Athletics' general manager whose pathbreaking use of statistics was made famous in the book and subsequent film *Moneyball*), Lester Rodney (sports editor of the *Daily Worker*, the Communist Party newspaper, who played a key role in exposing baseball's racial hypocrisy and pushing for integration as early as the 1930s), Nancy Faust (the longtime Chicago White Sox organist famous for ad-libbing theme songs for her team's players), Dr. Frank Jobe (who pioneered the Tommy John surgery), Ila Borders (the first woman to receive a college baseball scholarship, win a men's college game, and win a men's regular season professional game), Lisa Maria Fernandez (a four-time first-team college All American at UCLA and three-time Olympic medal–winning softball pitcher), Rachel Robinson (Jackie Robinson's widow and head of the Robinson Foundation), writers Arnold Hano and Roger Angell, and Sy Berger (designer of the first Topps' baseball cards in 1952).

Steve Dalkowski, often considered the fastest pitcher in baseball history, was inducted in 2009. Dalkowski pitched in the Orioles' farm system for nine erratic seasons (1957–65), typically leading the league in both strikeouts and walks. Wildness—of his fastball and his hard-drinking lifestyle—kept him out of the majors. After leaving baseball, he lost control of his life, scraped by as a migrant farmworker, was often homeless, and lost touch with his family. His sister, who found him and helped him get sober, accompanied him to the induction ceremony where, despite suffering from alcoholic dementia, the seventy-year-old Dalkowski signed autographs for the appreciative Reliquary audience.

Another inductee, Eddie "The King" Feigner, was perhaps the finest fast-pitch softball hurler ever—nearly ten thousand exhibition wins and 140,000 strikeouts while heading the King and His Court, a four-man fast-pitch squad. One-handed pitcher Jim Abbott and one-armed outfielder Pete Gray are part of the Reliquary's Shrine of the Eternals. So are players Moe Berg, Glenn Burke (the first former player to come out of the closet), Jimmy Piersall, Luis Tiant, Bob Uecker, Mark Fidrych, Fernando Valenzuela, Bill "Spaceman" Lee, Minnie Minoso, Bill Buckner, Jim "Mudcat" Grant, Manny Mota, Lefty O'Doul, Maury Wills, Tommy John, and Dick Allen. Except O'Doul, Wills, John, and Allen, none have the statistical credentials to get into Cooperstown, but each made a contribution to the sport that Reliquary members considered sufficiently unconventional or pathbreaking to be honored.

Another is Shoeless Joe Jackson, who was unfairly banned from baseball for life by Commissioner Kenesaw Landis for his association with the 1919 Black Sox scandal in which his teammates participated in a conspiracy to fix the World Series, despite his exceptional play, including setting a World Series record with twelve hits. Jackson's outstanding career was abruptly halted in his prime, but his accomplishments were recalled at the 2002 Reliquary event.

A handful of the Eternals—Veeck, Miller, Roberto Clemente, Jackie Robinson, Yogi Berra, Casey Stengel, Dizzy Dean, broadcasters Vin Scully and Bob Costas, and Negro League luminaries Buck O'Neil, Andrew "Rube" Foster, Satchel Paige, and Josh Gibson—have dual citizenship in the Reliquary and the Cooperstown Hall of Fame.

Cannon graduated from San Francisco State University in 1974, worked as an editor for magazines about antique cars, experimental film, and avant-garde arts, and founded a local film festival before starting a new career as a librarian.[97] He loved jazz almost as much as he loved baseball. Under Cannon's guidance, in 2019 the Reliquary commissioned a jazz suite, "Stealin' Home," composed by Bobby Bradford to celebrate the life of Jackie Robinson, who grew up in Pasadena.[98]

For years Cannon collected odd baseball artifacts to create a museum without walls—an iconoclastic alternative to the official Baseball Hall of Fame and Museum in Cooperstown. (A reliquary is a container for holy relics.) The quirky assortment of memorabilia include the hair curlers that Dock Ellis wore during batting practice in Pittsburgh, a jockstrap worn by three-foot-seven-inch Eddie Gaedel (who had one at bat for the St. Louis Browns in

1951 in a stunt conceived by Veeck), a rubber model of pitcher Mordecai "Three Finger" Brown's missing finger, several baseballs signed by Mother Teresa, a mid-nineteenth-century soil sample from Elysian Fields in Hoboken, NJ, where the first baseball game ever played between two organized teams took place in 1846, and a sacristy box that a priest used in 1948 to give the last rites to Babe Ruth (who died nearly a month later).

Cannon kept these and other artifacts at his home and in a storage unit, occasionally mounting exhibitions at Southern California libraries. Under Cannon's guidance, the Reliquary worked with academic and amateur historians to retrieve and reveal little-known aspects of baseball's past. Several exhibits were designed to preserve the history of amateur Latino and Japanese American baseball in Southern California. In 2015, Whittier College outside Los Angeles agreed to become the collection's permanent home. "I was interested in things that other museums weren't interested in collecting," Cannon explained. "Like, if they wanted bats and gloves, I wanted things to keep famous stories alive. It was more interesting to find a desiccated hot dog that Babe Ruth partially digested than a signed baseball or bat."[99]

"Baseball has so many wonderful relationships between the history of baseball and culture, politics and gender issues," Cannon said. "I try to draw parallels between how you can view what was going on with baseball, and the society at large. A lot of people who come to see the exhibits are not even into baseball, but they liked how we point out its effects on society."[100]

Similar to Veeck, Cannon liked to poke fun at the baseball establishment and had a talent for bringing people together around his passion for the sport. He received no pay for leading the Reliquary, operating it on a shoestring budget raised from foundations, government arts agencies, and members' $25 annual dues. Cannon died of cancer in 2020 at age sixty-six. Other volunteers, including Joe Price and Canon's widow, Mary, have assumed responsibility for keeping the Reliquary going.

"Baseball is often called the game of statistics," said Ron Shelton, a former minor league player who wrote and directed the film Bull Durham, "but the Reliquary is more about remembering the magic than the numbers."[101]

CHAPTER NINE

Baseball Justice: An Unfinished Agenda

B aseball rebels have influenced America beyond the ballpark. As we enter the third decade of the twenty-first century, how can baseball contribute to the ongoing struggle for social justice and a more humane society?

Here we will focus on issues around racism, sexism, and homophobia, but there are related matters that should be part of an agenda for baseball justice. For example, it is time for MLB to improve the pay and working conditions in the sweatshop factory in Costa Rica that it co-owns with Rawlings and which produces all baseballs used by MLB teams. The Major League Baseball Players Association (MLBPA) fought hard to overturn the reserve clause and dismantle the semifeudal system that ruled professional baseball for most of its history, but minor league players still live under that system and endure miserable pay and working conditions. Minor league players need to unionize.

The MLBPA should join the AFL-CIO and demonstrate its solidarity with other unions in their attempts to improve their lives and lift American workers out of poverty and into the middle class. During the off-season, why not encourage MLBPA members to show up at union picket lines, urge Congress to raise the federal minimum wage, or support legislation making it easier for workers to unionize?

It is time to end government subsidies for baseball's team owners. At least twenty of the thirty owners of major league teams are billionaires. Most of the team owners inherited their wealth from their families, primarily through real estate and banking. One of the interesting paradoxes about MLB is that baseball stadiums are increasingly named for big corporations while many of them are built with large government subsidies, what some call "corporate welfare." Politicians provide huge taxpayer-funded handouts to professional teams owned by some of the richest men in the country, who then make additional millions by selling naming rights to even bigger corporations to affix their brand on ballparks, like Citi Field in New York, Target Field in Minnesota, Coors Field in Denver, Minute Maid Park in Houston, T-Mobile Park in Seattle, and Citizens Bank Park in Philadelphia.

Owning an MLB team is highly lucrative. Between 2011 and 2020, the average value of the teams increased from $523 million to $1.9 billion, ranging from the Miami Marlins (worth $990 million) to the New York Yankees ($5.2 billion), according to *Forbes* magazine. The Yankees, Dodgers, Red Sox, Giants, and Cubs are all worth over $3 billion.[1] In 2018, MLB received $2.7 billion from national television money that it shared equally with the thirty teams. Each team also raises local revenue, primarily from sales of tickets, food, clothing, and parking as well as naming rights and revenues from local TV deals. These local revenues totaled $7.29 billion in 2018—an average of $243 million per team.

Politicians and corporate boosters justify handing over large sums of public funds to these wealthy tycoons by arguing that building baseball stadiums will help revitalize declining cities and catalyze new jobs. But dozens of economic studies over several decades have documented that this is a myth. Meanwhile, many cities lack sufficient funds to provide adequate schools, infrastructure, housing, and other basic services. Some elected officials and fans have resisted this trend, arguing that the costs of subsidizing a professional sports franchise outweigh the benefits.

In the arenas of race, gender, and sexuality, baseball has made significant progress, but more must be done to align the sport with the growing movements for social justice.

Black Lives Matter in Baseball, Too

Perhaps it is no accident that MLB is Black Lives Matter (BLM) backward. Since 2004, MLB has celebrated Jackie Robinson Day, which commemorates the day—April 15, in 1947—that Robinson broke baseball's color line. At every major league ballpark, every player, coach, manager, and umpire wears Robinson's uniform number, 42. For the MLB, it is an opportunity to congratulate itself for being a forerunner of social change and racial justice.

Even so, like the rest of the country, baseball is having its own reckoning with iconic figures from its racist past. If MLB wants to live up to the memory of Jackie Robinson, who was an activist as well as an athlete, it needs to do more than offer rhetoric that Black Lives Matter; it must match its words with deeds.

In 1965, Black football players and their white allies (including Buffalo Bills quarterback Jack Kemp, later a Republican politician) pressured the American Football League to move its All-Star game out of New Orleans because of its racial segregation. The Black players who showed up in New Orleans for the game were treated so shabbily (by cab drivers, hotel clerks, restaurant waiters, and others) that they refused to play in the All-Star game the next day. Their boycott forced the league to reschedule the game in Houston two days later.[2]

In a 1990 referendum, Arizona voters opposed making Martin Luther King Jr. Day a paid holiday like the rest of the country, angering many Americans and catalyzing a boycott in protest. To avoid a public controversy, NFL owners voted to withdraw the 1993 Super Bowl from Phoenix and move it to the Rose Bowl in Pasadena, California. By losing the Super Bowl, the Phoenix-area economy missed out on between $200 million and $250 million. In 1992, the holiday was again placed on the ballot; 62 percent of Arizona voters approved the measure, and the NFL scheduled the 1996 Super Bowl at Phoenix's Sun Devil Stadium.[3]

In 2016, the NBA pulled its All-Star game out of Charlotte, North Carolina, after players and human rights groups expressed outrage over the state's controversial law to ban transgender people from using bathrooms in accordance with their gender identities. "We do not believe we can successfully host our All-Star festivities in Charlotte in the climate created by the current law," said the NBA statement.[4] The state legislature quickly repealed the law, and the NBA scheduled its 2019 All-Star game in Charlotte.[5]

In 2010, however, MLB balked at moving the next year's All-Star game out of Phoenix, despite protests from some players (including Carlos Beltran, Adrian Gonzalez, Albert Pujols, and David Ortiz), the players union, and immigrant rights groups over Arizona's anti-immigrant law, SB 1070, which allowed police to racially profile Latinos and criminalize the failure to carry immigration documents. Arizona Diamondbacks owner Ken Kendrick, while feigning concern about the controversy, substantially funded the Arizona Republican Party that created the law. MLB held its 2011 All-Star game in Phoenix as planned, and no players boycotted the game.

Ten years later, however, the political climate had changed. In early 2021, Georgia's Republican-dominated state legislature and its Republican governor passed a law restricting voting access in the state—a move designed to restrict voting among African Americans, fueled by false claims that the 2020 election for president and two US Senate seats in Georgia were stolen. Civil rights groups and the MLBPA (the players union) weighed in, urging MLB to move the All-Star game, scheduled for July, from Atlanta to protest the voter suppression law—and to warn Georgia's business leaders and politicians that other sporting events (like the Masters Tournament) and major conventions could also face boycotts. The protest was also designed to send a message to major corporations and politicians in other states thinking about adopting similar voter suppression laws.

On March 31 that year—the day before the start of the baseball season— President Joe Biden said that he would "strongly support" Major League Baseball moving its All-Star Game from Atlanta to protest the state's voter suppression law. "This is Jim Crow on steroids, what they're doing in Georgia," Biden said, using the All-Star game as a way to put pressure on Georgia's major businesses as well as its politicians.[6] Dave Roberts, manager of the World Series–winning Dodgers, who was scheduled the manage the National League All-Star team, said he might decline the honor and boycott the game if it was held in Atlanta.[7]

Tony Clark, the executive director of the players union, echoed Biden's protest. "Players are very much aware" of the voting restrictions, he said.[8] Two days later, MLB Commissioner Rob Manfred announced that it would move the All-Star game to another city.[9] Georgia's Republican Governor Brian Kemp claimed that MLB had "caved to fear and lies from liberal activists," even though Georgia's largest corporations, including Delta and Coca-Cola, weighed in against the voter suppression legislation.[10] Manfred understood that MLB could not bathe in the glory of Jackie Robinson and ignore efforts by contemporary politicians to turn back the clock on voting rights.

As described in the first part of this book, throughout its history, baseball owners, players, and reporters have taken sides on racial issues. As America's reckoning with systemic racism continues, baseball can take a stand for racial justice.

One way to demonstrate a commitment to racial justice is for the baseball establishment to elect Curt Flood to the Hall of Fame. Starting in 1970, Flood's courageous and principled stand against the reserve clause—proclaiming that it was a form of indentured servitude and that without the freedom to negotiate for better contracts ballplayers were "well-paid slaves"—laid the groundwork for a baseball revolution. Since Flood died in 1997, he's been a Hall of Fame candidate three times (in 2003, 2005, and 2007), but the Veterans Committee failed to vote him in each time, leaving him a victim of the same anti-union corporate baseball establishment that kept out players union executive director Marvin Miller for many years.

After being blacklisted by baseball's corporate plutocrats for over three decades, Miller was finally elected to the Hall of Fame in December 2019.[11] It seemed obvious to many baseball experts, including many sportswriters, that Flood should join him in the Cooperstown shrine.[12] There's been a growing movement to pressure the Hall of Fame to give Flood his due—partly as a result of Black Lives Matter and partly the result of efforts by the players union to educate the current generation of players and the public about Flood's significance. In 2020, the MLBPA announced an annual Curt Flood Award, given to "a former player, living or deceased, who in the image of Flood demonstrated a selfless, longtime devotion to the Players Association and advancement of Players' rights."[13] In 2020, fifty years after he challenged the baseball establishment over the reserve clause, over one hundred members of Congress signed a letter to Jane Forbes Clark, chair of the Hall of Fame, urging the Golden Age Committee to elect Flood. A year later, the Congress members sent Clark a reminder letter that they still believed Flood should be in the Hall of Fame.[14]

At a 2020 press conference to announce the letter, Congressman David Trone, a Maryland Democrat, said, "Curt Flood sacrificed his own career so players after him could have free agency, leaving one of the biggest impacts on the game to this day." Added Senator Roy Blunt, a Missouri Republican, "As a lifelong Cardinals fan, I have always admired the talent he brought to the game and his bravery off the field. He deserves to be honored with his rightful place alongside America's greatest baseball players."[15]

At a news conference in 2020, MLBPA's president Tony Clark said, "If the Hall of Fame is a museum that is reflective of our game's history and historic performances, [Flood's] enshrinement would be an affirmation of Curt's contribution to our game and our history."[16] Representatives from players unions from the NFL, NBA, MLB, and NHL, and the MLBPA also issued a joint statement: "Curt Flood's historic challenge of the reserve clause a half century ago transcended baseball. He courageously sacrificed his career to take a stand for the rights of all players in professional sports, bringing the issue of free agency to the forefront of national discussion."[17]

In December 2019, when pitcher Gerrit Cole signed his $324 million, nine-year contract with the New York Yankees, he paid tribute to Miller and Flood. "Challenging the reserve clause was essential to the blossoming sport we have today, which I believe brings out the genuine competitiveness that we have in baseball," Cole said, adding, "I just think it's so important that players know the other sacrifices that players made in order to keep the integrity of the game where it is, and so I hope everybody has that conversation about Curt Flood on the bus."[18]

Rather than simply look at his batting and fielding statistics, said MLBPA executive director Tony Clark, they should base their decision on Flood's overall contribution to baseball. "If the Hall of Fame recognizes the individuals with the biggest impact on our game," said Clark, "it is undeniable that Curt should be in the Hall of Fame."[19] Every professional athlete since the 1970s—including those enshrined in the Baseball Hall of Fame—owes Flood a debt of gratitude. They should all be enlisted in a campaign to put Flood in Cooperstown to draw attention to his life and legacy.

Since 2017, many cities have removed statues of Confederate figures, including Generals Robert E. Lee and P. G. T. Beauregard and Confederate President Jefferson Davis. Maryland Governor Larry Hogan, a Republican, directed the dismantling of a State House statue of Roger Taney, the Supreme Court Chief Justice whose 1857 *Dred Scott* decision ruled that blacks could not be American citizens. Tennessee officials ordered a bust of Nathan Bedford Forrest, a Confederate General and Ku Klux Klan leader removed from the state capitol building. The Atlanta Board of Education changed the name of Forrest Hill Academy, a high school named for Forrest, to Hank Aaron New Beginnings Academy.[20] Other school boards have renamed schools named for figures with ties to slavery, the Klan, and other racist aspects of American history. These actions are part of a growing controversy over buildings, statues, and awards honoring racists—a controversy that the baseball establishment could not escape.

In June 2020, the Minnesota Twins removed a statue of former owner Calvin Griffith from Target Field in Minneapolis, the city where a police officer's murder of an unarmed Black man, George Floyd, triggered a nationwide uprising against racial injustice. Griffith, who inherited the Washington Senators from his father in 1955 and moved the team to the Twin Cities in 1961, had already been the subject of controversy for racist remarks. At a Lions Club dinner in 1978, unaware a reporter was present, Griffith said, "I'll tell you why we came to Minnesota. It was when we found out you only had 15,000 blacks here. Black people don't go to ballgames."[21]

After the *Star-Tribune* quoted those remarks the next day, the team's star player, Rod Carew, asked to be traded and was soon playing for the California (now Los Angeles) Angels. In response to the Twins' decision to remove the statue, Carew, a Hall of Fame first baseman who retired in 1985, said, "While we cannot change history, perhaps we can learn from it."[22]

The Baseball Writers Association of America (BWAA) has recently sought to distance itself from two other iconic and powerful baseball figures who were racists. Each year the BWAA bestows a MVP award to an athlete in both the American League and National League. Upon his death in 1944, the BWAA named the award for longtime Baseball Commissioner Kenesaw Mountain Landis. But several former winners objected to keeping that name in light of Landis's strong opposition to baseball integration. "Why is it on there?" asked Barry Larkin, a Black shortstop and Hall of Famer for the Cincinnati Reds, referring to Landis's name and visage. "I was always aware of his name and what that meant to slowing the color line in Major League Baseball, of the racial injustice and inequality that Black players had to go through."[23] Mike Schmidt, a white Hall of Fame third baseman for the Philadelphia Phillies who won the MVP award three times, agreed. "If you're looking to expose individuals in baseball's history who promoted racism by continuing to close baseball's doors to men of color, Kenesaw Landis would be a candidate," he said. "Looking back to baseball in the early 1900s, this was the norm. It doesn't make it right, though."[24] In October 2020, the BWAA announced that its members had voted to remove Landis's name from the trophy, effective immediately.

In 1962, the BWAA named its annual baseball writers award after J. G. Taylor Spink, publisher of the influential *Sporting News*, long known as the "Bible of Baseball," from 1914 to 1962. Spink was also the first recipient of the award. Each week, the *Sporting News* provided fans with more news, features, analysis, and box scores of major league games than were available anywhere else. Spink was as dictatorial running the newspaper as Landis was running the sport itself. He was also one of Landis's biggest boosters and an adamant foe of dismantling baseball's Jim Crow system. In 1947—three years after Landis died and the same year that Robinson crossed baseball's color line— Spink authored a highly sympathetic biography, *Judge Landis and Twenty-Five Years of Baseball*.

"Spink defended segregated baseball with his silence. If need be, he did so in words," explained Daryl Grigsby in his 2010 book, *Celebrating Ourselves: African-Americans and the Promise of Baseball*. "In August 1942 he wrote an editorial saying that baseball did not have a color line, but that segregation was in the best interests of both blacks and whites because the mixing of races would create riots in the stands."[25] In a column titled, "No Good from Raising the Race Issue," Spink called on baseball to stop any attempt to integrate the game.[26]

When baseball finally integrated, the *Sporting News* sought to discredit the idea. In 1947, after Robinson joined the Dodgers, and Larry Doby joined the Indians to become the first Black player in the American League, the *Sporting News* ran another editorial on segregation: "Once Again, That Negro Question." It quoted an unidentified player who complained about the end of all-white teams: "Let us not discriminate against the white player because he is white."[27] Later that year, after the St. Louis Browns became the third team to integrate, hiring Negro League stars Willard Brown and Hank Thompson, the *Sporting News* ran an article gloating about their mediocre performance under the headline "Browns Negro Players Bat Only .194 and .178."[28]

Former winners of the Spink Award weighed in on the controversy. "I think they should change the name of it. . . . I was never aware of that, but now knowing that, I feel very strongly about it," said legendary baseball writer and broadcaster Peter Gammons, recipient of the 2004 award. Paul Hagen, the 2013 winner, said, "You certainly don't want to whitewash history, but then again, you don't want to honor a racist." Claire Smith, the 2017 winner and the first woman inducted into the Hall of Fame writers' wing, said, "If Mississippi can change the flag, and Confederate statues can be removed from state capitals, we can do this."[29] In February 2021, the BWAA removed Spink's name from the award.

The BWAA hasn't discussed putting other names on these two awards. But it might consider renaming the MVP award after Hall of Fame slugger Frank Robinson (MLB's first Black manager and the only player ever to be named the MVP in both leagues) and renaming the writer's award after Wendell Smith (the crusading journalist for the *Pittsburgh Courier* who helped lead the movement to end Jim Crow baseball).

So far, no one has called on the Baseball Hall of Fame to remove the most blatantly racist players from its hallowed halls. It is not hard to identify Hall of Famers who were segregationists and racists, among them Rogers Hornsby and Tris Speaker. Some researchers believe that both of these outstanding players were members of the Ku Klux Klan, although the evidence is inconclusive. For many years it was widely accepted that Ty Cobb, one of the greatest players in baseball history and the first player inducted into the Hall of Fame in 1936, was a virulent bigot who took out his racist rage through physical assaults on Black people, a view popularized in the 1994 Hollywood film *Cobb* starring Tommy Lee Jones. Wrote one baseball historian, "Once you've already let in Ty Cobb, how can you exclude anyone else?"[30] But subsequent research has raised questions about those claims, arguing that he's been misunderstood.[31]

If any Hall of Fame figure deserves being ousted, it is probably Cap Anson, who was enshrined in Cooperstown in 1939. As discussed in chapter 1, Anson, the Chicago White Stockings' player-manager, established baseball's color line in the 1880s. "He was relentless in that cause," said John Thorn, MLB's official historian.

Tom Yawkey, the owner of the Boston Red Sox from 1933 to 1976, was well-known for his opposition to baseball integration. The Red Sox were the last team to put a Black player on their roster. They waited until 1959, twelve years after Jackie Robinson broke baseball's apartheid system. Despite his racism, his fellow owners orchestrated his election to the Hall of Fame in 1980. In 2018, however, the Red Sox asked the city of Boston to change the name of a two-block street outside Fenway Park from Yawkey Way to Jersey Street to distance the team from Yawkey's racist legacy.

Such symbolic gestures are important ways to influence how Americans think about race, but equally important is whether the people who own and manage baseball reflect the diversity of those who play it. In that regard, baseball has struck out in promoting people of color, particularly Black Americans.

At the start of the 2021 season, Latinos composed 28.1 percent, African Americans composed 7.6 percent, and Asians composed 1.4 percent of all major league players.[32] Six of the thirty MLB managers (20 percent) were people of color—three African Americans (the Astros' Dusty Baker, the Dodgers' Dave Roberts, and the Indians' DeMarlo Hale, who served as acting manager) and three Latinos—the Mets' Luis Rojas, the Nationals' Dave Martinez, and the Blue Jays' Charlie Montoyo). MLB has been more inclusive in hiring coaches; 40.5 percent are Black, Latino, or Asian.

In a sport in which 37.6 percent of major league rosters are players of color, only 19.8 percent of senior administrators and 13.3 percent of general managers are Black, Latino, or Asian. In 2017, former Yankees star Derek Jeter became the first African American CEO of an MLB team when he was hired by the Marlins. No others were named in the subsequent three years. In 2021, Ken Williams of the Chicago White Sox was the only African American in charge of baseball operations—a position called executive vice president or general manager. In 2021, besides Williams, the only people of color filling that position were Al Avila of the Tigers, Farhan Zaidi of the Giants, and the Marlins' Kim Ng. Among the eight openings for that position during the 2020 to 2021 off-season, none were filled by African Americans. During the previous two decades, the only other Black general managers hired were Tony Reagins of the Angels, Michael Hill of the Marlins, and Dave Stewart of the Diamondbacks.

Arte Moreno, who is Latino, purchased the Angels in 2003 and remains the only nonwhite majority team owner in MLB. In 2021, there were no Black people among the principal owners of the thirty MLB teams. Jeter had a small ownership share of the Marlins, Los Angeles Lakers icon Magic Johnson had small share of the Dodgers, and NFL quarterback Patrick Mahomes and businesswoman Karen Daniel (former chair of the Greater Kansas City Chamber of Commerce) held small shares of the Kansas City Royals. In fact, there's only one Black majority owner in all of professional baseball. In 2020 Brandon Bellamy, a real estate developer, became the owner of the new Gastonia, North Carolina, team in the independent Atlanta League. (There were 150 minor league teams at the time.)

After George Floyd was killed beneath the knee of a white Minneapolis police officer in May 2020, a group of current and former Black baseball players created the Players Alliance. They introduced themselves to the world in mid-June with a "Black Lives Matter" video. Their mission, as stated on their website, is "to use our collective voice and platform to create increased opportunities for the Black community in every aspect of our game and beyond."[33] The group met with support from many white players and executives. Aaron Boone, the New York Yankees white manager, posted a message on Instagram announcing that he was joining the group and donating two days of his salary to express his solidarity.

The announcement was somewhat vague about how MLB and MLBPA will partner with the Players Alliance. Here are several ways (not all of which require money) to translate these good intentions into action:

First, MLB should train and hire more Black, Latino, and Asian managers, coaches, executives, and general managers in the minor leagues to create a pipeline into the major leagues.

Second, to rebuild Black support for baseball, MLB should do more to help financially strapped cities and inner-city schools restore and expand baseball fields, pay for baseball coaches in public middle schools and high schools, and fund Little League and other youth programs in communities of color. They should also encourage the training of Black and brown minor and major leaguers to become Little League coaches and middle school and high school coaches after they retire.

Third, following LeBron James's lead, players and MLBPA should participate in and help fund voter registration and get-out-the-vote drives, particularly in Black and brown communities that face ongoing voter suppression efforts. They should also join forces with James's group, More Than a Vote, to oppose the wave of state-level legislation aimed at restricting voter access, which disproportionately disenfranchises Black, Latino, and low-income voters.

Fourth, Major league players and their union should support efforts by workers inside and outside baseball to unionize. Union membership improves pay and working conditions (including those related to unnecessary dangers due to the COVID-19 pandemic) among the nation's most vulnerable people, who are disproportionately Black and brown. Let's see more players, who owe their high salaries and benefits to the union, expressing their solidarity with other workers on social media and even on picket lines.

A League of Their Own?

For decades, MLB was an old boys club. Top executives were drawn from former players, who hired their friends (or friends of friends) for other top jobs, including managers, who in turn hired their friends and former teammates as coaches. It has been difficult for women to break into that culture. During 2019 and 2020, for example, MLB teams had thirteen vacant general manager positions. Kim Ng, hired as general manager for the Miami Marlins in 2021, was the only woman and the only person of color in that group. She is MLB's first female general manager.[34]

The tide is slowly turning. MLB has made significant strides in creating training programs and a pipeline for women to assume key roles in the minor and major leagues. A growing number of women have been hired for top jobs in the executive suites and as coaches.

Organized baseball has taken steps to address the toxic sexist culture that has come to light in the wake of the #MeToo movement in America's workplaces. MLB set up an anonymous hotline, Speak Up, to get reports of sexist misconduct. It adopted a new code of conduct and sponsored antiharassment and discrimination training workshops for top executives of every team. In 2020, MLB hired Michele Meyer-Shipp as its new chief people and culture officer to oversee these efforts. Clear and swift discipline will send a signal that MLB is serious about holding executives, coaches, managers, and players accountable.

In 2018, the Astros acquired relief pitcher Robert Osuna while he was serving a seventy-five-game suspension as a result of accusations of domestic violence. The next year, after the Astros clinched the pennant, assistant general manager Brandon Taubman yelled at a group of female reporters in the clubhouse, "Thank God we got Osuna! I'm so fucking glad we got Osuna!"[35] A few days later, Taubman's outburst was reported in *Sports Illustrated*. Days after that, the Astros suspended and then fired him.

In 2021, the Mets fired general manager Jared Porter after only thirty-seven days on the job after he acknowledged sending sexually explicit text messages, including nude photos, to a female reporter in 2016 when he was working for the Cubs. The Mets also fired hitting coach Ryan Ellis after multiple female employees filed complaints of sexual harassment against him. MLB suspended Mickey Callaway while it investigated an alleged pattern of sexual harassment and stalking of female employees and reporters while he was a coach for the Indians, Mets manager, and Angels pitching coach. Top employees for the Chicago Cubs, Arizona Diamondbacks, and other teams have also been accused of sexual harassment.

It is easier to promote and encourage women to take management-level jobs in baseball when there is a critical mass of women working for the same team and sharing their experiences on different teams. To foster that networking, in 2019 Jen Wolf, a life skills coordinator in the Cleveland Indians' farm system, began contacting other women working in organized baseball. She started a WhatsApp group for women to talk, vent, and help each other. It began with ten women and grew quickly as women invited other women. The group includes minor and major league coaches, scouts, media relations staff, baseball operations executives, and others. "Being able to mentor other women that are coming into the game is huge," Wolf told the *New York Times*. "I didn't have that. I had mentors, but not really female mentors."[36]

As more women join the ranks of baseball professionals, they feel more empowered to seek changes. For example, Wolf recalled having to use an empty umpires' locker room at the Mets' minor league facility in Port St. Lucie, Florida, because there were no accommodations for women. That has now changed.

Baseball fans have long wondered whether a woman would ever join the rosters of MLB teams. As we documented earlier, women have a proud history of playing baseball. A few have played on all-men's college teams, and a handful have played for minor league clubs, but none have gotten as far as the top-tier minor leagues. Is this because women don't have the strength, skills, or competitive will to make it to the major leagues? Is it due to the baseball establishment's stereotypes about women and their indifference to scouting, recruiting, and training potential female ballplayers? Is the absence of women in major league baseball due to the reality that highly talented female ballplayers are both overtly and subtly discouraged from playing baseball and redirected instead into playing softball, severely limiting the pipeline of potential MLB athletes?

The conventional wisdom is that boys play baseball and girls play softball. Girls who display a talent for baseball while playing in Little League or other youth leagues are discouraged from continuing in high school. As an eleven-year-old, Sarah Domin was the only girl and the best hitter on her coed youth league team in upstate New York. She was often asked why she doesn't play softball. "Baseball is more fun," she explained.[37]

But it is difficult for young girls to challenge that cultural conditioning. Baseball for All estimates that 100,000 girls play youth baseball every year, but according to the National Federation of State High School Associations, only 1,284 girls played baseball in high school during the 2018 season. In contrast, 482,740 American boys played high school baseball that year. Girls get channeled into softball, particularly since that's where the college scholarships are. In 2018, only 2,183 boys played fast-pitch softball in high school, but 362,038 girls did.

High school softball is a feeder into college, so not surprisingly, women's fast-pitch softball at the college level has seen a major increase, in part because of that cultural conditioning and in part because of the growing number of college scholarships for women softball players.

In 1982, the NCAA sponsored the first Women's College World Series, which gave the sport greater exposure and led to growing participation. That year, only 752 colleges and universities (55 percent of all NCAA member institutions) offered the sport, and 7,465 women participated. By 2018,

1,114 colleges and universities (90 percent of NCAA members) offered intercollegiate women's fast-pitch softball, attracting 20,316 female athletes.[38] These numbers don't even include the growing number of women's teams and athletes participating in club sports on college campuses. Women's College World Series drew large crowds and impressive television ratings.

Women's softball was an Olympic sport from 1996 to 2008, removed for the 2012 and 2016 games, and added for the 2020 games, although the competition was postponed to 2021 due to the COVID-19 pandemic.[39] To support the US team, Major League Baseball sponsored a series of exhibition games in advance of the Olympic games and invited the women's team to train at the old Dodgers complex in Vero Beach, Florida.

The growing numbers of women playing fast-pitch softball in high school and college laid the foundation for a professional league. The first effort was the International Women's Professional Softball Association (IWPSA), founded in 1976 with ten teams in cities across the country. Each team played a 120-game schedule in sixty doubleheaders. The USA Softball Women's national team won gold medals at the International Softball Federation's World Championship in 1986 and at the Pan American Games the next year, further expanding interest in the sport. With financial backing from the Cowles family, owner of Cowles Media Company, the Women's Professional Softball League was launched in 1995 with two teams composed of former college athletes. They were barnstorming teams that played exhibition games in Midwestern cities. In 1997 the project was renamed the Women's Pro Fastpitch (WPF), beginning with six teams, and the following year became the Women's Professional Softball League. Nine of its games were televised on ESPN, attracting more than three million viewers, but the league suspended play in 2002. Two years later, the league was reincarnated as National Pro Fastpitch (NPF) with five teams—the Aussie Peppers of Minnesota, Canadian Wild of Southern Illinois, Chicago Bandits, Cleveland Comets, and California Commotion—composed of players from the United States, Canada, Mexico, and Australia.

By 2019, NPF had six teams and a per-player pay scale of between $3,000 and $10,000 for the fifty-game season.[40] To earn a reasonable full-year salary, players sign on with teams in Japan and compete in the NPF during summers. Many players hold other jobs in sports or other fields. The COVID-19 pandemic forced the NPF to cancel its 2020 and 2021 seasons.

The biggest star in women's softball, six-foot-three pitcher Monica Abbott, played for the University of Tennessee and holds the NCAA records for career wins, shutouts, and strikeouts. Her fastball has been clocked at over seventy miles per hour. Between 2005 and 2010, she led Team USA to four World Cup of Softball championships, pitched the US to a gold medal at the 2007 Pan Am Games, and pitched a perfect game in the 2008 Olympics. She turned professional in 2007, playing in the NFP, but moved to Japan to play for a team sponsored by Toyota. In 2016, the Houston Scrap Yard Dawgs signed Abbott to a six-year $1 million contract—the most lucrative contract paid to a woman athlete by an American professional team.

In 2020, women softball players announced the formation of a new player-run league, Athletes Unlimited. The players would be paid a minimum of $10,000 with bonuses of up to $35,000. Each player would receive a share of the league's profits for twenty years—although they did not expect the league to be profitable in its first few years.[41]

Most women who play baseball or softball, whether amateur or professional, do so in all-women leagues. This provides a supportive culture for female athletes, including lesbians. But despite the upsurge of women's participation in softball and baseball, the stigma and stereotypes have not disappeared.

Malaika Underwood was an infielder on the 2008 and 2014 Women's World Cup teams and a member of the US women's national baseball team, which won a gold medal at the 2015 Pan American Games. When asked to discuss female athletes she shared that "she regrets that she sometimes capitulates to the impulse to be 'proactively heterosexual,' often making certain to mention that she has a boyfriend early in the conversation 'to establish that I'm not gay without them questioning it.'"[42]

Outfielder Tamara Holmes played Little League in Albany, California, and high school baseball in Berkeley. At the University of California at Berkeley, she played softball and basketball where, she recalled, "There is a higher chance of having gay members on the team," which made her more comfortable as a black lesbian.[43] In 1996, she joined the Colorado Silver Bullets, an all-female professional baseball team, even though she hadn't played competitive baseball since high school. (The Bullets only lasted from 1994 to 1997.) She graduated from Berkeley in 2001 and three years later played for the US team in the first Women's World Cup baseball tournament. She played on subsequent World Cup teams every two years until 2014, and for the US team in the 2015 Pan American Games. She was not publicly out of the closet, however, until she married her wife in 2016. Holmes became a firefighter and athletic trainer in Oakland after her athletic career ended.

Lauren Lappin grew up in Southern California and was an outstanding high school athlete. She knew she was gay in high school but dated men to avoid having to come out. "Hearing people talk about gay people or lesbians in a negative connotation was something that was pretty regular throughout high school and even in college," said Lappin, "Looking back, I think it was more of just the stereotype that all softball players are lesbians had something to do with it."[44] She was an All-American softball player at Stanford, graduating in 2006. She didn't come out publicly until 2008, after Vicky Galindo, her teammate on the silver-medal winning US Olympic team, told her teammates that she was a lesbian.[45]

In 2010, Lappin played on the US national team, which won the world championship. She then became a full-time professional, playing for the USSSA Pride, a team in the NPF league, then in its sixth season. She retired in 2015. She also spent several years as an assistant coach at Northwestern University.[46]

In 2018, Aleshia Ocasio, a Black Puerto Rican, graduated from the University of Florida, where she played for the NCAA Division I Softball champions. She came out as bisexual in college, explaining, "Playing in this sport and being around the same people every day who a lot of identify as LGBTQ+, I'm blessed to say that I've been comfortable with the process of coming out and being in an environment where I feel supported."[47] In 2019 she joined the Chicago Bandits, a NPF team, and was outspoken on behalf of the Black Lives Matter movement.

There are no women players in the NBA, NFL, NHL, or MLS. Women don't compete directly with men in professional golf or tennis. Might baseball be different? Women have played on men's baseball teams in college and in the minor leagues. Is it possible that the next generation of outstanding athletes like Abbott, Underwood, Holmes, Lappin, and Ocasio might someday play in the major leagues?

Whether or not that is in the cards, creating a viable women's professional baseball league—a new league of their own—is within reach. There is currently no baseball counterpart to professional women's basketball or soccer. The pipeline of female baseball players is currently much smaller than it is for softball, but some advocates believe that it could be possible to develop and sustain a professional women's baseball league within a generation. Doing so, however, would require a major change of thinking among high school and college administrators, who view baseball and softball to be so similar that they are "separate but equal" for purposes of Title IX. But they are, in fact, two different sports. Many female athletes might prefer the windmill pitching, shorter distances, and large balls that are part of softball. But that doesn't mean that there aren't girls and young women who can pitch overhand, hit a hardball thrown eighty or more miles an hour, and run ninety feet between bases.

In 1996, Justine Siegal (who later became the first female coach for an MLB team) started Baseball for All, a nonprofit organization that encourages girls to pursue baseball beyond the Little League level. It began as a four-team all-women's baseball league in Cleveland and has expanded since then. Baseball For All sponsored the first national girls' baseball tournament for girls ages ten to thirteen in Orlando, Florida, attracting hundreds of players from around the country. The 2019 event, played at Beyer Stadium in Rockford, Illinois, home of the AAGPBL's Rockford Peaches, expanded to include girls from seven to eighteen, attracting 350 participants.

In 2017, USA Baseball and MLB launched a new baseball tournament for girls ages eleven to thirteen called Trailblazers, held in Los Angeles area. By 2019, the two-day event attracted girls from twenty-one states, Canada, and Puerto Rico, whose expenses were covered by MLB. In 2018, MLB sponsored Girls Baseball Breakthrough Series (GBBS) aimed at identifying and grooming young girls to play baseball. The first Women's Baseball World Cup tournament has been held every two years since 2004. By 2016, twelve countries sent teams to the tournament. The US Baseball Women's National Team represented the United States at these events and at the Pan American Games in 2015, the first year women's baseball was included in that tournament.

Creating a large pipeline for women's baseball will require significant expansion of organized leagues. In Little League and other youth leagues (like the San Francisco Bay Sox baseball team for ages six to sixteen), high school programs, and even college programs, girls and women can play on mixed-gender teams as well as participate on all-female teams. More resources must be provided for more girls to begin playing baseball as adolescents and then be encouraged to continue playing baseball in high school and in college. That means that high school and college administrators can no longer allow women's softball to be counted as the equivalent of baseball when it comes to calculating the funding for men's and women's sports.

Out of the Closet, Into the Locker Room

In recent decades, America has made significant strides in advancing LGBTQ rights. One sign of progress is that young Americans—those born since the 1990s—are much less homophobic than older generations. In 2019, for example, 83 percent of Americans ages eighteen to twenty-nine, compared with 47 percent of Americans over sixty-five years of age, supported same-sex marriage. Younger gay people are more willing to come out of the closet, which in turn encourages straight Americans to accept homosexuality and support LGBTQ rights legislation.

Umpire Dave Pallone's 1990 memoir, *Behind the Mask: My Double Life in Baseball,* was shocking for stating that there were enough closeted gay major leaguers to field an All-Star team. Pallone did not name names. But his book and subsequent comments triggered a guessing game to identify gay players wearing big league uniforms.

In 2001, *Details* magazine quoted Mets manager Bobby Valentine that professional baseball is "probably ready for an openly gay player," adding, "the players are diverse enough now that I think they could handle it."[48] A *New York Post* gossip columnist speculated that Valentine's comments were a "pre-emptory strike" meant to pave the way for one of his players to come out. "There is a persistent rumor around town," the columnist wrote, "that one Mets star who spends a lot of time with pretty models in clubs is actually gay and has started to think about declaring his sexual orientation."[49] The rumors focused on the Mets' star catcher Mike Piazza, who felt compelled to hold an impromptu press conference. "I'm not gay," Piazza announced. "I'm hetero-sexual." He also said that players would accept an openly gay teammate. "In this day and age," Piazza told reporters, "it's irrelevant. I don't think it would be a problem at all."[50]

Polls show that fans support openly gay athletes playing professional sports. Acknowledging that the issue of gays in pro sports was on people's minds, in 2001 ESPN conducted a poll, asking, "If a player on your favorite professional sports team announced he or she was gay or lesbian, how would this affect your attitude towards that player?"[51] Only 17 percent said they would turn against the player, 63 percent said it would make no difference, and 20 percent said they would become a bigger fan. By 2015, a national poll found that 73 percent of Americans said they would support a pro sports team signing an openly gay or lesbian athlete, while fewer than one-fifth

(19 percent) said they would oppose it. The poll found broad support across the political spectrum, including 54 percent of white evangelical Protestants.

In 2013, Turnkey Sports and Entertainment asked sports executives how they thought fans would react to openly gay athletes on pro teams. Eighty-five percent thought that fans would be indifferent, 5 percent believed that fans would be supportive, and 5 percent thought fans would be less supportive of a team with an openly gay athlete.

"I think the time is coming for a team to have an active gay player," Arizona Diamondbacks president Derrick Hall told *USA Today* in 2016. "I'm confident there are players playing now that are gay. I'm looking forward to that day when we can point to one or many players, and say, there's an example of our inclusion, openness and acceptance."[52]

Most gay ballplayers still feel that coming out while in uniform puts their career in jeopardy. In retrospect, some say that they wish they had come out during their playing days, but the few minor league players who have done so have not remained in pro baseball very long.

MLB, including many of its minor league franchises, has sought to change the cultural climate for players and fans alike by monitoring and discouraging bigotry among players, reaching out to the LGBTQ community, and supporting gay players. But homophobia remains a serious problem in society and in baseball at the college and professional levels.

On August 8, 2000, security guards at Dodger Stadium ejected a lesbian couple, Danielle Goldey and Meredith Kott, for kissing during the game, allegedly saying that young children should not be exposed to "those people."[53] The couple talked to a lawyer about suing the team, but before they took any action, the Dodgers not only apologized but donated 5,000 tickets to gay rights groups and invited the couple to sit behind home plate. Then, on September 6, the LA Gay & Lesbian Center sponsored a "Gay and Lesbian Night at Dodger Stadium," believed to be the first "gay night" at a major league game.

The following season, the Chicago Cubs sponsored "Gay Days," which later became "Out at Wrigley." (In 2009, when the Ricketts family purchased the Cubs, Laura Ricketts became the first openly LGBTQ person to own a professional sports team. And Billie Jean King is part-owner of the Los Angeles Dodgers).

By 2021, out of thirty MLB teams, only the Texas Rangers have never hosted an LGBTQ Pride event of some kind. But, according to Billy Bean, team executives have initiated talks with Dallas' LGBTQ Resource Center to begin a partnership.[54] (The city's other professional sports teams, including the Dallas Mavericks, Dallas Stars, Dallas FC, and Dallas Wings, all host Pride celebrations.)

In 2019, the Yankees celebrated the fiftieth anniversary of the protest at the Stonewall Inn (considered the start of modern gay rights movement) by unveiling a plaque behind the centerfield fence commemorating the historic protest and awarding the first annual Yankees-Stonewall Scholarships to five New York City public school students in a pregame ceremony. In 2021, the Oakland A's announced that its annual Pride Night celebration would be known as Glenn Burke Pride Night. That year, too, at its annual Pride Day, the San Francisco Giants players wore baseball caps with rainbow pride colors in their logos and a pride-colored *SF* patch on their jerseys. It was an unprecedented display of support for LGBTQ fans. Before the game, the Giants honored gay former San Francisco City Council member and state legislator Tom Ammiano, and transgender activist Honey Mahogany sang the national anthem.

MLB took a major step when it hired Billy Bean in 2014 to help educate players and team executives about LGBTQ issues, including stereotypes and defamatory words and statements. That year, MLB issued a strongly worded statement denouncing Arizona Senate Bill 1062, called the Religious Freedom Act, which would allow businesses the right to refuse service to anyone based on the business owner's religious beliefs without fear of lawsuits. Critics claimed that it would lead to widespread discrimination against homosexuals. MLB's statement cited its "zero-tolerance policy for harassment or discrimination based on sexual orientation, as reflected by our collective bargaining agreement with the MLB Players Association."[55] MLB's statement, which generated substantial news coverage, helped persuade Governor Jan Brewer, a conservative Republican, to veto the legislation.

In 2016, MLB forged a partnership with the National Gay and Lesbian Chamber of Commerce to help LGBTQ-owned businesses bid on contracts within professional baseball. The Mets announced that a portion of the proceeds from ticket sales will go to the LGBTQ Network's Safe Schools Initiative in nearby Queens and Long Island. A growing number of teams now have openly gay top-tier executives. Erik Braverman is the Dodgers' senior vice president of marketing communications and broadcasting. Greg Bader serves as the Baltimore Orioles' senior vice president of administration and experience. Roscoe Mapps is vice president of external affairs for the San Francisco Giants, and Nona Lee is the Arizona Diamondbacks' executive vice president and chief legal officer. Bean has started a program to recruit and mentor more LGBTQ people to work for baseball teams' front offices at the major and minor league levels.

What is stopping gay professional baseball players from coming out publicly? The biggest obstacle is the workplace environment, especially among teammates. Certainly there are gay players in the majors who would like to come out, but so far they have calculated that the personal or financial costs outweigh the benefits. They fear being ostracized by fellow players, harassed by fans, and perhaps traded by their team's management or dropped entirely. They may lose some commercial endorsements, although it is possible that some gay-friendly companies would look favorably about having gay players as spokespeople for their products.

There is a strong fundamentalist Christian current within baseball, which could make life uncomfortable for out players. One study discovered that "major league baseball players are far and away the most overtly religious group of athletes of the four major sporting leagues."[56]

In 2012, Detroit Tigers outfielder Torii Hunter told a *Los Angeles Times* reporter that an out teammate could divide a team. "For me, as a Christian . . . I will be uncomfortable because in all my teachings and all my learning, biblically, it's not right," he said. "It will be difficult and uncomfortable."[57] Several sports columnists criticized Hunter's remarks, but there was no official response from MLB.

In 2015, Houston Astros slugger Lance Berkman, an evangelical Christian, campaigned against the city's Equal Rights Ordinance, designed to protect LGBTQ rights. "To me," Berkman said at the time, "tolerance is the virtue that's killing this country." The ordinance was defeated. Two years later, the St. Louis Cardinals, one of Berkman's former teams, invited him to speak at "Christian Day," held in July 2017 at Busch Stadium. A St. Louis gay rights group, the Pride Center, issued a statement saying it was "disappointed by the decision of the St. Louis Cardinals to provide a public platform for Berkman, an individual whose words and actions towards the LGBTQ+ are divisive and demeaning."[58]

Tyler Dunnington, who spent a year with a Cardinals minor league franchise in 2014, also spoke out about the invitation to Berkman, expressing his "disappointment" and expressing hope that "in the future, they will reconsider giving a platform to someone who thinks tolerance is a bad thing." But the Cardinals went through with the invitation, claiming that "Lance Berkman participated in Christian Day when he was a Cardinals player, and we welcome him back this year to discuss his faith." At that point, the Cardinals were still one of the holdouts to never hold a Pride Night, but they did so later that year.[59]

Some pro ballplayers have not been shy about expressing homophobic slurs and voicing their opposition to having openly gay teammates. In the internet age, antigay comments are hard to keep secret, and such remarks by ballplayers almost inevitably became news stories. MLB has increasingly expressed its official opposition to public expressions of homophobia among players. Several teams have fined or suspended players and managers for using antigay slurs, although the sanctions have been uneven. Team executives and players have expressed more support for the LBGTQ community and for having openly gay players on their rosters.

In 1999, Atlanta Braves pitcher John Rocker told *Sports Illustrated* he didn't want to take the New York subway because he might encounter "some queer with AIDS." Commissioner Bud Selig suspended him for seventy-three days, fined him $20,000, and ordered him to undergo sensitivity training.[60]

In the 2001 season, Chicago Cubs pitcher Julian Tavarez called San Francisco Giants fans "a bunch of faggots" after they booed him during a game. Rather than issue a fine or suspension, Selig simply deferred to the Cubs management, which issued a statement criticizing Tavarez and imposed a fine. Prompted by Cubs manager Don Baylor, the next day Tavarez apologized to the city of San Francisco.[61]

In 2003, the *Denver Post* asked Colorado Rockies pitcher Todd Jones for his reaction to the Broadway play *Take Me Out*, a Tony award-winning Broadway play about a celebrated New York City baseball hero who announces that he's gay. Jones said, "I wouldn't want a gay guy being around me." The Rockies issued a statement distancing the team from Jones's comments, but neither the Commissioner nor the team imposed any punishment.[62]

In 2006, Chicago White Sox manager Ozzie Guillen got angry at a column by *Sun-Times* writer Jay Mariotti and called the columnist a "fucking fag." Selig ordered Guillen to undergo four hours of sensitivity training after which Guillen told reporter, "I think the guy learned more from me than I learned from him."[63] That same year, the Toronto Blue Jays suspended Yunel Escobar for three games for writing a homophobic slur in Spanish on his eye black.

There are indicators that the climate is changing among players, teams, and fans. *Outsports* reported that the COVID-19–shortened sixty-game 2020 baseball season was the first season without any players involved in on-field antigay controversies since it began monitoring the issue in 2016 season.

In fact, the opposite occurred. During the 2020 season, veteran Cincinnati Reds announcer Thom Brennaman used a gay slur over a hot mic. He was quickly suspended and then resigned under pressure. Several Reds players and manager David Bell publicly denounced Brennaman's remarks. Pitcher Amir Garrett tweeted, "To the LGBTQ community just know I am with you, and whoever is against you, is against me. I'm sorry for what was said today." Reds slugger Joey Votto said, "It's too bad that there are people out there that have been held down and oppressed and had terrible experiences in their lives because of that word."[64]

Some players and managers have been voicing similar sentiments for at least the past two decades. In 2003, Colorado Rockies star Mark Grace told the *Denver Post* that most ballplayers wouldn't be threatened by the idea of a gay teammate. "I've played for 16 years, and I'm sure I've had homosexual teammates that I didn't know about. If one out of six or seven men are homosexual—do the math." He thought some players might be fearful of having a gay teammate but said, "I think if you're intelligent at all, you'd understand that homosexuals are just like us."[65]

Asked about having a gay teammate, Ken Griffey Jr. told *Sports Illustrated* in 2005: "Wouldn't bother me at all. If you can play, you can play."[66] In 2015, Eno Sarris of FanGraphs collected quotes from major leaguers—including Oakland Athletics players Sam Fuld, Josh Reddick, and Sonny Gray, and Padres players Justin Upton and Tyson Ross—who said they believe that MLB is ready for an openly gay player, and as discussed in chapter 8, Sean Doolittle has been outspoken in support of the LGBTQ community on and off the field.

"When I was playing, homosexuality was a taboo topic. We never talked openly about it," Billy Bean explained. "That's changed. Players, staff and executives all know LGBTQ folks. They have different images of gay people now. There's more understanding and less fear. Today's players want to know if their teammates can help their teams win."[67]

Asked in 2002 about the likelihood of a gay player coming out of the closet, Philadelphia Phillies manager Larry Bowa told the Associated Press, "If it was me, I'd probably wait until my career was over. I'm sure it would depend on who the player was. If he hits .340, it probably would be easier than if he hits .220."[68] Former MLB umpire Dave Pallone echoed similar sentiments: "I hope it's a player whose name rolls off somebody's tongue. That's what will do the most good."[69]

If a superstar came out first, it would be easier for average players to come out of the closet. The most likely candidates are among the growing number of openly gay college players, the best of whom could ascend the professional ranks into the majors. Several college players have laid the groundwork for that to happen. Of course, if several gay ballplayers came out simultaneously, no single player would have to confront the abuse (as well as bask in the cheers) on his own, as Jackie Robinson did. "The world has changed," Billy Bean observed. "Gay athletes in high school, college, and the minors now have role models, like Carl [Nassib, the NFL player] and Luke [Prokop, the NHL draft pick]. They have people like me they can talk to."[70]

"I think we're getting close" to having an openly gay player on a major league roster, said Bean. "We're making incredible strides."[71] For significant change to occur, the right person (or persons) has to mix with the right cultural and social conditions. The Black people of Montgomery, and the national news media, were ready when Rosa Parks refused to move to the back of the bus in 1955. Gay patrons at the Stonewall Inn didn't show up one night in 1969 planning to protest mistreatment by police, but when the NYPD raided the bar, years of pent-up anger was unleashed, and the confrontation became a turning point in the gay rights movement.

But the time is never exactly right. No matter how much injustice people experience, some will argue that society isn't ready for a major breakthrough. As Jon Buzinski, the founder of *Outsports*, observed, "Everybody will say, 'We aren't ready.' Society was not ready for Jackie Robinson. If you are going to wait for everybody to be ready, nobody will do it."[72]

Foreword

1. Martin Luther King Jr., "Hall of Fame Testimonial Dinner" (speech), July 20, 1962, quoted in Rampersad, *Jackie Robinson*, 7.
2. Dreier and Elias, *Baseball Rebels*, 12.

Introduction

3. Doolitte, "These Refugees."
4. "Editorial: Short Takes on Human Athletes, Car-Racing Doldrums and Anti-Privacy Conspirators," *St. Louis Post-Dispatch*, February 24, 2017, https://www.stltoday.com/opinion/editorial/editorial-short-takes-on-human-athletes-car-racing-doldrums-and-anti-privacy-conspirators/article_8956c2cc-31ae-5e1b-b2ea-562a90080483.html.
5. Posnanski, *The Baseball 100*, 639.
6. Jones, "Dutch Leonard,"
7. Briley, "Baseball and the Cold War, 15–18.
8. Marc Lacey, "Lasorda Speaks for Constitutional Amendment to Ban Flag Desecration," *Los Angeles Times*, July 9, 1998, https://www.latimes.com/archives/la-xpm-1998-jul-09-mn-2240-story.html.
9. Andrew Joseph, "Curt Schilling Says That Hillary Clinton 'Should Be Buried Under a Jail Somewhere,'" *USA Today*, March 2, 2016, https://ftw.usatoday.com/2016/03/curt-schilling-hillary-clinton-buried-under-jail.

Chapter One. Battling Jim Crow

1. Tygiel, *Past Time*, 6.
2. Hingston, "13 Things."
3. Hingston, "13 Things."
4. Waskie, "Octavius Catto Biography."
5. Waskie, "Octavius Catto Biography."
6. "Catto Addresses State House."
7. Waskie, "Octavius Catto Biography."

8. Gordon, "Octavius Catto."

9. Coval, "Playing for Keeps."

10. "Forging Citizenship and Opportunity."

11. Grigsby, *Celebrating Ourselves*, 33.

12. Wyman, "The Philadelphia Catto," 100.

13. Casway, "September 3, 1869."

14. Casway, "September 3, 1869."

15. Segal, "An Unbreakable Game," 467–94.

16. Biddle and Dubin, *Tasting Freedom*, 373.

17. Biddle and Dubin, *Tasting Freedom*, 373.

18. Biddle and Dubin, *Tasting Freedom*, 373

19. Casway, *The Culture and Ethnicity*, 38.

20. Duthiers, "Octavius Valentine Catto."

21. Zang, *Fleet Walker's Divided Heart*, 30.

22. *Toledo Daily Blade*, March 15, 1883, 3.

23. *Toledo Daily Blade*, March 15, 1883, 3.

24. *Sporting Life*, April 8, 1885, 5.

25. Husman, "August 10, 1883."

26. Zang, *Fleet Walker's Divided Heart*, 43.

27. Husman, "Fleet Walker."

28. Zang, *Fleet Walker's Divided Heart*, 42.

29. Zang, *Fleet Walker's Divided Heart*, 97.

30. Walker, *Our Home Colony*.

31. Zang, *Fleet Walker's Divided Heart*, 106.

Chapter Two. Building Black Institutions

1. *Lynching in America.*

2. Peterson, *Only the Ball Was White*, 103.

3. Odzer, "Rube Foster."

4. Hogan, *Forgotten History*, 145.

5. Tabbert, "American Giant."

6. Rogosin, *Invisible Men*, 68.

7. Lester, *Rube Foster in His Time*, 99.

8. Katz, *The American Negro*, 56.

9. Cottrell, *Best Pitcher in Baseball*, 106.

10. Trembanis, "They Opened the Door Too Late," 67.

11. "Monument to Racial Industry," 5.

12. Hogan, *Shades of Glory*, 160.

13. Ross, *Manning the Race*, 37.

14. Pietrusza, *Judge and Jury*, 413.

15. O'Toole, *The Best Man Plays*, 23.

16. Luke, *Willie Wells*, ix.

17. Holway, "Million Dollar Infield."

18. Fleitz, *Ghosts in the Gallery*, 197–98.

19. Riley, *Dandy, Day and the Devil*, 108.

20. Holway, "Frank 'Doc' Sykes."

21. Quoted in Hogan, *Forgotten History*, 122.

22. Holway, "Frank 'Doc' Sykes."

23. Deangelo McDaniel, "Scottsboro Boys Record," *The Decatur Daily*, September 30, 2007, http://archive.decaturdaily.com/decaturdaily/news/070930/scottsboro.shtml.

24. Quoted in Hogan, *Forgotten History*, 125.

Chapter Three. Before Jackie Robinson

1. Broun repeated his remarks in his syndicated column. Broun, "It Seems to Me."

2. Lamb, *Conspiracy of Silence*, 5.

3. Ruck, "Crossing the Color Line," 327.

4. Green et al., *Jackie Robinson Story*.

5. Myrdal, *An American Dilemma*, 21.

6. Horowitz, "Negro and White"; Zeitlin and Weyher, "Black and White," 430–67.

7. Little, "Why FDR Didn't Support."

8. Naison, *Communists in Harlem*; Solomon, *Cry Was Unity* Like others in that CP orbit, some of these Black artists and intellectuals later became disillusioned with communism and some denounced it publicly. See, for example, Smethurst, "Don't Say Goodbye," 1224–37.

9. ExecOrder No8802.

10. Tygiel, *Extra Bases*, 69.

11. Quoted in Mitcheli, *The Defender*, 244.

12. Tygiel, *Baseball's Great Experiment*, 69; Wendell Smith, "Plan to Boycott Yankees," *Pittsburgh Courier*, April 14, 1945; "Baseball Ban Draws Pickets at 1st Game," *New York Amsterdam News*, April 21, 1945; "Pickets Protest Baseball Bigotry," *Afro-American*, April 28, 1945; "Picket Yankee Stadium Game," *Chicago Defender*, April 28, 1945.

13. James G. Thompson, "Should I Sacrifice to Live 'Half-American?'" *Pittsburgh Courier*, January 31, 1942, 3; Goldman, "The Double Victory Campaign," 405–8.

14. "Labor Union to Protest Major League Color Ban at New York World Fair," *Pittsburgh Courier*, May 25, 1940, 16; "10,000 at Fair Petition to End Baseball Jim Crow," *Daily Worker*, July 25, 1940.

15. McReynolds, "Nate Moreland," 55–64.

16. Essington, *Integration of the Pacific Coast League*, 36–37.

17. "Labor Calls on Landis to Remove Color Ban in Major Leagues," *Pittsburgh Courier*, June 13, 1942, 15; "Seamen Demand Landis Lift Ban," *Daily Worker*, June 5, 1942; "Removal of Baseball Jim-Crow Against Negroes Sought by Strong White Forces," *Atlanta Daily World*, June 7, 1942; "Organized Labor Joins Fight on Major League Bias: Judge Landis Petitioned by Unions 2,000 Maritime Workers, Wholesalers Ask for Justice," *New York Amsterdam News*, June 13, 1942; "Color Ban in Baseball Hit by Packinghouse Men," *Chicago Defender*, July 11, 1942.

18. "Czar Landis Denies Rule Against Negroes in Majors," *Austin Statesman*, July 17, 1942; "You May Hire All Negro Players, No Ban Exists, Landis Tells Durocher," *New York Herald Tribune*, July 17, 1942.

19. "Drive on Jim Crow Gains Momentum," *Sunday Worker*, June 28, 1942.

20. "No Baseball Rule Against Hiring Negroes—Landis," *Elmira (New York) Star-Gazette*, July 17, 1942; Fetter, "Party Line," 375–402; Fetter, "From 'Stooge' to 'Czar,'" 29–63.

21. "Landis Denies Audience to Negro Group," *Detroit Free Press*, December 4, 1942; "CIO's Request to Ask Majors to Hire Negroes Turned Down," *Hartford Courant*, December 4, 1942; "Landis Rebuffs Plea for Negro Play in Majors: Asks Fair Play for Ball Stars/Bob Considine, Famous White Sports Writer, Urges Negro Players Be Given Their Chance," *New York Amsterdam Star-News*, December 12, 1942.

22. "Wrigley Sees 'Negroes in Big Leagues Soon': Cubs' Owner Says It Has 'Got To Come'/Would Put Negro Player on His Team if Fans Demanded Same," *Chicago Defender*, December 26, 1942; Lamb, *Conspiracy of Silence*, 218–21.

23. "Send Resolution on Negroes in Major Baseball to FDR," *Chicago Defender*, February 20, 1943;

24. This discussion of Wendell Smith relies on the following sources: Carroll, "Crusading Journalist's Last Campaign," 38–54; Carroll, "'It Couldn't Be,'" 5–23; Lamb, *Conspiracy of Silence*; Lamb, "What's Wrong with Baseball," 189–203; Wiggins, "Wendell Smith," 5; McTaggart, "Writing Baseball into History," 113–132; Andrew Schall, "Wendell Smith: The Pittsburgh Journalist Who Made Jackie Robinson Mainstream," *Pittsburgh Post-Gazette*, June 5, 2011; "Wendell Smith, Sportswriter, Jackie Robinson Booster, Dies," *New York Times*, November 27, 1972.

25. "Satchel Outhurls Dizzy!" *Pittsburgh Courier*, October 27, 1934."

26. "Dizzy Dean Rates 'Satch' Greatest Pitcher," *Pittsburgh Courier*, September 24, 1938, 17.

27. Wendell Smith, "'Would Be A Mad Scramble For Negro Players If Okayed'—Hartnett: Discrimination Has No Place In Baseball—These Cubs Agree," *Pittsburgh Courier*, August 12, 1939, 37.

28. Wendell Smith, "Smitty's Sport Spurts: A Strange Tribe," *Pittsburgh Courier*, May 14, 1938, 17.

29. Wendell Smith, "General Public Must Be Changed," *Pittsburgh Courier*, February 25, 1939.

30. McGregor, *Calculus of Color*, 65.

31. Wendell Smith, "Smitty's Sports Spurts," *Pittsburgh Courier*, March 24, 1945.

32. Lamb, *Conspiracy of Silence*, 235.

33. Silber, *Press Box Red*, 6; Duberman, *Paul Robeson*, 282–83.

34. Wendell Smith, "Publishers Place Case of Negro Players Before Big League Owners: Judge Landis Says No Official Race Ban Exists in Majors," *Pittsburgh Courier*, December 11, 1943, 1; "Robeson Sees Labor as Salvation of Negro Race: Praises CIO Plan to Better Racial Conditions Here," *Pittsburgh Courier*, December 25, 1943, 11.

35. Wendell Smith, "Smitty's Sport Spurts," *Pittsburgh Courier*, December 2, 1944.

36. Silber, *Press Box Red*, 6.

37. Silber, *Press Box Red*, 7

38. Silber, *Press Box Red*, 8–9.

39. Silber, *Press Box Red*, 151.

40. Quoted in Tygiel, *Baseball's Great Experiment*, 37.

41. Silber, *Press Box Red*, 79–80.

42. Zirin, "Interview with 'Red' Rodney."

43. Silber, *Press Box Red*, 79.

44. Silber, *Press Box Red*, 67.

45. Silber, *Press Box Red*, 166

46. Silber, *Press Box Red*, 144.

47. Silber, *Press Box Red*, 147.

48. Silber, *Press Box Red*, 144.

49. Silber, *Press Box Red*, 146.

50. Silber, *Press Box Red*, 61.

51. Silber, *Press Box Red*, 81.

52. Silber, *Press Box Red*, 68.

53. Dickson, *Bill Veeck*, 45.

54. Veeck, *Veeck as in Wreck*, 177

55. Veeck, *Veeck as in Wreck*, 177–78.

56. Dickson, *Bill Veeck*, 79

57. Veeck, *Veeck as in Wreck*, 171–72; Dickson, *Bill Veeck*, 79 Baseball historians disagree about whether Veeck's story about trying to purchase the Phillies is accurate. His biographer, Paul Dickson, believes it is true, but the debate can be found in these articles: Gerlach et al., "Baseball Myth Exploded"; Tygiel, "Revisiting Bill Veeck"; Warrington and Macht, "Veracity of Veeck."

58. Quoted in Tygiel, *Baseball's Great Experiment*, 69.

59. Fimrite, "Sam Lacy."

60. Lowenfish, *Branch Rickey*, 363.

61. "Two Negroes Are Tried Out by the Dodgers but They Fail to Impress President Rickey," *New York Times*, April 8, 1945.

62. Nowlin, *Tom Yawkey*; Nowlin, ed., *Pumpsie & Progress*.

63. Ric Roberts, "Chandler's Views on Player Ban Sought: New Czar Must Face Bias Issue," *Pittsburgh Courier*, May 5, 1945, 12.

64. This profile of Nahem draws on Dreier, "Sam Nahem: The Right-Handed Lefty," 184–201.

65. Dreier, "Sam Nahem," *Society for American Baseball Research*.

66. Eskenazi, "'Subway' Sam Nahem."

67. Eskenazi, "Artful Dodger."

68. Eskenazi, "Artful Dodger."

69. "Oise Nine Beats Third Army," *New York Times*, September 6, 1945.

70. "All Stars Win European Title," 12.

71. Weintraub, *Victory Season*.

72. "71st Division Wins ETO Game by 9 to 2," *New York Times*, September 3, 1945; "All Stars Win European Title"; "Third Army Loses to All-Stars, 2-1: Four-Hit Hurling of Leo [*sic*] Day of Newark Squares GI Series of One Each," *New York Times*, September 4, 1945; "Third Army Nine Loses to Oise," Plainfield (New Jersey) *Courier News*, September 6, 1945; "Third Army Nine Evens Series," *Des Moines Register*, September 7, 1945.

Chapter Four. Crossing the Color Line

1. McCue, "Branch Rickey."

2. Lowenfish, *Branch Rickey*, 325

3. Lowenfish, *Branch Rickey*, 15.

4. John McMurray, "Branch Rickey Revolutionized Baseball in More Ways Than One," *Investor's Business Daily*, April 12, 2017, https://www.investors.com/news/management/leaders-and-success/branch-rickey-revolutionized-baseball-in-more-ways-than-one/.

5. Allen St. John, "There Was Another Side to the Color Line: Green," *Los Angeles Times*, March 30, 1997. For more on Rickey's motives for pursuing integration, see Lowenfish, *Branch Rickey*.

6. Lowenfish, *Branch Rickey*, 379.

7. Rampersad, *Jackie Robinson*, 91. See also Tygiel, *Baseball's Great Experiment*, 61–62.

8. The story of Robinson's court martial, including the quotes, is found in Rampersad, *Jackie Robinson*, 102–9.

9. Robinson, *Baseball Has Done It*.

10. Lamb, *Blackout*, 75. Sanford is the town where Trayvon Martin, an unarmed seventeen-year-old Black man, was fatally shot by a vigilante in 2012, sparking a wave of national protest. See Peter Dreier, "Sanford and Its Sons: From Jackie Robinson to Trayvon Martin," *Huffington Post*, July 14, 2013, https://www.huffpost.com/entry/sanford-and-its-sons-from_b_3595577.

11. Lamb, *Conspiracy of Silence*, 312.

12. Tygiel, *Baseball's Great Experiment*, 109.

13. Rampersad, *Jackie Robinson*, 139.

14. Tygiel, *Baseball's Great Experiment*, 188.

15. Rampersad, *Jackie Robinson*, 172.

16. Haft, "10 Significant Moments."

17. Dreier, "Half a Century Before Colin Kaepernick."

18. *Hearings Regarding Communist Infiltration*, 479.

19. Duberman, *Paul Robeson*, 211.

20. Robinson with Duckett, *I Never Had It Made*, 83.

21. *Hearings Regarding Communist Infiltration*, 481.

22. *Hearings Regarding Communist Infiltration*, 481.

23. *Hearings Regarding Communist Infiltration*, 481.

24. *Hearings Regarding Communist Infiltration*, 481.

25. Golenbock, *Bums*, 223.

26. Arthur Daley, "Sports of the Times: Jackie Robinson and the Ku Klux Klan," *New York Times*, Jan 18, 1949, 29.

27. "Ku Klux Seeking to Bar Dodgers' Two Negro Stars," *Hartford Courant*, January 15, 1949.

28. "Jackie Robinson Pleased at Big Atlanta Ovation," *Boston Globe*, April 9, 1949.

29. Green et al., *Jackie Robinson Story*.

30. Schutz, *Jackie Robinson*, 105.

31. Gross, "Why They Boo."

32. Quoted in Schutz, *Jackie Robinson*, 102.

33. Kevin Kernan, "Larry Is Stuff of Legends," *New York Post*, July 28, 2002, https://nypost.com/2002/07/28/lary-is-stuff-of-legends-struggles-of-doby-a-lesson-for-any-time/.

34. Tye, "Satchel Paige."

35. Francis, "When Ted Williams Changed History."

36. Munzel, "14 Negro Players."

37. Dickson, *Bill Veeck*, 173.

38. Dickson, *Bill Veeck*, 225.

39. Nowlin, "Sam Jethroe."

40. Nowlin, "Sam Jethroe."

41. Nowlin, "Sam Jethroe."

42. Nowlin, "Sam Jethroe."

43. See Dreier, "Joe Black;" Black and Schoffner, *Joe Black*; Black, *Ain't Nobody Better*.

44. Rampersad, *Jackie Robinson*, 302.

45. Rampersad, *Jackie Robinson*, 367.

46. Rampersad, *Jackie Robinson*, 344; Schutz, *Jackie Robinson*, 120.

47. Rampersad, *Jackie Robinson*, 351.

48. Michael Beschloss, "Jackie Robinson and Nixon: Life and Death of a Political Friendship," *New York Times*, June 6, 2014, https://www.nytimes.com/2014/06/07/upshot/jackie-robinson-and-nixon-life-and-death-of-a-political-friendship.html.

49. Naze, *Reclaiming 42*, 65; Tinsley, "Jackie Robinson."

50. Bryant, "Unsanitized Story of Jackie Robinson."

51. Remnick, "Recalling Muhammad Ali."

52. Rampersad, *Jackie Robinson*, 415.

53. Quoted in Tygiel, *Baseball's Great Experiment*, 340.

54. Quoted in Tygiel, *Baseball's Great Experiment*, 341.

55. Briley, "Do Not Go Gently."

56. Rampersad, *Jackie Robinson*, 459.

57. Robinson with Duckett, *I Never Had It Made*, 268–69.

58. Robinson with Duckett, *I Never Had It Made*, 85–86.

59. Robinson with Duckett, *I Never Had It Made*, xxiv.

Chapter Five. Defending Civil Rights

1. Dreier, "Pumpsie Green."

2. Aaron with Wheeler, *I Had a Hammer*.

3. Bryant, "Atlanta Pro Sports and Integration."

4. "New Film Shows Hank Aaron's Lifetime of Overcoming Racism," *USA Today*, February 27, 2016, https://www.usatoday.com/story/sports/mlb/2016/02/27/new-film-shows-hank-aarons-lifetime-of-overcoming-racism/81031802/.

5. Baseball Reference, "Vic Power."

6. Drouzas, "Baseball and Biscuits."

7. Aaron, *I Had a Hammer*, 154.

8. Davis, "Baseball's Reluctant Challenge," 146.

9. Davis, "Baseball's Reluctant Challenge," 162.

10. Maraniss, "No Gentle Saint."

11. Varela, "What Would Clemente Do?."

12. Florio and Shapiro, "When King Died."

13. Francis, "National Tragedy Brought Baseball."

14. White, *Uppity*, 29.

15. White, "When Baseball Defied Segregation."

16. White, *Uppity*, 34.

17. Davis, "Baseball's Reluctant Challenge," 144.

18. Florio and Shapiro, *One Nation Under Baseball*, 19.

19. White, "When Baseball Defied Segregation."

20. Dave Anderson, "Sports of The Times; Bill White Keeps Fighting, His Way," *New York Times*, February 5, 1989, https://www.nytimes.com/1989/02/05/sports/sports-of-the-times-bill-white-keeps-fighting-his-way.html.

21. White, "When Baseball Defied Segregation."

22. White, *Uppity*, 89.

23. White, *Uppity*, 183–84.

24. White, *Uppity*, 185.

25. Claire Smith, "White Says He's No Diplomat and He Makes No Apologies," *New York Times*, September 17, 1990, C4.

26. Smith, "Baseball's Angry Man," 56.

27. Smith, "Baseball's Angry Man," 53.

28. Smith, "White Says He's No Diplomat," C4.

29. Smith, "Baseball's Angry Man," 30.

30. Smith, "Baseball's Angry Man," 56.

31. Smith, "White Says He's No Diplomat," C4.

32. "NL Prexy Bill White," 46.

33. White, *Uppity*, 7.

34. White, *Uppity*, 47.

35. Korr, *End of Baseball*; Burk, *Marvin Miller*; Lowenfish, *Imperfect Diamond*; Helyar, *Lords of the Realm*.

36. Flood with Carter, *The Way It Is*, 24.

37. Flood with Carter, *The Way It Is*, 24.

38. "Baseball's Best Centerfielder."

39. Snyder, *Well-Paid Slave*, 65.

40. Snyder, *Well-Paid Slave*, 65.

41. Judy Pace Flood, interview.

42. Flood with Carter, *The Way It Is*, 158.

43. Abrams, "Before the Flood"; Nathanson, "Who Exempted Baseball"; Nathanson, interview.

44. Barra, "How Curt Flood Changed Baseball."

45. Kevin Blackistone, "Baseball's Hall of Fame Cannot Be Complete Without Curt Flood," *Washington Post*, December 25, 2019, https://www.washingtonpost.com/sports/mlb/baseballs-hall-of-fame-cannot-be-complete-without-curt-flood/2019/12/23/68e9a526-25b7-11ea-ad73-2fd294520e97_story.html.

46. Snyder, *Well-Paid Slave*, 76.

47. Snyder, *Well-Paid Slave*, 94.

48. Clyde Haberman, "The Athlete Who Made LeBron James Possible," *New York Times*, October 5, 2014, https://www.nytimes.com/2014/10/06/us/curt-flood-the-athlete-who-made-lebron-james-possible.html.

49. Snyder, *Well-Paid Slave*, 162.

50. Snyder, *Well-Paid Slave*, 165.

51. Miller, *Whole Different Ballgame*, 238.

52. Curt Flood, interview from Ken Burns' 1994 documentary "Baseball," https://www.youtube.com/watch?v=tM9FIMwXeVk.

53. Helyar, *Lords of the Realm*, 583.

54. Ross Newhan, "Player Champion Flood Dead at 59," *Los Angeles Times*, January 21, 1997, https://www.latimes.com/archives/la-xpm-1997-01-21-sp-20694 -story.html.

55. Grant, *Black Aces*, 5.

56. Grant, *Black Aces*, 17.

57. Holtzclaw and Leonoudakis, *Baseball Pioneers*, 61.

58. Grant, *Black Aces*, 199.

59. Grant, *Black Aces*, 210.

60. Grant, *Black Aces*, 209.

61. Grant, *Black Aces*, 210.

62. Holtzclaw and Leonoudakis, *Baseball Pioneers*, 64.

63. Grant, *Black Aces*, 216.

64. Brown, "Mudcat Grant," 6.

65. Brown, "Mudcat Grant," 7.

66. Brown, "Mudcat Grant," 11.

67. Holtzclaw and Leonoudakis, *Baseball Pioneers*, 67.

68. Holtzclaw and Leonoudakis, *Baseball Pioneers*, 63.

69. Holtzclaw and Leonoudakis, *Baseball Pioneers*, 104–5.

70. Ira Berkow, "A Baseball Legend Wrestles with Removing His Former Boss's Statue," *New York Times*, June 30, 2020, https://www.nytimes.com/2020/06/30 /sports/baseball/rod-carew-minneapolis-george-floyd-protests.html.

71. Grant, *Black Aces*, 224.

72. Holtzclaw and Leonoudakis, *Baseball Pioneers*, 74.

73. Florio and Shapiro, *One Nation Under Baseball*, 97.

74. Florio and Shapiro, *One Nation Under Baseball*, 97–98.

75. Richard Goldstein, "Mudcat Grant, American League's First Black 20-Game Winner, Dies at 85," *New York Times*, June 12, 2021, https://www.nytimes.com/2021 /06/12/obituaries/mudcat-grant-dead.html.

76. Grant, *Black Aces*, 132.

77. Grant, *Black Aces*, 2.

78. Grant, *Black Aces*, 2.

79. Grant, *Black Aces*, 465.

80. Tyler Kepner, "The Hall of Fame Kept Dick Allen WaitingHe Ran Out of Time," *New York Times*, December 9, 2020, https://www.nytimes.com/2020/12/09 /sports/baseball/dick-allen-hall-of-fame.html.

81. Allen and Whitaker, *Crash*, 15.

82. Briley, "Times Were A'Changin," 162.

83. Allen and Whitaker, *Crash*, 13.

84. Alberston, "Race and Baseball in Philadelphia."

85. Florio and Shapiro, *One Nation Under Baseball*, 70.

86. Allen and Whitaker, *Crash*, 51.

87. Kashatus, *September Swoon*, 113.

88. Allen and Whitaker, *Crash*, 6.

89. Florio and Shapiro, *One Nation Under Baseball*, 83.

90. Florio and Shapiro, *One Nation Under Baseball*, 84.

91. Sandy Grady, "Allen Asked Mauch to Give Him Release," *Philadelphia Evening Bulletin*, July 9, 1965, 25.

92. Jacobson, "'Richie' Allen, Whitey's Ways, and Me," 27.

93. Kashatus, *September Swoon*, 180.

94. Allen and Whitaker, *Crash*, 80.

95. Briley, "Times Were A'Changin'," 206.

96. Allen and Whitaker, *Crash*, 78.

97. Banks, "Richie Allen," 93.

98. Kashatus, "Dick Allen, the Phillies, and Racism," 176.

99. Conlin, "For One Great Ballplayer."

100. Florio and Shapiro, *One Nation Under Baseball*, 165.

101. Banks, "Richie Allen," 93.

102. Banks, "Richie Allen," 94.

103. Kashatus, "Dick Allen, the Phillies, and Racism," 177.

104. Allen and Whitaker, *Crash*, 145.

105. Allen and Whitaker, *Crash*, 163.

106. Baseball Reference, "Second Dead-Ball Era."

107. Nathanson, "Dick Allen Preferred Not To," 1–41.

108. James, *The Politics of Glory*, 322–25.

109. Nathanson, *God Almighty Hisself*, 330.

110. Alberston, "Race and Baseball in Philadelphia."

111. Liptak, "Flashing Back with Stan Bahnsen."

112. Kashatus, "Mike Schmidt," 38.

113. Kashatus, "Dick Allen, the Phillies, and Racism," 186.

114. Allen Barra, "The Best Player Eligible for the Hall of Fame," *Wall Street Journal*, July 28, 2005, https://www.wsj.com/articles/SB112249995911597879.

115. "Cardinals Sacrifice Richie Allen's Homerun Power to Shore Up Team's No 1 Headache in '70: Defense," *Jefferson City (Missouri) Post Tribune*, October 6, 1970, 9.

116. Wright, "Dick Allen."

117. Bob Nightengale, "Dick Allen's Hard Road May Take Hall of Fame Turn," *USA Today*, December 2, 2014, https://www.usatoday.com/story/sports/mlb/2014/12/02/dick-allen-hall-of-fame-phillies/19798077/.

118. Allen and Whitaker, *Crash*, 186.

119. Alberston, "Race and Baseball in Philadelphia."

120. Nathanson, *God Almighty Hisself*, 7.

121. Nathanson, *God Almighty Hisself*, 3.

122. Allen and Whitaker, *Crash*, 185.

123. Nathanson, *God Almighty Hisself*, 5.

124. Alberston, "Race and Baseball in Philadelphia."

125. Allen and Whitaker, *Crash*, 34.

126. Blount, Jr., "Swinging in His Own Groove," 37.

127. Gmelch, *Playing with Tigers*, 125–26.

128. Gmelch, *Playing with Tigers*, 163.

129. Gmelch, *Playing with Tigers*, 184.

130. Gmelch, *Playing with Tigers*, 184.

131. Gmelch, *Playing with Tigers*, 184.

132. George Gmelch, "Life in Rocky Mount with the Klan," *Burlington Advance Star*, 1967.

133. Gmelch, *Playing with Tigers*, 197.

134. Gmelch, interview.

135. Gmelch, interview.

136. Gmelch, interview.

Chapter Six. Women in Baseball

1. "Casey Candaele Discusses His Mother."

2. Spalding, America's National Game, quoted in Ring, *A Game of Their Own*.

3. Shattuck, "Playing a Man's Game"; Craig, "Vassar and Beyond."

4. Shattuck, "Playing a Man's Game."

5. Shattuck, "Playing a Man's Game."

6. Shattuck, "Playing a Man's Game"; Craig, "Vassar and Beyond."

7. Rader, Baseball.

8. Gregorich, "You Can't Play in Skirts," 39–43.

9. Hanlon, "Queen Lizzie."

10. "Girl Babe Ruth Made Eligible in Legion Tourney," *New York Daily News*, July 1, 1928.

11. Berlage, *Women in Baseball*.

12. Gregorich, "You Can't Play in Skirts," 39–43.

13. Horwitz, "Woman Who (Maybe) Struck Out."

14. Minsberg, Talya, "Overlooked No More: Jackie Mitchell, Who Fanned Two of Baseball's Greats," *New York Times*, November 7, 2018, https://www.nytimes.com/2018/11/07/obituaries/jackie-mitchell-overlooked.html.

15. Sources for this chapter include the following: Ardell, *Breaking into Baseball*; Ardell, "Mamie 'Peanut' Johnson," 181–92; Arson, "Dames in the Dirt"; Berlage, *Women in Baseball*; Borders, *Making My Pitch*; Browne, *Girls of Summer*; Cohen, *No Girls in the Clubhouse*; Davis, "No League of Their Own," 74–96; Sopan Deb, "Big-League Baseball's First Woman, on a Stage of Her Own," *New York Times*, June 11, 2019; Everbach, "Breaking Baseball Barriers," 13–33; Fidler, *Origins and History*; Halper, "Written Out of History"; Heaphy and May, *Encyclopedia of Women and Baseball*; Johnson, *When Women Played Hardball*; Kimmel, "Baseball and the Reconstitution"; "League

History"; Madden, *Record Book*; Madden, *Women of the All-American*; Pierman, "Baseball, Conduct, and True Womanhood"; Richard, "Playing with the Boys"; Ring, *Game of Their Own*; Ring, *Stolen Bases*; Sargent, *We Were the All-American Girls*; Shattuck, *Bloomer Girls*; Shattuck, "Playing a Man's Game"; Shire, "Why Can't American Women Play Baseball?"; Williams, *All-American Girls*.

16. Moran, "Former Pro Baseball Player"; Stimson, "Louise Youngen Plays Ball"; Jack Moran, "A League of Her Own," Eugene (Oregon) *Register-Guard*, January 14, 2018, https://www.registerguard.com/rg/news/local/36336701-75/former-pro-baseball-player-lois-youngen-of-eugene-still-in-a-league-of-her-own.html.csp; Kylee O'Connor, "Lois Youngen Reflects on Her 36 Years as Administrator, Instructor and Coach at UO," *Daily Emerald*, May 16, 2016, https://www.dailyemerald.com/sports/q-a-lois-youngen-reflects-on-her-years-as-administrator/article_78b8b2d2-4efe-57be-a1cf-269c6b4b5451.html.

17. Stimson, "Louise Youngen Plays Ball."

18. Fidler, *Origins and History*, 185.

19. Fidler, *Origins and History*, 36.

20. Moran, "Former Pro Baseball Player."

21. Turner, *Heroes, Bums and Ordinary Men*.

22. Fidler, *Origins and History*, 59.

23. Andrea Moret, "Back at the Plate Again: Four Decades After the All American Girls Professional Baseball League Disbanded, Its Players Are Recalled in 'A League of Their Own,'" *Los Angeles Times*, June 28, 1992, https://www.latimes.com/archives/la-xpm-1992-06-28-ca-2121-story.html.

24. Moret, "Back at the Plate Again."

25. Turner, *Heroes, Bums and Ordinary Men*.

26. Turner, *Heroes, Bums and Ordinary Men*.

27. Turner, *Heroes, Bums and Ordinary Men*.

28. Jack Stenbuck, "Home Runs And Lipstick," *Baltimore Sun*, June 1946.

29. Turner, *Heroes, Bums and Ordinary Men*.

30. O'Keefe, "Casey Candaele Shares Story."

31. O'Keefe, "Casey Candaele Discusses His Mother."

32. Pierman, "Baseball, Conduct, and True Womanhood," 68–85.

33. Heaphy and May, *Encyclopedia of Women and Baseball*; "Mabel B. Holle," *State Journal-Register*, December 12, 2011; Rogers, "Mabel Holle and the All-American Girls"; Jessica Tobacman, "Longtime PE Teacher Led Way in Girls Sports," *Chicago Tribune*, December 15, 2011.

34. Candaele, interview.

35. Johnson, *When Women Played Hardball*, 140.

36. Quoted in de la Cretaz, "Hidden Queer History."

37. Kevin Cruley, "St. Charles Honors AAGPBL Star Donahue," *Kane County Chronicle*, March 26, 2010, https://www.kcchronicle.com/2010/03/26/st-charles-honors-aagpbl-star-donahue/aszs8ma/.

38. Donahue, interview.

39. Gazdziak, "Obituary: Terry Donahue."

40. Quoted in de la Cretaz, "Hidden Queer History"

41. Jack Rejtman, "A Legend with a Sense of Humor," *Tampa Bay Times*, March 30, 1993.

42. Douglas Martin, "Millie Deegan, 82, Pioneer in Women's Baseball League," *New York Times*, July 28, 2002, https://www.nytimes.com/2002/07/28/sports/millie-deegan-82-pioneer-in-women-s-baseball-league.html.

43. Rogers, "Mabel Holle"; Tobacman, "Longtime PE Teacher"; "Mabel B. Holle," *State Journal-Register*, December 12, 2011.

44. Brydum, "JoJo D'Angelo."

45. Cahn, *Coming on Strong*, 186.

46. Jodi Hausen, "A Bozeman Baseball Legend Dies At 82," *Bozeman Daily Chronicle*, November 30, 2010, https://www.bozemandailychronicle.com/news/a-bozeman-baseball-legend-dies-at/article_2a8ef4be-fc24-11df-8511-001cc4c03286.html; Samoray, "Jean Cione."

47. "Marietta 'Polly' Huitt," *Palm Beach* (Florida) *Post*, December 30, 2007.

48. Carter, "Animal Lover.'"

49. de la Cretaz, "Hidden Queer History."

50. "Caito, Ricki," *Arizona Republic*, January 12, 2011

51. This section on female black ballplayers relies on the following sources: Ackmann, *Curveball*; Ardell, "Mamie 'Peanuts' Johnson"; Berlage, *Women in Baseball*; Sophan Deb, "Big-League Baseball's First Woman, on a Stage of Her Own," *New York Times*, June 11, 2019; Everbach, "Breaking Baseball Barriers"; Lanctot, *Negro League Baseball*; Davis, "No League of Their Own"; Richard, "Playing with the Boys."

52. Lanctot, *Negro League Baseball*, 381.

53. de la Cretaz, "Hidden Queer History."

54. Lanctot, *Negro League Baseball*, 382.

55. Wayne Coffey, "Mamie (Peanut) Johnson, the Only Female Pitcher in the History of the Negro Leagues, Watches Mo'ne Davis Hurl Shutout in Opener of Little League World Series," *New York Daily News*, August 16, 2014, https://www.nydailynews.com/sports/baseball/coffey-mamie-peanut-johnson-watches-mo-davis-hurl-shutout-opener-league-world-series-article-1.1905448.

56. The discussion of Little League draws on the following sources: Abrams, "Twelve-Year-Old Girl's Lawsuit"; Megan Grindstaff, "Ambra Offutt Made It OK for Girls to Play Little League," *Nashville Tennessean*, June 29, 2014, https://www.tennessean.com/story/sports/baseball/2014/06/29/ambra-offutt-little-league-girls-lawsuit/11727583/; "How Little League Gender Barrier"; Chelsea Janes, "The Girls Who Fought for the Right to Play in Little League Look Back, 40 Years Later," *Washington Post*, June 13, 2014, https://www.washingtonpost.com/sports/othersports/the-girls-who-fought-for-the-right-to-play-in-little-league-look-back-40-years-later/2014/08/13/f86e4c88-2234-11e4-8593-da634b334390_story.

html; Mike Tierney, "A Novelty No Longer," *New York Times*, August 13, 2014, https://www.nytimes.com/2014/08/14/sports/girls-in-little-league-world-series -become-less-of-a-novelty.html.

57. Bowman, "Little League of Her Own."

58. Janes, "Girls Who Fought."

59. Grindstaff, "Ambra Offutt Made It OK."

60. Joseph B Treaster, "Little League Baseball Yields to 'Social Climate' and Accepts Girls," *New York Times*, June 13, 1974 https://www.nytimes.com/1974/06/13 /archives/little-league-baseball-yields-to-social-climate-and-accepts-girls.html.

61. Janes, "Girls Who Fought."

62. Janes, "Girls Who Fought."

63. Janes, "Girls Who Fought."

64. Abrams, "Twelve-Year-Old Girl's Lawsuit."

65. National Federation of State High School Associations, Sports Participation Surveys.

66. National Federation of State High School Associations, Sports Participation Surveys.

67. NCAA Sports Sponsorship and Participation Rates Database.

68. Borders, *Making My Pitch*.

69. Borders, *Making My Pitch*, 13.

70. Barbie Ludovise, "Despite Taunts, She's Undaunted About Crossing These Borders," *Los Angeles Times*, February 5, 1993, https://www.latimes.com/archives /la-xpm-1993-02-05-sp-1125-story.html.

71. Cohen, *No Girls in the Clubhouse*, 120.

72. Martin Beck, "SCC Baseball Signs a Woman, Makes History," *Los Angeles Times*, February 4, 1993, https://www.latimes.com/archives/la-xpm-1993-02-04 -sp-1186-story.html; Cohen, *No Girls in the Clubhouse*, 122.

73. Cohen, *No Girls in the Clubhouse*, 124.

74. Jeff Miller, "Miller: Ila Borders Is a Brave Pioneer You Should Remember," *Orange County Register*, March 3, 2017, https://www.ocregister.com/2017/03/03 /miller-ila-borders-is-a-brave-pioneer-you-should-remember/.

75. "Ila Borders Gives Herself the Hook, Retires," *Los Angeles Times*, July 1, 2000, https://www.latimes.com/archives/la-xpm-2000-jul-01-sp-46812-story.html.

76. Barry Faulkner, "Borders Aims to Inspire with Book," *Daily Pilot*, May 25, 2017, https://www.latimes.com/socal/daily-pilot/sports/tn-dpt-sp-ila-borders-20170525 -story.html.

77. Borders, *Making My Pitch*, 23.

78. Borders, *Making My Pitch*, 49.

79. Borders, *Making My Pitch*, 159.

80. Borders, *Making My Pitch*, 183.

81. Borders, *Making My Pitch*, 183.

82. Borders, *Making My Pitch*, 203.

83. Borders, *Making My Pitch*, 212.

84. Garcia, "Baseball Options For Girls"; Graham, "'League of Their Own'"; Ingemi, "How Young Talented Team Canada"; Oberteuffer, "AACC Men's Baseball Team"; Shipnuck, "Love of the Game"; Pete Warner, "NCAA's Only Female Baseball Pitcher Overcomes Harassment, Pursues Dream At Umaine-Presque Isle," *Bangor Daily News*, May 3, 2014, https://bangordailynews.com/2014/05/03/sports/baseball/ncaas-only-female-baseball-pitcher-overcomes-harassment-pursues-dream-at-umaine-presque-isle; Jimmy Watson, "BPCC Baseball to Sign Female Pitcher," *Shreveport Times*, February 3, 2015, https://www.shreveporttimes.com/story/sports/college/2015/02/03/bpcc-baseball-sign-female-pitcher/22807031/; "Ashton Lansdell Following Baseball Dream"; Tom King, "A Historic Step For Rivier Baseball In Works For This Spring," *Nashua Telegram*, September 29, 2019, https://www.nashuatelegraph.com/sports/local-sports/2019/09/29/a-historic-step-for-rivier-baseball-in-works-for-this-spring; Lauren Kirschman, "Meet The First Woman To Earn A Baseball Scholarship In The Northwest Athletic Conference," *News Tribune*, February 23, 2021 https://www.thenewstribune.com/sports/article249377190.html; Brad Elliott Schlossman, "Zoe Hicks Makes Expedition League History in Whiskey Jacks' First Grand Forks Game," *Grand Forks Herald*, May 28, 2021, https://www.grandforksherald.com/sports/baseball/7050945-Zoe-Hicks-makes-Expedition-League-history-in-Whiskey-Jacks-first-Grand-Forks-game; Jim Ha, "Lyndhurst's Jorge Ready To Make History As College Baseball Player," *The Observer*, March 30, 2021, https://www.theobserver.com/2021/03/lyndhursts-jorge-ready-to-make-history-as-college-baseball-player/.

85. Rosen, "Breaking the Grass Ceiling."

86. For example, see Justin McCurry and Lawrence Donegan, "Eri Yoshida Wins Plaudits as First Japanese Woman in US Baseball League," *The Guardian*, August 8, 2010, https://www.theguardian.com/world/2010/aug/08/eri-yoshida-japan-woman-us-baseball; Des Bielder, "In Historic Move, Two Female Players Signed By Minor League Baseball Team," *Washington Post*, June 30, 2016, https://www.washingtonpost.com/news/early-lead/wp/2016/06/30/in-historic-move-two-female-players-signed-by-minor-league-baseball-team/?utm_term=.17f0fa47ed5e.

87. Rubin, "Japan's 'Knuckle Princess.'"

88. David Wharton and Melissa Rohlin, "Photo Raises Issue of Sexual Orientation in Softball," *Los Angeles Times*, June 2, 2010, https://www.latimes.com/archives/la-xpm-2010-jun-02-la-sp-kagan-softball-20100603-story.html.

89. Jennifer Fermino, "Does a Picture of Elena Kagan Playing Softball Suggest She's a Lesbian?" *New York Post*, May 13, 2010, https://nypost.com/2010/05/13/does-a-picture-of-elena-kagan-playing-softball-suggest-shes-a-lesbian/.

90. Hays, "Stereotypes Haunt Softball"; Ed Pilkington, "Photo of US Court Hopeful Elena Kagan Sparks Debate over Sexuality," *The Guardian*, May 14, 2010, https://www.theguardian.com/world/2010/may/14/elena-kagan-baseball-photograph.

91. Donaldson, "I Avoided a Lesbian Stereotype."

92. Donaldson, "I Avoided a Lesbian Stereotype."

93. Adam Jude, "Spokane's Christine Wren Went to Bat for Future Generations as a Professional Umpire in the 1970s," *Spokesman Review*, July 18, 2020.

94. Postema, *You've Got to Have Balls.*

95. Hanks, "Perry Barber"; "Perry Barber Receives."

96. "Perry Barber, 1 of 8 Women."

97. Tyler Kepner and James Wagner, "Kim Ng Has Been Ready for Years," *New York Times*, November 18, 2020, https://www.nytimes.com/2020/11/18/sports/baseball/kim-ng-miami-marlins.html.

98. Kepner and Wagner, "Kim Ng Has Been Ready."

99. Kepner and Wagner, "Kim Ng Has Been Ready."

100. This discussion of Manley draws on Overmyer, *Queen of the Negro Leagues*, and Newman, *Black Baseball.*

101. Lindsay Berra, "The Yankees Hired a Hitting CoachHer Name Is Rachel," *New York Times*, November 22, 2019, https://www.nytimes.com/2019/11/22/sports/baseball/yankees-woman-coach-hitting.html.

102. Juliette Macur, "The First Black Woman to Coach in Pro Baseball Thanks Her Mom for the Job," *New York Times*, March 3, 2021, https://www.nytimes.com/2021/03/03/sports/baseball/bianca-smith-red.html.

103. Gilger and Wallace, *There's No Crying*; Lannin, *Who Let Them In?*; Rice, "Tribute to Women"; Rau, "Why Are Women."

104. Sowell, "Is She or Isn't He?," 228–37.

105. Ardell, *Breaking into Baseball*, 196.

106. Ardell, *Breaking into Baseball*, 198; Richard Goldstein, "Mary Garber, Sportswriter, Dies at 92," *New York Times*, September 22, 2008, https://www.nytimes.com/2008/09/23/sports/23garber.html.

107. Brendan Kennedy, "Pioneering Toronto Star Baseball Writer Alison Gordon Dead At 72," *Toronto Star*, February 12, 2015, https://www.thestar.com/sports/baseball/2015/02/12/pioneering-toronto-star-baseball-writer-alison-gordon-dead-at-72.html.

108. Catherine Porter, "Baseball Writer Alison Gordon an Unlikely Feminist Pioneer," *Toronto Star*, February 12, 2015, https://www.thestar.com/news/world/2015/02/12/baseball-writer-alison-gordon-an-unlikely-feminist-pioneer-porter.html.

109. Ardell, *Breaking into Baseball*, 204.

110. Ardell, *Breaking into Baseball*, 202.

111. David Waldstein, "In a First, an M.L.B. Game Will Be Called Entirely by Women," *New York Times*, July 15, 2021, https://www.nytimes.com/2021/07/15/sports/baseball/mlb-all-woman-broadcast.html.

Chapter Seven. Gay Men in Baseball

1. Dreier, "Is Baseball Ready."

2. Victory Institute, "Out for America."

3. Andrew Flores, Charles Gossett, Gabriele Magni, and Andrew Reynolds, "11 Openly LGBTQ Lawmakers Will Take Their Seats in The Next Congress; That's a Record in Both Numbers and Diversity," *Washington Post*, November 30, 2020, https://www.washingtonpost.com/politics/2020/11/30/11-lgbtq-legislators-will -take-their-seats-next-congress-largest-most-diverse-group-ever/.

4. Kyle Dropp and Jon Cohen, "Acceptance of Gay People in Military Grows Dramatically," *Washington Post*, July 19, 2008, http://www.washingtonpost.com /wp-dyn/content/article/2008/07/18/AR2008071802561.html; McCarthy, "U.S. Support for Gay Marriage."

5. Rick Telander, "Gay and Proud: Megan Rapinoe Is the Current Face of Athletic Excellence," *Chicago Sun-Times*, July 9, 2019, https://chicago.suntimes .com/2019/7/9/20688286/gay-megan-rapinoe-uswnt-womens-world-cup-fifa -equality-lesbian-bird-wnba.

6. "At Least 185 Out LGBTQ Athletes."

7. Buzinski, "Meet the 16."

8. Sam Borden, "Freed of a Secret's Burden, a Soccer Player Looks Ahead," *New York Times*, March 29, 2013, https://www.nytimes.com/2013/03/29/sports /soccer/robbie-rogers-feels-free-after-revealing-he-is-gay.html?pagewanted=2; Billy Witz, "Milestone for Gay Athletes as Rogers Plays for Galaxy," *New York Times*, May 27, 2013 https://www.nytimes.com/2013/05/28/sports/soccer/milestone -for-gay-athletes-as-robbie-rogers-plays-for-galaxy.html.

9. Wagoner, "President Obama Congratulates."

10. Michael Blinn, "Raiders' Carl Nassib Comes Out as Gay in Historic NFL Moment," *New York Post*, June 21, 2021, https://nypost.com/2021/06/21/raiders -carl-nassib-comes-out-as-gay-in-historic-nfl-moment/; Jeré Longman and Alanis Thames, "Carl Nassib Is Seeking His Path as an Out Athlete," *New York Times*, June 25, 2021, https://www.nytimes.com/2021/06/25/sports/carl-nassib-football.html.

11. Emmanuel Morgan, "Carl Nassib Made History, but Also a Big Play," *New York Times*, September 19, 2021, https://www.nytimes.com/2021/09/19/sports /football/carl-nassib-raiders-gay.html.

12. Jeré Longman, "An N.H.L. Prospect Is the First Such Player to Announce He's Gay," *New York Times*, July 19, 2021, https://www.nytimes.com/2021/07/19 /sports/hockey/luke-prokop-nhl-announces-gay.html.

13. Burke with Sherman, *Out at Home*; Jennifer Frey, "Once a Promising Ballplayer, Glenn Burke Is Dying of AIDS," *New York Times*, October 18, 1994, https:// archive.nytimes.com/www.nytimes.com/library/sports/baseball/090699bbo -bean-burke.html; Jerry Crowe, "When Glory Has Soured: Former Dodger Glenn Burke Battles AIDS As He Struggles to Survive Life on the Streets," *Los Angeles*

Times, August 30, 1994, https://www.latimes.com/archives/la-xpm-1994-08-30
-sp-32908-story.html; John Branch, "MLB to Honor Glenn Burke as a Gay Pioneer
in Baseball," *New York Times*, July 14, 2014, https://www.nytimes.com/2014/07/15
/sports/baseball/mlb-to-recognize-glenn-burke-as-a-gay-pioneer-in-baseball.
html; Buzinski, "30 LGBTQ Athletes"; Byron Williams, "The Glenn Burke Story
Is a Tragedy with a Local Flavor," *East Bay Times*, November 5, 2010, https://
www.eastbaytimes.com/2010/11/05/byron-williams-the-glenn-burke-story-is-a
-tragedy-with-a-local-flavor/; Sarah Kaplan, "The Trials of Baseball's First Openly
Gay Player, Glenn Burke, Four Decades Ago," *Washington Post*, August 17, 2015,
https://www.washingtonpost.com/news/morning-mix/wp/2015/08/17/the
-trials-of-baseballs-first-openly-gay-player-glenn-burke-four-decades-ago/?utm
_term=.64218a71a968; Alexander, *When Baseball Isn't White*; Hollander, "On Being
Gay"; Mooallem, "History of the High Five."

14. Smith, "The Double Life."
15. Larry Sushan, "A Superstar at Merritt?" *Oakland Tribune*, February 24, 1972.
16. Baseball Reference, "Glenn Burke."
17. Crowe, "When Glory Has Soured."
18. Burke with Sherman, *Out at Home*, 80.
19. Burke with Sherman, *Out at Home*, 10.
20. Frey, "Once a Promising Ballplayer."
21. Frey, "Once a Promising Ballplayer."
22. Frey, "Once a Promising Ballplayer."
23. The younger Lasorda died of AIDS in 1991, although his death certificate lists
pneumonia as his cause of death. "My son wasn't gay," his father insisted, "No way."
Richmond, "Brief Life and Complicated Death."
24. Kaplan, "Trials of Baseball's First."
25. Branch, "MLB to Honor Glenn Burke."
26. Frey, "Once a Promising Ballplayer."
27. Smith, "The Double Life."
28. Smith, "The Double Life."
29. *Out: The Glenn Burke Story*.
30. Smith, "The Double Life."
31. Smith, "The Double Life."
32. Smith, "The Double Life."
33. Frey, "Once a Promising Ballplayer."
34. *Out: The Glenn Burke Story*.
35. Glenn Burke's Family at Game as A's Honor Him on Pride Night," *USA Today*,
June 17, 2015, https://www.usatoday.com/story/sports/mlb/2015/06/17/glenn
-burke-family-at-game-as-honor-him-on-pride-night/28902199/.
36. Footer, "MLB Names Bean."

37. Robert Lipsyte, "A Major League Player's Life of Isolation and Secret Fear," *New York Times*, September 6, 1999, https://www.nytimes.com/1999/09/06/sports/baseball-a-major-league-player-s-life-of-isolation-and-secret-fear.html.

38. Bean, *Going the Other Way*, 101.

39. Bean, *Going the Other Way*, 110.

40. Bean, *Going the Other Way*, 105.

41. Bean, *Going the Other Way*, 122.

42. Bean, *Going the Other Way*, 128.

43. Bean, *Going the Other Way*, 146.

44. Bean, interview by Diane Sawyer.

45. Buster Olney, "Bean's Friends and Former Teammates Give Him Their Unconditional Acceptance," *New York Times*, September 7, 1999, https://www.nytimes.com/1999/09/07/sports/baseball-bean-s-friends-former-teammates-give-him-their-unconditional-acceptance.html.

46. Brad Ausmus, interview.

47. Bean, *Going the Other Way*, 241.

48. Buzinski, "John Dillinger."

49. Buzinski, "John Dillinger."

50. Zeigler, "Gay Cardinals Minor League Player."

51. Cindy Boren, "Cardinals Looking into Allegation That Players Discussed Killing Gay People," *Washington Post*, March 17, 2016, https://www.washingtonpost.com/news/early-lead/wp/2016/03/17/cardinals-looking-into-allegation-that-players-discussed-killing-gay-people/.

52. Zeigler, "Gay Cardinals Minor League Player."

53. Greenberg, "CMU Investigates Homophobic Remarks"; "Colorado Mesa Baseball Coach Apologizes"; Howe, "Colorado Baseball Coach"; Saxon, "Cardinals Taking Allegations.'"

54. Baseball Reference, "Jason Burch."

55. Zeigler, "Gay Cardinals Minor League Player."

56. Zeigler, "Gay Cardinals Minor League Player."

57. Zeigler, "Openly Gay Pitcher Sean Conroy"; "Sean Conroy Becomes First"; Scott Gleeson, "Is MLB Ready for Gay Player? First Open Pro Sean Conroy Discusses Concerns," *USA Today*, July 21, 2015, https://www.usatoday.com/story/sports/2015/07/21/sean-conroy-openly-gay-baseball-player-mlb/30441119/; Lindbergh and Miller, "Now Starting"; Finkel, "Story of How Sean Conroy"; Rymer, "1 Year Later."

58. Rymer, "1 Year Later."

59. Lindbergh and Miller, "Now Starting."

60. Lindbergh and Miller, *Only Rule Is It Has to Work*.

61. Gleeson, "Is MLB Ready for Gay Player?."

62. Rymer, "1 Year Later."

63. Leff and Rodriguez, "Pitcher Sean Conroy Makes History." The Stompers also signed and played three women: Kelsie Whitmore, Stacy Piagno, and Anna Kimbrel-lIt also hired Jen Ramos as assistant general manager, the first openly trans person to be a professional baseball executive. Gibbs, "Meet Jen Ramos."

64. Gleeson, "Is MLB Ready for Gay Player?."

65. Tom Haudricourt, "Brewers Minor-Leaguer Makes Baseball History by Coming Out Publicly as Gay," *Milwaukee Journal Sentinel*, August 15, 2015, http://archive.jsonline.com/sports/brewers/brewers-minor-leaguer-makes-baseball-history-by-coming-out-publicly-as-gay-b99557156z1-321977731.html; Cindy Boren, "A Milwaukee Brewers Minor-Leaguer Makes Baseball History by Coming Out as Gay," *Washington Post*, August 16, 201,5 https://www.washingtonpost.com/news/early-lead/wp/2015/08/16/a-milwaukee-brewers-minor-leaguer-makes-baseball-history-by-coming-out-as-gay/?postshare=2811439792040637; Billy Witz, "David Denson, Gay Baseball Prospect, Achieves a Key Victory: Being Himself," *New York Times*, August 21, 2015, https://www.nytimes.com/2015/08/22/sports/baseball/david-denson-baseball-prospect-achieves-a-key-victory-being-himself.html; "Former Southland star David Denson is First Openly Gay MLB Prospect," *Los Angeles Times*, August 16, 2015, https://www.latimes.com/sports/mlb/la-sp-gay-minor-league-baseball-player-20150816-story.html?_amp=true.

66. Haudricourt, "Brewers Minor-Leaguer."

67. Hine, "Meet the First Openly Gay."

68. Haudricourt, "Brewers Minor-Leaguer."

69. Haudricourt, Brewers Minor-Leaguer."

70. Haudricourt, Brewers Minor-Leaguer."

71. Haudricourt, "Brewers Minor-Leaguer."

72. Haudricourt, "Brewers Minor-Leaguer."

73. Haudricourt, "Brewers Minor-Leaguer."

74. Boren, "Milwaukee Brewers."

75. Haudricourt, "Brewers Minor-Leaguer."

76. Haudricourt, "Brewers Minor-Leaguer."

77. Tim Haudricourt, "Brewers Say Denson Would be Welcome in Clubhouse," *Milwaukee Journal Sentinel*, August 16, 2015, http://archive.jsonline.com/blogs/sports/321993101.html.

78. Haudricourt, "Brewers Say Denson."

79. Haudricourt, "Brewers Say Denson."

80. Haudricourt, "Brewers Minor-Leaguer."

81. Haudricourt, "Brewers Minor-Leaguer."

82. Tom Haudricourt and Todd Rosiak, "First Openly Gay Player David Denson Retires from Baseball," *Milwaukee Journal Sentinel*, March 21, 2017,

83. https://www.jsonline.com/story/sports/mlb/brewers/2017/03/21/notes-first-openly-gay-player-david-denson-retires-baseball/99432260/.

84. Zeigler, "This Gay Baseball Player."

85. Zeigler, "This Gay Baseball Player."

86. Zeigler, "This Gay Baseball Player."

87. Zeigler, "This Gay Baseball Player."

88. Zeigler, "This Gay Baseball Player."

89. Santana, "Transition from Straight to Gay Teams."

90. Pallone, *Behind the Mask*.

91. Eno, "Dave Pallone."

92. Neyer, "Chat with Dave Pallone."

93. Buzinski, "MLB Umpire Dale Scott"; Howie Kussoy, "How Ground-Breaking Baseball Umpire Came Out as Gay," *New York Post*, December 2, 2014, https://nypost .com/2014/12/02/how-ground-breaking-baseball-umpire-came-out-as-gay/; John Branch, "A Longtime Umpire Says He Is Gay," *New York Times*, December 2, 2014 https://www.nytimes.com/2014/12/03/sports/baseball/dale-scott-baseball -umpire-comes-out-as-gay.html.

Chapter Eight. Modern-Day Rebels

1. "Tom Seaver Says U.S. Should Leave Vietnam," *New York Times*, October 11, 1969, 4, https://timesmachine.nytimes.com/timesmachine/1969/10/11/83781878 .html?pageNumber=4.

2. Travers, *Last Icon*, 106; Candaele and Dreier, "Tom Seaver."

3. William C. Rhoden, "Delgado Makes a Stand by Taking a Seat," *New York Times*, July 21, 2004, https://www.nytimes.com/2004/07/21/sports/sports-of-the-times -delgado-makes-a-stand-by-taking-a-seat.html.

4. Ben Walker, "Blue Jays Star Delgado Protests War in Iraq," *Pittsburgh Post-Gazette*, July 21, 2004, https://www.post-gazette.com/sports/pirates/2004/07/22/Blue-Jays -star-Delgado-protests-U-S-war-in-Iraq/stories/200407220163.

5. Associated Press, "Delgado to Stand."

6. D. Torres, "Baseball Player Sits Down for God Bless America," *Narkive News Group*, n.d., https://alt.politics.greens.narkive.com/IWe9IC30/baseball-player-sits -down-for-god-bless-america.

7. Steve Wilstein, "Patriotism, Protest at Stadium," *Los Angeles Times*, July 25, 2004.

8. Zirin, "Silencing of Carlos Delgado."

9. "Delgado To Stand."

10. Brendan Kennedy, "Carlos Delgado Calls MLB's Lack of Latin American Managers 'Really Sad,'" *The Star*, May 23, 2016, https://www.thestar.com/sports /bluejays/2016/05/23/carlos-delgado-calls-mlbs-lack-of-latin-american -managers-really-sad.html.

11. Frye, "Billie Jean King."

12. LaFeber, *Michael Jordan*; Crowley, "Muhammad Ali."

13. Paul Davies, "Tiger Has World by Tail," *Philadelphia Daily News*, April 14, 1997.

14. Smith, "Chosen One."

15. Dreier and Candaele, "Where Are the Jocks for Justice?"

16. Scott Gleeson, "Fox News' Laura Ingraham Tells LeBron James, Kevin Durant: 'Shut Up and Dribble,'" *USA Today*, February 16, 2008, https://www.usatoday .com/story/sports/nba/2018/02/16/fox-laura-ingraham-tells-lebron-james-kevin -durant-shut-up-and-dribble/344393002/.

17. Rohlin, "LeBron James Calls Out."

18. Rohlin, "LeBron James Calls Out."

19. Des Bieler, "Lebron James, Told by Laura Ingraham to 'Shut Up and Dribble,' Calls Her Out over Drew Brees," *Washington Post*, June 4, 2020, https:// www.washingtonpost.com/sports/2020/06/04/lebron-james-calls-out-laura -ingraham-over-drew-brees/.

20. Eugene Scott, "President Trump Says NFL Players Who Protest Shouldn't Be in the Game—and Maybe Not Even in the Country," *Washington Post*, May 24, 2018, https://www.washingtonpost.com/news/the-fix/wp/2018/05/23/president -trump-wanted-consequences-for-nfl-players-who-protest-racism-before-games -today-he-got-them.

21. Lindsay H. Jones, "Broncos' Brandon Marshall Calls President Trump's National Anthem Remarks 'Disgusting,'" *USA Today*, May 24, 2018, https://www .usatoday.com/story/sports/nfl/broncos/2018/05/24/brandon-marshall -president-donald-trump-national-anthem-protest-kneel/642242002/.

22. Michelle R Martinelli, "U.S. Soccer is Forcing Players to 'Stand Respectfully' for National Anthem," *USA Today*, March 4, 2017, https://ftw.usatoday.com/2017/03 /national-anthem-protest-us-soccer-megan-rapinoe-colin-kaepernick-racial -injustice-lgbtq.

23. Rodrigo, "Ali Krieger Defends Teammate Rapinoe."

24. Gregory, "You Have to Take a Stand."

25. Andrew Das, "U.S. Soccer Repeals National Anthem Policy," *New York Times*, June 9, 2020, https://www.nytimes.com/2020/06/09/sports/soccer/us-soccer -anthem-uswnt.html.

26. Dylan Hernandez, "Dodgers' Adrian Gonzalez Chose Not to Stay in a Trump Hotel, But He Didn't Want It to Be News," *Los Angeles Times*, October 17, 2016.

27. McCarthy, "Tonight's Results."

28. McCarthy, "Was the 'Swamp.'"

29. Saxon, "Dexter Fowler Unapologetic."

30. Rodgers, "A's Rookie Bruce Maxwell."

31. Cindy Boren, "'My Decision Had Been Coming for a Long Time," *Denver Post*, October 29, 2017, https://www.denverpost.com/2017/10/29/bruce-maxwell -arrested-gun-charge-oakland-athletics/.

32. Dreier and Candaele, "Red Sox Should Not Visit"; Michael Tackett, "Trump Welcomes the Red Sox to the White House, but Not All of Them Are There," *New York Times*, May 9, 2019, https://www.nytimes.com/2019/05/09/us/politics/boston-red-sox-white-house-visit.html.

33. Adam Gilgore, "Nationals Owner Mark Lerner Says Trump 'Has Every Right to Come' to World Series," *Washington Post*, October 25, 2019, https://www.washingtonpost.com/sports/2019/10/25/nationals-owner-mark-lerner-says-trump-has-every-right-come-world-series.

34. Jesse Dougherty, "Ian Desmond, in Powerful Instagram Post on Race and Inclusion, Opts Out of 2020 Season," *Washington Post*, June 30, 2020, https://www.washingtonpost.com/sports/2020/06/30/ian-desmond-powerful-instagram-post-race-inclusion-opts-out-2020-season/.

35. Dougherty, "Ian Desmond."

36. Dougherty, "Ian Desmond."

37. Dougherty, "Ian Desmond."

38. Gaydos, "White Sox Pitcher Lucas Giolito."

39. Rivera, "Giants' Gabe Kapler."

40. "Pablo Sandoval, Hunter Pence."

41. Chuck Schilken, "Trump Tweets 'The Game Is Over for Me' If Players Kneel During the National Anthem," *Los Angeles Times*, July 21, 2020, https://www.latimes.com/sports/story/2020-07-21/national-anthem-kneel-trump-san-francisco-giants-gabe-kapler.

42. Bob Nightengale, "Giants' Gabe Kapler Responds to President Trump: 'Nothing More Patriotic Than Peaceful Protests,'" *USA Today*, July 21, 2020, https://www.usatoday.com/story/sports/mlb/giants/2020/07/21/giants-manager-gabe-kapler-responds-president-donald-trump-criticisms/5483937002/.

43. Maria Torres, "Angels' Keynan Middleton Kneels During National Anthem, Wants to Be a 'Voice for Unity,'" *Los Angeles Times*, July 20, 2020, https://www.latimes.com/sports/angels/story/2020-07-20/angels-reliever-keynan-middleton-kneels-during-national-anthem.

44. Fieldstadt, "San Francisco Giants Manager."

45. Pickman, "Bucks Players Issue Statement."

46. Pickman, "Bucks Players Issue Statement."

47. Andrew Wagner, "Christian Yelich, Brewers United with Bucks in Decision Not to Play Wednesday Night," *Wisconsin State Journal*, August 27, 2020.

48. Wagner, "Christian Yelich, Brewers."

49. Wagner, "Christian Yelich, Brewers."

50. Wagner, "Christian Yelich, Brewers."

51. Tom Haudricourt, "Brewers Decide to Follow Bucks' Lead and Vote Not to Play Wednesday Night, "*Milwaukee Journal Sentinel*, August 26, 2020, https://www.jsonline.com/story/sports/mlb/brewers/2020/08/26/brewers-follow-bucks-vote-not-play-protest-kenosha-shooting/3442042001/.

52. Rich Maese and Emily Guskin, "Most Americans Support Athletes Speaking Out, Say Anthem Protests Are Appropriate, Post Poll Finds," *Washington Post*, September 10, 2020, https://www.washingtonpost.com/sports/2020/09/10/poll-nfl-anthem -protests/.

53. Emma Baccallieri, "An Activist and a Bookworm, Sean Doolittle Is the Conscience of Baseball," *Washington Post*, April 2, 2020, https://www.si.com /mlb/2020/04/02/sean-doolittle-washington-nationals.

54. Tyler Kepner, "Off the Mound, Sean Doolittle Brings Relief to the Ostracized," *New York Times*, March 12, 2016, https://www.nytimes.com/2016/03/13/sports /baseball/off-the-mound-sean-doolittle-brings-relief-to-the-ostracized.html.

55. Reimer, "Sean Doolittle Challenged U.S."

56. "MLB Player Sean Doolittle Pitches."

57. Mike Digiovanna, "Whether on the Mound or For Refugees in Need, Relief Is a Calling for the A's' Sean Doolittle," *Los Angeles Times*, February 20, 2017, https:// www.latimes.com/sports/nba/la-sp-mlb-sean-doolittle-refugees-20170217-story .html.

58. Ted Berg, "A's Closer and Girlfriend Buying up Tickets to Team's LGBT Pride Night to Donate to LGBTQ Youth," *USA Today*, April 1, 2015, https://ftw .usatoday.com/2015/04/oakland-athletics-sean-doolittle-girlfriend-eireann-dolan -lgbt-pride-night-mlb; Ron Leuty, "Pride, Prejudice and An A's Player's Big LGBT Pitch," *San Francisco Business Times*, June 13, 2016, https://www.bizjournals.com /sanfrancisco/blog/2016/06/lgbt-pride-night-oakland-athletics-sean-doolittle .html.

59. Dan Steinberg, "Sean Doolittle: 'There's No Place for Racism, Insensitive Language or Even Casual Homophobia'" *Washington Post*, July 30, 2018, https:// www.washingtonpost.com/news/dc-sports-bog/wp/2018/07/30/sean-doolittle -theres-no-place-for-racism-insensitive-language-or-even-casual-homophobia.

60. Majoros, "Ally and Baseball Pro Sean Doolittle."

61. Majoros, "Ally and Baseball Pro Sean Doolittle."

62. Buzinski, "Nationals Pitcher Sean Doolittle."

63. Nicole Puglise, "Athletes on Trump's 'Locker Room Banter': That's Not How We Talk at Work," *The Guardian*, October 10, 2016, https://www.theguardian.com /us-news/2016/oct/10/donald-trump-locker-room-banter-athletes-reaction.

64. Blau, "Not 'Locker Room' Talk."

65. Doolittle, "These Refugees Are Fleeing."

66. Digiovanna, "Whether on the Mound."

67. Dickey, "All-Star Athlete Speaks Out."

68. Doolittle, "The C'Ville I Knew."

69. Jorge Castillo, "U-Va Product Sean Doolittle on Charlottesville Rally: 'It's the Worst Kind of Hatred It's Disgusting,'" *Washington Post*, August 12, 2017, https:// www.washingtonpost.com/news/nationals-journal/wp/2017/08/12/u-va-alum -sean-doolittle-on-charlottesville-rally-its-the-worst-kind-of-hatred-its-disgusting/.

70. Sean Doolittle, "MLB Players Love Our Caps; The People Who Make Them for Us Deserve Fair Wages," *Washington Post*, February 28, 2019, https://www .washingtonpost.com/outlook/mlb-players-love-our-caps-the-people-who -make-them-for-us-deserve-fair-wages/2019/02/28/73568324-3acd-11e9-aaae -69364b2ed137_story.html.

71. Gibbs, "This MLB Power Couple."

72. Gabe Lacques, "Sean Doolittle: 'You're an (Expletive)' If Critical of Daniel Hudson's Paternity Leave," *USA Today*, October 12, 2019, https://www .usatoday.com/story/sports/mlb/nationals/2019/10/12/sean-doolittle-final -word-daniel-hudson-paternity-leave-critics/3964849002/.

73. Jesse Dougherty, "Sean Doolittle on Declining White House Invite: 'I Don't Want to Hang Out with Somebody Who Talks Like That,'" *Washington Post*, November 2, 2019, https://www.washingtonpost.com/sports/2019/11/01/sean -doolittle-declining-white-house-invite-i-dont-want-hang-out-with-somebody-who -talks-like-that/; Dreier, "World Series Winners."

74. David Nakamura and Jesse Dougherty, "Nationals Embraced by Trump at White House, Where They Can't Escape Politics," *Washington Post*, November 4, 2019, https://www.washingtonpost.com/sports/2019/11/04/washington-nationals -white-house-visit/.

75. Dougherty, "Sean Doolittle on Declining."

76. Kepner, "Off the Mound."

77. Chelsea Janes, "Sean Doolittle and Eireann Dolan May Be Baseball's Most 'Woke' Couple," *Washington Post*, March 27, 2018, https://www.washingtonpost .com/sports/nationals/sean-doolittle-and-eireann-dolan-may-be-baseballs-most -woke-couple/2018/03/27/646b32ca-2dda-11e8-8688-e053ba58f1e4_story.html.

78. Selbe, "Nationals Players Pledge."

79. Silverman, "Leftist Star Pitcher Sean Doolittle."

80. Hall, "Sean Doolittle Stresses Importance."

81. Hall, "Sean Doolittle Stresses Importance."

82. "Nationals Sean Doolittle Makes Statement."

83. Jesse Dougherty, "Sean Doolittle Wants to Be a Better Ally. He Will Protest with His Teammates, If They Choose To," *Washington Post*, July 22, 2020, https://www.washingtonpost.com/sports/2020/07/22/sean-doolittle-met-john -lewis-2018-now-nat-is-ready-stir-up-good-trouble/.

84. Dougherty, "Sean Doolittle Wants."

85. Baccellieri, "Activist and a Bookworm."

86. Baccellieri, "Activist and a Bookworm."

87. "MLB Player Sean Doolittle Pitches."

88. Froeba, "Washington Nationals Major League Baseball Player."

89. McCauley, "Sean Doolittle Gets Lesson."

90. Doolittle and Dolan, "Stand Up."

91. Frank, "Honored with Act of Valor Award."

92. Doolittle, "The Yellow Ribbon Event."

93. Crasnick, "Sean Doolittle on Bruce Maxwell."

94. Crasnick, "Sean Doolittle on Bruce Maxwell."

95. Mike Hiserman, "Maybe It's the $25 That Really Counts," *Los Angeles Times*, May 11, 2003, https://www.latimes.com/archives/la-xpm-2003-may-11-sp -briefing11-story.html.

96. Ardell, "The Baseball Reliquary," 22; Peter Dreier, "'Not Exactly Cooperstown' Celebrates Baseball's Rebels and Renegades," *Huffington Post*, February 13, 2014, http://www.huffingtonpost.com/peter-dreier/not-exactly-cooperstown-baseball -rebels_b_4781969.html.

97. Richard Sandomir, "Terry Cannon, Creator of an Alternative to Cooperstown, Dies at 66," *New York Times*, August 14, 2020, https://www.nytimes.com/2020 /08/09/sports/baseball/terry-cannon-dead.html; Jim Alexander, "Alexander: Terry Cannon Was a Baseball Subversive, in the Best of Ways," *Orange County Register*, August 4, 2020, https://www.ocregister.com/2020/08/03/alexander-terry-cannon -was-a-baseball-subversive-in-the-best-of-ways/.

98. R.J. Smith, "An L.A. Jazz Legend Pays Homage to Jackie Robinson, with a Pitch from a Library Assistant," *Los Angeles Times*, September 25, 2019, https:// www.latimes.com/entertainment-arts/music/story/2019-09-25/bobby-bradford -jackie-robinson-stealin-home.

99. "Terry Cannon Captures the Magic."

100. "Terry Cannon Captures the Magic."

101. "Terry Cannon Captures the Magic."

Chapter Nine. Baseball Justice: An Unfinished Agenda

1. Ozanian, Baseball's Most Valuable Teams."

2. Graves, "When Racism Drove."

3. Walker, "When Arizona Lost."

4. Scott Cacciola and Alan Blinder, "N.B.A. to Move All-Star Game From North Carolina," *New York Times*, July 21, 2016, https://www.nytimes.com/2016/07/22 /sports/basketball/nba-all-star-game-moves-charlotte-transgender-bathroom-law .html.

5. Trotta, "NBA Returns All-Star Game."

6. Zolan Kanno-Youngs, "Biden Says He Would Support Moving All-Star Game Over Georgia Voting Law," *New York Times*, April 1, 2021, https://www.nytimes .com/2021/04/01/us/politics/biden-espn-baseball-georgia.html.

7. Bill Shaikin, "Dodgers' Dave Roberts Says He'd Consider Not Managing 2021 All-Star Game in Atlanta," *Los Angeles Times*, March 26, 2021, https://www .latimes.com/sports/dodgers/story/2021-03-26/dodgers-dave-roberts-georgia -voting-rights-mlb-all-star-game.

8. Kanno-Youngs, "Biden Says He Would Support."

9. James Wagner and Kevin Draper, "Baseball Pulls All-Star Game from Georgia in Response to Voting Law," *New York Times*, April 2, 2021, https://www.nytimes .com/2021/04/02/us/politics/mlb-all-star-game-moved.html.

10. Nick Corasaniti, "Kemp Lashes M.L.B. as Republicans Defend Georgia's Voting Law," *New York Times*, April 3, 2021, https://www.nytimes.com/2021/04/03/us /politics/mlb-georgia-voting-kemp.html.

11. Dreier, "Baseball's Hall of Fame"; Des Bieler, "Union Leader Marvin Miller is Finally Elected to the Baseball Hall of Fame," *Washington Post*, December 8, 2019, https://www.washingtonpost.com/sports/2019/12/08/union-leader-marvin -miller-finally-elected-baseball-hall-fame/.

12. Dreier, "The Ballplayer Who Fought"; Hill, "Curt Flood Belongs"; Jonathan Abrams, "The Sacrifice," *New York Times*, August 23, 2021, https://www.nytimes .com/2021/08/18/sports/curt-flood-free-agency.html; Benjamin Hochman, "Without Flood, the Hall Is Flawed," *St. Louis Post-Dispatch*, May 1, 2021, https:// www.stltoday.com/sports/columns/benjamin-hochman/hochman-without -flood-the-hall-is-flawed-former-cardinal-and-trailblazer-deserves-to-be-in/article _adcf21b8-c7de-5ae1-bdf2-0d718d2148e3.html; Vincent Davis, "Baseball Pioneer Curt Flood Is Deserving of Hall of Fame Induction," *New York Amsterdam News*, July 22, 2021, http://amsterdamnews.com/news/2021/jul/22/baseball-pioneer -curt-flood-deserving-hall-fame-in/; Bill Fletcher, "Curt Flood Deserves Induction into Baseball Hall of Fame Too," *Daytona Times*, December 27, 2019, https://www .daytonatimes.com/columnists/curt-flood-deserves-induction-into-baseball-hall -of-fame-too/article_f58ec42b-33f7-5345-9242-0507d130e411.html.

13. "Players Association Introduces."

14. "Letter for Curt Flood's Nomination."

15. Rhoden, "Members of Congress Unite"; James E. Clyburn and David Trone, "Why This Is the Year Baseball Should Correct Its Mistake and Put Curt Flood in the Hall of Fame," *Washington Post*, October 7, 2020 https://www.washingtonpost.com /opinions/2020/10/07/curt-flood-baseball-hall-of-fame/.

16. Rhoden, "Push for Curt Flood's Enshrinement."

17. Bradford William Davis, "Congress Calls for Curt Flood's Induction to the Hall of Fame," *New York Daily News*, February 28, 2020, https://www.nydailynews .com/sports/baseball/ny-20200228-w2dammmixnblzkfntovu4qy76q-story.html.

18. Kristie Ackert, "Gerrit Cole Knows His Labor History, Thanks Curt Flood and Marvin Miller," *New York Daily News*, December 18, 2019, https://www .nydailynews.com/sports/baseball/yankees/ny-gerrit-cole-free-agency-marvin -miller-curt-flood-20191218-sweqaznlajcudci4bhslbik43a-story.html.

19. Tony Clark, interview.

20. Cindy Boren, "Hank Aaron's Name Will Replace a Confederate General's on an Atlanta School," *Washington Post*, April 15, 2021, https://www.washingtonpost.com /sports/2021/04/15/hank-aaron-school-confederate-renamed/?outputType=amp.

21. Dan Martin, "Twins Remove Statue of Calvin Griffith: Owner Who Moved Team for 'White People,'" *New York Daily News*, June 19, 2020, https://nypost.com/2020/06/19/twins-remove-statue-of-calvin-griffith-who-moved-team-for-white-people/.

22. Martin, "Twins Remove Statue"; Carew, "Statement from Rod Carew,"

23. Ben Walker, "Former MLB Commissioner Kenesaw Mountain Landis Name Pulled Off MVP Plaques After More Than 75 Years," *Chicago Tribune*, October 3, 2020, https://www.chicagotribune.com/sports/breaking/ct-mlb-mvp-kenesaw-mountain-landis-bbwaa-20201003-gktpsmihnbdqbc46yiap64cu3e-story.html.

24. Michael Errigo, "Baseball MVPs Want Kenesaw Mountain Landis's Name Removed from Award," *Washington Post*, June 30, 2020, https://www.washingtonpost.com/sports/2020/06/30/baseball-mvps-want-kenesaw-mountain-landiss-name-removed-award/.

25. Grigsby, *Celebrating Ourselves.*

26. Bob Nightengale, "It's Time to Remove J.G. Taylor Spink's Name Off Baseball Writers' Award Over His Racist Views," *USA Today*, July 1, 2020, https://www.usatoday.com/story/sports/mlb/columnist/bob-nightengale/2020/07/01/j-g-taylor-spink-baseball-writers-award-racism/5356572002/.

27. Fagan, "*Sporting News* Supports Proposal."

28. Fagan, "*Sporting News* Supports Proposal."

29. Nightengale, "It's Time to Remove."

30. Bill Pennington, "Hall of Fame Has Always Made Room for Infamy," *New York Times*, January 8, 2013 https://www.nytimes.com/2013/01/09/sports/baseball/baseball-hall-of-fame-has-always-made-room-for-infamy.html.

31. Kyle Smith, "How Ty Cobb Was Framed as a Racist," *New York Post*, May 31, 2015 https://nypost.com/2015/05/31/how-ty-cobb-was-framed-as-a-racist/; Trip, "Fake History?" Bill Dow, "90 Years Ago, Detroit Tigers Legend Ty Cobb Challenged Myths Of Being Maniacal Racist," *Detroit Free Press*, May 16, 2020, https://www.freep.com/story/sports/mlb/tigers/2020/05/16/ty-cobb-detroit-tigers-racist-hamtramck-stadium-negro-leagues/3110323001/; George Hunter, "In Defense of Ty Cobb, Perhaps the Detroit Tigers' Most Infamous and Misunderstood Ballplayer, *Detroit Metro Times*, March 25, 2020, https://www.metrotimes.com/detroit/in-defense-of-ty-cobb-perhaps-detroits-most-infamous-and-misunderstood-ballplayer/Content?oid=24181608.

32. The data in these paragraphs are drawn from Lapchick, *2021 Racial and Gender Report Card.*

33. Players Alliance, *Allies of the Alliance*; Larry Stone, "'We're Going to Get It Right': Mariners' Dee Gordon, Players Alliance Work toward Equality for Black Players in Baseball," *Seattle Times*, August 18, 2020, https://www.seattletimes.com/sports/mariners/were-going-to-get-it-right-mariners-dee-gordon-players-alliance-work-toward-equality-for-black-players-in-baseball/.

34. James Wagner, "Hailed as a Trailblazer, Kim Ng Stands Alone," *New York Times*, January 29, 2021, https://www.nytimes.com/2021/01/29/sports/baseball /mlb-diversity-kim-ng.html?action=click&module=RelatedLinks&pgtype=Article.

35. Hoffman, "Brandon Taubman."

36. James Wagner, "'They Just Get It': How Women in M.L.B. Found Support in a Group Text," *New York Times*, October 19, 2020, https://www.nytimes .com/2020/10/19/sports/baseball/mlb-women-coaches.html.

37. Danny Jim, "Why More Girls Are Answering the Call of 'Play ball!'" *Christian Science Monitor*, August 1, 2019, https://www.csmonitor.com/The-Culture /2019/0801/Why-more-girls-are-answering-the-call-of-Play-ball.

38. NCAA *Sports Sponsorship*.

39. Men's baseball became an Olympic sport in 1992, but (like women's softball) was dropped again in the 2008 gamesBoth sports were restored to Olympic competition for the 2020 games that, due to the pandemic, were played in 2021 in Japan.

40. Hays, "Monica Abbott Wants Change."

41. Thomas, "What If Pro Sports Leagues."

42. Ring, *Game of Their Own*, 192.

43. Ring, *Game of Their Own*, 65.

44. Hays, "Stereotypes Haunt Softball."

45. Scott Reid, "Olympian Comes to Terms with Sexual Identity," *Orange County Register*, August 20, 2018, https://web.archive.org/web/20080823221453/http:// www.ocregister.com/articles/lappin-team-going-2131876-people-family; Connolly, "League of Her Own"; "Why Did You Come Out."

46. Hays, "Stereotypes Haunt Softball."

47. Juan Pimiento, "Black, Puerto Rican, Out and Proud: Aleshia Ocasio Blazes a New Trail in the World of Softball," *Chicago Tribune*, June 25, 2019, https://www.chicagotribune.com/voice-it/ct-fds-voiceit-ocasio-20190625 -pvy6u7w4l5bufgbyk4xkoevnry-story.html; Murtaugh, "Softball Player Reflects."

48. Dreier, "Is Baseball Ready."

49. Neal Travis, "In and Out with the Mets," *New York Post*, May 20, 2002, https:// pagesix.com/2002/05/20/in-and-out-with-the-mets/.

50. Maaddi, "Mets' Piazza."

51. Buzinski, "Are Fans Ready."

52. Bob Nightengale, "MLB Ready to Welcome First Openly Gay Active Player," *USA Today*, March 9, 2016, https://www.usatoday.com/story/sports/mlb/2016/03 /08/mlb-first-openly-gay-active-player-reaction/81508232.

53. Bill Plaschke, "Dodgers Don't Kiss This Off," *Los Angeles Times*, August 24, 2000, https://www.latimes.com/archives/la-xpm-2000-aug-24-sp-9565-story.html.

54. Billy Bean, interview.

55. MLB Criticizes Arizona Rights Bill," *Seattle Times*, February 26, 2014, https:// www.seattletimes.com/sports/mlb-criticizes-arizona-rights-bill/.

56. Burge, "I Want to Thank God."

57. Kevin Baxter, "In Pro Sports, Gay Athletes Still Feel Unwelcome," *Los Angeles Times*, December 29, 2012, https://www.latimes.com/sports/la-xpm-2012-dec-29 -la-sp-sports-homophobia-20121230-story.html; LaCaruba, "Getting Open."

58. Joe Holleman, "Lance Berkman Appearance at Cardinals 'Christian Day' Raises Ire with LGBT Group," *StLouis Post-Dispatch*, June 13, 2017, https://www .stltoday.com/news/local/columns/joe-holleman/lance-berkman-appearance-at -cardinals-christian-day-raises-ire-with-lgbt-group/article_7144f227-09e5-5791 -a95c-230cc4b0daa9.html.

59. Zeigler, "St. Louis Cardinals Stand."

60. Murray Chass, "Baseball Suspends Rocker till May for Comments," *New York Times*, January 31, 2000, https://archive.nytimes.com/www.nytimes.com/learning /students/pop/articles/020100bbn-braves.html.

61. Knapp, "Tavarez Trips"; Gwen Knapp, "Tavarez Trips Over His Own Tongue," *SF Gate*, April 29, 2001, https://www.sfgate.com/sports/knapp/article/Tavarez -trips-over-his-own-tongue-3327307.php.

62. "Pitcher Todd Jones."

63. "Guillen Apologizes"; Morrissey, *Ozzie's School of Management.*

64. Bobby Nightengale, "'Everyone Should Be Offended by It': Cincinnati Reds Players React to Thom Brennaman's On-Air Slur," *Cincinnati Enquirer*, August 20, 2020, https://www.cincinnati.com/story/sports/mlb/reds/2020/08/20/cincinnati-reds -players-react-thom-brennaman-air-homophobic-slur/3401419001/.

65. "Pitcher Todd Jones."

66. Wertheim, "Gays in Sports."

67. Billy Bean, interview.

68. Maaddi, "Mets' Piazza."

69. Neyer, "A Chat with Dave Pallone."

70. Billy Bean, interview.

71. Billy Bean, interview.

72. Tom D'Angelo, "Gay Issue Remains in Closet," *Palm Beach Post*, May 26, 2002.

Aaron, Hank, with Lonnie Wheeler. *I Had a Hammer: The Hank Aaron Story*. New York: Harper, 2007.

Abrams, Douglas E. "The Twelve-Year-Old Girl's Lawsuit That Changed America: The Continuing Impact of *Now v. Little League Baseball, Inc.* at 40," *Virginia Journal of Social Policy & the Law* 241 (Winter 2012). https://scholarship.law .missouri.edu/cgi/viewcontent.cgi?article=1505&context=facpubs.

Abrams, Roger. "Arbitrator Seitz Sets the Players Free," *Baseball Research Journal* (Fall 2009). https://sabr.org/research/arbitrator-seitz-sets-players-free.

———. "Before the Flood: The History of Baseball's Antitrust Exemption." *Marquette Sports Law Review* 9, (1999): 307. http://scholarship.law.marquette .edu/sportslaw/vol9/iss2/7.

———. *Legal Bases: Baseball and the Law*. Philadelphia: Temple University Press, 1998.

Ackmann, Martha. *Curveball: The Remarkable Story of Toni Stone, the First Woman to Play Professional Baseball in the Negro League*. Chicago: Lawrence Hill Books, 2010.

Albertson, Matt. "Race and Baseball in Philadelphia, Part 1: Octavius Catto and the Pythian Base Ball Club." *Philliedelphia*, February 11, 2016. https://www .philliedelphia.com/2016/02/race-and-baseball-in-philadelphia-part-1 -octavius-catto.html.

———. "Race and Baseball in Philadelphia, Part 3: Dick Allen in Philadelphia." *Philliedelphia*, March 11, 2016. https://www.philliedelphia.com/2016/03 /race-and-baseball-in-philadelphia-part-3-dick-allen.html.

Alexander, Lisa Doris. *When Baseball Isn't White, Straight and Male*. Jefferson, NC: McFarland, 2013.

"All Stars Win European Title in GI Playoff." *The Sporting News*, September 13, 1945.

Allen, Dick, and Tim Whitaker. *Crash: The Life and Times of Dick Allen*. New York: Ticknor and Fields, 1989.

Anderson, Eric. *In the Game: Gay Athletes and the Cult of Masculinity*. Albany: SUNY Press, 2005.

Ardell, Jean Hastings. "The Baseball Reliquary: The Left Coast's Alternative to Interpreting Baseball History." In *The Cooperstown Symposium on Baseball and American Culture 2007-2008*, edited by William M. Simons, 22–37. Jefferson, NC: McFarland, 2009.

———. *Breaking into Baseball: Women and the National Pastime.* Carbondale, IL: Southern Illinois University Press, 2005.

———. "Mamie 'Peanut' Johnson: The Last Female Voice of the Negro Leagues." *NINE: A Journal of Baseball History and Culture* 10, no. 1 (Fall 2001): 181–92.

Armour, Mark. "Baseball Integration, 1947–1986." *Society of American Baseball Research*, n.d. https://sabr.org/bioproj/topic/integration-1947-1986.

Arson, Anne. "Dames in the Dirt: Women's Baseball Before 1945." *The National Pastime* (2012). https://sabr.org/research/dames-dirt-womans-baseball-1945.

"Ashton Lansdell Following Baseball Dream in the NJCAA." *National Junior College Athletic Association*, August 9, 2019. https://www.njcaa.org/sports/bsb/2019 -20/releases/20190808h6049q.

Associated Press. "Delgado to Stand with Mets during 'God Bless America.'" *ESPN*, November 28, 2005. https://www.espn.com/mlb/news/story?id=2239461.

"At Least 185 Out LGBTQ Athletes Were at the Tokyo Summer Olympics, More than Triple the Number in Rio," *Outsports*, August 15, 2021. https://www .outsports.com/olympics/2021/7/12/22565574/tokyo-summer-olympics -lgbtq-gay-athletes-list.

Ausmus, Brad. Interview by Diane Sawyer. *20/20*. Aired December 8, 1999 on ABC News. http://greginhollywood.com/flashback-video-when-baseballs-billy -bean-was-interviewed-by-diane-sawyer-in-1999-84227.

Baccellieri, Emma. "An Activist and a Bookworm, Sean Doolittle Is the Conscience of Baseball." *Sports Illustrated*, April 2, 2020. https://www.si.com/mlb/2020 /04/02/sean-doolittle-washington-nationals.

Baldassaro, Lawrence, and Richard Johnson, eds. *The American Game: Baseball and Ethnicity.* Carbondale, IL: Southern Illinois University Press, 2002.

Banks, Lacy J. "Richie Allen: 'I'm My Own Man.'" *Ebony*, July 1970, 88–95.

Barnes, Katie. "Pro Baseball Player Ila Borders Blazed Trails with Each Pitch She Threw." *ESPN*, March 31, 2017. http://www.espn.com/espnw/culture /article/19042822/pro-baseball-player-ila-borders-blazed-trails-pitch-threw.

Barra, Allen. "How Curt Flood Changed Baseball and Killed His Career in the Process." *Atlantic*, July 12, 2011. https://www.theatlantic.com/entertainment /archive/2011/07/how-curt-flood-changed-baseball-and-killed-his-career -in-the-process/241783/.

"Baseball League President White & Racism." *Morning Edition.* NPR, June 10, 1992.

Baseball Reference. "Glenn Burke." n.d. https://www.baseball-reference.com /register/player.fcgi?id=burke-001gle.

———. "Jason Burch." n.d. https://www.baseball-reference.com/register/player .fcgi?id=burch-001rob.

———. "Second Dead-Ball Era." n.d. https://www.baseball-reference.com/bullpen /Second_Deadball_Era.

———. "Vic Power." n.d. https://www.baseball-reference.com/bullpen/V%C3 %ADc_Power.

"Baseball's Best Centerfielder." *Sports Illustrated*, August 19, 1968.

Bean, Billy. *Going the Other Way: Lessons from a Life In and Out of Major-League Baseball*. New York: Marlowe & Company, 2003.

———. Interview by Diane Sawyer. *20/20*. Aired December 8, 1999 on ABC News. https://www.youtube.com/watch?v=08GDdTcEflA.

———. Interview by Peter Dreier, August 16, 2021.

Beck, Peggy. "Working in the Shadows of Rickey and Robinson: Bill Veeck, Larry Doby, and the Advancement of Black Players in Baseball." In *The Cooperstown Symposium on Baseball and American Culture, 1997*, edited by Peter M. Rutkoff. Jefferson, NC: McFarland, 2000.

Belz, Kate Harrison. "The Girl Who Struck Out Babe Ruth." *Chattanooga Memory Project*, n.d.

Berlage, Gail Ingham. *Women in Baseball: The Forgotten History*. Westport, CT: Praeger, 1994.

Biddle, Daniel R., and Murray Dubin. *Tasting Freedom: Octavius Catto and the Battle for Equality in Civil War America*. Philadelphia: Temple University Press, 2010.

Black, Joe. *Ain't Nobody Better than You*. Scottsdale, AZ: Ironwood Lithographers, 1983.

Black, Martha Jo, and Chuck Schoffner. *Joe Black: More Than a Dodger*. Chicago: Chicago Review Press, 2015.

Blau, Max. "Not 'Locker Room' Talk: Athletes Push Back against Trump's Remark." *CNN*, October 10, 2016. https://www.cnn.com/2016/10/10/politics/locker-room-talk-athletes-respond-trnd/index.html.

"Blazing Baseball Trails from Field to Executive Suite." *All Things Considered*. NPR, April 14, 2011. https://www.npr.org/2011/04/15/135418480/bill-whites-baseball-days-on-the-field-and-on-a-mic.

Blount, Roy, Jr. "Swinging in His Own Groove." *Sports Illustrated*, September 10, 1973.

Blum, Ronald. "Negro League Players Gain Pension Eligibility." *Indiana Gazette*, January 20, 1997, 17.

Borders, Ila Jane, with Jean Hastings Ardell. *Making My Pitch: A Woman's Baseball Odyssey*. Lincoln: University of Nebraska Press, 2017.

Bowman, Emma. "A Little League of Her Own: The First Girl in Little League Baseball." *Morning Edition*. NPR, March 30, 2018. https://www.npr.org/2018/03/30/597960442/a-little-league-of-her-own-the-first-girl-in-little-league-baseball.

Briley, Ron. "Baseball and the Cold War: An Examination of Values." *OAH Magazine of History* 2, no. 1 (Summer 1986): 15–18.

———. "Do Not Go Gently into That Good Night: Race, the Baseball Establishment, and the Retirements of Bob Feller and Jackie Robinson," in *Class at Bat, Gender on Deck, and Race in the Hole*. Jefferson, NC: McFarland, 2003.

———. "The Times Were A'Changin': Baseball as a Symbol of American Values in Transition, 1963–1964." *Class at Bat, Gender on Deck, and Race in the Hole.* Jefferson, NC: McFarland, 2003.

Brown, Robert S. "Mudcat Grant and the Protest of the National Anthem." Paper presented at 30th Cooperstown Symposium on Baseball and American Culture, Cooperstown, NY, May 30–June 1, 2018.

Browne, Lois. *Girls of Summer: In Their Own League.* New York: HarperCollins, 1992.

Bryant, Howard. "Atlanta Pro Sports and Integration." *ESPN*, January 12, 2011. https://www.espn.com/espn/commentary/news/story?id=6015125.

———. *The Last Hero: A Life of Henry Aaron.* New York: Anchor, 2011.

———. *Shut Out: A Story of Race and Baseball in Boston.* New York: Routledge, 2002.

———. "The Unsanitized Story of Jackie Robinson." *ESPN*, April 11, 2016. https://www.espn.com/mlb/story/_/id/15182338/how-story-real-jackie-robinson-shows-deeper-more-painful-side-civil-rights-legend.

Brydum, Sunnivie. "JoJo D'Angelo, Real Life Inspiration for 'A League of Their Own,' Dies at 88." *Pride*, September 3, 2013. https://www.pride.com/box-office/2013/09/03/jojo-dangelo-real-life-inspiration-league-their-own-dies-88.

Burge, Ryan P. "I Want to Thank God for Allowing My Team to Win: An Analysis of Sports and Christianity." *Religion in Public*, February 12, 2018. https://religioninpublic.blog/2018/02/12/i-want-thank-god-for-allowing-my-team-to-win-an-analysis-of-sports-and-christianity/.

Burk, Robert F., *Marvin Miller, Baseball Revolutionary.* Urbana, IL: University of Illinois Press, 2015.

Burke, Glenn, with Erik Sherman. *Out at Home: The True Story of Glenn Burke, Baseball's First Openly Gay Player.* New York: Berkley Books, 1995.

Jim Buzinski. "Are Fans Ready to Accept an Openly Gay Player in MLB?" *Outsports*, June 18, 2002. https://www.outsports.com/2013/5/27/4371234/are-fans-ready-to-accept-an-openly-gay-player-in-mlb.

———. "John Dillinger, On Living Life in Baseball's Closet." *Outsports*, October 24, 2012. https://www.sbnation.com/2012/10/24/3545938/john-dillinger-interview-outsports.

———. "Meet the 16 Out Gay and Bi Football Players in the NFL's 102-Year History." *Outsports*, September 9, 2021. https://www.outsports.com/2019/9/5/20850457/nfl-history-gay-bi-players.

———. "MLB Umpire Dale Scott Comes Out as Gay in Quietest Way Possible." *Outsports*, December 2, 2014. https://www.outsports.com/2014/12/2/7295993/major-league-baseball-umpire-dale-scott-gay-coming-out.

———. "Nationals Pitcher Sean Doolittle: 'Homophobic Slurs are Still Used to Make People Feel Soft or Weak.'" *Outsports*, July 30, 2018. https://www

.outsports.com/2018/7/30/17632762/washigton-nationals-pitcher-sean
-doolittle-rebuts-homophobic-racist-slurs.

——. "Poll: Large Majority of Americans Favor Openly Gay Athletes." *Outsports,*
January 27, 2015. https://www.outsports.com/2015/1/27/7904811/poll
-large-majority-americans-favor-openly-gay-athletes.

——. "Poll: 90% of Sports Executives Say Fans Don't Care If Athlete is Gay."
Outsports, June 5, 2013. https://www.outsports.com/2013/6/5/4398034
/poll-sports-executives-gay-athlete-player-favorite-team.

——. "30 LGBTQ Athletes Who Showed 'Stonewall Spirit': Glenn Burke."
Outsports, June 6, 2019. https://www.outsports.com/2019/6/6/18649970
/stonewall-spirit-gay-mlb-glenn-burke-baseball.

Cahn, Susan K. *Coming on Strong: Gender and Sexuality in Twentieth-Century
Women's Sports.* Cambridge, MA: Harvard University Press, 1994.

"Casey Candaele Discusses His Mother, Helen Callaghan Candaele." Facebook,
July 1, 2017. https://www.facebook.com/Mariners/videos/casey-candaele
-discusses-his-mother-helen-callaghan-candaele-/10155351176268979/.

Candaele, Kelly. Interview by Peter Dreier, May 20, 2020.

Candaele, Kelly, and Peter Dreier. "Tom Seaver's Major League Protest." *The Nation,*
September 11, 2020. https://www.thenation.com/article/society/tom-seaver
-vietnam-protest/.

Carew, Rod. *Statement from Rod Carew on Calvin Griffith,* n.d. https://kstp.com
/kstpImages/repository/cs/files/STATEMENT%20FROM%20ROD
%20CAREW%20ON%20CALVIN%20GRIFFITH.pdf.

Carroll, Brian. "A Crusading Journalist's Last Campaign: Wendell Smith and the
Desegregation of Baseball's Spring Training." *Communication and Social Change*
1 (2007): 38–54.

——. "'It Couldn't Be Any Other Way': The Great Dilemma for the Black Press
and Negro League Baseball." *Black Ball: A Negro Leagues Journal* 5 (2012):
5–23.

Carter, Dan T. *Scottsboro: A Tragedy of the American South.* Baton Rouge, LA:
Louisiana State University Press, 2007.

Casway, Jerrold I. *The Culture and Ethnicity of Nineteenth Century Baseball.* Jefferson,
NC: McFarland, 2017.

——. "Octavius Catto and the Pythians of Philadelphia." *Phindie,* March 21, 2010.
http://phindie.com/octavius-catto-and-the-pythians-of-philadelphia/.

——. "September 3, 1869: Inter-Racial Baseball in Philadelphia." *Society of
American Baseball Research,* n.d. https://sabr.org/gamesproj/game/september
-3-1869-inter-racial-baseball-philadelphia.

"Catto Addresses State House in Philadelphia." *Christian Recorder,* April 22, 1865.

Clark, Tony. Interview by Peter Dreier, July 29, 2021.

Cohen, Marilyn. *No Girls in the Clubhouse: The Exclusion of Women from Baseball.*
Jefferson, NC: McFarland, 2009.

"Colorado Mesa Baseball Coach Apologizes for Anti-Gay Remark." *Sports Illustrated*, March 25, 2016. https://www.si.com/mlb/2016/03/25 /tyler-dunnington-sean-mckinney-anti-gay-apology.

Conlin, Bill. "For One Great Ballplayer, Philadelphia Was a Perpetual Traffic Jam." *Deadspin*, January 10, 2014. https://thestacks.deadspin.com/for-one-great -ballplayer-philadelphia-was-a-perpetual-1498843343.

Connolly, Shannon. "A League of Her Own." *The Advocate*, August 26, 2008.

Cook, William A. *Lady Moguls: A History of Women Who Have Owned Major League Baseball Teams*. Mechanicsburg, PA: Sunbury Press, 2015.

Corbett, Warren. "Bill White." *Society of American Baseball Research*, n.d. https:// sabr.org/bioproj/person/c3eea582.

Cottrell, Robert Charles. *The Best Pitcher in Baseball: The Life of Rube Foster, Negro League Giant*. New York: New York University Press, 2004.

Coval, Jennifer. "Playing for Keeps: The Pythian Base Ball Club of Philadelphia." *Historical Society of Pennsylvania*, n.d. https://hsp.org/education/unit-plans /baseball-and-race-in-post-bellum-pennsylvania/pythians-base-ball-club -playing-for-keeps.

Craig, Mary. "Jackie Mitchell: Beyond Babe Ruth." *Beyond the Box Score*, July 27, 2017. https://www.beyondtheboxscore.com/2017/7/27/16023858/jackie -mitchell-female-pitcher-babe-ruth-lou-gehrig.

———. "Vassar and Beyond: Women and Baseball in the 1800s." *SB Nation*, September 19, 2017. "https://www.beyondtheboxscore.com/2017/9/19 /16323942/women-baseball-history-vassar-suffrage-abolition.

Crasnick, Jerry. "Sean Doolittle on Bruce Maxwell, Respecting Veterans and Defining Patriotism in a Polarized America." *ESPN*, September 30, 2017. https://www.espn.com/mlb/story/_/id/20851364/sean-doolittle-bruce -maxwell-respecting-veterans-defining-patriotism-polarized-america.

Crowley, Michael. "Muhammad Ali Was a Rebel. Michael Jordan Is a Brand Name." *Nieman Reports*, September 15, 1999. https://niemanreports.org/articles /muhammad-ali-was-a-rebel-michael-jordan-is-a-brand-name/.

D'Ambrosio, Rich. "Dick Allen." *Society of American Baseball Research*, n.d. https:// sabr.org/bioproj/person/92ed657e.

Davis, Amira Rose. "No League of Their Own: Baseball, Black Women, and the Politics of Representation." *Radical History Review* 125 (May 2016): 74–96.

Davis, Jack. "Baseball's Reluctant Challenge: Desegregating Major League Spring Training Sites, 1961–1964." *Journal of Sport History* 19, no. 2 (Summer, 1992): 144–62.

Dean, Margaret Lazarus. "The Imaginary Athlete." *Michigan Quarterly Review* 46, no. 1 (Winter 2007). https://quod.lib.umich.edu/cgi/t/text/text-idx?cc=mqr ;c=mqr;c=mqrarchive;idno=act2080.0046.112;g=mqrg;rgn=main;view =text;xc=1.

De La Cruz, Britni. "The First Woman Is Inducted into the Writers' Wing of the Baseball Hall of Fame, and She Won't Be the Last." *Vogue*, August 1, 2017. https://www.vogue.com/article/claire-smith-baseball-hall-of-fame-women -sportswriters.

De la Cretaz, Britni. "The Hidden Queer History Behind 'A League of Their Own.'" *Narratively*, June 30, 2018. https://narratively.com/the-hidden-queer-history -behind-a-league-of-their-own/.

Dickey, Jack. "All-Star Athlete Speaks Out on Immigration." *Time*, June 5, 2017. https://time.com/collection/american-voices-2017/4714382/sean-dolittle -american-voices/.

Dickson, Paul. *Bill Veeck: Baseball's Greatest Maverick*. New York: Walker Publishing, 2012.

Dixon, Phil S. *Andrew "Rube" Foster: A Harvest on Field's Freedom*. Bloomington, IN: Xlibris, 2010.

Donahue, Terry. Interview by James Smither for the All American Girls Professional Baseball League Veterans History Project. Grand Valley State University, 2010. https://digitalcollections.library.gvsu.edu/document/29693.

Donaldson, Zoe. "I Avoided a Lesbian Stereotype for as Long as I Could." *Oprah Magazine*, June 6, 2019. https://www.oprahmag.com/life/a27758418/lesbian -identity-pride-month-essay/.

Doolittle, Sean. "The C'Ville I knew from my time at @UVA is a diverse and accepting community. It's no place for Nazis. People say 'if we don't give them attention they'll go." Twitter, August 13, 2017, https://twitter.com /whatwouldDOOdo/status/896612535587282944.

———. "These refugees are fleeing civil wars, terrorism, religious persecution, and are thoroughly vetted for 2yrs. A refugee ban is a bad idea..." Twitter, January 28, 2017. https://twitter.com/whatwouldDOOdo/ status/825565333805162497.

———. "The yellow ribbon event was a reminder that as long as we have an all-volunteer military, it's on us—the civilians at home—to advocate for our military." Twitter, January 26, 2020. https://twitter.com/whatwouldDOOdo /status/1221596484765921281.

Doolittle, Sean, and Eireann Dolan. "Stand Up: A's Pitcher Sean Doolittle's Quest to Properly Help Veterans with 'Bad Paper.'" *Sports Illustrated*, May 25, 2017.

Dreier, Peter. "The Ballplayer Who Fought for Free Agency." *The Nation*, August 27, 2021. https://www.thenation.com/article/activism/the-ballplayer-who -fought-for-free-agency/.

———. "Baseball's Hall of Fame Finally Admits Labor Pioneer Marvin Miller." *The Nation*, December 10, 2019. https://www.thenation.com/article/archive /marvin-miller-hall-fame/.

———. "Half a Century Before Colin Kaepernick, Jackie Robinson Said, 'I Cannot Stand and Sing the Anthem.'" *The Nation*, July 18. 2019. https://www.thenation.com/article/huac-jackie-robinson-paul-robeson/.

———. "Is Baseball Ready for a Gay Jackie Robinson?" *In These Times*, August 15, 2003. https://inthesetimes.com/article/is-baseball-ready-for-a-gay-jackie-robinson.

———. "Joe Black." *Society for American Baseball Research*, March 2021. https://sabr.org/bioproj/person/joe-black/.

———. *The 100 Greatest Americans of the 20th Century: A Social Justice Hall of Fame.* New York: Nation Books, 2012.

———. "Pumpsie Green: The Last of the Firsts." *Beyond Chron*, July 18, 2019. https://beyondchron.org/pumpsie-green-the-last-of-the-firsts/.

———. "Sam Nahem." *Society for American Baseball Research*, n.d. https://sabr.org/bioproj/person/sam-nahem/.

———. "Sam Nahem: The Right-Handed Lefty Who Integrated Military Baseball in World War II." In *The Cooperstown Symposium on Baseball and American Culture, 2017–2018*, edited by William M. Simons. Jefferson, NC: McFarland, 2019.

———. "The World Series Winners Should Not Visit the White House." *The Nation*, November 1, 2019. https://www.thenation.com/article/world-series-washington-nationals-trump/.

Dreier, Peter, and Kelly Candaele. "The Red Sox Should Not Visit the White House." *The Nation*, October 30, 2018. https://www.thenation.com/article/red-sox-world-series-donald-trump/.

———. "Where Are the Jocks for Justice?" *The Nation*, June 10, 2004. https://www.thenation.com/article/archive/where-are-jocks-justice/.

Drouzas, Frank. "Baseball and Biscuits and Gravy: Bay Area Racism and the National Pastime." *Tampa Bay Weekly Challenger*, July 11, 2019. https://theweeklychallenger.com/baseball-and-biscuits-and-gravy-bay-area-racism-and-the-national-pastime/.

Duberman, Martin. *Paul Robeson.* New York: New Press, 1995.

Duru, N. Jeremi. "Exploring Jethroe's Injustice: The Impact of an Ex-Ballplayer's Legal Quest for a Pension on the Movement for Restorative Racial Justice." *University of Cincinnati Law Review* 76 (Spring 2008). https://papers.ssrn.com/sol3/papers.cfm?abstract_id=1114209.

———. "Sam Jethroe's Last Hit." In *The Politics of Baseball*, edited by Ron Briley. Jefferson, NC: McFarland, 2010.

Duthiers, Vladimir. "Octavius Valentine Catto Honored in Philadelphia." *CBS News*, September 26, 2017. https://www.cbsnews.com/news/octavius-valentine-catto-receives-special-honor-in-philadelphia/.

Eig, Jonathan. *Opening Day: The Story of Jackie Robinson's First Season.* New York: Simon & Schuster, 2008.

Elias, Robert, ed. *Baseball and the American Dream: Race, Class, Gender and the National Pastime*. New York: Routledge, 2011.

———. *The Empire Strikes Out: How Baseball Sold U.S. Foreign Policy and Promoted the American Way Abroad*. New York: The New Press, 2010.

Elias, Robert, and Peter Dreier. *Major League Rebels: Baseball Battles Over Workers' Rights and American Empire*. Lanham, MD: Rowman & Littlefield, 2022.

Ennis, Dawn. "Play Ball! All But 2 MLB Teams are Hosting Pride Events This Season," *Outsports*, April 10, 2019. https://www.outsports.com/2019/3/28/18285393/baseball-mlb-opening-day-hosting-pride-events.

Eno, Greg. "Dave Pallone: MLB's First Gay Umpire Now Preaching Respect." *Bleacher Report*, June 12, 2010. https://bleacherreport.com/articles/405128-dave-pallone-mlbs-first-gay-umpire-now-preaching-respect.

Ephross, Peter, with Martin Abramowitz. *Jewish Major Leaguers in Their Own Words: Oral Histories of 23 Players*. Jefferson, NC: McFarland, 2012.

Eskenazi, Joe. "Artful Dodger: Baseball's 'Subway' Sam Strikes Out Batters, and with the Ladies' Too." *J Weekly*, October 23, 2003. jweekly.com/article/full/20827/artful-dodger.

———. "'Subway' Sam Nahem, Ballplayer and Union Man, Dies at 88," *J Weekly*, April 23, 2004. jweekly.com/article/full/22430/-subway-sam-nahem-ballplayer-and-union-man-dies-at-88.

Essington, Amy. "Effa Manley." *Society for American Baseball Research*, n.d. https://sabr.org/node/27089.

———. *The Integration of the Pacific Coast League*. Lincoln: University of Nebraska Press, 2018.

Everbach, Tracy. "Breaking Baseball Barriers: The 1953–54 Negro League and the Expansion of Women's Public Roles." *American Journalism* 22, no. 1 (2005): 13–33.

Exec. Order No. 8802, Prohibition of Discrimination in the Defense Industry (June 25, 1941). https://www.ourdocuments.gov/doc.php?flash=false&doc=72&page=transcript.

Fagan, Ryan. "*Sporting News* Supports Proposal to Remove J.G. Taylor Spink Name from BBWAA Award." *The Sporting News*, January 27, 2021. https://www.sportingnews.com/ca/mlb/news/mlb-taylor-spink-award-hall-of-fame-bbwaa-vote/10cld2vr8ixwm1560qx3rl49ml.

Fetter, Henry. "The Party Line and the Color Line: The American Communist Party, the 'Daily Worker,' and Jackie Robinson." *Journal of Sport History* 28, no. 3 (Fall 2001): 375–402.

———. "From 'Stooge' to 'Czar': Judge Landis, the *Daily Worker*, and the Integration of Baseball." *American Communist History* 6, no. 1 (September 13, 2007): 29–63 http://doi.org/10.1080/14743890701400811.

Fieldstadt, Elisha. "San Francisco Giants Manager, Several Team Members Take a Knee During National Anthem." *NBC Sports*, July 21, 2020. https://www

.nbcnews.com/news/us-news/san-francisco-giants-manager-several-team
-members-take-knee-during-n1234447.

Fidler, Merrie A. *The Origins and History of the All-American Girls Professional Baseball League.* Jefferson, NC: McFarland, 2006.

Fimrite, Ron. "Sam Lacy: Black Crusader a Resolute Writer Helped Bring Change to Sports." *Sports Illustrated*, October 29, 1990. https://vault.si.com/vault /1990/10/29/sam-lacy-black-crusader-a-resolute-writer-helped-bring -change-to-sports.

Finch, Jennie, with Ann Killion. *Throw Like a Girl.* Chicago: Triumph Books, 2011.

Finkel, Lena. "The Story of How Sean Conroy Became the First Openly Gay Pro-Baseball Player." *Femestella*, August 5, 2016.

Fleitz, David L. *Ghosts in the Gallery at Cooperstown: Sixteen Forgotten Members of the Hall of Fame.* Jefferson, NC: McFarland, 2004.

Flood, Curt. Interview by Ken Burns, dir., *Baseball.* Episode 8, "A Whole New Ballgame." Aired September 27, 1994, on PBS. Available from Negro Leagues Baseball Museum. https://www.youtube.com/watch?v=tM9FIMwXeVk.

Flood, Curt, with Richard Carter. *The Way It Is.* New York: Pocket Books, 1971.

Flood, Judy Pace. Interview by Peter Dreier, June 15, 2021.

Florio, John, and Ouisie Shapiro. *One Nation Under Baseball: How the 1960s Collided with the National Pastime.* Lincoln: University of Nebraska Press, 2017.

———. "When King Died, Baseball Struck Out." *The Undefeated*, April 4, 2018. https://theundefeated.com/features/when-martin-luther-king-died-major -league-baseball-struck-out/.

Footer, Alyson. "MLB Names Bean Its First Ambassador for Inclusion." *MLB.com*, July 15, 2014. https://www.mlb.com/news/billy-bean-is-mlbs-first -ambassador-for-inclusion/c-84795004.

"Forging Citizenship and Opportunity—Octavius Catto's Legacy." *Independence Hall Association*, n.d. https://catto.ushistory.org/.

Francis, Bill. "National Tragedy Brought Baseball to Halt for Two Days in 1968." *Baseballhall.org*, n.d.

———. "When Ted Williams Changed History." *Baseball America*, July 15, 2016. https://www.baseballamerica.com/stories/when-ted-williams-changed -history/.

Frank, Noah. "Honored with Act of Valor Award, Doolittle Presses Sports Leagues to Do More for Veterans." *WTOP*, December 5, 2018. https://wtop.com /washington-nationals/2018/12/honored-with-act-of-valor-award-doolittle -presses-sports-leagues-to-do-more-for-veterans/.

Frisch, Paul A. "Wells, Willie." In *African American National Biography*, edited by Henry Louis Gates Jr. and Evelyn Brooks Higginbotham. New York: Oxford University Press, 2006.

Froeba, Kristine. "Washington Nationals Major League Baseball Player Sean Doolittle Reads to Military Children." *Military Times*, June 24, 2019. https://

www.militarytimes.com/2019/06/24/baseballs-washington-nationals-sean
-doolittle-hosts-military-children/.

Frye, Andy. "Billie Jean King: Today's Athletes and Companies Are Promoting
'Good Change.'" *Forbes*, May 10, 2021. https://www.forbes.com/sites
/andyfrye/2021/05/10/billie-jean-king-todays-athletes-and-companies-are
-promoting-good-change/?sh=1c5aa0bece63.

Gallagher, Tom. "Lester Rodney, the *Daily Worker*, and the Integration of Baseball."
In *The National Pastime: A Review of Baseball History*. Cooperstown, NY:
Society for American Baseball Research, 1999.

Garcia, Megan. "Baseball Options for Girls, Women Expanding." *MLB.com*, April 9,
2021. https://www.mlb.com/news/baseball-options-for-girls-and-women
-after-little-league-expanding.

Gaydos, Ryan. "White Sox Pitcher Lucas Giolito Speaks Out on Racism Amid
Protests: 'It's Time to Do Better.'" *Fox News*, June 1, 2020. https://www
.foxnews.com/sports/white-sox-lucas-giolito-racism-amid-protests.

Gazdziak, Sam. "Obituary: Terry Donahue (1925–2019)." *RIP Baseball*, March 17,
2019. https://ripbaseball.com/2019/03/17/obituary-terry-donahue-1925
-2019/.

Gems, Gerald R. *Before Jackie Robinson: The Transcendent Role of Black Sporting
Pioneers*. Lincoln: University of Nebraska Press, 2017.

Gerlach, Larry, David Jordan, and John Rossi. "A Baseball Myth Exploded: Bill
Veeck and the 1943 Sale of the Phillies." *The National Pastime* 18 (1998).
https://sabr.org/research/article/a-baseball-myth-exploded-bill-veeck-and
-the-1943-sale-of-the-phillies/.

Gibbs, Lindsay. "Meet Jen Ramos, The First Openly Non-Binary Executive in Pro
Sports." *Think Progress*, February 27, 2017. https://thinkprogress.org/meet-jen
-ramos-the-first-openly-non-binary-executive-in-pro-sports-11553c02878a/.

———. "This MLB Power Couple is Fighting to Save 200 Union Jobs." *Think
Progress*, February 20, 2019. https://thinkprogress.org/baseball-couple-union
-campaign-003ec8963027/.

Gilger, Kristin, and Julia Wallace. *There's No Crying in Newsrooms: What Women
Have Learned about What It Takes to Lead*. Lanham, MD: Rowman &
Littlefield, 2019.

Gitlin, Todd. *Occupy Nation: The Roots, the Spirit, and the Promise of Occupy Wall
Street*. New York: IT Books, 2012.

Gladstone, Douglas. *Bitter Cup of Coffee: How MLB and the Players Association
Threw 874 Retirees a Curve*. Tarentum, PA: Word Association Publishers, 2010.

———. "MLB Isn't Paying Pensions to Herb Washington and Other Persons of
Color." *Bleacher Report*, July 17, 2012. https://bleacherreport.com/articles
/1261542-mlb-isnt-paying-pensions-to-herb-washington-and-other-persons
-of-color.

Gmelch, George. *Beyond the Smile: The Working Lives of Caribbean Tourism*. Bloomington, IN: Indiana University Press, 2003.

———. *Inside Pitch: Life in Professional Baseball*. Lincoln: University of Nebraska Press, 2006.

———. Interview by Peter Dreier, March 7, 2021.

———. *The Irish Tinkers: The Urbanization of an Itinerant People*. Long Grove, IL: Waveland Press, 1985.

———. *Playing with Tigers: A Minor League Chronicle of the Sixties*. Lincoln: University of Nebraska Press, 2016.

Gmelch, George, and Daniel Nathan, eds. *Baseball Beyond Our Borders: An International Pastime*. Lincoln: University of Nebraska Press, 2017.

Gmelch, George, and J. J. Weiner. *In the Ballpark: The Working Lives of Baseball People*. Lincoln: University of Nebraska Press, 2006.

Gmelch, Sharon Bohn, and George Gmelch. *Irish Travellers: The Unsettled Life*. Bloomington, IN: Indiana University Press, 2014.

———. *The Parish Behind God's Back: The Changing Culture of Rural Barbados*. Long Grove IL: Waveland Press, 2012.

Goldman, Doron. "The Double Victory Campaign and the Campaign to Integrate Baseball." In *Who's on First? Replacement Players in World War II*, edited by Marc Z. Aaron and Bill Nowlin, 405–8. Phoenix: Society of American Baseball Research, 2015. www.sabr.org/research/article/goldman-double-victory-campaign-and-campaign-integrate-baseball.

Goldman, Steve. "The Genius: Foster Made Negro League Baseball Successful." *MLB.com*, n.d. http://mlb.mlb.com/mlb/history/mlb_negro_leagues_story.jsp?story=foster_rube.

Golenbock, Peter. *Bums: An Oral History of the Brooklyn Dodgers*. New York: Dover Publications.

Gordon, Patrick. "Octavius Catto, the Pythians, and Early Black Baseball in Philadelphia." *Philadelphia Baseball Review*, July 18, 2016. http://www.philadelphiabaseballreview.com/2016/07/octavius-catto-pythians-and-early-black.html.

Graham, Pat. "'A League of Their Own' Inspired Baseball Pioneer Croteau." Associated Press, April 17, 2020. https://apnews.com/article/madonna-mlb-baseball-sports-general-sports-ea3462213c68d73563458e0af0e468e9.

Grant, Jim. *The Black Aces*. Farmingdale, NY: Black Aces, LLC., 2006.

Graves, Neil. "When Racism Drove the AFL All-Star Game Out of New Orleans," *The Undefeated*, January 27, 2017. https://theundefeated.com/features/when-racism-drove-the-afl-all-star-game-out-of-new-orleans/.

Green, Alfred E., dir., Arther Mann, writer, and Lawrence Taylor, writer. *The Jackie Robinson Story*. Released May 1950 by United Artists.

Greenberg, Kalie. "CMU Investigates Homophobic Remarks." *KJCT8*, March 18, 2016.

Gregorich, Barbara. "You Can't Play in Skirts: Alta Weiss, Baseball Player." *Timeline: The Magazine of the Ohio Historical Society*, July/August 1994.

Gregory, Sean. "You Have to Take a Stand.' Soccer Phenom Alex Morgan Wants the Respect—and Money—Female Players Deserve." *Time*, May 23, 2019. https://time.com/5594356/alex-morgan-world-cup/.

Grigsby, Daryl Russell. *Celebrating Ourselves: African Americans and the Promise of Baseball*. Indianapolis, IN: Dog Ear Publishing, 2010.

Grim, Ryan. *We've Got People: From Jesse Jackson to Alexandria Ocasio-Cortez, the End of Big Money and the Rise of a Movement*. Washington, DC: Strong Arm Press, 2019.

Gross, Milton. "Why They Boo Jackie Robinson." *Sport*, February 1953.

"Guillen Apologizes for Use of Homosexual Slur." *ESPN*, June 22, 2006. https://www.espn.com/mlb/news/story?id=2494491.

Haft, Chris. "10 Significant Moments from Jackie's Life." *MLB.com*, April 14, 2021. https://www.mlb.com/news/jackie-robinson-significant-moments.

Hall, Alex. "Sean Doolittle Stresses Importance of Health Safety in Plans for 2020 MLB Season." *Athletics Nation*, May 13, 2020. https://www.athleticsnation.com/2020/5/13/21257778/sean-doolittle-coronavirus-health-safety-twitter-2020-mlb.

Halper, Donna L. "Written Out of History: Women Baseball Writers, 1905–1945." In *The Cooperstown Symposium on Baseball and American Culture, 2017–2018*, edited by William M. Simons. Jefferson, NC: McFarland, 2019.

Hanks, Stephen. "Perry Barber: You Gotta Love the Ump!" *Village Voice*, August 5, 1986. https://stephenhanks.medium.com/authors-flashback-perry-barber-you-gotta-love-the-ump-7253f39fa240.

Hanlon, John. "Queen Lizzie Plays First Base." *Sports Illustrated*, June 21, 1965. https://Vault.Si.Com/Vault/1965/06/21/Queen-Lizzie-Plays-First-Base.

Hays, Graham. "Monica Abbott Wants Change After Signing $1 Million Contract with NPF Expansion Team." *ESPN*, May 4, 2016. https://www.espn.com/espnw/sports/story/_/id/15464430/pitcher-monica-abbott-signs-1-million-contract-national-pro-fastpitch-expansion-team.

———. "Stereotypes Haunt Softball." *ESPN*, October 11, 2010. https://www.espn.com/college-sports/columns/story?columnist=hays_graham&id=5671978.

Heaphy, Leslie A., and Mel Anthony May, eds. *Encyclopedia of Women and Baseball*. Jefferson, NC: McFarland, 2006.

Hearings Regarding Communist Infiltration of Minority Groups, 81st Cong. (1949) (sworn testimony of Jack Roosevelt Robinson). https://babel.hathitrust.org/cgi/pt?id=uc1.31210019443231&view=1up&seq=61.

Helyar, John. *Lords of the Realm: The Real History of Baseball*. New York: Ballantine Books, 1994.

Hensler, Paul. *The New Boys of Summer: Baseball's Radical Transformation in the Late Sixties*. Lanham, MD: Rowman & Littlefield, 2017.

Hickey, John. "What Would Doo Do When It Comes to Owners' Reopening Plan? It's a Tough One." *Sports Illustrated*, May 11, 2020. https://www.si.com/mlb /athletics/news/what-would-doo-do-when-it-comes-to-owners-reopening -plan-its-a-tough-one.

Hill, Jemele. "Curt Flood Belongs in the Hall of Fame." *The Atlantic*, February 10, 2021. https://www.theatlantic.com/ideas/archive/2021/02/curt-floods-fight -was-about-so-much-more-than-baseball/617931/.

Hill, Justice B. "A True Pioneer: Fleet Walker Is First African-American to Play in Major Leagues." *MLB.com*, n.d. http://mlb.mlb.com/mlb/history/mlb_negro _leagues_profile.jsp?player=walker_fleetwood.

Hine, Chris. "Meet the First Openly Gay Professional Baseball Player." *Esquire*, June 27, 2016. https://www.esquire.com/news-politics/a45822/david-denson-gay -baseball-player/.

Hingston, Sandy. "13 Things You Might Not Know About Octavius Catto." *Philadelphia*, June 10, 2016. https://www.phillymag.com/news/2016/06/10 /octavius-catto-memorial/.

Hoffman, Benjamin. "Brandon Taubman, Astros Executive, Is Fired Over Outburst." *Sports Illustrated*, October 24, 2019. https://www.si.com/mlb/2019/10/22 /houston-astros-roberto-osuna-suspension.

Hogan, Lawrence. *The Forgotten History of African American Baseball*. Westport, CT: Praeger, 2014.

———. *Shades of Glory: The Negro Leagues and the Story of African-American Baseball*. Washington, DC: National Geographic, 2006.

Hollander, Russell. "On Being Gay in Major League Baseball." In *The Cooperstown Symposium on Baseball and American Culture: 2002*, edited by William M. Simons. Jefferson, NC: McFarland, 2002.

Holtzclaw, Kelly, and Jon Leonoudakis. *Baseball Pioneers*. Sherman Oaks, CA: Facetious, Inc., 2018.

Holway, John B. "Frank 'Doc' Sykes as Told to John Holway." *The National Pastime Museum*, July 8, 2013.

———. "Million Dollar Infield." *BaseballGuru.com*, n.d. http://baseballguru.com /jholway/analysisjholway48.html.

———. "Willie Wells: A Devil of a Shortstop." *Baseball Research Journal* 17 (1988): 50–53.

Horowitz, Roger. "Negro and White, Unite and Fight!" *A Social History of Industrial Unionism in Meatpacking, 1930-90*. Urbana, IL: University of Illinois Press, 1997.

Horwitz, Tony. "The Woman Who (Maybe) Struck Out Babe Ruth and Lou Gehrig." *Smithsonian Magazine*, July 2013. https://www.smithsonianmag.com /history/the-woman-who-maybe-struck-out-babe-ruth-and-lou-gehrig -4759182/.

Howe, Ryan. "Colorado Baseball Coach Who Said 'We Kill Gay People' Apologizes." *OutFront*, May 28, 2016. https://www.outfrontmagazine.com /trending/colorado-baseball-coach-said-kill-gay-people-apologizes/.

"How the Little League Gender Barrier Was Broken." *Portable Press*, July 23, 2014. https://www.portablepress.com/blog/2014/07/little-league-gender-barrier -broken/.

Hunzinger, Erica. "Major League Baseball Is Trying to Bring More Women into Front Offices and Fields." *All Things Considered*. NPR, April 8, 2019. https:// www.npr.org/2019/04/08/711169787/major-league-baseball-is-trying-to -bring-more-women-into-game-related-roles.

Husman, John. "August 10, 1883: Cap Anson vs. Fleet Walker." *Society for American Baseball Research*, 2013. https://sabr.org/gamesproj/game/august-10-1883 -cap-anson-vs-fleet-walker/.

———. "Fleet Walker." *Society of American Baseball Research*, n.d. https://sabr.org /bioproj/person/9fc5f867.

Ingemi, Marisa. "How Young Talented Team Canada Is Prepping for Women's Baseball World Cup." *SportsNet*, March 3, 2021. https://www.sportsnet.ca /baseball/article/young-talented-team-canada-prepping-womens-baseball -world-cup/.

Jacobson, Matthew F. "'Richie' Allen, Whitey's Ways, and Me: A Political Education in the 1960s." In *In the Game: Race, Identity, and Sports in the Twentieth Century*, edited by Amy Bass, 21–32. New York: Palgrave Macmillan, 2005.

Jacobson, Steve. *Carrying Jackie's Torch*. Chicago: Lawrence Hill Books, 2007.

James, Bill. *The Politics of Glory: How Baseball's Hall of Fame Really Works*. New York: Macmillan, 1994.

Johnson, Susan E. *When Women Played Hardball*. Seattle: Seal Press, 1994.

Jones, David. "Dutch Leonard." *Society for American Baseball Research*, n.d. https:// sabr.org/bioproj/person/dutch-leonard/.

Kahn, Harvey M. "Playing Hardball: Brushing Off the Memory of a Civil Rights Giant." *Readex Report*, n.d. http://www.readex.com/readex-report/playing -hardball-brushing-memory-civil-rights-giant.

Kashatus, William C. "Dick Allen, the Phillies, and Racism." *NINE: Journal of Baseball History and Culture* 9, no. 2 (Spring 2001): 151–91. https://muse.jhu .edu/article/24119/pdf.

———. *Mike Schmidt: Philadelphia's Hall of Fame Third Baseman*. Jefferson, NC: McFarland, 1999.

———. *September Swoon: Richie Allen, the '64 Phillies, and Racial Integration*. University Park: Pennsylvania State University Press, 2004.

Katz, William Loren. *The American Negro: His History and Literature*. New York: American Anti-Slavery Society, 1968.

Kelly, Matt. "Negro National League Is Founded." *National Baseball Hall of Fame*, n.d. https://baseballhall.org/discover-more/stories/inside-pitch/negro -national-league-is-founded.

Khan, Abraham Iqubal. *Curt Flood in the Media: Baseball, Race, and the Demise of the Activist-Athlete*. Jackson, MS: University Press of Mississippi, 2016.

Kimmel, Michael. "Baseball and the Reconstitution of American Masculinity, 1880–1920." In *Baseball History from Outside the Lines*, edited by John E. Dreifort. Lincoln: University of Nebraska Press, 2001.

Klima, John. *The Game Must Go On: Hank Greenberg, Pete Gray, and the Great Days of Baseball on the Home Front in WWII*. New York: St. Martin's Press, 2015.

Korr, Charles P. *The End of Baseball as We Knew It: The Players Union, 1960–81*. Urbana, IL: University of Illinois Press, 2002.

Kuklick, Bruce. *To Every Thing a Season: Shibe Park and Urban Philadelphia, 1909–1976*. Princeton: Princeton University Press, 1993.

LaCaruba, Paul Michael. "Getting Open: A Study of Homosexuality in Men's Professional Team Sports in North America." *Seton Hall Law School Student Scholarship* 508 (2014). https://scholarship.shu.edu/cgi/viewcontent.cgi ?article=1508&context=student_scholarship.

LaFeber, Walter. *Michael Jordan and the New Global Capitalism*. New York: Norton, 2002.

Laing, Jeff. "Philadelphia, October 1866: The Center of the Baseball Universe." *The National Pastime* (2013). https://sabr.org/research/philadelphia-october-1866 -center-baseball-universe.

Lamb, Chris. *Blackout: The Untold Story of Jackie Robinson's First Spring Training*. Lincoln: University of Nebraska Press, 2006.

———. *Conspiracy of Silence: Sportswriters and the Long Campaign to Desegregate Baseball*. Lincoln: University of Nebraska Press, 2012.

———. "'What's Wrong with Baseball': The *Pittsburgh Courier* and the Beginning of its Campaign to Integrate the National Pastime." *The Western Journal of Black Studies* 26 (2002): 189–203.

Lamberti, Chris. "South Side Baseball Legend." *White Sox Observer*, March 28, 2012. http://www.chicagonow.com/white-sox-observer/2012/03/south-side -baseball-legend-rube-foster/.

Lanctot, Neal. *Negro League Baseball: The Rise and Ruin of a Black Institution*. Philadelphia: University of Pennsylvania Press, 2004.

Lannin, Joanne. *Who Let Them In?: Pathbreaking Women in Sports Journalism*. Lanham, MD: Rowman & Littlefield, 2022.

Lapchick, Richard. *The 2019 Racial and Gender Report Card: Major League Baseball*. The University of Central Florida, April 15, 2019. https://docs.wixstatic.com /ugd/7d86e5_e943e1c08a514661a86b449dea5bcfd2.pdf.

"League History." *All-American Girls Professional Baseball League*, n.d. http://www .aagpbl.org/history/league-history.

Leff, Lisa, and Olga Rodriguez. "Pitcher Sean Conroy Makes History as Baseball's First Openly Active Gay Pro." Associated Press, June 25, 2015. https://www.nbcbayarea.com/news/local/Pitcher-Sean-Conroy-Makes-History-as-Sports-First-Openly-Gay-Pro-309933491.html.

Lester, Larry. *Rube Foster in His Time: On the Field and in the Papers with Black Baseball's Greatest Visionary*. Jefferson, NC: McFarland, 2012.

"Letter for Curt Flood's Nomination and Induction into the Baseball Hall of Fame." June 28, 2021. https://trone.house.gov/2021/06/28/letter-for-curt-floods-nomination-and-induction-into-the-baseball-hall-of-fame/.

Lindbergh, Ben, and Sam Miller. "Now Starting for the Sonoma Stompers." *Slate*, May 3, 2016. https://slate.com/culture/2016/05/sean-conroy-the-first-openly-gay-player-in-pro-baseball-history-was-signed-by-accident-heres-how-it-happened.html.

———. *The Only Rule Is It Has to Work: Our Wild Experiment Building a New Kind of Baseball Team*. New York: Henry Holt & Company, 2016.

Liptak, Mark. "Flashing Back . . . with Stan Bahnsen." *White Sox Interactive*, August 2, 2014.

Little, Becky. "Why FDR Didn't Support Eleanor Roosevelt's Anti-Lynching Campaign." *History.com*, January 31, 2019. https://www.history.com/news/fdr-eleanor-roosevelt-anti-lynching-bill.

Long, Michael G. *First Class Citizenship: The Civil Rights Letters of Jackie Robinson*. New York: Times Books, 2007.

Lowenfish, Lee. *Branch Rickey: Baseball's Ferocious Gentleman*. Lincoln: University of Nebraska Press, 2007.

———. *The Imperfect Diamond: A History of Baseball's Labor Wars*. Lincoln: Bison Books, 2010.

Luke, Bob. *The Most Famous Woman in Baseball: Effa Manley and the Negro Leagues*. Washington, DC: Potomac Books, 2011.

———. *Willie Wells: "El Diablo" of the Negro Leagues*. Austin, TX: University of Texas Press, 2007.

Lynching in America: Confronting the Legacy of Racial Terror. Equal Justice Initiative, 2017. https://lynchinginamerica.eji.org/report/.

Maaddi, Rob. "Mets' Piazza: 'I'm Not Gay.'" Associated Press, May 21, 2002. https://www.apnews.com/8cfb273686366a8efc992bf3f7f966f8.

Madden, W. C. *The All-Americans Girls Professional Baseball League Record Book*. Jefferson, NC: McFarland, 2000.

———. *The Women of the All-American Girls Professional Baseball League: A Biographical Dictionary*. Jefferson, NC: McFarland, 1997.

Majoros, Kevin. "Ally and Baseball Pro Sean Doolittle Wears Pride on His Cleats." *Washington Blade*, June 20, 2019. https://www.washingtonblade.com/2019/06/20/ally-and-baseball-pro-sean-doolittle-wears-pride-on-his-cleats/.

Maraniss, David. "No Gentle Saint." *The Undefeated*, May 31, 2016. https://
theundefeated.com/features/roberto-clemente-was-a-fierce-critic-of-both
-baseball-and-american-society/.

McAlevey, Jane. *No Shortcuts: Organizing for Power in the New Gilded Age.* New
York: Oxford University Press, 2016.

McCarthy, Brandon. "Tonight's result affects me none because I'm rich, white and
male. Yet, it'll be a long time until I'm able to sleep peacefully." Twitter, November
9, 2016. https://twitter.com/bmccarthy32/status/796278973072216064.

———. "Was the 'swamp' Goldman Sachs itself?" Twitter, March 14, 2017. https://
twitter.com/bmccarthy32/status/841846756463718400.

McCarthy, Justin. "U.S. Support for Gay Marriage Stable, at 63%." *Gallup*, May 22,
2019. https://news.gallup.com/poll/257705/support-gay-marriage-stable.
aspx.

McCauley, Janie. "Sean Doolittle Gets Lesson on Gen. James Doolittle." *ESPN*,
August 22, 2013. http://www.espn.com/espn/wire/_/section/mlb/id
/9592565.

McCue, Andy. "Branch Rickey." *Society for American Baseball Research*, n.d. https://
sabr.org/bioproj/person/branch-rickey.

McGovern, Jen. "Fan Perspectives on Race and Baseball in the City of Brotherly
Love." *The National Pastime* (2013). https://sabr.org/research/fan
-perspectives-race-and-baseball-city-brotherly-love.

McGregor, Robert Kuhn. *A Calculus of Color: The Integration of Baseball's American
League.* Jefferson, NC: McFarland, 2015.

McReynolds, John. "Nate Moreland: A Mystery to Historians." *The National
Pastime*, no. 19 (1999): 55–64.

McTaggart, Ursula. "Writing Baseball into History: The *Pittsburgh Courier*,
Integration, and Baseball in a War of Position." *American Studies* 47 (2006):
113–32.

Mead, William B. *Baseball Goes to War.* Washington, DC: Farragut Publishing Co.,
1985.

Messner, Michael. *Taking the Field: Women, Men and Sports.* Minneapolis: University
of Minnesota Press, 2002.

Miller, Marvin. *A Whole Different Ballgame: The Sport and Business of Baseball.* New
York: Birch Lane Press, 1991.

Miller, Toby. *Sport/Sex.* Philadelphia: Temple University Press, 2001.

Mitcheli, Ethan, *The Defender: How the Legendary Black Newspaper Changed
America.* New York: Houghton Mifflin Harcourt, 2016.

"MLB Player Sean Doolittle Pitches for Independent Bookstores." *CBS News*,
September 21, 2019. https://www.cbsnews.com/news/washington-nationals
-star-sean-doolittle-pitches-for-independent-bookstores-mlb-2019-09-21/.

Moffi, Larry, and Jonathan Kronstadt. *Crossing the Line: Black Major Leaguers,
1947–1959.* Iowa City: University Press of Iowa, 1994.

"A Monument to Racial Industry." *Half-Century Magazine*, November–December 1922.

Mooallem, Jon. "History of the High Five." *ESPN*, August 8, 2011. https://www .espn.com/espn/story/_/page/Mag15historyofthehighfive/who-invented -high-five.

Moran, Jack. "Former Pro Baseball Player Still in A League of Her Own." Associated Press, January 20, 2018. https://apnews.com/article/ a1772829503f4c828936de8fe80631dd.

Morrissey, Rich. *Ozzie's School of Management*. New York: Henry Holt & Company, 2012.

Munzel, Edgar. "14 Negro Players Give Tribe Corner on Colored Talent." *Sporting News*, April 13, 1949.

Murtaugh, Mackenzie. "Softball Player Reflects on Sexuality in Sports, Teamwork." *Windy City Times*, June 26, 2019. https://www.windycitytimes.com/lgbt /Softball-player-reflects-on-sexuality-in-sports-teamwork/66430.html.

Myrdal, Gunnar. *An American Dilemma: The Negro Problem and Modern Democracy*. New York: Harper, 1944.

Naison, Mark. *Communists in Harlem during the Depression*. Urbana, IL: University of Illinois Press, 2004.

———. "Lefties and Righties: The Communist Party and Sports during the Great Depression." *Radical America* 13 (July/August, 1979).

Nathanson, Mitchell. "Dick Allen Preferred Not To: A Reconsideration of Baseball's Bartleby," *NINE: Journal of Baseball History and Culture* 22, no. 2 (Spring 2014): 1–41.

———. "Dick Allen's Second Act." *The National Pastime* (2013). https://sabr.org /research/dick-allen-s-second-act.

———. *God Almighty Hisself: The Life and Legacy of Dick Allen*. Philadelphia: University of Pennsylvania Press, 2016.

———. Interview by Peter Dreier, April 8, 2021.

———. "Who Exempted Baseball, Anyway? The Curious Development of the Antitrust Exemption that Never Was." *Harvard Journal of Sports and Entertainment Law* 4, no. 1 (2013).

National Federation of State High School Associations. *Sports Participation Surveys*. https://www.nfhs.org/sports-resource-content/high-school-participation -survey-archive/.

"Nationals Players to Cover Minor Leaguers' Lost Weekly Stipend Wages, Sean Doolittle Says." *ESPN*, June 1, 2020. https://www.espn.com/mlb/story/_/id /29251556/nationals-players-cover-minor-leaguers-lost-wages-sean-doolittle -says?platform=amp.

"Nationals Sean Doolittle Makes Statement on the Death of George Floyd." *NBC Sports*, June 29, 2020. https://www.nbcsports.com/washington/nationals /nationals-sean-doolittle-makes-statement-death-george-floyd.

National Visionary Leadership Project. "Mamie 'Peanut' Johnson." *Oral History Archive*. http://www.visionaryproject.com/johnsonmamie/.

Naze, David. *Reclaiming 42: Public Memory and the Reframing of Jackie Robinson's Radical Legacy*. Lincoln: University of Nebraska Press, 2019.

Newman, Roberta. *Black Baseball, Black Business: Race Enterprise and the Fate of the Segregated Dollar*. Oxford, MS: University Press of Mississippi, 2014.

Neyer, Rob. "A Chat with Dave Pallone, First MLB Umpire to Come Out as Gay." *Fox Sports*, December 3, 2014.

NCAA Sports Sponsorship and Participation Rates Database. http://www.ncaa .org/about/resources/research/ncaa-sports-sponsorship-and-participation -rates-database.

Nightingale, Dave. "The Human Side of Richie Allen." *Baseball Digest* 31 (July 1972): 16–24.

"NL Prexy Bill White Cites Baseball Racism." *Jet*, June 15, 1992, 46.

Norris, Christopher, "Black Athlete and Activist Enshrined Amid Debate on Race and Sports," *The Good Man Project*, September 26, 2017. https:// goodmenproject.com/featured-content/black-athlete-and-activist-enshrined -amid-debate-on-race-and-sports-cnorris/.

Nowlin, Bill, ed. *Pumpsie & Progress: The Red Sox, Race, and Redemption*. Burlington, MA: Rounder Books, 2010.

———. "Sam Jethroe." *Society for American Baseball Research*, n.d. https://sabr.org /bioproj/person/sam-jethroe/.

———. *Tom Yawkey: Patriarch of the Boston Red Sox*. Lincoln: University of Nebraska Press, 2018.

Oberteuffer, Ryan. "AACC Men's Baseball Team Has Female Pitcher." *Campus Current*, May 19, 2021. https://www.thecampuscurrent.com/10712/front -page/showcase/aacc-mens-baseball-team-has-female-pitcher/.

Odzer, Timothy. "Rube Foster." *Society of American Baseball Research*, n.d. https:// sabr.org/bioproj/person/fcf322f7.

O'Keefe, Colin. "Casy Candaele Shares Story of His Mother, Inspiration for 'A League of Their Own.'" *From the Corner of Edgar & Dave*, May 13, 2017. https://marinersblog.mlblogs.com/casey-candaele-shares-story-of-his-mother -inspiration-for-a-league-of-their-own-d5c987588841.

O'Toole, Andrew. *The Best Man Plays: Major League Baseball and the Black Athlete, 1901–2002*. Jefferson, NC: McFarland, 2003.

Out: The Glenn Burke Story. NBC Universal/Comcast SportsNet, 2010. https:// vimeo.com/171518513

Overmyer, James. *Queen of the Negro Leagues: Effa Manley and the Newark Eagles*. Lanham, MD: Rowman & Littlefield, 1998.

Ozanian, Mike. "Baseball's Most Valuable Teams." *Forbes*, March 26, 2021. https:// www.forbes.com/sites/mikeozanian/2021/03/26/baseballs-most-valuable -teams-new-york-yankees-on-top-at-525-billion/?sh=5801af2dd5ef.

"Pablo Sandoval, Hunter Pence Join Giants Kneeling during National Anthem."
    NBC Sports, July 21, 2020. https://www.nbcsports.com/bayarea/giants
    /pablo-sandoval-hunter-pence-join-giants-kneeling-during-national-anthem.

Paige, Satchel, and David Lipman. *Maybe I'll Pitch Forever: A Great Baseball Player
    Tells the Hilarious Story Behind the Legend*. Lincoln: University of Nebraska
    Press, 1993.

Pallone, Dave. *Behind the Mask: My Double Life in Baseball*. New York: Viking, 1990.

"Perry Barber, 1 of 8 Women to Umpire Professional Baseball." *MLB Network*,
    March 8, 2021. https://www.youtube.com/watch?v=EvsaKgC5pLo.

"Perry Barber Receives 2018 Dorothy Seymour Mills Lifetime Achievement
    Award." *Society for American Baseball Research*, April 24, 2020. https://sabr.org
    /latest/perry-barber-selected-winner-inaugural-dorothy-seymour-mills
    -lifetime-achievement-award/.

Peterson, Robert. *Only the Ball Was White: A History of Legendary Black Ballplayers
    and All-Black Professional Teams*. New York: Oxford University Press, 1992.

Peterson, Todd. "May the Best Man Win: The Black Ball Championships 1866–
    1923." *Baseball Research Journal* (Spring 2013). https://sabr.org/research
    /may-best-man-win-black-ball-championships-1866-1923.

Pickman, Ben. "Bucks Players Issue Statement on Decision to Sit Out: 'We Are
    Calling for Justice for Jacob Blake.'" *Sports Illustrated*, August 26, 2020. https://
    www.si.com/nba/2020/08/27/bucks-players-statement-decision-sit-out.

Pierman, Carol J. "Baseball, Conduct, and True Womanhood." *Women's Studies
    Quarterly*, 33, no. 1/2 (Summer 2005).

Pietrusza, David. *Judge and Jury: The Life and Times of Judge Kenesaw Mountain
    Landis*. Chicago: Diamond Communications, 2001.

"Pitcher Todd Jones Doesn't Like Gay People." *Outsports*, April 29, 2003. https://
    www.outsports.com/2013/2/26/4033832/pitcher-todd-jones-doesnt-like-gay
    -people.

Players Alliance. *Allies of the Alliance*. n.d. https://theplayersalliance.com/allies/.

"Players Association Introduces Annual Curt Flood Award as Part of 2020 Players
    Choice Awards." Major League Baseball Players Association, October 19, 2020.
    https://www.mlbplayers.com/post/players-association-introduces-annual
    -curt-flood-award-as-part-of-2020-players-choice-awards.

Polner, Murray. *Branch Rickey: A Biography*. New York: Atheneum, 1982.

Posnanski, Joe. *The Baseball 100*. New York: Simon & Schuster, 2021.

Postema, Pam. *You've Got to Have Balls to Make It in This League: My Life as an
    Umpire*. New York: Simon & Schuster, 1992.

Rader, Benjamin G. *Baseball: A History of America's Game*, 4th edition. Urbana, IL:
    University of Illinois Press, 2018.

Rampersad, Arnold. *Jackie Robinson: A Biography*. New York: Alfred Knopf, 1997.

Randhawa, Manny. "South Side and Negro Leagues Go Way Back." *MLB.com*, n.d. https://www.mlb.com/news/negro-league-pioneer-rube-foster-among-many -who-left-impact-on-chicago/c-57490560.

Rau, Melanie. "Why Are Women Sports Journalists Still on the Sidelines?" *Vox*, December 28, 2019. https://www.voxmagazine.com/magazine/female-sports -reporters-sidelined/article_e1a252f4-1cae-11ea-a4f4-5755f88350e7.html.

Regan, Barry. "Moses Fleetwood Walker: The Forgotten Man Who Actually Integrated Baseball." *Bleacher Report*, April 16, 2012. https://bleacherreport .com/articles/1147947-moses-fleetwood-walker-the-forgotten-man-who -actually-integrated-baseball.

Reimer, Alex. "Sean Doolittle Challenged U.S. To Become Functioning Society for Sports to Return, And We're Failing." *Forbes*, July 9, 2020. https://www.forbes .com/sites/alexreimer/2020/07/09/sean-doolittle-challenged-us-to-become -functioning-society-for-sports-to-return-and-were-failing/?sh=1ecc78ff5a64.

Remnick, David. "Recalling Muhammad Ali's Vietnam War Resistance in the Age of Trump." *The New Yorker*, September 24, 2017. https://www.newyorker.com /news/daily-comment/recalling-muhammad-alis-vietnam-war-resistance-in -the-age-of-trump.

Rhoden, William C. *Forty Million Dollar Slaves: The Rise, Fall, and Redemption of the Black Athlete*. New York: Crown Publishers, 2006.

———. "Members of Congress Unite in Call for Baseball Hall of Fame to Elect Curt Flood." *The Undefeated*, February 27, 2020. https://theundefeated.com /features/members-of-congress-unite-in-call-for-baseball-hall-of-fame-to-elect -curt-flood/.

———. "The Push for Curt Flood's Enshrinement into the Baseball Hall of Fame Intensifies." *The Undefeated*, December 25, 2019. https://theundefeated.com /features/cause-for-curt-flood-enshrinement-into-baseball-hall-of-fame -continues-fifty-years-since-letter.

Ribowsky, Mark. *Don't Look Back: Satchel Paige in the Shadows of Baseball*. New York: Simon & Schuster, 1994.

Rice, Ebonee. "A Tribute to Women in Journalism Who Cracked Glass Ceilings." *Ms.*, March 16, 2021. https://msmagazine.com/2021/03/16/women -journalism-media-ida-b-wells-ida-tarbell-alice-allison-dunnigan-k-connie -kang/.

Richard, A. J. "Playing with the Boys: Gender, Race, and Baseball in Post-War America." *Baseball Research Journal* (Spring 2019). https://sabr.org/research /playing-boys-gender-race-and-baseball-post-war-america.

Richmond, Peter. "The Brief Life and Complicated Death of Tommy Lasorda's Gay Son." *Deadspin*, April 30, 2013. https://thestacks.deadspin.com/the-brief-life -and-complicated-death-of-tommy-lasordas-485999366.

Riley, James A. *Dandy, Day and the Devil*. Dallas: TK Publishers, 1987.

Ring, Jennifer. *A Game of Their Own: Voices of Contemporary Women in Baseball.* Lincoln: University of Nebraska Press, 2015.

———. *Stolen Bases: Why American Girls Don't Play Baseball,* Urbana, IL: University of Illinois Press, 2003.

Rivera, Joe. "Giants' Gabe Kapler Explains Why He Kneeled during National Anthem." *The Sporting News,* July 21, 2020. https://www.sportingnews.com/us/mlb /news/giants-gabe-kapler-kneel-national-anthem/hy8jjixcxann1vju14s18zh4e.

Roberts, Robin, and C. Paul Rogers III. *The Whiz Kids and the 1950 Pennant.* Philadelphia: Temple University Press, 2000.

Robinson, Jackie. *Baseball Has Done It.* Philadelphia: J. B. Lippincott Company, 1964.

Robinson, Jackie, with Alfred Duckett. *I Never Had It Made: The Autobiography of Jackie Robinson.* New York: Fawcett, 1972.

Rodd, Scott. "LGBT Inclusion in Major League Baseball Is Long Overdue." *Think Progress,* April 4, 2016. https://thinkprogress.org/lgbt-inclusion-in-major -league-baseball-is-long-overdue-839297f49b5f/.

Rodgers, Joe. "A's Rookie Bruce Maxwell First MLB Player to Take a Knee for the Anthem." *Sporting News,* September 25, 2017.

Rodrigo, Chris Mills. "Ali Krieger Defends Teammate Rapinoe: Trump Angered by Women He 'Cannot Control or Grope.'" *The Hill,* June 26, 2019. https:// thehill.com/blogs/blog-briefing-room/news/450496-ali-krieger-defends -teammate-rapinoe-trump-angered-by-women-he.

Rogers, Betsy Jane. "Mabel Holle and the All-American Girls Professional Baseball League." *Rogers & Jones,* 2018. https://rogers-jones.com/2018/01/10/mabel -holle-the-all-american-girls-professional-ball-league/.

Rogosin, Donn. *Invisible Men: Life in Baseball's Negro Leagues.* Lincoln: University of Nebraska Press, 2020.

Rohlin, Melissa. "LeBron James Calls Out Laura Ingraham for Telling Him to 'Shut Up' While Defending Drew Brees." *Sports Illustrated,* June 4, 2020. https:// www.si.com/nba/lakers/news/lebron-james-calls-out-laura-ingraham-for -telling-him-to-shut-up-while-defending-drew-brees.

Rosen, Michael. "Breaking the Grass Ceiling: More Women Are Playing College Baseball Than Ever Before." *Sports Illustrated,* June 23, 2021. https://www .si.com/college/2021/06/23/womens-college-baseball-gaining-momentum.

Rosen, Ruth. *The World Split Open: How the Modern Women's Movement Changed America.* New York: Penguin Books, 2006.

Ross, Marlon Bryan. *Manning the Race: Reforming Black Men in the Jim Crow Era.* New York: New York University Press, 2004.

Rossi, Kevin. "Octavius Catto, Colin Kaepernick, and Athlete-Activists Turned Martyrs." *Sport in American History,* October 13, 2016. https://ussporthistory .com/2016/10/13/octavius-catto-colin-kaepernick-athlete-activists-turned -martyrs/.

Rothenberg, Mark. "Fighting for Equality on the Baseball Grounds." *National Baseball Hall of Fame*, n.d. https://baseballhall.org/discover/octavius-catto-philadelphia-black-baseball.

Rubin, Gideon. "Japan's 'Knuckle Princess' Aims at MLB." *ESPN*, August 3, 2011.

Ruck, Rob. "Crossing the Color Line." In *Shades of Glory: The Negro Leagues and the Story of African American Baseball*, edited by Lawrence Hogan. Washington, DC: National Geographic, 2006.

Rusinack, Kelly. "Baseball on the Radical Agenda: The *Daily Worker* and *Sunday Worker* Journalistic Campaign to Desegregate Major League Baseball, 1933–1947." In *Jackie Robinson: Race, Sports, and the American Dream*, edited by Joseph Dorinson and Joram Warmund. Armonk, NY: M. E. Sharpe, 1998.

Rusinack, Kelly, and Chris Lamb. "'A Sickening Red Tinge': The *Daily Worker's* Fight Against White Baseball." *Cultural Logic* 3, no. 1 (Fall 1999).

Ryczek, William. *Baseball on the Brink: The Crisis of 1968*. Jefferson, NC: McFarland, 2017.

Rymer, Zachary. "1 Year Later, Pro Baseball's 1st Openly Gay Player Still Leads by Example." *Bleacher Report*, August 3, 2013. https://bleacherreport.com/articles/2652165-1-year-later-pro-baseballs-1st-openly-gay-player-still-leads-by-example.

Samoray, Jeff. "Jean Cione." *Society for American Baseball Research*, n.d. https://sabr.org/node/27119.

Santana, Ryan Jordan. "Transition from Straight to Gay Teams Has Been Special for This Athlete." *Outsports*, June 6, 2018. https://www.outsports.com/2018/6/6/17433114/ryan-jordan-santana-gay-athlete-baseball-softball.

Sargent, James. "Marge and Helen Callaghan." *Society for American Baseball Research*, n.d. https://sabr.org/node/28032.

———. *We Were the All-American Girls: Interviews with Players of the AAGPBL, 1943–1954*. Jefferson, NC: McFarland, 2013.

Sarris, Eno. "Players' View: Is Baseball Ready for an Openly Gay Player?" *Fan Graphs*, June 18, 2016. https://blogs.fangraphs.com/players-view-is-baseball-ready-for-an-openly-gay-player/.

Saxon, Mark. "Cardinals Taking Allegations of Anti-Gay Comments 'Very Seriously.'" *ESPN*, March 16, 2015. https://abc7chicago.com/sports/cardinals-taking-allegations-of-anti-gay-comments-very-seriously/1248661/.

———. "Dexter Fowler Unapologetic for Criticism of Trump's Travel Ban." *ESPN*, February 20, 2017. https://abc7news.com/sports/dexter-fowler-unapologetic-for-criticism-of-trumps-travel-ban/1763719/.

Schutz, Christopher. *Jackie Robinson: An Integrated Life*. Lanham, MD: Rowman & Littlefield, 2016.

"Sean Conroy Becomes First Openly Gay Professional Baseball Player." *Sports Illustrated*, June 26, 2015. https://www.si.com/mlb/2015/06/26/openly-gay-professional-baseball-player-sean-conroy-sonoma-stompers.

Segal, Stephen. "An Unbreakable Game: Baseball and Its Inability to Bring About Equality during Reconstruction." *The Historian* 74, no. 3 (Fall 2012): 467–94.

Selbe, Nick. "Nationals Players Pledge to Compensate for Minor Leaguers Facing Pay Cuts." *Sports Illustrated*, June 1, 2020. https://www.si.com/mlb/2020/06 /01/washington-nationals-sean-doolittle-compensate-minor-league-pay-cuts.

Shattuck, Debra. *Bloomer Girls: Women Baseball Pioneers*. Urbana, IL: University of Illinois Press, 2017.

———. "Playing a Man's Game: Women and Baseball in the United States, 1866– 1954." In *Baseball History from Outside the Lines*, edited by John E. Dreifort. Lincoln: University of Nebraska Press, 2001.

Shipnuck, Alan. "For the Love of the Game." *Sports Illustrated*, November 14, 2005. https://vault.si.com/vault/2005/11/14/for-the-love-of-the-game.

Shire, Emily. "Why Can't American Women Play Baseball?" *Daily Beast*, June 24, 2015. https://www.thedailybeast.com/why-cant-american-women-play -baseball.

Silber, Irwin. *Press Box Red: The Story of Lester Rodney, the Communist Who Helped Break the Color Line in Sports*. Philadelphia: Temple University Press, 2003.

Silverman, Robert. "Leftist Star Pitcher Sean Doolittle and Wife Speak Out on MLB's Reopening Proposal." *Daily Beast*, April 11, 2020. https://www .thedailybeast.com/socialist-star-pitcher-sean-doolittle-and-wife-slam-mlbs -reckless-reopening-plan?fbclid=IwAR0A84SlPjrjU7OPsPyvIwuIaEAMCcG2 BMEQ0MfowC3S8Cv0u1JkzL9qgMc.

Skocpol, Theda, and Vanessa Williamson. *The Tea Party and the Remaking of Republican Conservatism*. New York: Oxford University Press, 2016.

Smethurst, James. "'Don't Say Goodbye to the Porkpie Hat': Langston Hughes, the Left, and the Black Arts Movement." *Callaloo* 25, no. 4 (August 2002), 1224–37.

Smith, Aaron X. "The Murder of Octavius Catto." *Encyclopedia of Greater Philadelphia*, 2015. https://philadelphiaencyclopedia.org/archive/murder-of -octavius-catto/.

Smith, Claire. "Baseball's Angry Man." *New York Times Magazine*, October 13, 1991, 53.

Smith, Gary. "The Chosen One." *Sports Illustrated*, December 23, 1996.

Smith, Michael. "The Double Life of a Gay Dodger." *Inside Sports*, October 1982. https://thestacks.deadspin.com/the-double-life-of-a-gay-dodger-493697377.

Snyder, Brad. *A Well-Paid Slave: Curt Flood's Fight for Free Agency in Professional Sports*. New York: Plume Books, 2006.

Solomon, Mark. *The Cry Was Unity: Communists and African Americans, 1917–36*. Jackson, MS: University Press of Mississippi, 1998.

Sowell, Mike. "Is She or Isn't He?: Exploring the Gender Identity Controversy Over the First Female Byline in a National Sports Publication." *Journalism History* 37, no. 4 (Winter 2012): 228–37.

Spalding, Albert. *America's National Game*, Reprint Edition. New York: Halo Books, 1991.

Stimson, Alex. "Louise Youngen Plays Ball." *MLB.com*, July 31, 2019.

Swanson, Krister. *Baseball's Power Shift: How the Players Union, the Fans, and the Media Changed American Sports*. Lincoln: University of Nebraska Press, 2016.

Swanson, Ryan. *When Baseball Went White: Reconstruction, Reconciliation, and Dreams of a National Pastime*. Lincoln: University of Nebraska Press, 2014.

Swartz, Cody. "Dick Allen: What Could Have Been." *Bleacher Report*, April 28, 2009. https://bleacherreport.com/articles/164255-dick-allen-what-could -have-been.

Tabbert, Christopher. "American Giant." *Chicago Sports Memories*, 2010. https:// chicagosportsmemories.blogspot.com/2010/04/american-giant.html.

"Terry Cannon Captures the Magic of America's Game with His Baseball Reliquary." *Pasadena Weekly*, July 13, 2017. https://pasadenaweekly.com /terry-cannon-captures-magic-americas-game-baseball-reliquary/.

Thielman, Jim. *Cool of the Evening: The 1965 Minnesota Twins*. Edina, MN: Kirk House Publishers, 2005.

Thomas, Louisa. "What If Pro Sports Leagues Were Controlled By Their Players? *New Yorker* June 3, 2021. https://www.newyorker.com/sports/sporting-scene /what-if-pro-sports-leagues-were-controlled-by-their-players.

Thorn, John. *Baseball in the Garden of Eden*. New York: Simon & Schuster, 2012.

Tinsley, Justin. "Jackie Robinson vs. Malcolm X." *The Undefeated*, May 25, 2016. https://theundefeated.com/features/jackie-robinson-vs-malcolm-x/.

Tolan, Sandy. *Me and Hank: A Boy and His Hero, Twenty-Five Years Later*. New York: Free Press, 2000.

Tomasik, Mark. "Bill White: Retrosimba Interview." *Retrosimba*, March 28, 2011. https://retrosimba.com/2011/03/28/bill-white-interviewed-about -autobiography/.

Travers, Steven. *The Last Icon: Tom Seaver and His Times*. Lanham, MD: Taylor Trade Publishing, 2011.

Trembanis, Sarah L. "'They Opened the Door Too Late': African Americans and Baseball, 1900–1947" (PhD diss., William & Mary, 2006). https://doi.org /10.21220/s2-srkh-wb23.

Trip, Steven Elliott. "Fake History? Charles Leerhsen and the Redemption of Ty Cobb." *NINE: Journal of Baseball History & Culture* 26, no. 1–2 (Fall–Spring 2017–2018): 226–38.

Trotta, Daniel. "NBA Returns All-Star Game to N. Carolina after Transgender Law Lifted." *Reuters*, May 24, 2017.

Turner, Dan. *Heroes, Bums and Ordinary Men: Profiles in Canadian Baseball*, Toronto: Doubleday Canada, 1988.

Tye, Larry. "Satchel Paige." *Society of American Baseball Research*, n.d. https://sabr .org/bioproj/person/satchel-paige/.

———. *Satchel: The Life and Times of an American Legend*. New York: Random House, 2010.

Tygiel, Jules. *Baseball's Great Experiment: Jackie Robinson and His Legacy*. New York: Oxford University Press, 1983.

———. *Extra Bases: Reflections on Jackie Robinson, Race, and Baseball History*. Lincoln, NE: Bison Books, 2002.

———. *Past Time*. New York: Oxford University Press. 2000.

———. "Revisiting Bill Veeck and the 1943 Phillies." *Baseball Research Journal* 35 (2007): 109–14.

Varela, Julio Ricardo. "What Would Clemente Do?" *Global Sports Matters*, July 22, 2020. https://globalsportmatters.com/culture/2020/07/22/what-would -roberto-clemente-do/.

Veeck, Bill, with Ed Linn. *Veeck as in Wreck*. New York: G. P. Putnam's Sons, 1962.

Victory Institute. "Out for America." https://outforamerica.org/.

Wagner, Andrew. "Christian Yelich, Brewers United with Bucks in Decision Not to Play Wednesday Night." *Wisconsin State Journal*, August 27, 2020.

Wagoner, Nick. "President Obama Congratulates Sam, Rams." *ESPN*, May 11, 2014. https://www.espn.com/blog/nfcwest/post/_/id/113616/president-obama -congratulates-sam-rams.

Walker, Moses Fleetwood. *Our Home Colony: A Treatise on the Past, Present and Future of the Negro Race in America*. Malabar, FL: P. E. Rieger, 1993.

Walker, Rhiannon. "When Arizona Lost the Super Bowl Because the State Didn't Recognize Martin Luther King Jr. Day." *The Undefeated*, March 22, 2017. https://theundefeated.com/features/when-arizona-lost-the-super-bowl -because-the-state-didnt-recognize-martin-luther-king-jr-day/.

Wancho, Joseph. "Mudcat Grant." *Society of American Baseball Research*, n.d. https:// sabr.org/bioproj/person/ba7b1b4d.

Warrington, Robert D., and Norman Macht. "The Veracity of Veeck." *Baseball Research Journal* (Fall 2013). https://sabr.org/journal/article/the-veracity-of -veeck/.

Washington, Linn. "Honoring Octavius V. Catto: Another History Lesson Trump Will Ignore." *Counterpunch*, September 29, 2017. https://www.counterpunch .org/2017/09/29/honoring-octavius-v-catto-another-history-lesson-trump -will-ignore/.

Waskie, Andy. "Octavius Catto Biography." *General Meade Society of Philadelphia*, 2015–2017. https://generalmeadesociety.org/octavius-catto-biography/.

Weintraub, Robert. *The Victory Season: The End of World War II and the Birth of Baseball's Golden Age*. New York: Little Brown & Co., 2013.

Wertheim, L. Jon. "Gays in Sports: A Poll." *Sports Illustrated*, April 18, 2005. https:// www.si.com/vault/2005/04/18/8257820/gays-in-sports-a-poll.

Wescott, Rich. "The Early Years of Philadelphia Baseball." *The National Pastime* (2013). https://sabr.org/research/early-years-philadelphia-baseball.

White, Bill. *Uppity: My Untold Story About the Games People Play*. New York: Grand Central Publishing, 2011.

———. "When Baseball Defied Segregation Off the Field." *CNN.com*, May 14, 2011. http://www.cnn.com/2011/OPINION/05/14/white.baseball.desegregation/index.html.

"Why Did You Come Out as an Openly LGBTQ Olympic Athlete?" *The Athlete's Village*, December 18, 2018. https://www.youtube.com/watch?v=tTwa70vhtS0.

Wiggins, David K. "Wendell Smith, The *Pittsburgh Courier-Journal* and the Campaign to Include Blacks in Organized Baseball 1933–1945." *Journal of Sport History* 10, no. 2 (Summer 1983): 5–29.

Wiggins, David K., and Patrick B. Miller, eds. *The Unlevel Playing Field*. Urbana, IL: University of Illinois Press, 2003.

Williams, Kat. *The All-American Girls After the AAGPBL: How Playing Pro Ball Shaped Their Lives*. Jefferson, NC: McFarland, 2017.

Wilson, Lyle K. "Mr. Foster Comes to Washington." *The National Pastime* 17 (1998): 107–11.

Wright, Craig R. "Dick Allen: Another View." *White Sox Interactive*, August 1, 2014.

Wyman, Rachel. "The Philadelphia Catto: Bridging the Racial Gap in the City of Brotherly Love" (honors thesis, Union College, 2016).

Yellin, Emily. *Our Mothers' War: American Women at Home and at the Front during World War II*. New York: Free Press, 2005.

Zang, David W. *Fleet Walker's Divided Heart: The Life of Baseball's First Black Major Leaguer*. Lincoln: University of Nebraska Press, 1995.

Zeigler, Cyd. *Fair Play: How LGBT Athletes Are Claiming Their Rightful Place in Sports*. New York: Akashic Books, 2016.

———. "Gay Cardinals Minor League Player Quit Baseball When Teammates Said Gays Should Be Killed." *Outsports*, March 16, 2016. https://www.outsports.com/2016/3/16/11243142/gay-baseball-cardinals-tyler-dunnington.

———. "Openly Gay Pitcher Sean Conroy Gets Pro Baseball Start This Thursday." *Outsports*, June 22, 2015. https://www.outsports.com/2015/6/22/8824663/gay-baseball-pitcher-sean-conroy-sonoma.

———. "St. Louis Cardinals Stand by Lance Berkman, Say They 'Welcome Him Back.'" *Outsports*, June 12, 2017. https://www.outsports.com/2017/6/12/15789708/st-louis-cardinals-lance-berkman-gay.

———. "This Gay Baseball Player Just Came Put on Live TV." *Outsports*, April 24, 2017. https://www.outsports.com/2017/4/24/15416098/gay-baseball-ryan-jordan-santana.

Zeitlin, Maurice, and L. Frank Weyher. "Black and White, Unite and Fight: Interracial Working-Class Solidarity and Racial Employment Equality." *American Journal of Sociology* 107 (September 2001): 430–67.

Zirin, Dave. "An Interview with 'Red' Rodney." *Counterpunch*, April 3, 2004.

―――. *People's History of Sports in the United States: 250 Years of Politics, Protest, People, and Play*. New York: New Press, 2009.

―――. "The Silencing of Carlos Delgado." *The Nation*, December 7, 2005. www .thenation.com/article/archive/silencing-carlos-delgado/.

―――. *What's My Name, Fool? Sports and Resistance in the United States*. Chicago: Haymarket Books, 2005.